# Designing and Building Parallel Programs

# Designing and Building Parallel Programs

## Concepts and Tools for Parallel Software Engineering

**Ian T. Foster**

**Addison-Wesley Publishing Company**

Reading, Massachusetts • Menlo Park, California
New York • Don Mills, Ontario • Wokingham, England
Amsterdam • Bonn • Sydney • Singapore
Tokyo • Madrid • San Juan • Milan • Paris

The cover image shows a finite element mesh for an assembly part, decomposed for 16 processors using the spectral bisection partitioning algorithm. The finite element mesh was constructed by M. S. Shephard and the partition by Z. Johan.

*Acquisitions Editor:* Thomas E. Stone
*Assistant Editor:* Kathleen Billus
*Production Supervisor:* Nancy H. Fenton
*Cover Designer:* Eileen Hoff
*Senior Manufacturing Manager:* Roy E. Logan
*Production:* Superscript Editorial Production Services
*Composition:* Windfall Software (Paul C. Anagnostopoulos, Debra Wasserman), using ZzTEX
*Copy Editor:* Laura K. Michaels
*Proofreader:* Nev Hanke

Library of Congress Cataloging-in-Publication Data
Foster, Ian, 1959–
    Designing and building parallel programs : concepts and tools for
parallel software engineering / Ian Foster.
      p.  cm.
    Includes bibliographical references and index.
    ISBN 0-201-57594-9
    1. Parallel programming (Computer science)    I. Title.
QA76.642.F67   1994
005.2—dc20                                  94-3661
                                                CIP

For more information about Addison-Wesley titles, please visit our gopher site via the Internet: gopher aw.com to connect to our on-line book information listing. To learn more about this title, please send email to dbpp@aw.com. An on-line version of this title is available via the World Wide Web at URL: http://www.mcs.anl.gov/dbpp.

Printed in the United States of America.

1 2 3 4 5 6 7 8 9 10–MA–98 97 96 95

# Preface

Welcome to *Designing and Building Parallel Programs*! My goal in this book is to provide a practitioner's guide for students, programmers, engineers, and scientists who wish to design and build efficient and cost-effective programs for parallel and distributed computer systems. I cover both the techniques used to design parallel programs and the tools used to implement these programs. I assume familiarity with sequential programming, but no prior exposure to parallel computing.

*Designing and Building Parallel Programs* promotes a view of parallel programming as an engineering discipline, in which programs are developed in a methodical fashion and both cost and performance are considered in a design. This view is reflected in the structure of the book, which is divided into three parts. The first part, *Concepts*, provides a thorough discussion of parallel algorithm design, performance analysis, and program construction, with numerous examples to illustrate fundamental principles. The second part, *Tools*, provides an in-depth treatment of four parallel programming tools: the parallel languages Compositional C++ (CC++), Fortran M (FM), and High Performance Fortran (HPF), and the Message Passing Interface (MPI) library. HPF and MPI are standard parallel programming systems, and CC++ and FM are modern languages particularly well-suited for parallel software engineering. Part II also describes tools for collecting and analyzing performance data. The third part, *Resources* surveys some fundamental parallel algorithms and provides many pointers to other sources of information.

A unique feature of this book is that it is also a guide to a larger resource accessible via the Internet and the World Wide Web. *Designing and Building Parallel Programs (Online)* provides online access to the book's contents and also allows you to download the parallel tools described in the book, to access example programs and other educational materials, and to browse through a wealth of other online information on parallel and distributed computing. The online version is described in Chapter 13.

## How to Use This Book

In writing this book, I chose to decouple the presentation of fundamental parallel programming *concepts* from the discussion of the parallel *tools* used to realize these concepts in programs. This separation allowed me to present concepts in a tool-independent manner; hence, commonalities between different approaches are emphasized, and the book does not become a manual for a particular programming language.

However, this separation also has its dangers. In particular, it may encourage you to think that the concepts introduced in Part I can be studied independently of the practical discipline of writing parallel programs. This assumption would be a serious mistake. Parallel programming, like most engineering activities, is best learned by doing. Practical experience is essential! Hence, I recommend that chapters from Parts I and II be studied concurrently. This approach will enable you to acquire the hands-on experience needed to translate knowledge of the concepts introduced in the book into the intuition that makes a good programmer. For the same reason, I also recommend that you attempt as many of the end-of-chapter exercises as possible.

*Designing and Building Parallel Programs* can be used as both a textbook for students and a reference book for professionals. Because the hands-on aspects of parallel programming are so important, professionals may find it useful to approach the book with a programming problem in mind and make the development of a solution to this problem part of the learning process. The basic materials have been classroom tested. For example, I have used them to teach a two-quarter graduate-level course in parallel computing to students from both computer science and noncomputer science backgrounds. In the first quarter, students covered much of the material in this book; in the second quarter, they tackled a substantial programming project. Colleagues have used the same material to teach a one-semester undergraduate introduction to parallel computing, augmenting this book's treatment of design and programming with additional readings in parallel architecture and algorithms.

Your comments and suggestions are very welcome, and can help guide the evolution of both the printed and online versions of this text. You can send electronic mail to dbpp@mcs.anl.gov. Or, you can write to

Designing and Building Parallel Programs
c/o Addison-Wesley Publishing Co.
1 Jacob Way
Reading, MA 01867
U.S.A.

Please consider submitting example programs, course materials, case studies, and the like: these can be integrated into the online version, to the benefit of other readers.

## Acknowledgments

It is a pleasure to thank the colleagues with whom and from whom I have gained the insights that I have tried to distill in this book: in particular Mani Chandy, Bill Gropp, Carl Kesselman, Ewing Lusk, John Michalakes, Ross Overbeek, Rick Stevens, Steven

Taylor, Steven Tuecke, and Patrick Worley. In addition, I am grateful to the many people who reviewed the text. Enrique Castro-Leon, Alok Choudhary, Carl Kesselman, Rick Kendall, Ewing Lusk, Rob Schreiber, and Rick Stevens reviewed one or more chapters. Gail Pieper, Brian Toonen, and Steven Tuecke were kind enough to read the entire text. Addison-Wesley's anonymous reviewers also provided invaluable comments. Nikos Drakos provided the `latex2html` software used to construct the online version, and Cris Perez helped run it. Brian Toonen tested all the programs and helped in other ways too numerous to mention. Carl Kesselman made major contributions to Chapter 5. Last but certainly not least, the staff at Addison-Wesley and associated companies were always a pleasure to work with. In addition to my editor Tom Stone, I would like to thank Paul Anagnostopoulos, Kathleen Billus, Nancy Fenton, Laura Michaels, Ann Knight, and Debra Wasserman for their expert and efficient handling of this project.

Many of the tools and techniques described in this book stem from the pioneering work of the National Science Foundation's Center for Research on Parallel Computation, without which this book would not have been possible. I am also grateful to the Office of Scientific Computing of the U.S. Department of Energy for their continued support.

The online version provides access here to other educational resources related to parallel and distributed computing. See Chapter 13 for more information about the online version.

# Contents

# Terminology

All logarithms in this book are to base 2; hence $\log N$ should be read as $\log_2 N$.

The notation $\mathcal{O}$ is used in the formal sense: A problem has size $\mathcal{O}(f(N))$ if and only if there exists some constant $c$ and some minimum problem size $N_0$ such that for all $N > N_0$, $\text{size}(N) \leq c \times f(N)$.

Various symbols are assumed to have the following conventional meanings, unless stated otherwise.

| | |
|---|---|
| $N$ | Problem size |
| $P$ | Number of processors |
| $t_s$ | Message startup cost |
| $t_w$ | Per-word message transfer cost |
| $t_c$ | Per-element computation cost |
| $\lfloor V \rfloor$ | Largest integer not larger than $V$ |
| $\lceil V \rceil$ | Smallest integer not smaller than $V$ |

# Concepts

The first part of this book comprises four chapters that deal with the design of parallel programs. Chapter 1 briefly introduces parallel computation and the importance of concurrency, scalability, locality, and modularity in parallel algorithm design. It also introduces the machine model and programming model used when developing parallel algorithms in subsequent chapters.

Chapter 2 presents a design methodology for parallel programs whereby the design process is divided into distinct partition, communication, agglomeration, and mapping phases. It introduces commonly used techniques and shows how these apply to realistic problems. It also presents design checklists for each phase. Case studies illustrate the application of the design methodology.

Chapter 3 describes how to analyze the performance of parallel algorithms and parallel programs, and shows how simple performance models can be used to assist in the evaluation of both design alternatives and program implementations. It also shows how performance models can account for characteristics of realistic interconnection networks.

Finally, Chapter 4 considers the issues that arise when parallel algorithms are combined to develop larger programs. It reviews the basic principles of modular design and discusses how these apply to parallel programs. It also examines different approaches to the composition of parallel program modules and shows how to model the performance of multicomponent programs.

# Parallel Computers
# and Computation

In this chapter, we review the role of parallelism in computing and introduce the parallel machine and programming models that will serve as the basis for subsequent discussion of algorithm design, performance analysis, and implementation.

After studying this chapter, you should be aware of the importance of concurrency, scalability, locality, and modularity in parallel program design. You should also be familiar with the idealized multicomputer model for which we shall design parallel algorithms, and the computation and communication abstractions that we shall use when describing parallel algorithms.

## 1.1 Parallelism and Computing

A *parallel computer* is a set of processors that are able to work cooperatively to solve a computational problem. This definition is broad enough to include parallel supercomputers that have hundreds or thousands of processors, networks of workstations, multiple-processor workstations, and embedded systems. Parallel computers are interesting because they offer the potential to concentrate computational resources—whether processors, memory, or I/O bandwidth—on important computational problems.

Parallelism has sometimes been viewed as a rare and exotic subarea of computing, interesting but of little relevance to the average programmer. A study of trends in applications, computer architecture, and networking shows that this view is no longer tenable. Parallelism is becoming ubiquitous, and parallel programming is becoming central to the programming enterprise.

### 1.1.1 Trends in Applications

As computers become ever faster, it can be tempting to suppose that they will eventually become "fast enough" and that appetite for increased computing power will be sated. However, history suggests that as a particular technology satisfies known applications, new applications will arise that are enabled by that technology and that will demand the development of new technology. As an amusing illustration of this phenomenon, a report prepared for the British government in the late 1940s concluded that Great Britain's computational requirements could be met by two or perhaps three computers. In those days, computers were used primarily for computing ballistics tables. The authors of the report did not consider other applications in science and engineering, let alone the commercial applications that would soon come to dominate computing. Similarly, the initial prospectus for Cray Research predicted a market for ten supercomputers; many hundreds have since been sold.

Traditionally, developments at the high end of computing have been motivated by numerical simulations of complex systems such as weather, climate, mechanical devices, electronic circuits, manufacturing processes, and chemical reactions. However, the most significant forces driving the development of faster computers today are emerging commercial applications that require a computer to be able to process large amounts of data in sophisticated ways. These applications include video conferencing, collaborative work environments, computer-aided diagnosis in medicine, parallel databases used for decision support, and advanced graphics and virtual reality, particularly in the entertainment industry. For example, the integration of parallel computation, high-performance networking, and multimedia technologies is leading to the development of *video servers,* computers designed to serve hundreds or thousands of simultaneous requests for real-time video. Each video stream can involve both data transfer rates of many megabytes per second and large amounts of processing for encoding and decoding. In graphics, three-dimensional data sets are now approaching $10^9$ volume elements (1024 on a side). At 200 operations per element, a display updated 30 times per second requires a computer capable of $6.4 \times 10^{12}$ operations per second.

Although commercial applications may define the architecture of most future parallel computers, traditional scientific applications will remain important users of parallel computing technology. Indeed, as nonlinear effects place limits on the insights offered by purely theoretical investigations and as experimentation becomes more costly or impractical, computational studies of complex systems are becoming ever more important. Computational costs typically increase as the fourth power or more of the "resolution" that determines accuracy, so these studies have a seemingly insatiable demand for more computer power. They are also often characterized by large memory and input/output requirements. For example, a ten-year simulation of the earth's climate using a state-of-the-art model may involve $10^{16}$ floating-point operations—ten days at an execution speed of $10^{10}$ floating-point operations per second (10 gigaflops). This same simulation can easily generate a hundred gigabytes ($10^{11}$ bytes) or more of data. Yet as Table 1.1 shows, scientists can easily imagine refinements to these models that would increase these computational requirements 10,000 times.

In summary, the need for faster computers is driven by the demands of both data-intensive applications in commerce and computation-intensive applications in science and engineering. Increasingly, the requirements of these fields are merging, as scientific and engineering applications become more data intensive and commercial applications perform more sophisticated computations.

### 1.1.2  Trends in Computer Design

The performance of the fastest computers has grown exponentially from 1945 to the present, averaging a factor of 10 every five years. While the first computers performed

**Table 1.1**  Various refinements proposed to climate models, and the increased computational requirements associated with these refinements. Altogether, these refinements could increase computational requirements by a factor of between $10^4$ and $10^7$.

| Current State | Needed Capability | Cost |
|---|---|---|
| 100-km resolution | 10-km resolution | $10^2$–$10^3$ |
| Simple process representations | Improved process representations | 2–10 |
| Simple ocean | Fully coupled ocean | 2–5 |
| Simple atmospheric chemistry | Improved atmospheric chemistry | 2–5 |
| Limited biosphere | Comprehensive biosphere | about 2 |
| Tens of years | Hundreds of years | $10$–$10^2$ |

a few tens of floating-point operations per second, the parallel computers of the mid-1990s achieve tens of billions of operations per second (Figure 1.1). Similar trends can be observed in the low-end computers of different eras: the calculators, personal computers, and workstations. There is little to suggest that this growth will not continue. However, the computer architectures used to sustain this growth are changing radically—from sequential to parallel.

The performance of a computer depends directly on the time required to perform a basic operation and the number of these basic operations that can be performed concurrently. The time to perform a basic operation is ultimately limited by the "clock cycle" of the processor, that is, the time required to perform the most primitive operation. However, clock cycle times are decreasing slowly and appear to be approaching physical limits such as the speed of light (Figure 1.2). We cannot depend on faster processors to provide increased computational performance.

To circumvent these limitations, the designer may attempt to utilize internal concurrency in a chip, for example, by operating simultaneously on all 64 bits of two numbers that are to be multiplied. However, a fundamental result in Very Large Scale Integration (VLSI) complexity theory says that this strategy is expensive. This result states that for certain transitive computations (in which any output may depend on any input), the chip area $A$ and the time $T$ required to perform this computation are related so that $AT^2$ must exceed some problem-dependent function of problem size. This result can be explained informally by assuming that a computation must move a certain amount of information from one side of a square chip to the other. The amount of information that can be moved in a time unit is limited by the cross section of the chip, $\sqrt{A}$. This gives a transfer rate of $\sqrt{A}T$, from which the $AT^2$ relation is obtained. To decrease the time required to move the information by a certain factor, the cross section must be increased by the same factor, and hence the total area must be increased by the square of that factor.

This $AT^2$ result means that not only is it difficult to build individual components that operate faster, it may not even be desirable to do so. It may be cheaper to use more, slower components. For example, if we have an area $n^2A$ of silicon to use in a computer,

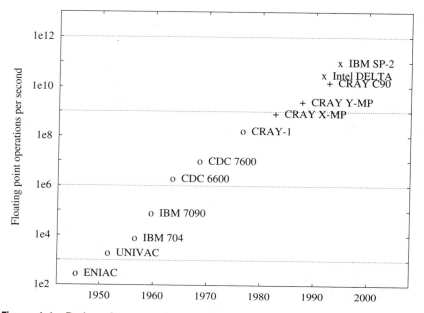

**Figure 1.1**    Peak performance of some of the fastest supercomputers, 1945–1995. The exponential growth flattened off somewhat in the 1980s but is accelerating again as massively parallel supercomputers become available. Here, "o" are uniprocessors, "+" denotes modestly parallel vector computers with 4–16 processors, and "x" denotes massively parallel computers with hundreds or thousands of processors. Typically, massively parallel computers achieve a lower proportion of their peak performance on realistic applications than do vector computers.

we can either build $n^2$ components, each of size $A$ and able to perform an operation in time $T$, or build a single component able to perform the same operation in time $T/n$. The multicomponent system is potentially $n$ times faster.

Computer designers use a variety of techniques to overcome these limitations on single computer performance, including pipelining (different stages of several instructions execute concurrently) and multiple function units (several multipliers, adders, etc., are controlled by a single instruction stream). Increasingly, designers are incorporating multiple "computers," each with its own processor, memory, and associated interconnection logic. This approach is facilitated by advances in VLSI technology that continue to decrease the number of components required to implement a computer. As the cost of a computer is (very approximately) proportional to the number of components that it contains, increased integration also increases the number of processors that can be included in a computer for a particular cost. The result is continued growth in processor counts (Figure 1.3).

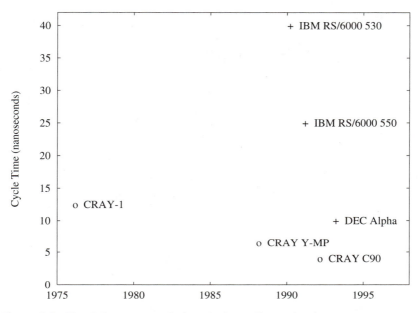

**Figure 1.2** Trends in computer clock cycle times. Conventional vector supercomputer cycle times (denoted "o") have decreased only by a factor of 3 in sixteen years, from the CRAY-1 (12.5 nanoseconds) to the C90 (4.0). RISC microprocessors (denoted "+") are fast approaching the same performance. Both architectures appear to be approaching physical limits.

### 1.1.3 Trends in Networking

Another important trend changing the face of computing is an enormous increase in the capabilities of the networks that connect computers. Not long ago, high-speed networks ran at 1.5 Mbits per second; by the end of the 1990s, bandwidths in excess of 1000 Mbits per second will be commonplace. Significant improvements in reliability are also expected. These trends make it feasible to develop applications that use physically distributed resources as if they were part of the same computer. A typical application of this sort may utilize processors on multiple remote computers, access a selection of remote databases, perform rendering on one or more graphics computers, and provide real-time output and control on a workstation.

We emphasize that computing on networked computers ("distributed computing") is not just a subfield of parallel computing. Distributed computing is deeply concerned with problems such as reliability, security, and heterogeneity that are generally regarded as tangential in parallel computing. (As Leslie Lamport has observed, "A distributed system is one in which the failure of a computer you didn't even know existed can render your own computer unusable.") Yet the basic task of developing programs that can run on many

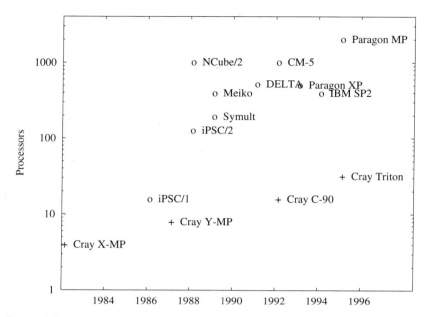

**Figure 1.3**    Number of processors in massively parallel computers ("o") and vector multiprocessors ("+"). In both cases, a steady increase in processor count is apparent. A similar trend is starting to occur in workstations, and personal computers can be expected to follow the same trend.

computers at once is a parallel computing problem. In this respect, the previously distinct worlds of parallel and distributed computing are converging.

### 1.1.4    Summary of Trends

This brief survey of trends in applications, computer architecture, and networking suggests a future in which parallelism pervades not only supercomputers but also workstations, personal computers, and networks. In this future, programs will be required to exploit the multiple processors located inside each computer and the additional processors available across a network. Because most existing algorithms are specialized for a single processor, this situation implies a need for new algorithms and program structures able to perform many operations at once. *Concurrency* becomes a fundamental requirement for algorithms and programs.

This survey also suggests a second fundamental lesson. It appears likely that processor counts will continue to increase—perhaps, as they do in some environments at present, by doubling each year or two. Hence, software systems can be expected to experience substantial increases in processor count over their lifetime. In this environment, *scalability*—resilience to increasing processor counts—is as important as portability for protecting software investments. A program able to use only a fixed number of processors is a bad program, as is a program able to execute on only a single computer. Scalability is a major theme that will be stressed throughout this book.

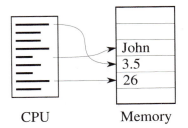

CPU                    Memory

**Figure 1.4**   The von Neumann computer. A central processing unit (CPU) executes a program that performs a sequence of read and write operations on an attached memory.

## 1.2   A Parallel Machine Model

The rapid penetration of computers into commerce, science, and education owed much to the early standardization on a single machine model, the von Neumann computer. A von Neumann computer comprises a central processing unit (CPU) connected to a storage unit (memory) (Figure 1.4). The CPU executes a stored program that specifies a sequence of read and write operations on the memory. This simple model has proved remarkably robust. Its persistence over more than forty years has allowed the study of such important topics as algorithms and programming languages to proceed to a large extent independently of developments in computer architecture. Consequently, programmers can be trained in the abstract art of "programming" rather than the craft of "programming machine X" and can design algorithms for an abstract von Neumann machine, confident that these algorithms will execute on most target computers with reasonable efficiency.

Our study of parallel programming will be most rewarding if we can identify a parallel machine model that is as general and useful as the von Neumann sequential machine model. This machine model must be both simple and realistic: *simple* to facilitate understanding and programming, and *realistic* to ensure that programs developed for the model execute with reasonable efficiency on real computers.

### 1.2.1   The Multicomputer

A parallel machine model called the *multicomputer* fits these requirements. As illustrated in Figure 1.5, a multicomputer comprises a number of von Neumann computers, or *nodes*, linked by an *interconnection network*. Each computer executes its own program. This program may access local memory and may send and receive messages over the network. Messages are used to communicate with other computers or, equivalently, to read and write remote memories. In the idealized network, the cost of sending a message between two nodes is independent of both node location and other network traffic, but does depend on message length.

A defining attribute of the multicomputer model is that accesses to local (same-node) memory are less expensive than accesses to remote (different-node) memory. That is, read and write are less costly than send and receive. Hence, it is desirable that accesses to local data be more frequent than accesses to remote data. This property, called *locality*, is a third fundamental requirement for parallel software, in addition to concurrency and scalability.

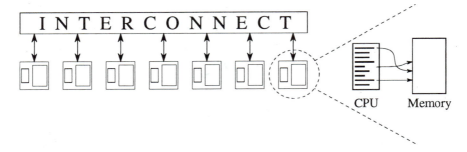

**Figure 1.5**   The multicomputer, an idealized parallel computer model. Each node consists of a von Neumann machine: a CPU and memory. A node can communicate with other nodes by sending and receiving messages over an interconnection network.

The importance of locality depends on the ratio of remote to local access costs. This ratio can vary from 10:1 to 1000:1 or greater, depending on the relative performance of the local computer, the network, and the mechanisms used to move data to and from the network.

## 1.2.2   Other Machine Models

We review important parallel computer architectures (several are illustrated in Figure 1.6) and discuss briefly how these differ from the idealized multicomputer model.

The multicomputer is most similar to what is often called the *distributed-memory MIMD* (multiple instruction multiple data) computer. MIMD means that each processor can execute a separate stream of instructions on its own local data; distributed memory means that memory is distributed among the processors, rather than placed in a central location. The principal difference between a multicomputer and the distributed-memory MIMD computer is that in the latter, the cost of sending a message between two nodes may not be independent of node location and other network traffic. These issues are discussed in Chapter 3. Examples of this class of machine include the IBM SP, Intel Paragon, Thinking Machines CM5, Cray T3D, Meiko CS-2, and nCUBE.

Another important class of parallel computer is the *multiprocessor*, or shared-memory MIMD computer. In multiprocessors, all processors share access to a common memory, typically via a bus or a hierarchy of buses. In the idealized Parallel Random Access Machine (PRAM) model, often used in theoretical studies of parallel algorithms, any processor can access any memory element in the same amount of time. In practice, scaling this architecture usually introduces some form of memory hierarchy; in particular, the frequency with which the shared memory is accessed may be reduced by storing copies of frequently used data items in a *cache* associated with each processor. Access to this cache is much faster than access to the shared memory; hence, locality is usually important, and the differences between multicomputers and multiprocessors are really just questions of degree. Programs developed for multicomputers can also execute efficiently on multiprocessors, because shared memory permits an efficient implementation of message passing.

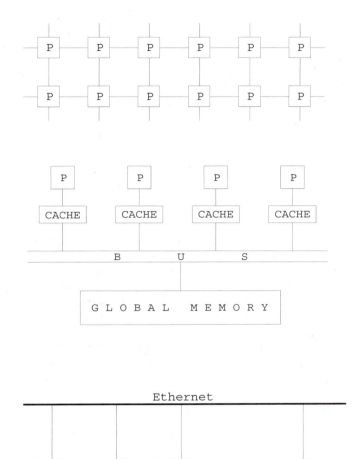

**Figure 1.6**  Classes of parallel computer architecture. From top to bottom: a distributed-memory MIMD computer with a mesh interconnect, a shared-memory multiprocessor, and a local area network (in this case, an Ethernet). In each case, P denotes an independent processor.

Examples of this class of machine include the Silicon Graphics Challenge, Sequent Symmetry, and the many multiprocessor workstations.

A more specialized class of parallel computer is the *SIMD* (single instruction multiple data) computer. In SIMD machines, all processors execute the same instruction stream on a different piece of data. This approach can reduce both hardware and software complexity but is appropriate only for specialized problems characterized by a high degree of regularity, for example, image processing and certain numerical simulations. Multicomputer algorithms *cannot* in general be executed efficiently on SIMD computers. The MasPar MP is an example of this class of machine.

Two classes of computer system that are sometimes used as parallel computers are the local area network (LAN), in which computers in close physical proximity (e.g., the same building) are connected by a fast network, and the wide area network (WAN), in which geographically distributed computers are connected. Although systems of this sort introduce additional concerns such as reliability and security, they can be viewed for many purposes as multicomputers, albeit with high remote-access costs. Ethernet and asynchronous transfer mode (ATM) are commonly used network technologies.

## 1.3   A Parallel Programming Model

The von Neumann machine model assumes a processor able to execute sequences of instructions. An instruction can specify, in addition to various arithmetic operations, the address of a datum to be read or written in memory and/or the address of the next instruction to be executed. While it is possible to program a computer in terms of this basic model by writing machine language, this method is for most purposes prohibitively complex, because we must keep track of millions of memory locations and organize the execution of thousands of machine instructions. Hence, modular design techniques are applied, whereby complex programs are constructed from simple components, and components are structured in terms of higher-level abstractions such as data structures, iterative loops, and procedures. Abstractions such as procedures make the exploitation of modularity easier by allowing objects to be manipulated without concern for their internal structure. So do high-level languages such as Fortran, Pascal, C, and Ada, which allow designs expressed in terms of these abstractions to be translated automatically into executable code.

Parallel programming introduces additional sources of complexity: if we were to program at the lowest level, not only would the number of instructions executed increase, but we would also need to manage explicitly the execution of thousands of processors and coordinate millions of interprocessor interactions. Hence, abstraction and modularity are at least as important as in sequential programming. In fact, we shall emphasize *modularity* as a fourth fundamental requirement for parallel software, in addition to concurrency, scalability, and locality.

### 1.3.1   Tasks and Channels

We consider next the question of which abstractions are appropriate and useful in a parallel programming model. Clearly, mechanisms are needed that allow explicit discussion about concurrency and locality and that facilitate development of scalable and modular programs. Also needed are abstractions that are simple to work with and that match the architectural model, the multicomputer. While numerous possible abstractions could be considered for this purpose, two fit these requirements particularly well: the *task* and *channel*. These are illustrated in Figure 1.7 and can be summarized as follows:

1. A parallel computation consists of one or more tasks. Tasks execute concurrently. The number of tasks can vary during program execution.

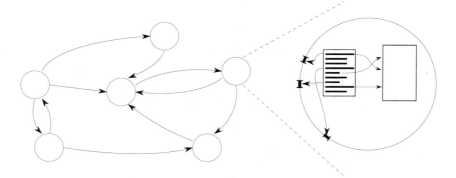

**Figure 1.7**    A simple parallel programming model. The figure shows both the instantaneous state of a computation and a detailed picture of a single task. A computation consists of a set of tasks (represented by circles) connected by channels (arrows). A task encapsulates a program and local memory and defines a set of ports that define its interface to its environment. A channel is a message queue into which a sender can place messages and from which a receiver can remove messages, "blocking" if messages are not available.

2. A task encapsulates a sequential program and local memory. (In effect, it is a virtual von Neumann machine.) In addition, a set of *inports* and *outports* define its interface to its environment.

3. A task can perform four basic actions in addition to reading and writing its local memory (Figure 1.8): send messages on its outports, receive messages on its inports, create new tasks, and terminate.

4. A send operation is asynchronous: it completes immediately. A receive operation is synchronous: it causes execution of the task to block until a message is available.

5. Outport/inport pairs can be connected by message queues called *channels*. Channels can be created and deleted, and references to channels (ports) can be included in messages, so connectivity can vary dynamically.

6. Tasks can be mapped to physical processors in various ways; the mapping employed does not affect the semantics of a program. In particular, multiple tasks can be mapped to a single processor. (We can also imagine a single task being mapped to multiple processors, but that possibility is not considered here.)

The task abstraction provides a mechanism for talking about locality: data contained in a task's local memory are "close"; other data are "remote." The channel abstraction provides a mechanism for indicating that computation in one task requires data in another task in order to proceed. (This is termed a *data dependency*). The following simple example illustrates some of these features.

Send a message:

Receive a message:

Create tasks:

Terminate:

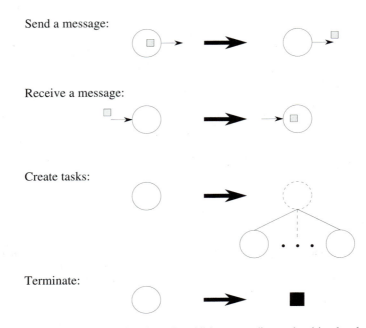

**Figure 1.8**   The four basic task actions. In addition to reading and writing local memory, a task can send a message, receive a message, create new tasks (suspending until they terminate), and terminate.

---

**EXAMPLE 1.1** (Bridge Construction)    Consider the following real-world problem. A bridge is to be assembled from girders being constructed at a foundry. These two activities are organized by providing trucks to transport girders from the foundry to the bridge site. This situation is illustrated in Figure 1.9(a), with the foundry and bridge represented as tasks and the stream of trucks as a channel. Notice that this approach allows assembly of the bridge and construction of girders to proceed in parallel without any explicit coordination: the foundry crew puts girders on trucks as they are produced, and the assembly crew adds girders to the bridge as and when they arrive.

A disadvantage of this scheme is that the foundry may produce girders much faster than the assembly crew can use them. To prevent the bridge site from overflowing with girders, the assembly crew instead can explicitly request more girders when stocks run low. This refined approach is illustrated in Figure 1.9(b), with the stream of requests represented as a second channel. The second channel can also be used to shut down the flow of girders when the bridge is complete.

---

We now examine some other properties of this task/channel programming model: performance, mapping independence, modularity, and determinism.

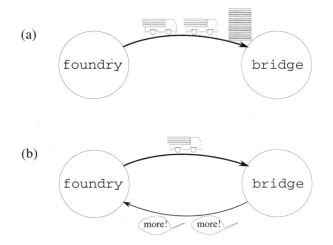

**Figure 1.9**   Two solutions to the bridge construction problem. Both represent the foundry and the bridge assembly site as separate tasks, `foundry` and `bridge`. The first uses a single channel on which girders generated by `foundry` are transported as fast as they are generated. If `foundry` generates girders faster than they are consumed by `bridge`, then girders accumulate at the construction site. The second solution uses a second channel to pass flow control messages from `bridge` to `foundry` so as to avoid overflow.

**Performance**   Sequential programming abstractions such as procedures and data structures are effective because they can be mapped simply and efficiently to the von Neumann computer. The task and channel have a similarly direct mapping to the multicomputer. A task represents a piece of code that can be executed sequentially, on a single processor. If two tasks that share a channel are mapped to different processors, the channel connection is implemented as interprocessor communication; if they are mapped to the same processor, some more efficient mechanism can be used.

**Mapping Independence**   Because tasks interact using the same mechanism (channels) regardless of task location, the result computed by a program does not depend on where tasks execute. Hence, algorithms can be designed and implemented without concern for the number of processors on which they will execute; in fact, algorithms are frequently designed that create many more tasks than processors. This is a straightforward way of achieving *scalability*: as the number of processors increases, the number of tasks per processor is reduced but the algorithm itself need not be modified. The creation of more tasks than processors can also serve to mask communication delays, by providing other computation that can be performed while communication is performed to access remote data.

**Modularity**   In modular program design, various components of a program are developed separately, as independent modules, and then combined to obtain a complete program. Interactions between modules are restricted to well-defined interfaces. Hence,

(a)

(b)

(c)

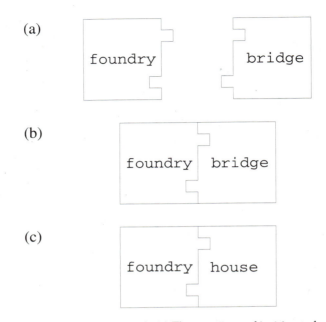

**Figure 1.10**    The task as building block. (a) The `foundry` and `bridge` tasks are building blocks with complementary interfaces. (b) Hence, the two tasks can be plugged together to form a complete program. (c) Tasks are interchangeable: another task with a compatible interface can be substituted to obtain a different program.

module implementations can be changed without modifying other components, and the properties of a program can be determined from the specifications for its modules and the code that plugs these modules together. When successfully applied, modular design reduces program complexity and facilitates code reuse.

The task is a natural building block for modular design. As illustrated in Figure 1.10, a task encapsulates both data and the code that operates on those data; the ports on which it sends and receives messages constitute its interface. Hence, the advantages of modular design summarized in the previous paragraph are directly accessible in the task/channel model.

Strong similarities exist between the task/channel model and the popular object-oriented programming paradigm. Tasks, like objects, encapsulate data and the code that operates on those data. Distinguishing features of the task/channel model are its concurrency, its use of channels rather than method calls to specify interactions, and its lack of support for inheritance.

**Determinism**    An algorithm or program is deterministic if execution with a particular input always yields the same output. It is nondeterministic if multiple executions with the same input can give different outputs. Although nondeterminism is sometimes useful and must be supported, a parallel programming model that makes it easy to write deterministic programs is highly desirable. Deterministic programs tend to be easier to understand. Also, when checking for correctness, only one execution sequence of a parallel program needs to be considered, rather than all possible executions.

The "arms-length" interactions supported by the task/channel model makes determinism relatively easy to guarantee. As we shall see in Part II when we consider programming tools, it suffices to verify that each channel has a single sender and a single receiver and that a task receiving on a channel blocks until a receive operation is complete. These conditions can be relaxed when nondeterministic interactions are required.

In the bridge construction example, determinism means that the same bridge will be constructed regardless of the rates at which the foundry builds girders and the assembly crew puts girders together. If the assembly crew runs ahead of the foundry, it will block, waiting for girders to arrive. Hence, it simply suspends its operations until more girders are available, rather than attempting to continue construction with half-completed girders. Similarly, if the foundry produces girders faster than the assembly crew can use them, these girders simply accumulate until they are needed. Determinism would be guaranteed even if several bridges were constructed simultaneously: As long as girders destined for different bridges travel on distinct channels, they cannot be confused.

### 1.3.2 Other Programming Models

In subsequent chapters, the task/channel model will often be used to describe algorithms. However, this model is certainly not the only approach that can be taken to representing parallel computation. Many other models have been proposed, differing in their flexibility, task interaction mechanisms, task granularities, and support for locality, scalability, and modularity. Here, we review several alternatives.

**Message Passing**     Message passing is probably the most widely used parallel programming model today. Message-passing programs, like task/channel programs, create multiple tasks, with each task encapsulating local data. Each task is identified by a unique name, and tasks interact by sending and receiving messages to and from named tasks. In this respect, message passing is really just a minor variation on the task/channel model, differing only in the mechanism used for data transfer. For example, rather than sending a message on "channel ch," we may send a message to "task 17." We study the message-passing model in more detail in Chapter 8, where we discuss the *Message Passing Interface*. In that chapter, we explain that the definition of channels is a useful discipline even when designing message-passing programs, because it forces us to conceptualize the communication structure of a parallel program.

The message-passing model does not preclude the dynamic creation of tasks, the execution of multiple tasks per processor, or the execution of different programs by different tasks. However, in practice most message-passing systems create a fixed number of identical tasks at program startup and do not allow tasks to be created or destroyed during program execution. These systems are said to implement a *single program multiple data* (SPMD) programming model because each task executes the same program but operates on different data. As explained in subsequent chapters, the SPMD model is sufficient for a wide range of parallel programming problems but does hinder some parallel algorithm developments.

**Data Parallelism**    Another commonly used parallel programming model, data parallelism, calls for exploitation of the concurrency that derives from the application of the same operation to multiple elements of a data structure, for example, "add 2 to all elements of this array," or "increase the salary of all employees with 5 years service." A data-parallel program consists of a sequence of such operations. As each operation on each data element can be thought of as an independent task, the natural granularity of a data-parallel computation is small, and the concept of "locality" does not arise naturally. Hence, data-parallel compilers often require the programmer to provide information about how data are to be distributed over processors, in other words, how data are to be partitioned into tasks. The compiler can then translate the data-parallel program into an SPMD formulation, thereby generating communication code automatically. We discuss the data-parallel model in more detail in Chapter 7 under the topic of *High Performance Fortran*. In that chapter, we show that the algorithm design and analysis techniques developed for the task/channel model apply directly to data-parallel programs; in particular, they provide the concepts required to understand the locality and scalability of data-parallel programs.

**Shared Memory**    In the shared-memory programming model, tasks share a common address space, which they read and write asynchronously. Various mechanisms such as locks and semaphores may be used to control access to the shared memory. An advantage of this model from the programmer's point of view is that the notion of data "ownership" is lacking, and hence there is no need to specify explicitly the communication of data from producers to consumers. This model can simplify program development. However, understanding and managing locality becomes more difficult, an important consideration (as noted earlier) on most shared-memory architectures. It can also be more difficult to write deterministic programs.

## 1.4    Parallel Algorithm Examples

We conclude this chapter by presenting four examples of parallel algorithms. We do not concern ourselves here with the process by which these algorithms are derived or with their efficiency; these issues are discussed in Chapters 2 and 3, respectively. The goal is simply to introduce parallel algorithms and their description in terms of tasks and channels.

The first two algorithms described have an SPMD structure, the third creates tasks dynamically during program execution, and the fourth uses a fixed number of tasks but has different tasks perform different functions.

### 1.4.1    Finite Differences

We first consider a one-dimensional finite difference problem, in which we have a vector $X^{(0)}$ of size $N$ and must compute $X^{(T)}$, where

$$0 < i < N - 1,\ 0 \leq t < T :\ X_i^{(t+1)} = \frac{X_{i-1}^{(t)} + 2X_i^{(t)} + X_{i+1}^{(t)}}{4}.$$

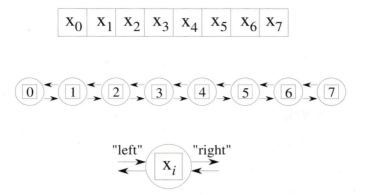

**Figure 1.11**   A parallel algorithm for the one-dimensional finite difference problem. From top to bottom: the one-dimensional vector $X$, where $N = 8$; the task structure, showing the 8 tasks, each encapsulating a single data value and connected to left and right neighbors via channels; and the structure of a single task, showing its two inports and outports.

That is, we must repeatedly update each element of $X$, with no element being updated in step $t + 1$ until its neighbors have been updated in step $t$.

A parallel algorithm for this problem creates $N$ tasks, one for each point in $X$. The $i$th task is given the value $X_i^{(0)}$ and is responsible for computing, in $T$ steps, the values $X_i^{(1)}, X_i^{(2)}, \ldots, X_i^{(T)}$. Hence, at step $t$, it must obtain the values $X_{i-1}^{(t)}$ and $X_{i+1}^{(t)}$ from tasks $i - 1$ and $i + 1$. We specify this data transfer by defining channels that link each task with "left" and "right" neighbors, as shown in Figure 1.11, and requiring that at step $t$, each task $i$ other than task 0 and task $N - 1$

1. sends its data $X_i^{(t)}$ on its left and right outports,
2. receives $X_{i-1}^{(t)}$ and $X_{i+1}^{(t)}$ from its left and right inports, and
3. uses these values to compute $X_i^{(t+1)}$.

Notice that the $N$ tasks can execute independently, with the only constraint on execution order being the synchronization enforced by the receive operations. This synchronization ensures that no data value is updated at step $t + 1$ until the data values in neighboring tasks have been updated at step $t$. Hence, execution is deterministic.

### 1.4.2   Pairwise Interactions

Our second example uses a similar channel structure but requires a more complex communication algorithm. Many problems require the computation of all $N(N - 1)$ pairwise interactions $I(X_i, X_j)$, $i \neq j$, between $N$ data, $X_0, \ldots, X_{N-1}$. Interactions may be symmetric, in which case $I(X_i, X_j) = \pm I(X_j, X_i)$ and only $N(N - 1)/2$ interactions need be computed. For example, in molecular dynamics we may require the total force vector $f_i$ acting on each atom $X_i$, defined as follows:

$$f_i = \sum_{j=0}^{N-1} F(X_i, X_j).$$

Each atom is represented by its mass and Cartesian coordinates. $F(X_i, X_j)$ denotes the mutual attraction or repulsion between atoms $X_i$ and $X_j$; in this example, $F(X_i, X_j) = -F(X_j, X_i)$, so interactions are symmetric.

A simple parallel algorithm for the general pairwise interactions problem might create $N$ tasks. Task $i$ is given the datum $X_i$ and is responsible for computing the interactions $\{I(X_i, X_j) \mid i \neq j\}$. One might think that as each task needs a datum from every other task, $N(N-1)$ channels would be needed to perform the necessary communications. However, a more economical structure is possible that uses only $N$ channels. These channels are used to connect the $N$ tasks in a unidirectional ring (Figure 1.12(a)). Hence, each task has one inport and one outport. Each task first initializes both a buffer (with the value of its local datum) and an accumulator that will maintain the result of the computation. It then repeatedly

1. sends the value contained in its buffer on its outport,
2. receives a datum on its inport into its buffer,
3. computes the interaction between this datum and its local datum, and
4. uses the computed interaction to update its local accumulator.

This send-receive-compute cycle is repeated $N - 1$ times, causing the $N$ data to flow around the ring. Every task sees every datum and is able to compute all $N - 1$ interactions involving its datum. The algorithm involves $N - 1$ communications per task.

It turns out that if interactions are symmetric, we can halve both the number of interactions computed and the number of communications by refining the communication structure. Assume for simplicity that $N$ is odd. An additional $N$ communication channels are created, linking each task to the task offset $\lfloor N/2 \rfloor$ around the ring (Figure 1.12(b)).

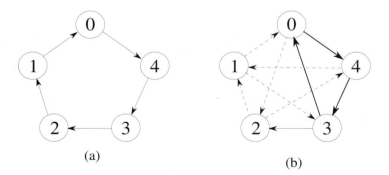

(a)                    (b)

**Figure 1.12**    Task structures for computing pairwise interactions for $N = 5$. (a) The unidirectional ring used in the simple, nonsymmetric algorithm. (b) The unidirectional ring with additional channels used to return accumulated values in the symmetric algorithm; the path taken by the accumulator used for task 0 is shown as a solid line.

```
procedure search(A)
begin
   if (solution(A)) then
      score = eval(A)
      report solution and score
   else
      foreach child A(i) of A
         search(A(i))
      endfor
   endif
end
```

**Algorithm 1.1**   A recursive formulation of a simple search algorithm. When called to expand a search tree node, this procedure checks to see whether the node in question represents a solution. If not, the algorithm makes recursive calls to the same procedure to expand each of the offspring nodes.

Each time an interaction $I(X_i, X_j)$ is computed between a local datum $X_i$ and an incoming datum $X_j$, this value is accumulated not only in the accumulator for $X_i$ but also in another accumulator that is circulated with $X_j$. After $\lfloor N/2 \rfloor$ steps, the accumulators associated with the circulated values are returned to their home task using the new channels and combined with the local accumulators. Hence, each symmetric interaction is computed only once: either as $I(X_i, X_j)$ on the node that holds $X_i$ or as $I(X_j, X_i)$ on the node that holds $X_j$.

## 1.4.3   Search

The next example illustrates the dynamic creation of tasks and channels during program execution. Algorithm 1.1 explores a search tree looking for nodes that correspond to "solutions." A parallel algorithm for this problem can be structured as follows. Initially, a single task is created for the root of the tree. A task evaluates its node and then, if that node is not a solution, creates a new task for each `search` call (subtree). A channel created for each new task is used to return to the new task's parent any solutions located in its subtree. Hence, new tasks and channels are created in a wavefront as the search progresses down the search tree (Figure 1.13).

## 1.4.4   Parameter Study

In so-called embarrassingly parallel problems, a computation consists of a number of tasks that can execute more or less independently, without communication. These problems are usually easy to adapt for parallel execution. An example is a parameter study, in which the same computation must be performed using a range of different input parameters. The parameter values are read from an input file, and the results of the different computations are written to an output file.

    If the execution time per problem is constant and each processor has the same computational power, then it suffices to partition available problems into equal-sized sets and

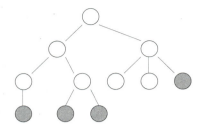

**Figure 1.13** Task structure for the search example. Each circle represents a node in the search tree and hence a call to the `search` procedure. A task is created for each node in the tree as it is explored. At any one time, some tasks are actively engaged in expanding the tree further (these are shaded in the figure); others have reached solution nodes and are terminating, or are waiting for their offspring to report back with solutions. The lines represent the channels used to return solutions.

allocate one such set to each processor. In other situations, we may choose to use the task structure illustrated in Figure 1.14. The input and output tasks are responsible for reading and writing the input and output files, respectively. Each worker task (typically one per processor) repeatedly requests parameter values from the input task, computes using these values, and sends results to the output task. Because execution times vary, the input and output tasks cannot expect to receive messages from the various workers in any particular order. Instead, a many-to-one communication structure is used that allows them to receive messages from the various workers in arrival order.

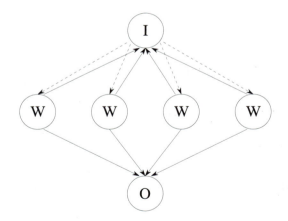

**Figure 1.14** Task structure for parameter study problem. Workers (W) request parameters from the input task (I) and send results to the output task (O). Note the many-to-one connections: this program is nondeterministic in that the input and output tasks receive data from workers in whatever order the data are generated. Reply channels, represented as dashed lines, are used to communicate parameters from the input task to workers.

The input task responds to a worker request by sending a parameter to that worker. Hence, a worker that has sent a request to the input task simply waits for the parameter to arrive on its reply channel. In some cases, efficiency can be improved by *prefetching*, that is, requesting the next parameter before it is needed. The worker can then perform computation while its request is being processed by the input task.

Because this program uses many-to-one communication structures, the order in which computations are performed is not necessarily determined. However, this nondeterminism affects only the allocation of problems to workers and the ordering of results in the output file, not the actual results computed.

## 1.5  Summary

This chapter has introduced four desirable attributes of parallel algorithms and software: concurrency, scalability, locality, and modularity. *Concurrency* refers to the ability to perform many actions simultaneously; this is essential if a program is to execute on many processors. *Scalability* indicates resilience to increasing processor counts and is equally important, as processor counts appear likely to grow in most environments. *Locality* means a high ratio of local memory accesses to remote memory accesses (communication); this is the key to high performance on multicomputer architectures. *Modularity*—the decomposition of complex entities into simpler components—is an essential aspect of software engineering, in parallel computing as well as sequential computing.

The multicomputer parallel machine model and the task/channel programming model introduced in this chapter will be used in subsequent discussion of parallel algorithm design, analysis, and implementation. The *multicomputer* consists of one or more von Neumann computers connected by an interconnection network. It is a simple and realistic machine model that provides a basis for the design of scalable and portable parallel programs. A programming model based on *tasks* and *channels* simplifies the programming of multicomputers by providing abstractions that allow us to talk about concurrency, locality, and communication in a machine-independent fashion, and by providing a basis for the modular construction of parallel programs.

### Exercises

Exercises 6–10 require you to describe a parallel algorithm. You should describe the task/channel structure created by the algorithm and provide a definition for each task, including its interface (inports and outports), its local data, and the actions it performs.

1. If today's workstations execute at $10^8$ operations per second, and performance increases at a rate of 25 percent per year, how long will it be before we have workstations capable of $10^9$ operations per second? $10^{12}$?

2. A climate model requires $10^{16}$ floating point operations for a ten-year simulation. How long would this computation take at $10^7$ floating point operations per second (10 Mflops)?

3. A climate model generates $10^{11}$ bytes of data in a ten-day simulation. How fast must data be transferred to secondary storage? What transfer rate is required if we are to search this data in ten minutes?

4. Consider a three-dimensional chip. Demonstrate that chip volume $V$ and computation time $T$ are related as $V^2T^3$, just as area $A$ and computation time are related as $AT^2$ in a two-dimensional chip.

5. Execute the parallel algorithm described in Section 1.4.1 by hand for $N = 4$, and satisfy yourself that execution is deterministic.

6. Adapt the parallel algorithm of Section 1.4.1 to deal with a two-dimensional finite difference problem in which the value of each point $x_{ij}$ in a two-dimensional grid of size $N \times N$ is updated as follows:

$$X_{i,j}^{(t+1)} = \frac{4X_{i,j}^{(t)} + X_{i-1,j}^{(t)} + X_{i,j-1}^{(t)} + X_{i+1,j}^{(t)} + X_{i,j+1}^{(t)}}{8}.$$

7. Describe a variant of the parallel algorithm of Section 1.4.2 that allows for the case when $N$ is even.

8. Describe a parallel algorithm for Hoare's quicksort algorithm [153] based on the parallel divide-and-conquer strategy employed in Section 1.4.3.

9. Describe a task/channel structure for a parallel database system in which $M$ concurrently executing users can generate requests to read and write data located in $N$ databases and requests to access different databases can be handled concurrently. You must use less than $M.N$ channels.

   Extend this structure to allow a user to request that a set of read and write operations be performed as an atomic operation, that is, without read or write operations generated by other tasks intervening.

10. Extend the parallel algorithms of Sections 1.4.1 and 1.4.3 to provide for the loading of initial data values in from disk and the writing out of the solutions to disk.

## Chapter Notes

Kauffman and Smarr [169] discuss the impact of high-performance computing on science. Levin [189] and several U.S. government reports [232, 233, 215] describe the so-called Grand Challenge problems that have motivated recent initiatives in high-performance computing. The computational requirements in Table 1.1 are derived from the project plan for the CHAMMP climate modeling program, which has adapted a range of climate models for execution on parallel computers [287]. Dewitt and Gray [79] discuss developments in parallel databases. Lawson [186] discusses industrial real-time applications of parallel computing. Worlton [299], Meindl [201], and Hennessy and Joupp [147] discuss trends in processor design and sequential and parallel computer architecture. Ullman [286] provides a succinct explanation of the $AT^2$ complexity results.

Goldstine and von Neumann [121] provide an early exposition of the von Neumann computer. Bailey [22] explains how this model derived from the automation of algorithms performed previously by "human computers." He argues that highly parallel computers are stimulating not only new algorithmic approaches, but also new ways of thinking about problems. Many researchers have proposed abstract machine models for parallel computing [67, 99, 288]. Snyder [268] explains why the multicomputer is a good choice. Early parallel computers with a multicomputer-like architecture include the Ultracomputer [252] and the Cosmic Cube [254]. Athas and Seitz [18] and Seitz [255] discuss developments in this area. Almasi and Gottlieb [11] and Hwang [156] provide good introductions to parallel computer architectures and interconnection networks. Hillis [150] describes SIMD computers. Fortune and Wylie [99] and JáJá [157] discuss the PRAM model. Comer [63] discusses LANs and WANs. Kahn [162] describes the ARPANET, an early WAN. The chapter notes in Chapter 3 provide additional references on parallel computer architecture.

The basic abstractions used to describe parallel algorithms have been developed in the course of many years of research in operating systems, distributed computing, and parallel computation. The use of channels was first explored by Hoare in Communicating Sequential Processes (CSP) [154] and is fundamental to the occam programming language [231, 280]. However, in CSP the task and channel structure is static, and both sender and receiver block until a communication has completed. This approach has proven too restrictive for general-purpose parallel programming. The task/channel model introduced in this chapter is described by Chandy and Foster [102], who also discuss the conditions under which the model can guarantee deterministic execution [51].

Seitz [254] and Gropp, Lusk, and Skjellum [126] describe the message-passing model (see also the chapter notes in Chapter 8). Ben Ari [32] and Karp and Babb [165] discuss shared-memory programming. Hillis and Steele [151] and Hatcher and Quinn [136] describe data-parallel programming; the chapter notes in Chapter 7 provide additional references. Other approaches that have generated considerable interest include Actors [5], concurrent logic programming [107], functional programming [146], Linda [48], and Unity [54]. Bal et al. [23] provide a useful survey of some of these approaches. Pancake and Bergmark [218] emphasize the importance of deterministic execution in parallel computing.

The online version provides access here to additional information on parallel applications, parallel computer architecture, and parallel programming models.

#  Designing Parallel Algorithms

Now that we have discussed what parallel algorithms look like, we are ready to examine how they can be designed. In this chapter, we show how a problem specification is translated into an algorithm that displays concurrency, scalability, and locality. Issues relating to modularity are discussed in Chapter 4.

Parallel algorithm design is not easily reduced to simple recipes. Rather, it requires the sort of integrative thought that is commonly referred to as "creativity." However, it *can* benefit from a methodical approach that maximizes the range of options considered, that provides mechanisms for evaluating alternatives, and that reduces the cost of backtracking from bad choices. We describe such an approach and illustrate its application to a range of problems. Our goal is to suggest a framework within which parallel algorithm design can be explored. In the process, we hope you will develop intuition as to what constitutes a good parallel algorithm.

After studying this chapter, you should be able to design simple parallel algorithms in a methodical fashion and recognize design flaws that compromise efficiency or scalability. You should be able to partition computations, using both domain and functional decomposition techniques, and know how to recognize and implement both local and global, static and dynamic, structured and unstructured, and synchronous and asynchronous communication structures. You should also be able to use agglomeration as a means of reducing communication and implementation costs and should be familiar with a range of load-balancing strategies.

## 2.1 Methodical Design

Most programming problems have several parallel solutions. The best solution may differ from that suggested by existing sequential algorithms. The design methodology that we describe is intended to foster an exploratory approach to design in which machine-independent issues such as concurrency are considered early and machine-specific aspects of design are delayed until late in the design process. This methodology structures the design process as four distinct stages: partitioning, communication, agglomeration, and mapping. (The acronym PCAM may serve as a useful reminder of this structure.) In the first two stages, we focus on concurrency and scalability and seek to discover algorithms with these qualities. In the third and fourth stages, attention shifts to locality and other performance-related issues. The four stages are illustrated in Figure 2.1 and can be summarized as follows:

1. *Partitioning.* The computation that is to be performed and the data operated on by this computation are decomposed into small tasks. Practical issues such as the number of processors in the target computer are ignored, and attention is focused on recognizing opportunities for parallel execution.

2. *Communication.* The communication required to coordinate task execution is determined, and appropriate communication structures and algorithms are defined.

3. *Agglomeration.* The task and communication structures defined in the first two stages of a design are evaluated with respect to performance requirements and implementation costs. If necessary, tasks are combined into larger tasks to improve performance or to reduce development costs.

4. *Mapping.* Each task is assigned to a processor in a manner that attempts to satisfy the competing goals of maximizing processor utilization and minimizing communication costs. Mapping can be specified statically or determined at runtime by load-balancing algorithms.

The outcome of this design process can be a program that creates and destroys tasks dynamically, using load-balancing techniques to control the mapping of tasks to processors. Alternatively, it can be an SPMD program that creates exactly one task per processor. The same process of algorithm discovery applies in both cases, although if the goal is to produce an SPMD program, issues associated with mapping are subsumed into the agglomeration phase of the design.

Algorithm design is presented here as a sequential activity. In practice, however, it is a highly parallel process, with many concerns being considered simultaneously. Also, although we seek to avoid backtracking, evaluation of a partial or complete design may require changes to design decisions made in previous steps.

The following sections provide a detailed examination of the four stages of the design process. We present basic principles, use examples to illustrate the application of these principles, and include design checklists that can be used to evaluate designs as they are developed. In the final sections of this chapter, we use three case studies to illustrate the application of these design techniques to realistic problems.

## 2.2   Partitioning

The partitioning stage of a design is intended to expose opportunities for parallel execution. Hence, the focus is on defining a large number of small tasks in order to yield what is termed a *fine-grained* decomposition of a problem. Just as fine sand is more easily poured than a pile of bricks, a fine-grained decomposition provides the greatest flexibility in terms of potential parallel algorithms. In later design stages, evaluation of communication requirements, the target architecture, or software engineering issues may lead us to forego opportunities for parallel execution identified at this stage. We then revisit the original par-

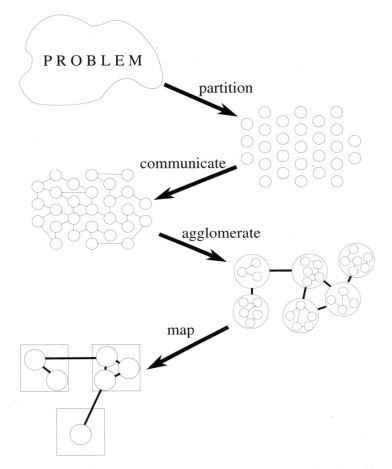

**Figure 2.1**  PCAM: a design methodology for parallel programs. Starting with a problem specification, we develop a partition, determine communication requirements, agglomerate tasks, and finally map tasks to processors.

tition and agglomerate tasks to increase their size, or granularity. However, in this first stage we wish to avoid prejudging alternative partitioning strategies.

A good partition divides into small pieces both the *computation* associated with a problem and the *data* on which this computation operates. When designing a partition, programmers most commonly first focus on the data associated with a problem, then determine an appropriate partition for the data, and finally work out how to associate computation with data. This partitioning technique is termed *domain decomposition*. The alternative approach—first decomposing the computation to be performed and then dealing with the data—is termed *functional decomposition*. These are complementary techniques which may be applied to different components of a single problem or even applied to the same problem to obtain alternative parallel algorithms.

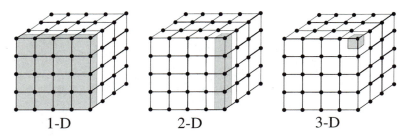

**Figure 2.2** Domain decompositions for a problem involving a three-dimensional grid. One-, two-, and three-dimensional decompositions are possible; in each case, data associated with a single task are shaded. A three-dimensional decomposition offers the greatest flexibility and is adopted in the early stages of a design.

In this first stage of a design, we seek to avoid replicating computation and data; that is, we seek to define tasks that partition both computation and data into disjoint sets. Like granularity, this is an aspect of the design that we may revisit later. It can be worthwhile replicating either computation or data if doing so allows us to reduce communication requirements.

### 2.2.1  Domain Decomposition

In the domain decomposition approach to problem partitioning, we seek first to decompose the data associated with a problem. If possible, we divide these data into small pieces of approximately equal size. Next, we partition the computation that is to be performed, typically by associating each operation with the data on which it operates. This partitioning yields a number of tasks, each comprising some data and a set of operations on that data. An operation may require data from several tasks. In this case, communication is required to move data between tasks. This requirement is addressed in the next phase of the design process.

The data that are decomposed may be the input to the program, the output computed by the program, or intermediate values maintained by the program. Different partitions may be possible, based on different data structures. Good rules of thumb are to focus first on the largest data structure or on the data structure that is accessed most frequently. Different phases of the computation may operate on different data structures or demand different decompositions for the same data structures. In this case, we treat each phase separately and then determine how the decompositions and parallel algorithms developed for each phase fit together. The issues that arise in this situation are discussed in Chapter 4.

Figure 2.2 illustrates domain decomposition in a simple problem involving a three-dimensional grid. (This grid could represent the state of the atmosphere in a weather model, or a three-dimensional space in an image-processing problem.) Computation is performed repeatedly on each grid point. Decompositions in the $x$, $y$, and/or $z$ dimensions are possible. In the early stages of a design, we favor the most aggressive decomposition possible, which in this case defines one task for each grid point. Each task maintains as its state the various values associated with its grid point and is responsible for the computation required to update that state.

### 2.2.2 Functional Decomposition

Functional decomposition represents a different and complementary way of thinking about problems. In this approach, the initial focus is on the computation that is to be performed rather than on the data manipulated by the computation. If we are successful in dividing this computation into disjoint tasks, we proceed to examine the data requirements of these tasks. These data requirements may be disjoint, in which case the partition is complete. Alternatively, they may overlap significantly, in which case considerable communication will be required to avoid replication of data. This is often a sign that a domain decomposition approach should be considered instead.

While domain decomposition forms the foundation for most parallel algorithms, functional decomposition is valuable as a different way of thinking about problems. For this reason alone, it should be considered when exploring possible parallel algorithms. A focus on the computations that are to be performed can sometimes reveal structure in a problem, and hence opportunities for optimization, that would not be obvious from a study of data alone.

As an example of a problem for which functional decomposition is most appropriate, consider Algorithm 1.1. This explores a search tree looking for nodes that correspond to "solutions." The algorithm does not have any obvious data structure that can be decomposed. However, a fine-grained partition can be obtained as described in Section 1.4.3. Initially, a single task is created for the root of the tree. A task evaluates its node and then, if that node is not a leaf, creates a new task for each `search` call (subtree). As illustrated in Figure 1.13, new tasks are created in a wavefront as the search tree is expanded.

Functional decomposition also has an important role to play as a program structuring technique. A functional decomposition that partitions not only the computation that is to be performed but also the code that performs that computation is likely to reduce the complexity of the overall design. This is often the case in computer models of complex systems, which may be structured as collections of simpler models connected via interfaces. For example, a simulation of the earth's climate may comprise components representing the atmosphere, ocean, hydrology, ice, carbon dioxide sources, and so on. While each component may be most naturally parallelized using domain decomposition techniques, the parallel algorithm as a whole is simpler if the system is first decomposed using functional decomposition techniques, even though this process does not yield a large number of tasks (Figure 2.3). This issue is explored in Chapter 4.

### 2.2.3 Partitioning Design Checklist

The partitioning phase of a design should produce one or more possible decompositions of a problem. Before proceeding to evaluate communication requirements, we use the following checklist to ensure that the design has no obvious flaws. Generally, all these questions should be answered in the affirmative.

1. Does your partition define at least an order of magnitude more tasks than there are processors in your target computer? If not, you have little flexibility in subsequent design stages.

2. Does your partition avoid redundant computation and storage requirements? If not, the resulting algorithm may not be scalable to deal with large problems.

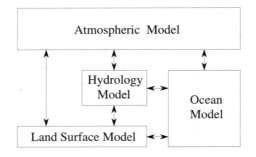

**Figure 2.3**  Functional decomposition in a computer model of climate. Each model component can be thought of as a separate task, to be parallelized by domain decomposition. Arrows represent exchanges of data between components during computation: the atmosphere model generates wind velocity data that are used by the ocean model, the ocean model generates sea surface temperature data that are used by the atmosphere model, and so on.

3. Are tasks of comparable size? If not, it may be hard to allocate each processor equal amounts of work.

4. Does the number of tasks scale with problem size? Ideally, an increase in problem size should increase the number of tasks rather than the size of individual tasks. If this is not the case, your parallel algorithm may not be able to solve larger problems when more processors are available.

5. Have you identified several alternative partitions? You can maximize flexibility in subsequent design stages by considering alternatives now. Remember to investigate both domain and functional decompositions.

Answers to these questions may suggest that, despite careful thought in this and subsequent design stages, we have a "bad" design. In this situation it is risky simply to push ahead with implementation. We should use the performance evaluation techniques described in Chapter 3 to determine whether the design meets our performance goals despite its apparent deficiencies. We may also wish to revisit the problem specification. Particularly in science and engineering applications, where the problem to be solved may involve a simulation of a complex physical process, the approximations and numerical techniques used to develop the simulation can strongly influence the ease of parallel implementation. In some cases, optimal sequential and parallel solutions to the same problem may use quite different solution techniques. While detailed discussion of these issues is beyond the scope of this book, we present several illustrative examples of them later in this chapter.

## 2.3   Communication

The tasks generated by a partition are intended to execute concurrently but cannot, in general, execute independently. The computation to be performed in one task will typically require data associated with another task. Data must then be transferred between tasks so as to allow computation to proceed. This information flow is specified in the *communication* phase of a design.

Recall from Chapter 1 that in our programming model, we conceptualize a need for communication between two tasks as a channel linking the tasks, on which one task can send messages and from which the other can receive. Hence, the communication associated with an algorithm can be specified in two phases. First, we define a channel structure that links, either directly or indirectly, tasks that require data (consumers) with tasks that possess those data (producers). Second, we specify the messages that are to be sent and received on these channels. Depending on our eventual implementation technology, we may not actually create these channels when coding the algorithm. For example, in a data-parallel language, we simply specify data-parallel operations and data distributions. Nevertheless, thinking in terms of tasks and channels helps us to think quantitatively about locality issues and communication costs.

The definition of a channel involves an intellectual cost and the sending of a message involves a physical cost. Hence, we avoid introducing unnecessary channels and communication operations. In addition, we seek to optimize performance by distributing communication operations over many tasks and by organizing communication operations in a way that permits concurrent execution.

In domain decomposition problems, communication requirements can be difficult to determine. Recall that this strategy produces tasks by first partitioning data structures into disjoint subsets and then associating with each datum those operations that operate solely on that datum. This part of the design is usually simple. However, some operations that require data from several tasks usually remain. Communication is then required to manage the data transfer necessary for these tasks to proceed. Organizing this communication in an efficient manner can be challenging. Even simple decompositions can have complex communication structures.

In contrast, communication requirements in parallel algorithms obtained by functional decomposition are often straightforward: they correspond to the data flow between tasks. For example, in a climate model broken down by functional decomposition into atmosphere model, ocean model, and so on, the communication requirements will correspond to the interfaces between the component submodels: the atmosphere model will produce values that are used by the ocean model, and so on (Figure 2.3).

In the following discussion, we use a variety of examples to show how communication requirements are identified and how channel structures and communication operations are introduced to satisfy these requirements. For clarity in exposition, we categorize communication patterns along four loosely orthogonal axes: local/global, structured/unstructured, static/dynamic, and synchronous/asynchronous.

- In *local* communication, each task communicates with a small set of other tasks (its "neighbors"); in contrast, *global* communication requires each task to communicate with many tasks.

- In *structured* communication, a task and its neighbors form a regular structure, such as a tree or grid; in contrast, *unstructured* communication networks may be arbitrary graphs.

- In *static* communication, the identity of communication partners does not change over time; in contrast, the identity of communication partners in *dynamic* communication structures may be determined by data computed at runtime and may be highly variable.

- In *synchronous* communication, producers and consumers execute in a coordinated fashion, with producer/consumer pairs cooperating in data transfer operations; in contrast, *asynchronous* communication may require that a consumer obtain data without the cooperation of the producer.

### 2.3.1   Local Communication

A local communication structure is obtained when an operation requires data from a small number of other tasks. It is then straightforward to define channels that link the task responsible for performing the operation (the consumer) with the tasks holding the required data (the producers) and to introduce appropriate send and receive operations in the producer and consumer tasks, respectively.

For illustrative purposes, we consider the communication requirements associated with a simple numerical computation, namely a Jacobi finite difference method. In this class of numerical method, a multidimensional grid is repeatedly updated by replacing the value at each point with some function of the values at a small, fixed number of neighboring points. The set of values required to update a single grid point is called that grid point's *stencil*. For example, the following expression uses a five-point stencil to update each element $X_{i,j}$ of a two-dimensional grid $X$:

$$X_{i,j}^{(t+1)} = \frac{4X_{i,j}^{(t)} + X_{i-1,j}^{(t)} + X_{i+1,j}^{(t)} + X_{i,j-1}^{(t)} + X_{i,j+1}^{(t)}}{8}. \tag{2.1}$$

This update is applied repeatedly to compute a sequence of values $X_{i,j}^{(1)}$, $X_{i,j}^{(2)}$, and so on. The notation $X_{i,j}^{(t)}$ denotes the value of grid point $X_{i,j}$ at step $t$.

Let us assume that a partition has used domain decomposition techniques to create a distinct task for each point in the two-dimensional grid. Hence, a task allocated the grid point $X_{i,j}$ must compute the sequence

$$X_{i,j}^{(1)}, \ X_{i,j}^{(2)}, \ X_{i,j}^{(3)}, \ \ldots.$$

This computation requires in turn the four corresponding sequences

$$X_{i-1,j}^{(0)}, \ X_{i-1,j}^{(1)}, \ X_{i-1,j}^{(2)}, \ \cdots$$
$$X_{i+1,j}^{(0)}, \ X_{i+1,j}^{(1)}, \ X_{i+1,j}^{(2)}, \ \cdots$$
$$X_{i,j-1}^{(0)}, \ X_{i,j-1}^{(1)}, \ X_{i,j-1}^{(2)}, \ \cdots$$
$$X_{i,j+1}^{(0)}, \ X_{i,j+1}^{(1)}, \ X_{i,j+1}^{(2)}, \ \cdots,$$

which are produced by the four tasks handling grid points $X_{i-1,j}$, $X_{i+1,j}$, $X_{i,j-1}$, and

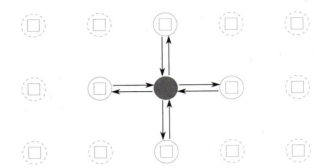

**Figure 2.4** Task and channel structure for a two-dimensional finite difference computation with five-point update stencil. In this simple fine-grained formulation, each task encapsulates a single element of a two-dimensional grid and must both send its value to four neighbors and receive values from four neighbors. Only the channels used by the shaded task are shown.

$X_{i,j+1}$, that is, by its four neighbors in the grid. For these values to be communicated, we define channels linking each task that requires a value with the task that generates that value. This yields the channel structure illustrated in Figure 2.4. Each task then executes the following logic:

```
for t = 0 to T − 1
    send X⁽ᵗ⁾ᵢ,ⱼ to each neighbor
    receive X⁽ᵗ⁾ᵢ₋₁,ⱼ, X⁽ᵗ⁾ᵢ₊₁,ⱼ, X⁽ᵗ⁾ᵢ,ⱼ₋₁, X⁽ᵗ⁾ᵢ,ⱼ₊₁ from neighbors
    compute X⁽ᵗ⁺¹⁾ᵢ,ⱼ using Equation 2.1
endfor
```

We observed earlier that the best sequential and parallel solutions to a problem may use different techniques. This situation arises in finite difference problems. In sequential computing, Gauss-Seidel update strategies are often preferred over Jacobi strategies because they allow solutions of comparable accuracy to be obtained using fewer iterations. In a Gauss-Seidel scheme, elements are updated in a particular order so that the computation of each element can use the most up-to-date value of other elements. For example, the Jacobi update of Equation 2.1 may be reformulated as follows (notice the use of values $X^{(t+1)}_{i-1,j}$ and $X^{(t+1)}_{i,j-1}$):

$$X^{(t+1)}_{i,j} = \frac{4X^{(t)}_{i,j} + X^{(t+1)}_{i-1,j} + X^{(t)}_{i+1,j} + X^{(t+1)}_{i,j-1} + X^{(t)}_{i,j+1}}{8}. \tag{2.2}$$

While Jacobi schemes are trivial to parallelize (all grid points can be updated concurrently), this is not the case for all Gauss-Seidel schemes. For example, the update scheme of Equation 2.2 allows only an average of around $N/2$ points within an $N \times N$ grid to be updated concurrently. Fortunately, many different Gauss-Seidel orderings are possible for most problems, and we are usually free to choose the ordering that maximizes available parallelism. In particular, we can choose to update first the odd-numbered elements

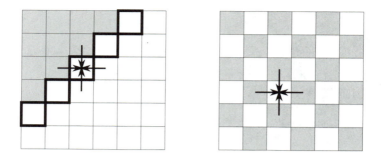

**Figure 2.5** Two finite difference update strategies, here applied on a two-dimensional grid with a five-point stencil. In both figures, shaded grid points have already been updated to step $t + 1$; unshaded grid points are still at step $t$. The arrows show data dependencies for one of the latter points. The figure on the left illustrates a simple Gauss-Seidel scheme and highlights the five grid points that can be updated at a particular point in time. In this scheme, the update proceeds in a wavefront from the top left corner to the bottom right. On the right, we show a red-black update scheme. Here, all the grid points at step $t$ can be updated concurrently.

and then the even-numbered elements of an array. Each update uses the most recent information, yet the updates to the odd-numbered points are independent and can proceed concurrently, as can the updates to the even-numbered points. This update strategy yields what is referred to as a *red-black* algorithm, since the points can be thought of as being colored as on a chess board: either red (odd) or black (even); points of the same color can be updated concurrently. Figure 2.5 illustrates both the Gauss-Seidel scheme of Equation 2.2 and a red-black scheme, and shows how the latter scheme increases opportunities for parallel execution.

This example indicates the important role that choice of solution strategy can play in determining the performance of a parallel program. While the simple Gauss-Seidel update strategy of Equation 2.2 may be appropriate in a sequential program, it is not ideal on a parallel computer. The Jacobi update strategy is efficient on a parallel computer but is inferior numerically. The red-black scheme combines the advantages of both approaches.

### 2.3.2  Global Communication

A *global communication* operation is one in which many tasks must participate. When such operations are implemented, it may not be sufficient simply to identify individual producer/consumer pairs. Such an approach may result in too many communications or may restrict opportunities for concurrent execution. For example, consider the problem of performing a *parallel reduction* operation, that is, an operation that reduces $N$ values distributed over $N$ tasks using a commutative associative operator such as addition:

$$S = \sum_{i=0}^{N-1} X_i.$$

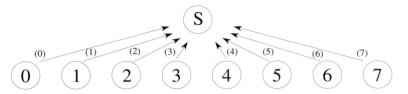

**Figure 2.6**   A centralized summation algorithm that uses a central manager task (S) to sum $N$ numbers distributed among $N$ tasks. Here, $N = 8$, and each of the 8 channels is labeled with the number of the step in which they are used.

Let us assume that a single "manager" task requires the result $S$ of this operation. Taking a purely local view of communication, we recognize that the manager requires values $X_0$, $X_1$, etc., from tasks 0, 1, etc. Hence, we could define a communication structure that allows each task to communicate its value to the manager independently. The manager would then receive the values and add them into an accumulator (Figure 2.6). However, because the manager can receive and sum only one number at a time, this approach takes $\mathcal{O}(N)$ time to sum $N$ numbers—not a very good parallel algorithm!

This example illustrates two general problems that can hinder efficient parallel execution in algorithms based on a purely local view of communication:

1. The algorithm is *centralized*: it does not distribute computation and communication. A single task (in this case, the manager task) must participate in every operation.

2. The algorithm is *sequential*: it does not allow multiple computation and communication operations to proceed concurrently.

We must address both these problems to develop a good parallel algorithm.

**Distributing Communication and Computation**   We first consider the problem of distributing the computation and communication associated with the summation. We can distribute the summation of the $N$ numbers by making each task $i$, $0 < i < N - 1$, compute the sum:

$$S_i = X_i + S_{i-1}.$$

The communication requirements associated with this algorithm can be satisfied by connecting the $N$ tasks in a one-dimensional array (Figure 2.7). Task $N - 1$ sends its value to

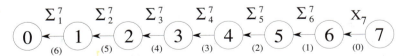

**Figure 2.7**   A summation algorithm that connects $N$ tasks in an array in order to sum $N$ numbers distributed among these tasks. Each channel is labeled with the number of the step in which it is used and the value that is communicated on it.

```
procedure divide_and_conquer
begin
   if base case then
      solve problem
   else
      partition problem into subproblems L and R
      solve problem L using divide-and-conquer
      solve problem R using divide-and-conquer
      combine solutions to problems L and R
   endif
end
```

**Algorithm 2.1**    The divide-and-conquer strategy, a technique commonly used to uncover parallelism in algorithms. This procedure provides a recursive formulation of the strategy. If we are dealing with a primitive ("base case") problem, the problem is solved. Otherwise, the problem is divided into two subproblems. If these subproblems are independent, they can be solved concurrently.

its neighbor in this array. Tasks 1 through $N - 2$ each wait to receive a partial sum from their right-hand neighbor, add this to their local value, and send the result to their left-hand neighbor. Task 0 receives a partial sum and adds this to its local value to obtain the complete sum. This algorithm distributes the $N - 1$ communications and additions, but permits concurrent execution only if multiple summation operations are to be performed. (The array of tasks can then be used as a pipeline, through which flow partial sums.) A single summation still takes $N - 1$ steps.

**Uncovering Concurrency: Divide and Conquer**    Opportunities for concurrent computation and communication can often be uncovered by applying a problem-solving strategy called *divide and conquer*. To solve a complex problem (such as summing $N$ numbers), we seek to partition it into two or more simpler problems of roughly equivalent size (e.g., summing $N/2$ numbers). This process is applied recursively to produce a set of subproblems that cannot be subdivided further (e.g., summing two numbers). The strategy is summarized in Algorithm 2.1. The divide-and-conquer technique is effective in parallel computing when the subproblems generated by problem partitioning can be solved concurrently. For example, in the summation problem, we can take advantage of the following identity ($N = 2^n$, $n > 0$, $n$ an integer):

$$\sum_{i=0}^{2^n-1} = \sum_{i=0}^{2^{n-1}-1} + \sum_{i=2^{n-1}}^{2^n-1}.$$

The two summations on the right-hand side can be performed concurrently. They can also be further decomposed if $n > 1$, to give the tree structure illustrated in Figure 2.8. Summations at the same level in this tree of height $n = \log N$ can be performed concurrently, so the complete summation can be achieved in $\log N$ rather than $N$ steps.

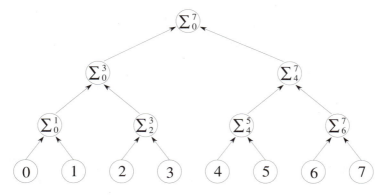

**Figure 2.8**   Tree structure for divide-and-conquer summation algorithm with $N = 8$. The $N$ numbers located in the tasks at the bottom of the diagram are communicated to the tasks in the row immediately above; these each perform an addition and then forward the result to the next level. The complete sum is available at the root of the tree after $\log N$ steps.

In summary, we observe that in developing an efficient parallel summation algorithm, we have distributed the $N - 1$ communication and computation operations required to perform the summation and have modified the order in which these operations are performed so that they can proceed concurrently. The result is a regular communication structure in which each task communicates with a small set of neighbors.

### 2.3.3   Unstructured and Dynamic Communication

The examples considered previously are all of static, structured communication, in which a task's communication partners form a regular pattern such as a tree or a grid and do not change over time. In other cases, communication patterns may be considerably more complex. For example, in finite element methods used in engineering calculations, the computational grid may be shaped to follow an irregular object or to provide high resolution in critical regions (Figure 2.9). Here, the channel structure representing the communication partners of each grid point is quite irregular and data-dependent and, furthermore, may change over time if the grid is refined as a simulation evolves.

Unstructured communication patterns do not generally cause conceptual difficulties in the early stages of a design. For example, it is straightforward to define a single task for each vertex in a finite element graph and to require communication for each edge. However, unstructured communication complicates the tasks of agglomeration and mapping. In particular, sophisticated algorithms can be required to determine an agglomeration strategy that both creates tasks of approximately equal size and minimizes communication requirements by creating the least number of intertask edges. Algorithms of this sort are discussed in Section 2.5.1. If communication requirements are dynamic, these algorithms must be applied frequently during program execution, and the cost of these algorithms must be weighed against their benefits.

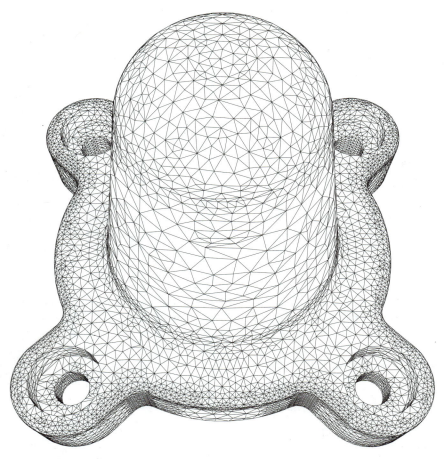

**Figure 2.9**   Example of a problem requiring unstructured communication. In this finite element mesh generated for an assembly part, each vertex is a grid point. An edge connecting two vertices represents a data dependency that will require communication if the vertices are located in different tasks. Notice that different vertices have varying numbers of neighbors. (Image courtesy of M. S. Shephard.)

### 2.3.4   Asynchronous Communication

The examples considered in the preceding section have all featured synchronous communication, in which both producers and consumers are aware when communication operations are required, and producers explicitly send data to consumers. In *asynchronous* communication, tasks that possess data (producers) are not able to determine when other tasks (consumers) may require data; hence, consumers must explicitly request data from producers.

This situation commonly occurs when a computation is structured as a set of tasks that must periodically read and/or write elements of a shared data structure. Let us assume

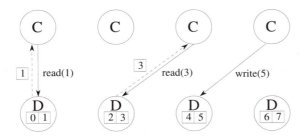

**Figure 2.10**   Using separate "data tasks" to service read and write requests on a distributed data structure. In this figure, four computation tasks (C) generate read and write requests to eight data items distributed among four data tasks (D). Solid lines represent requests; dashed lines represent replies. One compute task and one data task could be placed on each of four processors so as to distribute computation and data equitably.

that this data structure is too large or too frequently accessed to be encapsulated in a single task. Hence, a mechanism is needed that allows this data structure to be distributed while supporting asynchronous read and write operations on its components. Possible mechanisms include the following.

1. The data structure is distributed among the computational tasks. Each task both performs computation and generates requests for data located in other tasks. It also periodically interrupts its own computation and *polls* for pending requests.

2. The distributed data structure is encapsulated in a second set of tasks responsible only for responding to read and write requests (Figure 2.10).

3. On a computer that supports a shared-memory programming model, computational tasks can access shared data without any special arrangements. However, care must be taken to ensure that read and write operations on this shared data occur in the proper order.

Each strategy has advantages and disadvantages; in addition, the performance characteristics of each approach vary from machine to machine. The first strategy can result in convoluted, nonmodular programs because of the need to intersperse polling operations throughout application code. In addition, polling can be an expensive operation on some computers, in which case we must trade off the cost of frequent polling against the benefit of rapid response to remote requests. The second strategy is more modular: responsibility for the shared data structure is encapsulated in a separate set of tasks. However, this strategy makes it hard to exploit locality because, strictly speaking, there are no local data: all read and write operations require communication. Also, switching between the computation and data tasks can be expensive on some machines.

## 2.3.5   Communication Design Checklist

Having devised a partition and a communication structure for our parallel algorithm, we now evaluate our design using the following design checklist. As in Section 2.2.3, these are guidelines intended to identify nonscalable features, rather than hard and fast rules. However, we should be aware of when a design violates them and why.

1. Do all tasks perform about the same number of communication operations? Unbalanced communication requirements suggest a nonscalable construct. Revisit your design to see whether communication operations can be distributed more equitably. For example, if a frequently accessed data structure is encapsulated in a single task, consider distributing or replicating this data structure.

2. Does each task communicate only with a small number of neighbors? If each task must communicate with many other tasks, evaluate the possibility of formulating this global communication in terms of a local communication structure, as was done in the pairwise interactions algorithm of Section 1.4.2 and the summation algorithm of Section 2.3.2.

3. Are communication operations able to proceed concurrently? If not, your algorithm is likely to be inefficient and nonscalable. Try to use divide-and-conquer techniques to uncover concurrency, as in the summation algorithm of Section 2.3.2.

4. Is the computation associated with different tasks able to proceed concurrently? If not, your algorithm is likely to be inefficient and nonscalable. Consider whether you can reorder communication and computation operations. You may also wish to revisit your problem specification, as was done in moving from a simple Gauss-Seidel to a red-black algorithm in Section 2.3.1.

## 2.4  Agglomeration

In the first two stages of the design process, we partitioned the computation to be performed into a set of tasks and introduced communication to provide data required by these tasks. The resulting algorithm is still abstract in the sense that it is not specialized for efficient execution on any particular parallel computer. In fact, it may be highly inefficient if, for example, it creates many more tasks than there are processors on the target computer and this computer is not designed for efficient execution of small tasks.

In the third stage, *agglomeration,* we move from the abstract toward the concrete. We revisit decisions made in the partitioning and communication phases with a view to obtaining an algorithm that will execute efficiently on some class of parallel computer. In particular, we consider whether it is useful to combine, or *agglomerate*, tasks identified by the partitioning phase, so as to provide a smaller number of tasks, each of greater size (Figure 2.11). We also determine whether it is worthwhile to *replicate* data and/or computation.

The number of tasks yielded by the agglomeration phase, although reduced, may still be greater than the number of processors. In this case, our design remains somewhat abstract, since issues relating to the mapping of tasks to processors remain unresolved. Alternatively, we may choose during the agglomeration phase to reduce the number of tasks to exactly one per processor. We might do this, for example, because our target

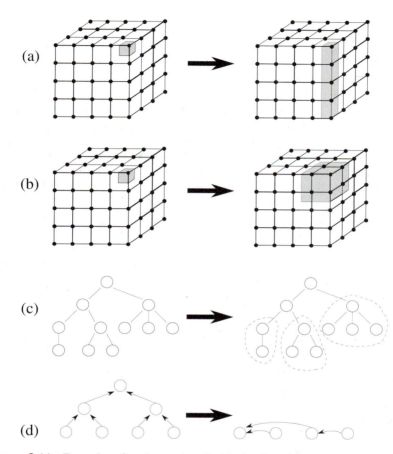

**Figure 2.11**    Examples of agglomeration. In (a), the size of tasks is increased by reducing the dimension of the decomposition from three to two. In (b), adjacent tasks are combined to yield a three-dimensional decomposition of higher granularity. In (c), subtrees in a divide-and-conquer structure are coalesced. In (d), nodes in a tree algorithm are combined.

parallel computer or program development environment demands an SPMD program. In this case, our design is already largely complete, since in defining $P$ tasks that will execute on $P$ processors, we have also addressed the mapping problem. In this section, we focus on general issues that arise when increasing task granularity. Specific issues relating to the generation of SPMD programs are discussed in Section 2.5.

Three sometimes-conflicting goals guide decisions concerning agglomeration and replication: reducing communication costs by increasing computation and communication *granularity*, retaining *flexibility* with respect to scalability and mapping decisions, and reducing *software engineering* costs. These goals are discussed in the next three subsections.

## 2.4.1   Increasing Granularity

In the partitioning phase of the design process, our efforts are focused on defining as many tasks as possible. This is a useful discipline because it forces us to consider a wide range of opportunities for parallel execution. We note, however, that defining a large number of fine-grained tasks does not necessarily produce an efficient parallel algorithm.

One critical issue influencing parallel performance is communication costs. On most parallel computers, we have to stop computing in order to send and receive messages. Because we typically would rather be computing, we can improve performance by reducing the amount of time spent communicating. Clearly, this performance improvement can be achieved by sending less data. Perhaps less obviously, it can also be achieved by using fewer messages, even if we send the same amount of data. This is because each communication incurs not only a cost proportional to the amount of data transferred but also a fixed startup cost. These issues are discussed in detail in Chapter 3, where we use analytic models to quantify communication costs.

In addition to communication costs, we may need to be concerned with task creation costs. For example, the performance of the fine-grained search algorithm illustrated in Figure 1.13, which creates one task for each search tree node, is sensitive to task creation costs.

**Surface-to-Volume Effects**   If the number of communication partners per task is small, we can often reduce both the number of communication operations and the total communication volume by increasing the granularity of our partition, that is, by agglomerating several tasks into one. This effect is illustrated in Figure 2.12. In this figure, the reduction in communication costs is due to a *surface-to-volume effect*. In other words, the communication requirements of a task are proportional to the surface of the subdomain on which it operates, while the computation requirements are proportional to the subdomain's volume. In a two-dimensional problem, the "surface" scales with the problem size while the "volume" scales as the problem size squared. Hence, the amount of communication performed for a unit of computation (the *communication/computation ratio*) decreases as task size increases. This effect is often visible when a partition is obtained by using domain decomposition techniques.

A consequence of surface-to-volume effects is that higher-dimensional decompositions are typically the most efficient, other things being equal, because they reduce the surface area (communication) required for a given volume (computation). Hence, from the viewpoint of efficiency it is usually best to increase granularity by agglomerating tasks in all dimensions rather than reducing the dimension of the decomposition. This issue is explored quantitatively in Example 3.4 in Chapter 3.

The design of an efficient agglomeration strategy can be difficult in problems with unstructured communications, such as the finite element problem of Figure 2.9. Specialized techniques that can be used in such cases are discussed in Section 2.5.1.

**Replicating Computation**   We can sometimes trade off replicated computation for reduced communication requirements and/or execution time. For an example, we consider

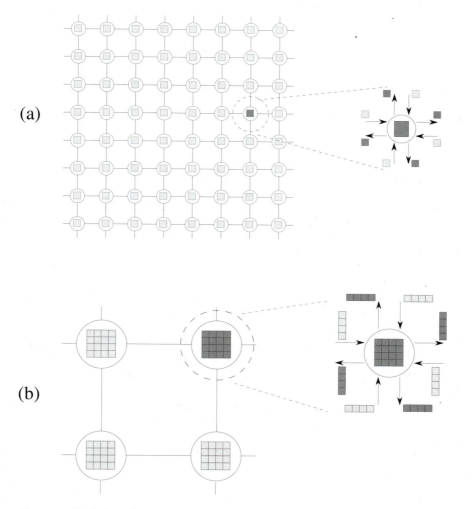

**Figure 2.12** Effect of increased granularity on communication costs in a two-dimensional finite difference problem with a five-point stencil. The figure shows fine- and coarse-grained two-dimensional partitions of this problem. In each case, a single task is exploded to show its outgoing messages (dark shading) and incoming messages (light shading). In (a), a computation on an $8 \times 8$ grid is partitioned into $8 \times 8 = 64$ tasks, each responsible for a single point, while in (b) the same computation is partioned into $2 \times 2 = 4$ tasks, each responsible for 16 points. In (a), $64 \times 4 = 256$ communications are required, 4 per task; these transfer a total of 256 data values. In (b), only $4 \times 4 = 16$ communications are required, and only $16 \times 4 = 64$ data values are transferred.

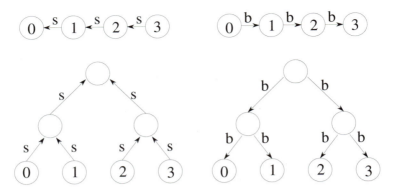

**Figure 2.13**   Using an array (above) and a tree (below) to perform a summation and a broadcast. On the left are the communications performed for the summation (s); on the right, the communications performed for the broadcast (b). After $2(N-1)$ or $2\log N$ steps, respectively, the sum of the $N$ values is replicated in each of the $N$ tasks.

a variant of the summation problem presented in Section 2.3.2, in which the sum must be replicated in each of the $N$ tasks that contribute to the sum.

A simple approach to distributing the sum is first to use either a ring- or tree-based algorithm to compute the sum in a single task, and then to *broadcast* the sum to each of the $N$ tasks. The broadcast can be performed using the same communication structure as the summation; hence, the complete operation can be performed in either $2(N-1)$ or $2\log N$ steps, depending on which communication structure is used (Figure 2.13).

These algorithms are optimal in the sense that they do not perform any unnecessary computation or communication. However, there also exist alternative algorithms that execute in less elapsed time, although at the expense of unnecessary (replicated) computation and communication. The basic idea is to perform multiple summations concurrently, with each concurrent summation producing a value in a different task.

We first consider a variant of the array summation algorithm based on this idea. In this variant, tasks are connected in a *ring* rather than an array, and all $N$ tasks execute the same algorithm so that $N$ partial sums are in motion simultaneously. After $N-1$ steps, the complete sum is replicated in every task. This strategy avoids the need for a subsequent broadcast operation, but at the expense of $(N-1)^2$ redundant additions and $(N-1)^2$ unnecessary communications. However, the summation and broadcast complete in $N-1$ rather than $2(N-1)$ steps. Hence, the strategy is faster if the processors would otherwise be idle waiting for the result of the summation.

The tree summation algorithm can be modified in a similar way to avoid the need for a separate broadcast. That is, multiple tree summations are performed concurrently so that after $\log N$ steps each task has a copy of the sum. One might expect this approach to result in $\mathcal{O}(N^2)$ additions and communications, as in the ring algorithm. However, in this case we can exploit redundancies in both computation and communication to perform the summation in just $\mathcal{O}(N \log N)$ operations. The resulting communication structure, termed

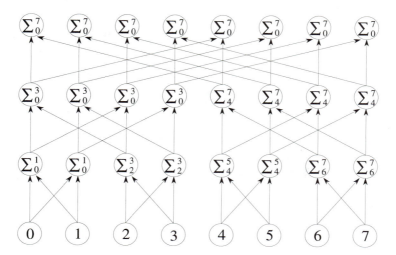

**Figure 2.14** The butterfly communication structure can be used to sum $N$ values in $\log N$ steps. Numbers located in the bottom row of tasks are propagated up through $\log N$ intermediate stages, thereby producing the complete sum in each task in the top row.

a *butterfly*, is illustrated in Figure 2.14. In each of the $\log N$ stages, each task receives data from two tasks, performs a single addition, and sends the result of this addition to two tasks in the next stage.

**Avoiding Communication** Agglomeration is almost always beneficial if analysis of communication requirements reveals that a set of tasks cannot execute concurrently. For example, consider the tree and butterfly structures illustrated in Figures 2.8 and 2.14. When a single summation problem is performed, only tasks at the same level in the tree or butterfly can execute concurrently. (Notice, however, that if many summations are to be performed, in principle all tasks can be kept busy by pipelining multiple summation operations.) Hence, tasks at different levels can be agglomerated without reducing opportunities for concurrent execution, thereby yielding the communication structures represented in Figure 2.15. The hypercube structure shown in this figure is a fundamental communication structure that has many applications in parallel computing. It is discussed in greater detail in Chapter 11.

### 2.4.2 Preserving Flexibility

It is easy when agglomerating tasks to make design decisions that limit unnecessarily an algorithm's scalability. For example, we might choose to decompose a multidimensional data structure in just a single dimension, reasoning that this provides more than enough concurrency for the number of processors available. However, this strategy is shortsighted

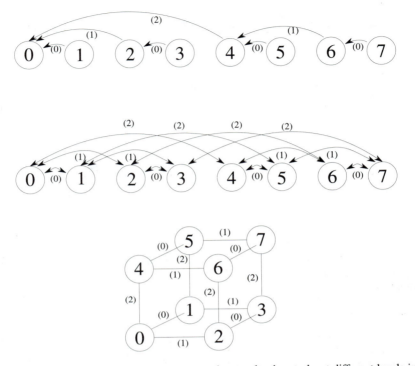

**Figure 2.15**    The communication structures that result when tasks at different levels in a tree or butterfly structure are agglomerated. From top to bottom: a tree, a butterfly, and an equivalent representation of the butterfly as a hypercube. In each case, $N = 8$, and each channel is labeled with the step in which it is used for communication.

if our program must ultimately be ported to larger parallel computers. It may also lead to a less efficient algorithm, as discussed in Section 2.4.1.

The ability to create a varying number of tasks is critical if a program is to be portable and scalable. As discussed in Chapter 1, good parallel algorithms are designed to be resilient to changes in processor count. This flexibility can also be useful when tuning a code for a particular computer. If tasks often block waiting for remote data, it can be advantageous to map several tasks to a processor. Then, a blocked task need not result in a processor becoming idle, since another task may be able to execute in its place. In this way, one task's communication is overlapped with another task's computation. This technique, termed *overlapping computation and communication,* is discussed in Chapter 3.

A third benefit of creating more tasks than processors is that doing so provides greater scope for mapping strategies that balance computational load over available processors. As a general rule of thumb, we could require that there be at least an order of magnitude more tasks than processors. This issue is discussed in the next section.

The optimal number of tasks is typically best determined by a combination of analytic modeling and empirical studies. Flexibility does not necessarily require that a design always create a large number of tasks. Granularity can be controlled by a compile-time or runtime parameter. What is important is that a design not incorporate unnecessary limits on the number of tasks that can be created.

### 2.4.3  Reducing Software Engineering Costs

So far, we have assumed that our choice of agglomeration strategy is determined solely by a desire to improve the efficiency and flexibility of a parallel algorithm. An additional concern, which can be particularly important when parallelizing existing sequential codes, is the relative development costs associated with different partitioning strategies. From this perspective, the most interesting strategies may be those that avoid extensive code changes. For example, in a code that operates on a multidimensional grid, it may be advantageous to avoid partitioning altogether in one dimension, if doing so allows existing routines to be reused unchanged in a parallel program.

Frequently, we are concerned with designing a parallel algorithm that must execute as part of a larger system. In this case, another software engineering issue that must be considered is the data distributions utilized by other program components. For example, the best algorithm for some program component may require that an input array data structure be decomposed in three dimensions, while a preceding phase of the computation generates a two-dimensional decomposition. Either one or both algorithms must be changed, or an explicit restructuring phase must be incorporated in the computation. Each approach has different performance characteristics. These issues are discussed in Chapter 4.

### 2.4.4  Agglomeration Design Checklist

We have now revised the partitioning and communication decisions developed in the first two design stages by agglomerating tasks and communication operations. We may have agglomerated tasks because analysis of communication requirements shows that the original partition created tasks that cannot execute concurrently. Alternatively, we may have used agglomeration to increase computation and communication granularity and/or to decrease software engineering costs, even though opportunities for concurrent execution are reduced. At this stage, we evaluate our design with respect to the following checklist. Several of these questions emphasize quantitative performance analysis, which becomes more important as we move from the abstract to the concrete; this topic is addressed in Chapter 3.

1. Has agglomeration reduced communication costs by increasing locality? If not, examine your algorithm to determine whether this could be achieved using an alternative agglomeration strategy.

2. If agglomeration has replicated computation, have you verified that the benefits of this replication outweigh its costs, for a range of problem sizes and processor counts?

3. If agglomeration replicates data, have you verified that this does not compromise the scalability of your algorithm by restricting the range of problem sizes or processor counts that it can address?

4. Has agglomeration yielded tasks with similar computation and communication costs? The larger the tasks created by agglomeration, the more important it is that they have similar costs. If we have created just one task per processor, then these tasks should have nearly identical costs.

5. Does the number of tasks still scale with problem size? If not, then your algorithm is no longer able to solve larger problems on larger parallel computers.

6. If agglomeration eliminated opportunities for concurrent execution, have you verified that there is sufficient concurrency for current and future target computers? An algorithm with insufficient concurrency may still be the most efficient, if other algorithms have excessive communication costs; performance models can be used to quantify these tradeoffs.

7. Can the number of tasks be reduced still further, without introducing load imbalances, increasing software engineering costs, or reducing scalability? Other things being equal, algorithms that create fewer larger-grained tasks are often simpler and more efficient than those that create many fine-grained tasks.

8. If you are parallelizing an existing sequential program, have you considered the cost of the modifications required to the sequential code? If these costs are high, consider alternative agglomeration strategies that increase opportunities for code reuse. If the resulting algorithms are less efficient, use performance modeling techniques to estimate cost tradeoffs.

## 2.5  Mapping

In the fourth and final stage of the parallel algorithm design process, we specify where each task is to execute. This mapping problem does not arise on uniprocessors or on shared-memory computers that provide automatic task scheduling. In these computers, a set of tasks and associated communication requirements is a sufficient specification for a parallel algorithm; operating system or hardware mechanisms can be relied upon to schedule executable tasks to available processors. Unfortunately, general-purpose mapping mechanisms have yet to be developed for scalable parallel computers. In general, mapping remains a difficult problem that must be explicitly addressed when designing parallel algorithms.

Our goal in developing mapping algorithms is normally to minimize total execution time. We use two strategies to achieve this goal:

1. We place tasks that are able to execute concurrently on *different* processors, so as to enhance concurrency.

2. We place tasks that communicate frequently on the *same* processor, so as to increase locality.

Clearly, these two strategies will sometimes conflict, in which case our design will involve tradeoffs. In addition, resource limitations may restrict the number of tasks that can be placed on a single processor.

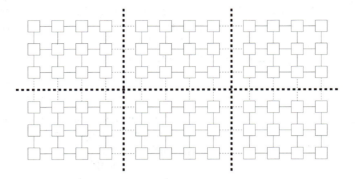

**Figure 2.16**  Mapping in a grid problem in which each task performs the same amount of computation and communicates only with its four neighbors. The heavy dashed lines delineate processor boundaries. The grid and associated computation is partitioned to give each processor the same amount of computation and to minimize off-processor communication.

The mapping problem is known to be *NP-complete*, meaning that no computationally tractable (polynomial-time) algorithm can exist for evaluating these tradeoffs in the general case. However, considerable knowledge has been gained on specialized strategies and heuristics and the classes of problem for which they are effective. In this section, we provide a rough classification of problems and present some representative techniques.

Many algorithms developed using domain decomposition techniques feature a fixed number of equal-sized tasks and structured local and global communication. In such cases, an efficient mapping is straightforward. We map tasks in a way that minimizes interprocessor communication (Figure 2.16); we may also choose to agglomerate tasks mapped to the same processor, if this has not already been done, to yield a total of $P$ coarse-grained tasks, one per processor.

In more complex domain decomposition-based algorithms with variable amounts of work per task and/or unstructured communication patterns, efficient agglomeration and mapping strategies may not be obvious to the programmer. Hence, we may employ *load balancing* algorithms that seek to identify efficient agglomeration and mapping strategies, typically by using heuristic techniques. The time required to execute these algorithms must be weighed against the benefits of reduced execution time. *Probabilistic load-balancing* methods will tend to have lower overhead than do methods that exploit structure in an application.

The most complex problems are those in which either the number of tasks or the amount of computation or communication per task changes dynamically during program execution. In the case of problems developed using domain decomposition techniques, we may use a *dynamic load-balancing* strategy in which a load-balancing algorithm is executed periodically to determine a new agglomeration and mapping. Because load balancing must be performed many times during program execution, *local* algorithms may be preferred that do not require global knowledge of computation state.

Algorithms based on functional decomposition often yield computations consisting of many short-lived tasks that coordinate with other tasks only at the start and end of execution. In this case, we can use *task-scheduling* algorithms, which allocate tasks to processors that are idle or that are likely to become idle.

## 2.5.1   Load-Balancing Algorithms

A wide variety of both general-purpose and application-specific load-balancing techniques have been proposed for use in parallel algorithms based on domain decomposition techniques. We review several representative approaches here (the chapter notes provide references to other methods), namely recursive bisection methods, local algorithms, probabilistic methods, and cyclic mappings. These techniques are all intended to agglomerate fine-grained tasks defined in an initial partition to yield one coarse-grained task per processor. Alternatively, we can think of them as partitioning our computational domain to yield one subdomain for each processor. For this reason, they are often referred to as *partitioning* algorithms.

**Recursive Bisection**    Recursive bisection techniques are used to partition a domain (e.g., a finite element grid) into subdomains of approximately equal computational cost while attempting to minimize communication costs, that is, the number of channels crossing task boundaries. A divide-and-conquer approach is taken. The domain is first cut in one dimension to yield two subdomains. Cuts are then made recursively in the new subdomains until we have as many subdomains as we require tasks. Notice that this recursive strategy allows the partitioning algorithm itself to be executed in parallel.

The most straightforward of the recursive bisection techniques is *recursive coordinate bisection*, which is normally applied to irregular grids that have a mostly local communication structure. This technique makes cuts based on the physical coordinates of grid points in the domain, at each step subdividing along the longer dimension so that if (for example) the cut is made along the $x$ dimension, grid points in one subdomain will all have an $x$-coordinate greater than grid points in the other. This approach has the advantages of being simple and inexpensive. It also does a good job of partitioning computation. A disadvantage is that it does not optimize communication performance. In particular, it can generate long, skinny subdomains, which if an algorithm has significant local communication will result in more messages than will a decomposition that generates square subdomains.

A variant of recursive bisection called *unbalanced recursive bisection* attempts to reduce communication costs by forming subgrids that have better aspect ratios. Instead of automatically dividing a grid in half, it considers the $P - 1$ partitions obtained by forming unbalanced subgrids with $1/P$ and $(P - 1)/P$ of the load, with $2/P$ and $(P - 2)/P$ of the load, and so on, and chooses the partition that minimizes partition aspect ratio. This method increases the cost of computing the partition but can reduce communication costs. Plate 1 shows a mapping onto 64 processors constructed by using unbalanced recursive bisection. In this instance, the grid in question is an irregular finite element mesh generated for a superconductivity simulation.

Another technique, called *recursive graph bisection*, can be useful in the case of more complex unstructured grids, for example, finite element meshes. This technique

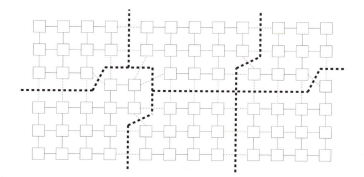

**Figure 2.17**  Load balancing in a grid problem. Variable numbers of grid points are placed on each processor so as to compensate for load imbalances. This sort of load distribution may arise if a local load-balancing scheme is used in which tasks exchange load information with neighbors and transfer grid points when load imbalances are detected.

uses connectivity information to reduce the number of grid edges crossing subdomain boundaries, and hence to reduce communication requirements. A grid is treated as a graph with $N$ vertices (grid points) $v_i$. The algorithm first identifies the two extremities of the graph, that is, the two vertices that are the most separated in terms of graph distance. (The graph distance between two vertices is the smallest number of edges that must be traversed to go between them.) Each vertex is then assigned to the subdomain corresponding to the closer extremity. Another algorithm called *recursive spectral bisection* is even better in many circumstances (see the chapter notes for references). Plate 2 shows a partition computed using the latter algorithm for the grid of Figure 2.9.

**Local Algorithms**    The techniques just described are relatively expensive because they require global knowledge of computation state. In contrast, local load-balancing algorithms compensate for changes in computational load using only information obtained from a small number of neighboring processors. For example, processors may be organized in a logical mesh; periodically, each processor compares its computational load with that of its neighbors in the mesh and transfers computation if the difference in load exceeds some threshold. Figure 2.17 and Plate 3 show load distributions produced by such schemes.

Because local algorithms are inexpensive to operate, they can be useful in situations in which load is constantly changing. However, they are typically less good at balancing load than global algorithms and, in particular, can be slow to adjust to major changes in load characteristics. For example, if a high load suddenly appears on one processor, multiple local load-balancing operations are required before load "diffuses" to other processors.

**Probabilistic Methods**    A particularly simple approach to load balancing is to allocate tasks to randomly selected processors. If the number of tasks is large, we can expect that each processor will be allocated about the same amount of computation. Advantages of

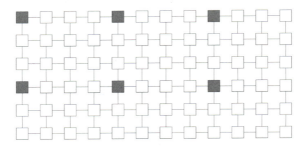

**Figure 2.18**    Using a cyclic mapping for load balancing in a grid problem, when executing on 12 processors. Tasks mapped to a single processor are shaded. Notice that with this mapping, all communications are with tasks located on different processors (assuming a five-point stencil).

this strategy are its low cost and scalability. Disadvantages are that off-processor communication is required for virtually every task and that acceptable load distribution is achieved only if there are many more tasks than there are processors. The strategy tends to be most effective when there is relatively little communication between tasks and/or little locality in communication patterns. In other cases, probabilistic methods tend to result in considerably more communication than do other techniques.

**Cyclic Mappings**    If we know both that computational load per grid point varies and that there is significant spatial locality in load levels, then a *cyclic* (or *scattered*, as it is sometimes called) mapping of tasks to processors can be appropriate. That is, each of $P$ processors is allocated every $P$th task according to some enumeration of the tasks (Figure 2.18). This technique is a form of probabilistic mapping. The goal is that, on average, each processor will be allocated about the same computational load. The benefits of improved load balance may need to be weighed against increased communication costs due to reduced locality. Block cyclic distributions are also possible, in which blocks of tasks are allocated to processors.

## 2.5.2  Task-Scheduling Algorithms

Task-scheduling algorithms can be used when a functional decomposition yields many tasks, each with weak locality requirements. A centralized or distributed task pool is maintained, into which new tasks are placed and from which tasks are taken for allocation to processors. In effect, we reformulate the parallel algorithm so that what were originally conceived of as tasks become data structures representing "problems," to be solved by a set of worker tasks, typically one per processor.

The most critical (and complicated) aspect of a task-scheduling algorithm is the strategy used to allocate problems to workers. Generally, the chosen strategy will represent a compromise between the conflicting requirements for independent operation (to

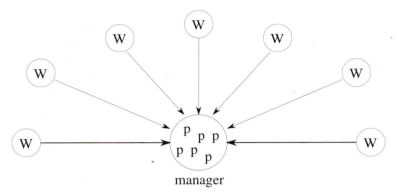

**Figure 2.19**   Manager/worker load-balancing structure. Workers repeatedly request and process problem descriptions; the manager maintains a pool of problem descriptions (p) and responds to requests from workers.

reduce communication costs) and global knowledge of computation state (to improve load balance). We discuss manager/worker, hierarchical manager/worker, and decentralized approaches.

**Manager/Worker**   Figure 2.19 illustrates a particularly simple task scheduling scheme that is nevertheless effective for moderate numbers of processors. This strategy was used previously in Section 1.4.4. A central manager task is given responsibility for problem allocation. Each worker repeatedly requests and executes a problem from the manager. Workers can also send new tasks to the manager for allocation to other workers. The efficiency of this strategy depends on the number of workers and the relative costs of obtaining and executing problems. Efficiency can be improved by prefetching problems so as to overlap computation and communication, and by caching problems in workers, so that workers communicate with the manager only when no problems are available locally.

**Hierarchical Manager/Worker**   A variant of the manager/worker scheme divides workers into disjoint sets, each with a submanager. Workers request tasks from submanagers, which themselves communicate periodically with the manager and with other submanagers to balance load between the sets of processors for which they are responsible.

**Decentralized Schemes**   In completely decentralized schemes, there is no central manager. Instead, a separate task pool is maintained on each processor, and idle workers request problems from other processors. In effect, the task pool becomes a distributed data structure that is accessed by the different tasks in an asynchronous fashion. A variety of access policies can be defined. For example, a worker may request work from a small number of predefined "neighbors" or may select other processors at random. In a hybrid centralized/distributed scheme, requests are sent to a central manager, which allocates them to workers in a round-robin fashion. Notice that while this manager will certainly be a bottleneck on large numbers of processors, it will typically be accessed less frequently than will the manager in a manager/worker scheduler and hence is a more scalable construct.

As noted in Section 2.3.4, access to a distributed data structure, such as the task pool maintained by a decentralized load-balancing scheme, can be provided in several different ways. Workers can be made responsible for both computing and managing the queue of problems. In this case, each worker must periodically poll to detect pending requests. Alternatively, computation and task pool management responsibilities can be encapsulated in separate tasks.

**Termination Detection**    Task-scheduling algorithms require a mechanism for determining when a search is complete; otherwise, idle workers will never stop requesting work from other workers. This *termination detection* operation is straightforward in centralized schemes, because the manager can easily determine when all workers are idle. It is more difficult in decentralized algorithms, because not only is there no central record of which workers are idle, but also messages in transit may be carrying tasks even when all workers appear to be idle. See the chapter notes for references to termination-detection algorithms.

### 2.5.3   Mapping Design Checklist

We have now completed our parallel algorithm design by specifying how tasks defined in previous design stages are mapped to processors. Our mapping decisions seek to balance conflicting requirements for equitable load distribution and low communication costs. When possible, we use a static mapping scheme that allocates each task to a single processor. However, when the number or size of tasks is variable or not known until runtime, we may use a dynamic load balancing scheme or reformulate the problem so that a task scheduling structure can be used to schedule computation.

The following checklist can serve as a basis for an informal evaluation of the mapping design.

1. If considering an SPMD design for a complex problem, have you also considered an algorithm based on dynamic task creation and deletion? The latter approach can yield a simpler algorithm (as will be illustrated in Section 2.7); however, performance can be problematic.

2. If considering a design based on dynamic task creation and deletion, have you also considered an SPMD algorithm? An SPMD algorithm provides greater control over the scheduling of communication and computation, but can be more complex.

3. If using a centralized load-balancing scheme, have you verified that the manager will not become a bottleneck? You may be able to reduce communication costs in these schemes by passing pointers to tasks, rather than the tasks themselves, to the manager.

4. If using a dynamic load-balancing scheme, have you evaluated the relative costs of different strategies? Be sure to include the implementation costs in your analysis. Probabilistic or cyclic mapping schemes are simple and should always be

considered, because they can avoid the need for repeated load-balancing operations.

5. If using probabilistic or cyclic methods, do you have a large enough number of tasks to ensure reasonable load balance? Typically, at least ten times as many tasks as processors are required.

We have now completed the design of one or more parallel algorithms designs for our problem. However, we are not quite ready to start writing code: several phases in the design process remain. First, we need to conduct some simple performance analyses in order to choose between alternative algorithms and to verify that our design meets performance goals. We should also think hard about the implementation costs of our designs, about opportunities for reusing existing code in their implementation, and about how algorithms fit into larger systems of which they may form a part. These issues are discussed in detail in Chapters 3 and 4.

## 2.6  Case Study: Atmosphere Model

In the next three sections, we develop parallel algorithms for atmosphere modeling, VLSI design, and computational chemistry problems. These case studies are intended to illustrate both the design principles presented in the text and the stepwise process by which realistic parallel algorithms are developed.

While the problems examined in these case studies are of considerable interest in their own right, our interest here is in their computational characteristics. The atmosphere modeling application is an example of a problem amenable to parallelization by using simple domain decomposition techniques. It is representative of a wide range of scientific and engineering computations. The VLSI design problem is an example of an irregular problem requiring load-balancing techniques. It is representative of many symbolic computing problems. Finally, the computational chemistry application is an example of a problem requiring asynchronous access to distributed data structures, a requirement that arises frequently in both numerical and symbolic computing.

In each case study, we first briefly introduce the problem being solved and then develop parallel algorithms. We restrict the problem descriptions to essential computational issues and omit details that would add to the length of the presentation without illustrating new principles. In particular, we do not say much about why the underlying scientific or engineering problem is formulated in the way described, or about alternative problem formulations that might admit to alternative parallelization strategies. The chapter notes provide pointers to detailed treatments of these topics.

### 2.6.1  Atmosphere Model Background

An *atmosphere model* is a computer program that simulates atmospheric processes (wind, clouds, precipitation, etc.) that influence weather or climate. It may be used to study the evolution of tornadoes, to predict tomorrow's weather, or to study the impact on climate of increased concentrations of atmospheric carbon dioxide. Like many numerical models

Conservation of momentum:

$$\frac{du}{dt} - \left( f + u\frac{\tan\phi}{a} \right) v = -\frac{1}{a\cos\phi}\frac{1}{\rho}\frac{\partial p}{\partial\lambda} + F_\lambda$$

$$\frac{dv}{dt} + \left( f + u\frac{\tan\phi}{a} \right) u = -\frac{1}{\rho a}\frac{\partial p}{\partial\phi} + F_\phi$$

Hydrostatic approximation:

$$g = -\frac{1}{\rho}\frac{\partial p}{\partial z}$$

Conservation of mass:

$$\frac{\partial\rho}{\partial t} = -\frac{1}{a\cos\phi}\left( \frac{\partial}{\partial\lambda}(\rho u) + \frac{\partial}{\partial\phi}(\rho v\cos\phi) \right) - \frac{\partial}{\partial z}(\rho w)$$

Conservation of energy:

$$C_p\frac{dT}{dt} - \frac{1}{\rho}\frac{dp}{dt} = Q$$

State equation (atmosphere):

$$p = \rho RT$$

**Figure 2.20**   The basic predictive equations used in atmospheric modeling, where $\phi$ and $\lambda$ are latitude and longitude, $z$ is height, $u$ and $v$ are horizontal components of velocity, $p$ is pressure, $\rho$ is density, $T$ is temperature, $f$ is Coriolis force, $g$ is gravity, $F$ and $Q$ are external forcing terms, $C_p$ is specific heat, and $a$ is the earth's radius.

of physical processes, an atmosphere model solves a set of partial differential equations, in this case describing the basic fluid dynamical behavior of the atmosphere (Figure 2.20). The behavior of these equations on a continuous space is approximated by their behavior on a finite set of regularly spaced points in that space. Typically, these points are located on a rectangular latitude-longitude grid of size $N_x \times N_y \times N_z$, with $N_z$ in the range 15–30, $N_x \approx 2N_y$, and $N_y$ in the range 50–500 (Figure 2.21). This grid is periodic in the $x$ and $y$ dimensions, meaning that grid point $G_{0,0,0}$ is viewed as being adjacent to $G_{0,N_y-1,0}$ and $G_{N_x-1,0,0}$. A vector of values is maintained at each grid point, representing quantities such as pressure, temperature, wind velocity, and humidity.

The atmosphere model performs a time integration to determine the state of the atmosphere at some future time, based on an initial state. This integration proceeds in a series of steps, with each step advancing the state of the computation by a fixed amount. We shall assume that the model uses a finite difference method (Section 2.3.1) to update grid values, with a nine-point stencil being used to compute atmospheric motion in the horizontal dimension, and a three-point stencil in the vertical (Figure 2.22).

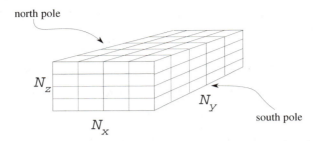

north pole

$N_z$

$N_y$

$N_x$

south pole

**Figure 2.21**   The three-dimensional grid used to represent the state of the atmosphere. Values maintained at each grid point represent quantities such as pressure and temperature.

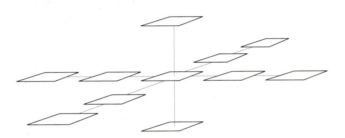

**Figure 2.22**   The finite difference stencils used in the atmosphere model. This figure shows for a single grid point both the nine-point stencil used to simulate horizontal motion and the three-point stencil used to simulate vertical motion.

The finite difference computations are concerned with the movement, or fluid dynamics, of the atmosphere. In addition to these dynamics calculations, the atmosphere model includes algorithms used to simulate processes such as radiation, convection, and precipitation. These calculations are collectively termed *physics* and use a range of numerical methods of varying complexity. Data dependencies within physics computations are restricted to within vertical columns.

Plate 4 illustrates one of the many phenomena that can be simulated using an atmospheric circulation model. This shows a potential temperature isosurface of two thunderstorm downdrafts that hit the ground as microbursts, then spread out and collide. The surfaces outline the boundaries of the cold downdrafted air. The collision region contains wind fields that are dangerous to landing aircraft. The grey tiles are 1-kilometer squares and the model domain is $16 \times 18$ km with 50 m resolution.

In summary, the atmosphere modeling example is primarily concerned with performing finite difference computations on a regular three-dimensional grid. In this respect, it is representative of a large class of scientific (numeric) computations. The simple, regular structure of the finite difference method makes it a useful pedagogical tool, and we shall use it repeatedly in the following chapters to illustrate issues in algorithm design and performance analysis.

### 2.6.2   Atmosphere Model Algorithm Design

We now develop parallel algorithms for the atmosphere modeling problem, proceeding in the stepwise fashion presented in earlier sections.

**Partition**    The grid used to represent state in the atmosphere model is a natural candidate for domain decomposition. Decompositions in the $x$, $y$, and/or $z$ dimensions are possible (Figure 2.2). Pursuant to our strategy of exposing the maximum concurrency possible, we initially favor the most aggressive decomposition possible, which in this case defines a task for each grid point. This task maintains as its state the various values associated with its grid point and is responsible for the computation required to update that state at each time step. Hence, we have a total of $N_x \times N_y \times N_z$ tasks, each with $\mathcal{O}(1)$ data and computation per time step.

**Communication**    The design checklist of Section 2.2.3 does not suggest any obvious deficiencies in our partition design, so we proceed to consider communication requirements. We identify three distinct communications:

1. *Finite difference stencils.* If we assume a fine-grained decomposition in which each task encapsulates a single grid point, the nine-point stencil used in the horizontal dimension requires that each task obtain values from eight neighboring tasks. The corresponding channel structure is illustrated in Figure 2.23. Similarly, the three-point stencil used in the vertical dimension requires that each task obtain values from two neighbors.

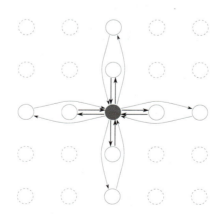

**Figure 2.23**   Task and channel structure for a two-dimensional finite difference computation with nine-point stencil, assuming one grid point per processor. Only the channels used by the shaded task are shown.

2. *Global operations.* The atmosphere model computes periodically the total mass of the atmosphere, in order to verify that the simulation is proceeding correctly. This quantity is defined as follows:

$$Total\ Mass = \sum_{i=0}^{N_x-1} \sum_{j=0}^{N_y-1} \sum_{k=0}^{N_z-1} M_{ijk}, \tag{2.3}$$

where $M_{ijk}$ denotes the mass at grid point $(i, j, k)$. This sum can be computed using one of the parallel summation algorithms presented in Section 2.4.1.

3. *Physics computations.* If each task encapsulates a single grid point, then the physics component of the atmosphere model requires considerable communication. For example, the total clear sky (TCS) at level $k \geq 1$ is defined as

$$\text{TCS}_k = \prod_{i=1}^{k}(1 - \text{cld}_i)TCS_1$$

$$= TCS_{k-1}(1 - \text{cld}_k),$$

where level 0 is the top of the atmosphere and $\text{cld}_i$ is the cloud fraction at level $i$. This *prefix product* operation can be performed in $\log N_z$ steps using a variant of the hypercube algorithm of Section 2.4.1. In total, the physics component of the model requires on the order of 30 communications per grid point and per time step.

Let us evaluate this design by using the checklist of Section 2.3.5. The communication associated with the finite difference stencil is distributed and hence can proceed concurrently. So is the communication required for the global communication operation, thanks to the distributed algorithm developed in Section 2.4.1. (We might also consider performing this global operation less frequently, since its value is intended only for diagnostic purposes.) The one component of our algorithm's communication structure that is problematic is the physics. However, we shall see that the need for this communication can be avoided by agglomeration.

**Agglomeration**   Our fine-grained domain decomposition of the atmosphere model has created $N_x \times N_y \times N_z$ tasks: between $10^5$ and $10^7$, depending on problem size. This is likely to be many more than we require and some degree of agglomeration can be considered. We identify three reasons for pursuing agglomeration:

1. As illustrated in Figure 2.24, a small amount of agglomeration (from one to four grid points per task) can reduce the communication requirements associated with the nine-point stencil from eight to four messages per task per time step.

2. Communication requirements in the horizontal dimension are relatively small: a total of four messages containing eight data values. In contrast, the vertical dimension requires communication not only for the finite difference stencil (2 messages, 2 data values) but also for various "physics" computations (30 messages).

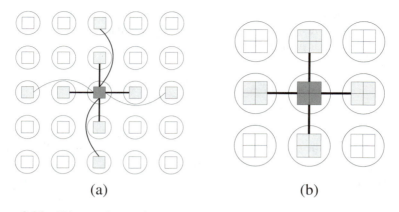

(a)                                    (b)

**Figure 2.24**    Using agglomeration to reduce communication requirements in the atmosphere model. In (a), each task handles a single point and hence must obtain data from eight other tasks in order to implement the nine-point stencil. In (b), granularity is increased to $2 \times 2$ points, meaning that only 4 communications are required per task.

These communications can be avoided by agglomerating tasks within each vertical column.

3. Agglomeration in the vertical is also desirable from a software engineering point of view. Horizontal dependencies are restricted to the dynamics component of the model; the physics component operates within individual columns only. Hence, a two-dimensional horizontal decomposition would allow existing sequential physics code to be reused in a parallel program without modification.

This analysis makes it appear sensible to refine our parallel algorithm to utilize a two-dimensional horizontal decomposition of the model grid in which each task encapsulates at least four grid points. Communication requirements are then reduced to those associated with the nine-point stencil and the summation operation. Notice that this algorithm can create at most $N_x \times N_y/4$ tasks: between $10^3$ and $10^5$, depending on problem size. This number is likely to be enough for most practical purposes.

**Mapping**    In the absence of load imbalances, the simple mapping strategy illustrated in Figure 2.16 can be used. It is clear from the figure that in this case, further agglomeration can be performed; in the limit, each processor can be assigned a single task responsible for many columns, thereby yielding an SPMD program.

This mapping strategy is efficient if each grid column task performs the same amount of computation at each time step. This assumption is valid for many finite difference problems but turns out to be invalid for some atmosphere models. The reason is that the cost of physics computations can vary significantly depending on model state variables. For example, radiation calculations are not performed at night, and clouds are formed only when humidity exceeds a certain threshold. The sort of variation in computational load that can result is illustrated in Plate 5.

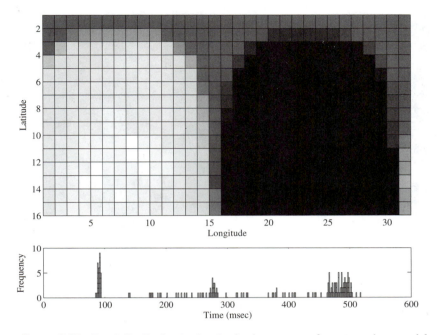

**Figure 2.25** Load distribution in the physics component of an atmosphere model in the absence of load balancing. In the top part of the figure, shading is used to indicate computational load in each of 16 × 32 processors. A strong spatial variation is evident. This effect is due to the night/day cycle (radiation calculations are performed only in sunlight); hence, there is a temporal variation also. The bottom part of the figure is a histogram showing the distribution of computation times, which vary by a factor of 5. These results were obtained by using a parallel version of the National Center for Atmospheric Research (NCAR) Community Climate Model (CCM2) on the 512-processor Intel DELTA computer.

Empirical studies suggest that these load imbalances can reduce computational efficiency by 20 percent or more (Figure 2.25; see also Plate 5). In many circumstances, this performance loss may be regarded as acceptable. However, if a model is to be used extensively, it is worthwhile to spend time improving efficiency. One approach is to use a form of cyclic mapping: for example, allocating each processor tasks from western and eastern and from northern and southern hemispheres. Figure 2.26 shows the reduction in load imbalance that can be achieved with this technique; this reduction must be weighed against the resulting increase in communication costs.

### 2.6.3 Atmosphere Model Summary

The design of a parallel atmosphere model has proved to be straightforward process, in that most design choices are clear-cut. A two-dimensional domain decomposition of the model

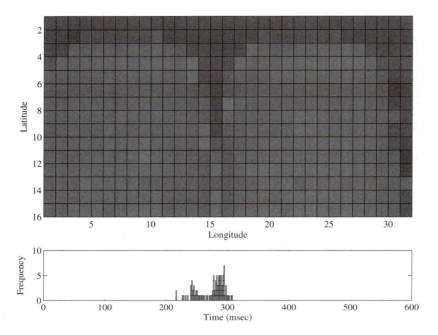

**Figure 2.26** Load distribution in the physics component of CCM2 when using a cyclic mapping. A comparison with Figure 2.25 shows that load imbalances are reduced significantly.

grid results in a need for both local communication between tasks handling neighboring grid points and a parallel summation operation.

One unanswered question concerns whether load-balancing algorithms should be incorporated into the model. Because load balancing adds to the complexity of the overall design, this decision requires both performance data (of the sort presented in Figure 2.25) and information about the expected use of the parallel model. Another question, addressed in Chapter 4, is how the atmosphere model will fit into a larger framework such as the climate model of Figure 2.3.

## 2.7  Case Study: Floorplan Optimization

Our second case study is an example of a highly irregular, symbolic problem. The solution that we develop incorporates a task scheduling algorithm.

### 2.7.1  Floorplan Background

VLSI is a process used to build electronic components such as microprocessors and memory chips comprising millions of transistors. The design of VLSI components is a computationally demanding process. Computers are used extensively to verify the correctness of a circuit design, to lay out a circuit in a two-dimensional area, and to generate the patterns used to test circuits once they have been fabricated. Many of these problems involve either an exhaustive or a heuristically guided search of a large space of possible solutions. Here, we consider a layout problem. The first stage of the VLSI design process typically produces a set of indivisible rectangular blocks called *cells*. In a second stage, interconnection information is used to determine the relative placements of these cells. In a third stage, implementations are selected for the various cells with the goal of optimizing the total area. It is the third stage, *floorplan optimization*, for which we shall develop a parallel algorithm. This is an important part of the design process, since the cost of a chip is usually dominated by its area.

VLSI floorplan optimization can be explained by analogy with the problem of designing a kitchen. Assume that we have decided on the components the kitchen is to contain (this action is stage 1 of the VLSI design process) and how these components are to be arranged (stage 2). For example, we may wish to have a stove, refrigerator, table, and sink and may require that the stove be next to the refrigerator and the table next to the sink. Assume also that we can choose among several possible models for each of these components, with different models having different shapes but occupying the same floor area. In the floorplan optimization phase of our kitchen design, we select models so as to make the best use of available floorspace.

In VLSI, a floorplan is represented as a pair of polar graphs, conventionally called the $\mathcal{G}$ and $\mathcal{H}$ graphs. (A polar graph is a directed acyclic graph with a single source and a single sink. The term *directed* means that edges have a direction, and *acyclic* means that there are no cycles.) These graphs specify which cells are adjacent in the vertical and horizontal directions, respectively. Each arc denotes a cell, and nodes (other than the source and sink) link cells that must have touching edges.

Although a cell has a fixed area, it may have several possible implementations with different aspect ratios. If we have $N$ cells, and if cell $c_i$ has $\mathcal{I}(c_i)$ implementations, then the total number of possible floorplan configurations is

$$\prod_{i=0}^{N-1} \mathcal{I}(c_i).$$

For example, Figure 2.27 shows a floorplan optimization problem with three cells and six possible configurations.

The problem then is to identify the configuration with the lowest area, where area is defined as the product of the maximum horizontal and vertical extents. This identification can be achieved by using a search algorithm to explore a search tree representing all possible configurations. As shown in Figure 2.28, level $i$ of this tree corresponds to the situation in which implementations have been chosen for $i$ cells. We can explore this search tree by using Algorithm 1.1. An initial call search(root) causes the entire tree to be visited, with the path used to get to each leaf node reported as a solution.

Algorithm 1.1 implements an *exhaustive search* that visits all nodes of the search tree. Unfortunately, this strategy is computationally infeasible for any but the smallest problems. For example, a problem with just 20 cells and 6 implementations per cell has

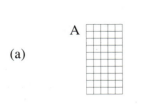
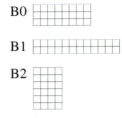
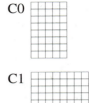

(a)

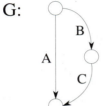
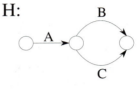

(b)

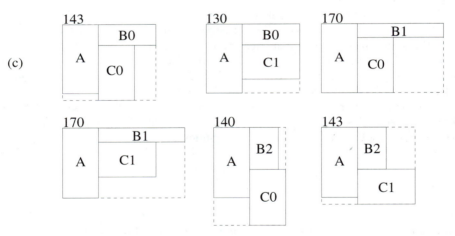

(c)

**Figure 2.27**  A floorplan optimization problem. The three cells A, B, and C, have 1, 3, and 2 implementations each, respectively. In (a) are the alternative implementations. In (b) are the $\mathcal{G}$ and $\mathcal{H}$ graphs, which state that B must be above C, and that A must be to the left of B and C, respectively. In (c) are the $1 \times 3 \times 2 = 6$ alternative floorplans that satisfy the constraints; each is labeled with its area. The lowest area floorplan is constructed from A, B0, and C1 and has an area of 130.

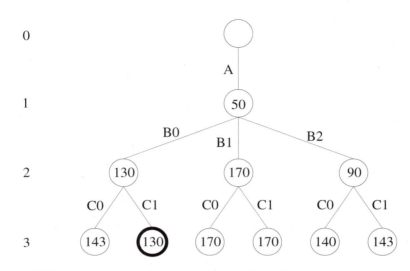

**Figure 2.28** Solving a floorplan optimization problem. This is the search tree corresponding to the problem illustrated in Figure 2.27. Level 0 is the root. At level 1, an implementation has been chosen for A; the three level 2 subtrees represent the choices for B and the level 3 leaves the choices for C. The number in each tree node represents the area of the associated (partial) solution. The optimal configuration is (A, B0, C1) and has area 130.

a search space of $6^{20} \approx 4 \times 10^{15}$ nodes. Fortunately, the number of nodes explored can be reduced considerably by using a technique called *branch-and-bound* search. The basic idea is to keep track of the best (lowest area) solution found so far. Before "expanding" a node (that is, looking at its subtrees), we check whether the area of the partial configuration represented by that node is already greater than that of the best known solution. If so, we know that this node cannot yield a better solution, and the subtree rooted at that node can be abandoned, or *pruned* (Figure 2.29). This approach is specified as Algorithm 2.2, with the global variable $A_{min}$ used to maintain a record of the best solution.

On a sequential computer, the `foreach` in Algorithm 2.2 can examine each subtree in turn, thereby giving a *depth-first* search algorithm that explores the tree depth-first and left-to-right. In this case, pruning can reduce the number of nodes explored enormously. In one experiment reported in the literature, the number of nodes explored in a typical 20-cell problem was reduced from $4 \times 10^{15}$ to $6 \times 10^6$. As we shall see, efficient pruning is a difficult problem in a parallel environment and, to a large extent, determines the structure of our parallel algorithm.

In summary, the fundamental operation to be performed in the floorplan optimization problem is branch-and-bound search. This is an interesting algorithm from a parallel computing perspective because of its irregular computational structure: the size and shape of the search tree that must be explored are not known ahead of time. Also, the need for pruning introduces a need both to manage the order in which the tree is explored and to acquire

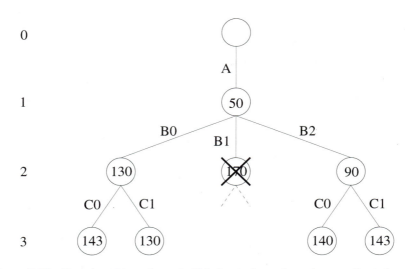

**Figure 2.29**   Branch-and-bound search. This figure shows the nodes actually explored in the example problem, assuming a depth-first and left-to-right search strategy. The subtree rooted at the second node on level 2 is pruned because the cost of this node (170) is greater than that of the cheapest solution already found (130).

and propagate global knowledge of computation state. In these respects this problem is typical of many algorithms in symbolic (nonnumeric) computing.

### 2.7.2   Floorplan Algorithm Design

**Partition**   Algorithm 2.2, like Algorithm 1.1, has no obvious data structure to which we can apply domain decomposition techniques. Hence, we use a fine-grained functional decomposition in which each search tree node is explored by a separate task. As noted earlier, this means that new tasks will be created in a wavefront as the search progresses down the search tree, which will tend to be explored in a *breadth-first* fashion. Notice that only tasks on the wavefront can execute concurrently. We also need to address the issue of how to manage the $A_{min}$ value, which must be accessed by all tasks. For now, we assume that it is encapsulated in a single task with which other tasks will communicate.

A quick review using the design checklist of Section 2.2.3 reveals one deficiency in this design. The breadth-first exploration strategy is likely to decrease performance dramatically by delaying discovery of solution nodes and hence reducing the amount of pruning that occurs, thereby leading to considerable redundant computation. We must bear this issue in mind in subsequent design phases.

**Communication**   In a parallel implementation of simple search (Algorithm 1.1), tasks can execute independently and need communicate only to report solutions. In contrast, branch-and-bound search requires communication during execution in order to obtain and update the search bound $A_{min}$. In designing a communication structure to achieve this

```
procedure b&b_search(A)
begin
   Amin = ∞
   score = eval(A)
   if(score < Amin) then
      if (leaf(A)) then
         Amin = score
         report solution and score
      else
         foreach child Ai of A
            b&b_search(Ai)
         endfor
      endif
   endif
end
```

**Algorithm 2.2**  Branch-and-bound search is similar to Algorithm 1.1 (simple search), but uses a search bound $A_{min}$ to prune the search.

goal, we need to trade off the benefits of frequent accesses to a centralized $A_{min}$ value (which tends to reduce the amount of the search tree that must be explored) against communication costs.

One approach is to encapsulate responsibility for maintaining $A_{min}$ in a centralized task, with which each task communicates when a solution is produced or a bound is required. This approach is simple and may even be efficient if communication is cheap, evaluating a node is expensive, and the number of processors is not too large. However, the centralized approach is inherently nonscalable. Since the manager must take a certain amount of time to process a request, the maximum rate at which it can service requests, and hence the maximum number of tasks that can execute concurrently, is bounded.

Various refinements to this centralized scheme can be imagined. We can modify Algorithm 2.2 to check $A_{min}$ only periodically, for example when a depth counter incremented on each recursive call is an integer multiple of a specified frequency parameter. Or, we can partition the tree into subtrees, each with its own $A_{min}$ submanager, and organize periodic exchanges of information between these submanagers. For example, submanagers can perform broadcast operations when they discover significantly better solutions.

**Agglomeration**  In the agglomeration phase of the design process we start to address practical issues relating to performance on target computers. In the floorplan optimization problem, this means we must address two potential deficiencies of the fine-grained algorithm that we have developed. The first will be familiar from earlier problems, that is, the cost of creating a large number of fine-grained tasks. This can be addressed using agglomeration, unless we believe that node evaluation is sufficiently expensive and task creation sufficiently cheap for the fine-grained algorithm to be efficient. For example, we can create one task for each search call in the foreach statement of Algorithm 2.2 until we reach a

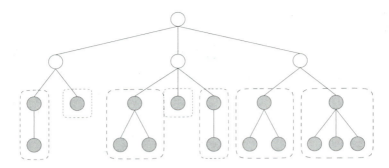

**Figure 2.30** Increasing granularity in a search problem. In this figure, we agglomerate by switching to a sequential search at level two in the search tree. A task is created for each subtree rooted at level two.

specified depth in the tree, and then switch to a depth-first strategy, thereby creating a single task that evaluates search calls in sequence (Figure 2.30). If the switch to depth-first search is performed at depth $D$ and cell $c_i$ has $\mathcal{I}(c_i)$ implementations, then in the absence of pruning this technique creates $\prod_{i=0}^{D-1} \mathcal{I}(c_i)$ tasks.

The second potential deficiency is more subtle and relates to the scheduling of tasks rather than to their creation. In the absence of explicit programmer control, we can assume that the tasks created to evaluate search tree nodes will execute either in the order that they are created or perhaps in a random order. In either case, the search tree tends to be explored in a breadth-first fashion. This is undesirable because it tends to reduce the effectiveness of pruning and hence cause redundant computation. The solution to this problem is to control the order in which search tree nodes are explored. That is, we must implement a task-scheduling algorithm. Because this is really a mapping issue, we discuss it under "Mapping."

**Mapping**    Recall that when we use a task-scheduling strategy, tasks (search tree nodes) become "problems" to be executed by one of a smaller number of "worker" tasks, typically one per processor. Workers generate new search problems as they expand nodes, and request new search problems each time they complete previously assigned problems. Requests can be handled using a centralized or decentralized strategy.

We can imagine a variety of alternative task-scheduling schemes for the floorplan optimization problem. One approach works in conjunction with the agglomeration scheme of Figure 2.30. A central manager first constructs a number of coarse-grained tasks, by exploring the search tree to depth $D$. These tasks are then assigned to idle workers in a demand-driven manner. Because each task can be represented by a short vector representing the path taken to its position in the tree, the data movement costs associated with this scheme are not high. Furthermore, because each processor executes one subtree at a time in a depth-first fashion, pruning is effective.

An interesting variant of this approach combines elements of both redundant work and cyclic mapping to avoid the need for a central manager. Every worker expands the tree to depth $D$. Then, each worker takes responsibility for a disjoint subset of the tasks generated. (This subset could be identified using a cyclic allocation strategy, for example.) Only if a worker becomes idle does it ask other workers for tasks.

A third strategy, more complex but also more general, is initially to allocate the root node to a single worker. Load balancing is then achieved by causing workers with empty queues to request problems from other workers. Each worker can then enforce a local depth-first search strategy, and hence increase the amount of pruning, by ordering its queue of search problems according to their depth in the tree. This method allows the worker to select problems far from the root for local execution and problems nearer to the root to hand to other workers.

Our choice of task scheduling strategy will depend on characteristics of our problem and target computer and can be determined by analysis and experiment. Notice that the communication structures used for task scheduling can be integrated with those proposed earlier for maintaining $A_{min}$. For example, a central manager used for task scheduling can also maintain and distribute an up-to-date search bound with each task. In decentralized schemes, the worker tasks that execute search problems can broadcast improved search bound values to other workers.

### 2.7.3  Floorplan Summary

The parallel algorithm designed in this case study is certainly more complex, and perhaps less obvious, than that developed for the atmosphere model. It is clear from the start that functional decomposition techniques should be used to define tasks, that responsibility for maintaining $A_{min}$ should be isolated from the rest of the computation, and that we can increase task granularity by switching from a parallel to a sequential evaluation strategy at a specified depth in the search tree. If we were concerned with parallelizing simple search, the design might be complete at this stage. However, the need to support pruning requires that we proceed with further refinements. In particular, we introduce a task-scheduling algorithm so that we can pursue depth-first search on each processor while exposing higher-level search tree nodes for idle workers.

## 2.8   Case Study: Computational Chemistry

Our third case study, like the first, is from computational science. It is an example of an application that accesses a distributed data structure in an asynchronous fashion and that is amenable to a functional decomposition.

### 2.8.1  Chemistry Background

Computational techniques are being used increasingly as an alternative to experiment in chemistry. In what is called *ab initio quantum chemistry*, computer programs are used to compute fundamental properties of atoms and molecules, such as bond strengths and reaction energies, from first principles, by solving various approximations to the Schrödinger equation that describes their basic structures. This approach allows the chemist to explore reaction pathways that would be hazardous or expensive to explore experimentally. One application for these techniques is in the investigation of biological processes. For example, Plate 6 shows a molecular model for the active site region in the enzyme malate dehydrogenase, a key enzyme in the conversion of glucose to the high-energy molecule ATP. This image is taken from a simulation of the transfer of a hydride anion from the substrate, malate, to a cofactor, nicotinamide adenine diphosphate. The two isosurfaces colored blue and brown represent lower and higher electron densities, respectively, calculated by using a combined quantum and classical mechanics methodology. The green, red, blue, and white balls are carbon, oxygen, nitrogen, and hydrogen atoms, respectively.

Fundamental to several methods used in quantum chemistry is the need to compute what is called the *Fock matrix*, a two-dimensional array representing the electronic structure of an atom or molecule. This matrix, which is represented here as F, has size $N \times N$ and is formed by evaluating the following summation for each element:

$$F_{ij} = \sum_{k=0}^{N-1} \sum_{l=0}^{N-1} D_{kl} \left( I_{ijkl} - \frac{1}{2} I_{ikjl} \right), \tag{2.4}$$

where D is a two-dimensional array of size $N \times N$ that is only read, not written, by this computation and the I represent integrals that are computed using elements $i$, $j$, $k$, and $l$ of a read-only, one-dimensional array A with $\mathcal{O}(N)$ elements. An integral can be thought of as an approximation to the repulsive force between two electrons.

Because Equation 2.4 includes a double summation, apparently $2N^2$ integrals must be computed for each element of F, for a total of $2N^4$ integrals. However, in practice it is possible to exploit redundancy in the integrals and symmetry in F and reduce this number to a total of $N^4/8$. When this is done, the algorithm can be reduced to the rather strange logic given as Algorithm 2.3. In principle, the calculation of each element of F requires access to all elements of D and A; furthermore, access patterns appear highly irregular. In this respect, the Fock matrix construction problem is representative of many numeric problems with irregular and nonlocal communication patterns.

For the molecular systems of interest to chemists, the problem size $N$ may be in the range $10^3 - 10^4$. Because the evaluation of an integral is a fairly expensive operation, involving $10^2 - 10^3$ operations, the construction of the Fock matrix may require $10^{14} - 10^{19}$ operations. In addition, most methods require that a series of Fock matrices be constructed, each representing a more accurate approximation to a molecule's electronic structure. These considerations have motivated a considerable amount of work on both efficient parallel algorithms for Fock matrix construction and improved methods that require the computation of less than $\mathcal{O}(N^4)$ integrals.

### 2.8.2 Chemistry Algorithm Design

**Partition**    Because the Fock matrix problem is concerned primarily with the symmetric two-dimensional matrices F and D, an obvious partitioning strategy is to apply domain decomposition techniques to these matrices to create $N(N + 1)/2$ tasks, each containing a single element from each matrix ($F_{ij}$, $D_{ij}$) and responsible for the operations required to compute its $F_{ij}$. This yields $N(N + 1)/2$ tasks, each with $\mathcal{O}(1)$ data and each responsible for computing $2N^2$ integrals, as specified in Equation 2.4.

```
procedure fock_build
begin
    for i = 1 to N
        for j = 1 to i
            for k = 1 to j
                for l = 1 to k
                    integral(i, j, k, l)
                endfor
            endfor
        endfor
    endfor
end

procedure integral(i, j, k, l)
begin
    I = compute_integral(i, j, k, l)
```

$F_{ij} = F_{ij} + D_{kl} I$

$F_{kl} = F_{kl} + D_{ij} I$

$F_{ik} = F_{ik} + D_{jl} I$

$F_{jl} = F_{jl} - (1/2) D_{ik} I$

$F_{il} = F_{il} - (1/2) D_{jk} I$

$F_{jk} = F_{jk} - (1/2) D_{il} I$

```
end
```

**Algorithm 2.3** Sequential Fock matrix construction algorithm. When symmetry is exploited in the computation, each of $N^4/8$ integrals can contribute to six elements of F.

This domain decomposition strategy is simple but suffers from a significant disadvantage: it cannot easily exploit redundancy and symmetry and, hence, performs eight times too many integral computations. Because an alternative algorithm based on functional decomposition techniques is significantly more efficient (it does not perform redundant computation and does not incur high communication costs), the domain decomposition algorithm is not considered further.

Quite a different parallel algorithm can be developed by focusing on the computation to be performed rather than on the data structures manipulated, in other words, by using a functional decomposition. When redundancy is considered, one naturally thinks of a computation as comprising a set of integrals (the integral procedure of Algorithm 2.3), each requiring six D elements and contributing to six F elements. Focusing on these computations, we define $N^4/8$ "computation" tasks, each responsible for one integral.

Having defined a functional decomposition, we next need to distribute data structures over tasks. However, we see no obvious criteria by which data elements might be associated with one computation task rather than another: each data element is accessed by many tasks. In effect, the F, D, and A arrays constitute large data structures that the computation tasks need to access in a distributed and asynchronous fashion. This situation suggests that

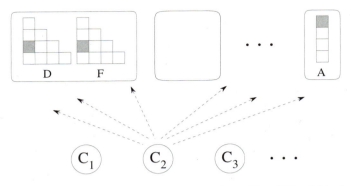

**Figure 2.31**    Functional decomposition of Fock matrix problem. This yields about $N^2/2$ data tasks, shown in the upper part of the figure, and $N^4/8$ computation tasks, shown in the lower part of the figure. Computation tasks send read and write requests to data tasks.

the techniques described in Section 2.3.4 for asynchronous communication may be useful. Hence, for now we simply define two sets of "data" tasks that are responsible only for responding to requests to read and write data values. These tasks encapsulate elements of the two-dimensional arrays D and F ($F_{ij}$, $D_{ij}$) and of the one-dimensional array A ($A_i$), respectively. In all, our partition yields a total of approximately $N^4/8$ computation tasks and $N^2/2$ data tasks (Figure 2.31).

**Communication and Agglomeration**    We have now defined $\mathcal{O}(N^4)$ computation tasks and $\mathcal{O}(N^2)$ data tasks. Each computation task must perform sixteen communications: six to obtain D matrix elements, four to obtain A matrix elements, and six to store F matrix elements. As the computational costs of different integrals can vary significantly, there does not appear to be any opportunity for organizing these communication operations into a regular structure, as is advocated in Section 2.3.2.

On many parallel computers, the cost of an integral will be comparable to the cost of a communication. Hence, communication requirements must be reduced by agglomeration. We describe two alternative strategies that can be used to achieve this goal. Their data requirements are illustrated in Figure 2.32.

1. *Total replication.* Communication costs can be cut dramatically by replicating the F and D matrices in each of $P$ tasks, one per processor of a parallel computer. Each task is given responsibility for $1/P$ of the integrals. Computation can then proceed in each task without any communication. The only coordination required is a final summation to accumulate partial F matrices. This can be achieved using a parallel vector reduction algorithm described in Section 11.2.

The technique of replicating data structures on each processor of a parallel computer is commonly used in parallel computing to reduce software engineering costs. It allows an existing sequential code to be adapted quickly for parallel execution, since there is no need to modify data structures. The principal disadvantage of the technique is that it is nonscalable. Because total memory requirements scale with the number of tasks created,

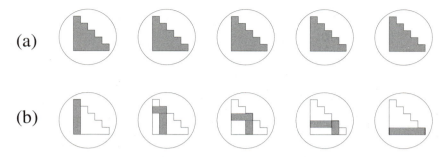

(a)

(b)

**Figure 2.32**    Agglomeration strategies for Fock matrix construction with $N = P = 5$, for (a) the total replication algorithm and (b) the partial replication algorithm. In each case, the five tasks are shown with shading used to represent the portion of the symmetric D and F matrices allocated to each task. In (a), each matrix is replicated in each task. In (b), each task is given a single row and column; this corresponds to a factor of two replication.

the largest problem that can be solved is determined not by the total amount of memory in a parallel computer, but by the amount available in a single processor. For example, on a 512-processor computer with 16 MB of memory per processor, an implementation of the quantum chemistry code DISCO that uses this strategy cannot solve problems with $N > 400$. In principle, it would be interesting to solve problems where $N$ is 10 times larger.

2. *Partial replication.* An alternative approach is as follows. First, we agglomerate computation in what seems an obvious way, namely, by making the inner loop of the procedure `fock_build` in Algorithm 2.3 into a task. This yields $\mathcal{O}(N^3)$ computation tasks, each responsible for $\mathcal{O}(N)$ integrals. Next, we examine the communication requirements of each such task. We find that there is considerable locality in the data required by these clusters of integrals: each cluster accesses the $i$th, $j$th, and $k$th row (and sometimes column) of D and F (Figure 2.33). To exploit this locality, we agglomerate data to create $N$ data tasks, each containing a row/column pair of the two-dimensional arrays D and F and all of the one-dimensional array A. In this scheme, each element of D and F is replicated once, and A is replicated $N$ times, so total storage requirements are increased from an average of $N$ to $3N$ per task. Because of this replication, each computation task now requires data from just three data tasks. Hence, the number of messages is reduced from $\mathcal{O}(N^4)$ to $\mathcal{O}(N^3)$. The total volume communicated remains $\mathcal{O}(N^4)$. Because the cost of communicating a word is typically much less than the cost of computing an integral, this is an efficient parallel algorithm.

**Mapping**    The "partial replication" Fock matrix construction algorithm creates $N$ data tasks and $N^3$ computation tasks. We use the notation $(i\ j\ k)$ to identify the computation task responsible for computing the $\mathcal{O}(N)$ integrals $I_{ijk*}$; this task requires data from data tasks $i$, $j$, and $k$. To complete the parallel algorithm, we must define a mapping of data and computation tasks to processors.

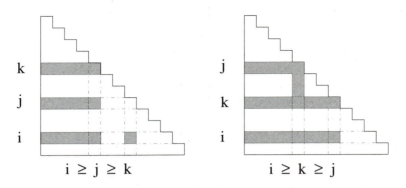

**Figure 2.33**   Data requirements for integral clusters. Each task accesses three rows (and sometimes columns) of the D and F matrices.

We assume $\mathcal{O}(N)$ processors. Since each data task will receive roughly the same number of requests, we allocate one data task to each processor. This leaves the problem of mapping computation tasks. We can imagine a variety of approaches:

1. A simple mapping, in which task $(i\ j\ k)$ is mapped to the same processor as data task $i$; since each task communicates with data tasks $i$, $j$, and $k$, off-processor communication requirements are reduced by one third. A disadvantage of this strategy is that since both the number of integrals in a task and the amount of computation per integral can vary, different processors may be allocated different amounts of computation.

2. A probabilistic mapping, in which computation tasks are mapped to processors at random or using a cyclic strategy.

3. A task-scheduling algorithm to allocate tasks to idle processors. Since a problem can be represented by three integers $(i, j, k)$ and multiple problems can easily be agglomerated into a single message, a simple centralized scheduler can be used. (Empirical studies suggest that a centralized scheduler performs well on up to a few hundred processors.)

4. Hybrid schemes in which, for example, tasks are allocated randomly to sets of processors, within which a manager/worker scheduler is used.

The best scheme will depend on performance requirements and on problem and machine characteristics.

### 2.8.3   Chemistry Summary

We have developed two alternative parallel algorithms for the Fock matrix construction problem.

1. The F and D matrices are replicated in each of $N$ tasks. Integral computations are distributed among the tasks, and a summation algorithm is used to sum F

matrix contributions accumulated in the different tasks. This algorithm is simple but nonscalable.

2. The F, D, and A matrices are partitioned among $N$ tasks, with a small amount of replication. Integral computations are agglomerated into $\mathcal{O}(N^3)$ tasks, each containing $\mathcal{O}(N)$ integrals. These tasks are mapped to processors either statically or using a task-scheduling scheme.

This case study illustrates some of the tradeoffs that can arise in the design process. The first algorithm slashes communication and software engineering costs; however, it is not scalable. In contrast, the second algorithm has higher communication costs but is highly scalable: its memory requirements increase only with problem size, not the number of processors. To choose between the two algorithms, we need to quantify their parallel performance and then to determine the importance of scalability, by assessing application requirements and the characteristics of the target parallel computer.

## 2.9  Summary

In this chapter, we have described a four-step approach to parallel algorithm design in which we start with a problem specification and proceed as follows:

1. We first *partition* a problem into many small pieces, or tasks. This partitioning can be achieved by using either domain or functional decomposition techniques.

2. Next, we organize the *communication* required to obtain data required for task execution. We can distinguish between local and global, static and dynamic, structured and unstructured, and synchronous and asynchronous communication structures.

3. Then, we use *agglomeration* to decrease communication and development costs, while maintaining flexibility if possible.

4. Finally, we *map* tasks to processors, typically with the goal of minimizing total execution time. Load balancing or task scheduling techniques can be used to improve mapping quality.

We have also provided *design checklists* that can be used to evaluate designs as they are developed. These informal questions are intended to highlight nonscalable or inefficient features in designs.

Successful application of this design methodology, together with the use of the performance modeling techniques described in Chapter 3, produces one or more parallel algorithms that balance in an appropriate fashion the potentially conflicting requirements for concurrency, scalability, and locality. The next stage in the design process is to consider how such algorithms fit into the larger context of a complete program. As we shall see in Chapter 4, additional concerns must be addressed at that level, which may require revisions to the designs of individual components. Agglomeration and mapping decisions are particularly prone to modification; therefore, we make these decisions last, when they can be most easily changed.

## Exercises

Some of the exercises in this chapter ask you to design parallel algorithms; others ask you to implement algorithms described in the text or designed by you. It is important to attempt both types of problem. Your implementations should use one of the tools described in Part II.

1. The component labeling problem in image processing is defined as follows. We are given a two-dimensional array of pixels valued 0 or 1. The 1-pixels must be labeled in such a way that two pixels have the same label if and only if they are in the same connected component. Two 1-pixels are in the same connected component if there is a path of contiguous 1-pixels linking them together. Two pixels are contiguous if they are adjacent vertically or horizontally. Develop a parallel algorithm based on the following approach. First, each 1-pixel is assigned a unique label (for example, its address). Then, each 1-pixel is updated to contain the minimum of its current label and those of its four neighbors. The second step is repeated until all adjacent 1-pixels have the same label.

2. Modify the algorithm in Exercise 1 to deal with the situation in which pixels are also contiguous when adjacent diagonally.

3. Implement the algorithm developed in Exercise 1 and measure its performance for a variety of array sizes and processor counts.

4. A compiler consists of six distinct stages. The tokenizer translates characters (input from one or more files) into tokens. The parser translates tokens into procedures. The canonicalizer translates procedures into a canonical form. The encoder translates procedures in this canonical form into low-level code. The optimizer rewrites this low-level code. Finally, the assembler generates object code. Apply domain and functional decomposition techniques to obtain two different parallel algorithms for the compiler. Compare and contrast the scalability and expected efficiency of the two algorithms.

5. Design and implement a parallel algorithm for a 1-D finite-difference algorithm with a three-point stencil. Study the performance of the resulting program as a function of problem size and processor count, assuming one task per processor.

6. Extend the algorithm and program developed in Exercise 5 to incorporate a simple convergence test: terminate execution when the difference between values computed at successive steps is less than a specified threshold for all grid points.

7. Design and implement parallel algorithms based on both 1-D and 2-D decompositions of a 2-D finite-difference algorithm with a five-point stencil. Study the performance of the resulting programs as a function of problem size and processor count, assuming one task per processor.

8. Using a parallel tool such as CC++ or Fortran M that supports multiple tasks per processor, study the performances of the programs developed in Exercises 5 and 7 for a fixed number of processors as the number of tasks is varied.

9. Implement the various parallel summation algorithms described in Section 2.3.2, and study their performance as a function of problem size and processor count. Account for any differences.

10. Design parallel algorithms for the Gauss-Seidel method shown in Section 2.3.1, for both 1-D and 2-D grids.

11. Implement the parallel Gauss-Seidel algorithms of Exercise 10. Quantify the available parallelism (a) in a single time step and (b) when performing $T$ time steps in a pipelined fashion.

12. The branch-and-bound search algorithm (Section 2.7) replicates the data defining the search problem on every processor. Is it worthwhile distributing these data? Explain.

13. An all-solutions search problem explores a search tree similar to that shown in Figure 2.28 in its entirety without the benefit of pruning. A function is applied to each leaf-node to determine whether it is a solution, and solutions are collected. Develop a parallel algorithm for this problem. Initially, assume that the cost of a node evaluation is a constant and that the tree is of uniform and known depth; then relax these assumptions.

14. A single-solution search is like the all-solutions search of Exercise 13, except that it terminates when a single solution is found. Develop a parallel algorithm for this problem.

15. Design a variant of the "partial replication" Fock matrix construction algorithm (Section 2.8) that can execute on $P$ processors, where $P > N$.

16. Design a variant of the "partial replication" Fock matrix construction algorithm (Section 2.8) that reduces communication requirements to less than two messages per task. Characterize the savings that can be achieved by this scheme as a function of available memory. *Hint*: Cache data.

17. Develop an analytic model for the maximum performance possible in a branch-and-bound search algorithm in which tasks poll a central manager for an up-to-date search bound.

18. Implement the branch-and-bound search algorithm studied in Exercise 17 and compare its performance with that of your model. Propose and investigate refinements to the centralized algorithm.

19. A deficiency of the parallel branch-and-bound search algorithm of Section 2.7 is that it does not provide a mechanism for informing workers when a search is complete. Hence, an idle worker will never stop requesting work from other workers. Design a mechanism that ensures that all workers cease execution some finite time after the last solution is reported.

20. Discuss the circumstances under which a random mapping of tasks to processors might be expected to be effective in the branch-and-bound search problem. When might it be expected to be ineffective?

21. Discuss the relative advantages and disadvantages of random and cyclic mappings of tasks to processors in the partial replication Fock matrix construction algorithm of Section 2.8.2.

22. Educate yourself about the basic operations employed in a relational database, and design parallel algorithms that could be used to perform these operations when a database is distributed over the processors of a multicomputer.

23. Without referring to Section 4.6, design parallel algorithms based on both 1-D and 2-D decompositions for the matrix multiplication problem, in which we compute $C = A.B$, where $C_{ij} = \sum_{k=0}^{N-1} A_{ik}.B_{kj}$.

## Chapter Notes

In this chapter, we have focused on the software engineering question of developing a parallel algorithm design from a given problem specification. We have assumed some familiarity with program design—from, for example, previous study in sequential programming. A classic article by Parnas and Clements [222] describes the benefits (and difficulties) of a rational design process. The chapter notes in Chapters 3 and 4 provide additional references to material on the related topics of performance analysis and modularity.

Relatively few authors have addressed the particular problems that arise when designing algorithms for realistic scalable parallel computers. Numerous books discuss parallel algorithm design in the context of the idealized PRAM model; see, for example, Akl [8], Gibbons and Reitter [119], and JáJá [157]. However, these techniques are for the most part not directly applicable to multicomputers. The books by Fox et al. [111, 113] and Kumar et al. [181] provide relevant material. Carriero and Gelernter [48] give an introduction to parallel program design in the Linda language. They distinguish between agenda, result, and specialist parallelism, which can be thought of as domain decomposition and two different forms of functional parallelism, respectively. See also the references in Chapter 12.

The mapping problem has received considerable attention in the computer science and scientific computing literature. Bokhari shows that it is *NP*-complete [39]. The recursive coordinate bisection algorithm is due to Berger and Bokhari [33], and the unbalanced recursive bisection algorithm is due to Jones and Plassmann [161]. A related algorithm is the recursive spectral bisection algorithm of Pothen, Simon, and Liou [230], which uses connectivity information to identify partitions of unstructured meshes with low communication requirements, at the cost of an eigenvalue computation. This algorithm has proven very effective, although more expensive than the other recursive algorithms. Simon [258] and Williams [293] compare different algorithms for partitioning unstructured meshes, including coordinate bisection, graph bisection, and spectral bisection. Barnard and Simon [28] describe a less expensive multilevel version of spectral bisection. The mesh in Figure 2.9 is generated using the finite octree technique of Shephard and Georges [256]. Fox et al. [111] and Nicol and Saltz [213] describe the use of cyclic decompositions. Lin and Keller [190] describe a local algorithm. The local algorithm described in the text is termed a *receiver-initiated* strategy. In an alternative *sender-initiated* strategy, workers with excess work send it to other workers. Tantawi and Towsley [279] compare sender-initiated and receiver-initiated strategies and show that the former gives better performance if workers are often idle and that the latter performs better when load is heavy. Other relevant papers include those by Berman and Snyder [34]; Chowdhury [61]; Cybenko [68]; Hac [131]; Heath, Rosenberg, and Smith [141]; Kumar, Grama, and Rao [180]; Lo [191]; and Sadayappan and Ercal [250]. Dijkstra, Seijen, and Gasteren [81], Rokusawa et al. [246], and Kumar et al. [179] describe distributed termination-detection algorithms.

Real atmosphere models are of course more complex than the system considered in Section 2.6. Washington and Parkinson [292] provide a good introduction to the numerical methods and algorithms used in climate modeling on sequential computers. A workshop held at the European Center for Medium-range Weather Forecasting surveyed issues involved in executing weather and climate models on parallel computers [155]. The parallel version of the Community Climate Model is described by Drake et al. [86]. Michalakes [206] analyzes load imbalances in climate models and Foster and Toonen [109] describe load-balancing algorithms.

Banerjee [26] describes parallel algorithms for VLSI design. Wimer et al. [294] and Arvindam et al. [17] describe branch-and-bound search algorithms and domain-specific optimizations that can improve performance on floorplanning problems. Reinefeld and Schnecke [243] describe the algorithm variant in which workers redundantly expand several tree levels before selecting nodes for local expansion. Kumar et al. [179, 181, 239] provide a wealth of material on the design, implementation, and analysis of parallel search algorithms. Quinn [234] also examines branch-and-bound search and describes and analyzes the performance of four different load balancing strategies. For a general introduction to search algorithms, see Nilsson [214], Pearl [225], and Kumar and Kanal [164].

Hehre et al. [142] provide an introduction to *ab initio* quantum chemistry. Feyereisen and Kendall [96] describe a replicated data algorithm for the Fock matrix construction problem. Colvin et al. [62] describe an algorithm based on domain decomposition techniques. An algorithm that uses distributed data structures and a centralized task scheduler is described by Harrison et al. [108, 135].

The online version provides access here to additional information on parallel program design and software engineering.

# 3 A Quantitative Basis for Design

In parallel programming, as in other engineering disciplines, the goal of the design process is not to optimize a single metric such as speed. Rather, a good design must optimize a problem-specific function of execution time, memory requirements, implementation costs, maintenance costs, and so on. Such design optimization involves tradeoffs between simplicity, performance, portability, and other factors.

Making informed design decisions about alternatives requires an understanding of their costs. In this chapter, we show how this understanding can be developed and formalized in mathematical *performance models*. These models can be used to compare the efficiency of different algorithms, to evaluate scalability, and to identify bottlenecks and other inefficiencies, all *before* we invest substantial effort in an implementation. Performance models can also be used to guide implementation efforts by showing where optimization is needed.

After studying this chapter, you should know how to develop performance models for parallel algorithms and be able to use these models to evaluate scalability and to choose between alternative algorithms. You also should know how to obtain reliable empirical data and how to use this data to validate models and implementations. Further, you should understand how network topology can affect communication performance, and you should know how to account for these effects in your models. Finally, you should be able to recognize and account for factors other than performance, factors such as implementation costs, that influence design choices.

## 3.1 Defining Performance

The task of the software engineer is to design and implement programs that satisfy user requirements for correctness and performance. However, the "performance" of a parallel program is a complex and multifaceted issue. We must consider, in addition to the execution time and scalability of the computational kernels, the mechanisms by which data are generated, stored, transmitted over networks, moved to and from disk, and passed between different stages of a computation. We must consider costs incurred at different phases of the software life cycle, including design, implementation, execution, and maintenance. Hence, the metrics by which we measure performance can be as diverse as execution time, parallel efficiency, memory requirements, throughput, latency, input/output rates, network throughput, design costs, implementation costs, verification costs, potential for reuse, hardware requirements, hardware costs, maintenance costs, portability, and scalability.

The relative importance of these diverse metrics will vary according to the nature of the problem at hand. A specification may provide hard numbers for some metrics, require that others be optimized, and ignore yet others. For example, the design specification for an operational weather forecasting system may specify maximum execution time ("the forecast must complete within four hours"), hardware costs, and implementation costs, and require that the fidelity of the model be maximized within these constraints. In addition, reliability is of particularly high importance, as may be scalability to future generations of computers.

In contrast, a group of engineers developing a parallel database search program for their own occasional use may be happy with anything that runs faster than an existing sequential program but may be tightly constrained as to how long they can spend on implementation. Here, scalability is less critical, but the code should adapt easily to changes in both the database system and computer technologies.

As a third example, consider an image-processing pipeline consisting of several concurrent stages, each performing a different transformation on a stream of images. Here, one may be concerned not with the total time required to process a certain number of images but rather with the number of images that can be processed per second (*throughput*) or the time that it takes a single image to pass through the pipeline (*latency*). Throughput would be important in a video compression application, while latency would be important if the program formed part of a sensor system that must react in real time to events detected in an image stream.

In other situations, the ratio of execution time to system cost may be important. For example, consider a bank that spends two hours every night on its overloaded mainframe computer running an analysis program that searches for fraudulent transactions. A version that runs in six hours on a parallel computer at one-twentieth the cost is significantly more cost effective even though the total execution time is greater.

Much of the material in the rest of this chapter is concerned with the modeling and measurement of just two aspects of algorithm performance: execution time and parallel scalability. We focus on these issues because they are frequently among the more problematic aspects of parallel program design and because they are the most easily formalized in mathematical models. However, these topics must be examined in the context of a broader design process that also addresses the other issues listed in this section.

## 3.2  Approaches to Performance Modeling

We introduce the topic of performance modeling by describing three techniques sometimes used to characterize the performance of parallel algorithms. We explain why each is inadequate for our purposes.

### 3.2.1 Amdahl's Law

A common observation regarding parallel processing is that every algorithm has a sequential component that will eventually limit the speedup that can be achieved on a parallel computer. (Speedup, as we shall soon define more formally, is the ratio between execution time on a single processor and execution time on multiple processors.) This observation is often codified as *Amdahl's law*, which can be stated as follows: if the sequential component of an algorithm accounts for $1/s$ of the program's execution time, then the maximum possible speedup that can be achieved on a parallel computer is $s$. For example, if the sequential component is 5 percent, then the maximum speedup that can be achieved is 20.

In the early days of parallel computing, it was widely believed that this effect would limit the utility of parallel computing to a small number of specialized applications. However, practical experience shows that this inherently sequential way of thinking is of little relevance to real problems. To understand why, let us consider a noncomputing problem. Assume that 999 of 1000 workers on an expressway construction project are idle while a single worker completes a "sequential component" of the project. We would not view this as an inherent attribute of the problem to be solved, but as a failure in management. For example, if the time required for a truck to pour concrete at a single point is a bottleneck, we could argue that the road should be under construction at several points simultaneously. Doing this would undoubtedly introduce some inefficiency—for example, some trucks would have to travel further to get to their point of work—but would allow the entire task to be finished more quickly. Similarly, it appears that almost all computational problems admit parallel solutions. The scalability of some solutions may be limited, but this is due to communication costs, idle time, or replicated computation rather than the existence of "sequential components."

Amdahl's law can be relevant when sequential programs are parallelized incrementally. In this approach to parallel software development, a sequential program is first profiled to identify computationally demanding components. These components are then adapted for parallel execution, one by one, until acceptable performance is achieved. Amdahl's law clearly applies in this situation, because the computational costs of the components that are not parallelized provide a lower bound on the execution time of the parallel program. Therefore, this "partial," or "incremental," parallelization strategy is generally effective only on small parallel computers. Amdahl's law can also be useful when analyzing the performance of data-parallel programs, in which some components may not be amenable to a data-parallel formulation (see Chapter 7).

### 3.2.2 Extrapolation from Observations

Descriptions of parallel algorithms often characterize performance by stating something like the following:

> We implemented the algorithm on parallel computer $X$ and achieved a speedup of 10.8 on 12 processors with problem size $N = 100$.

Presumably, this single data point on a small number of processors is intended as a measure of algorithm quality. A speedup of 10.8 on 12 processors may or may not be regarded as "good." However, a single performance measurement (or even several measurements) serves only to determine performance in one narrow region of what is a large multidimensional space, and is often a poor indicator of performance in other situations. What happens on 1000 processors? What if $N = 10$ or $N = 1000$? What if communication costs are ten times higher? Answering these questions requires a deeper understanding of the parallel algorithm.

The following three equations emphasize the limitations of observations as a tool for understanding parallel performance. Each is a simple performance model that specifies execution time $T$ as a function of processor count $P$ and problem size $N$. In each case, we assume that the total computation performed by an optimal sequential algorithm scales as $N + N^2$.

1. $T = N + N^2/P$. This algorithm partitions the computationally demanding $\mathcal{O}(N^2)$ component of the algorithm but replicates the $\mathcal{O}(N)$ component on every processor. There are no other sources of overhead.

2. $T = (N + N^2)/P + 100$. This algorithm partitions all the computation but introduces an additional cost of 100.

3. $T = (N + N^2)/P + 0.6P^2$. This algorithm also partitions all the computation but introduces an additional cost of $0.6P^2$.

These algorithms all achieve a speedup of about 10.8 when $P = 12$ and $N = 100$. However, they behave differently in other situations, as illustrated in Figure 3.1. With $N = 100$, all three algorithms perform poorly for larger $P$, although Algorithm (3) does noticeably worse than the other two. When $N = 1000$, Algorithm (2) is significantly better than Algorithm (1) for larger $P$.

### 3.2.3 Asymptotic Analysis

Textbooks frequently characterize the performance of parallel algorithms by stating something like the following:

> Asymptotic analysis reveals that the algorithm requires $\mathcal{O}(N \log N)$ time on $\mathcal{O}(N)$ processors.

That is, there exists a constant $c$ and minimum problem size $N_0$ such that for all $N > N_0$, $\text{cost}(N) \leq c\,N \log N$ on $N$ processors. This relationship tells how cost varies with $N$ when $N$ and $P$ are large.

While this information is interesting, it is often not directly relevant to the task of developing an efficient parallel program. Because it deals with large $N$ and $P$, it ignores lower-order terms that may be significant for problem sizes and processor counts of practical interest. For example, the actual cost of an algorithm with asymptotic complexity of $N \log N$ might be $10N + N \log N$. The $10N$ component is larger for $N < 1024$ and must be incorporated in a performance model if problems of interest are in this regime. A second deficiency of asymptotic analysis is that it says nothing about absolute cost. Asymptotic

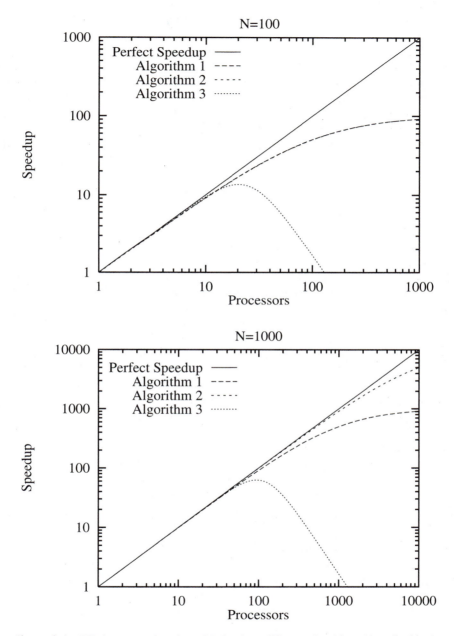

**Figure 3.1**   Efficiency as a function of *P* for three different algorithms (described in the text). The upper figure is for *N* = 100, and the lower figure is for *N* = 1000. Notice the use of logarithmic scales. When *N* = 100, Algorithms (1) and (2) are indistinguishable.

analysis would suggest that an algorithm with cost $1000N \log N$ is superior to an algorithm with cost $10N^2$. However, the latter is faster for $N < 996$, which again may be the regime of practical interest. A third deficiency is that such analyses frequently assume idealized machine models that are very different from the physical computers for which we develop programs. For example, they may assume the PRAM model, in which communication costs are assumed to be nil.

Asymptotic analysis has a role to play in parallel program design. However, when evaluating asymptotic results, we must be careful to identify the machine model for which the results are obtained, the coefficients that are likely to apply, and the $N$ and $P$ regime in which the analyses hold.

## 3.3  Developing Models

A good performance model, like a good scientific theory, is able to explain available observations and predict future circumstances, while abstracting unimportant details. Amdahl's law, empirical observations, and asymptotic analysis do not satisfy the first of these requirements. On the other hand, conventional computer system modeling techniques, which typically involve detailed simulations of individual hardware components, introduce too many details to be of practical use to parallel programmers. In the rest of this chapter, we introduce performance modeling techniques that provide an intermediate level of detail. These techniques are certainly not appropriate for all purposes: they are specialized for the multicomputer architecture and do not take into account, for example, cache behavior. However, they have been proven useful in a wide range of parallel algorithm design problems. The chapter notes provide references to other approaches.

The performance models considered here specify a metric such as execution time $T$ as a function of problem size $N$, number of processors $P$, number of tasks $U$, and other algorithm and hardware characteristics:

$$T = f(N, P, U, \ldots).$$

We define the *execution time* of a parallel program as the time that elapses from when the first processor starts executing on the problem to when the last processor completes execution. This definition is not entirely adequate for a timeshared parallel computer but suffices for our purposes. During execution, each processor is computing, communicating, or idling, as illustrated in Figure 3.2. $T_{\text{comp}}^i$, $T_{\text{comm}}^i$, and $T_{\text{idle}}^i$ are the time spent computing, communicating, and idling, respectively, on the $i$th processor. Hence, total execution time $T$ can be defined in two ways: as the sum of computation, communication, and idle times on an arbitrary processor $j$,

$$T = T_{\text{comp}}^j + T_{\text{comm}}^j + T_{\text{idle}}^j,$$

or as the sum of these times over all processors divided by the number of processors $P$,

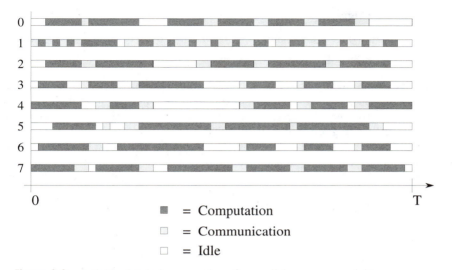

**Figure 3.2** Activity plot during execution of a parallel program on eight processors. Each processor spends its time computing, communicating, or idling. $T$ is the total execution time.

$$T = \frac{1}{P} \left( T_{\text{comp}} + T_{\text{comm}} + T_{\text{idle}} \right)$$

$$= \frac{1}{P} \left( \sum_{i=0}^{P-1} T_{\text{comp}}^{i} + \sum_{i=0}^{P-1} T_{\text{comm}}^{i} + \sum_{i=0}^{P-1} T_{\text{idle}}^{i} \right).$$

The latter definition is often more useful, since it is typically easier to determine the total computation and communication performed by a parallel algorithm rather than the time spent computing and communicating on individual processors.

Thus, the goal is to develop mathematical expressions that specify execution time as functions of $N$, $P$, etc. These models should be as simple as possible, while providing acceptable accuracy. We use the following techniques to reduce model complexity.

- We base our model on the idealized *multicomputer* parallel architecture model introduced in Chapter 1. Low-level hardware details such as memory hierarchies and the topology of the interconnection network are introduced only if there is evidence to suggest that they are important. (The latter issue is discussed in Section 3.7.)

- We use *scale analysis* to identify insignificant effects that can be ignored in the analysis. For example, if an algorithm consists of an initialization step followed by several thousand iterations of a computation step, then unless initialization is very expensive we consider only the computation step in our analysis.

- We use *empirical studies* to calibrate simple models rather than developing more complex models from first principles.

### 3.3.1  Execution Time

We first examine the three components of total execution time: computation time, communication time, and idle time.

**Computation Time**   The *computation time* of an algorithm ($T_{\text{comp}}$) is the time spent performing computation rather than communicating or idling. If we have a sequential program that performs the same computation as the parallel algorithm, we can determine $T_{\text{comp}}$ by timing that program. Otherwise, we may have to implement key kernels.

Computation time will normally depend on some measure of problem size, whether that size is represented by a single parameter $N$ or by a set of parameters, $N_1, N_2, \ldots, N_m$. If the parallel algorithm replicates computation, then computation time will also depend on the number of tasks or processors. In a heterogeneous parallel computer (such as a workstation network), computation time can vary according to the processor on which computation is performed.

Computation time will also depend on characteristics of processors and their memory systems. For example, scaling problem size or number of processors can change cache performance or the effectiveness of processor pipelining. As a consequence, one cannot automatically assume that total computation time will stay constant as the number of processors changes.

**Communication Time**   The *communication time* of an algorithm ($T_{\text{comm}}$) is the time that its tasks spend sending and receiving messages. Two distinct types of communication can be distinguished: interprocessor communication and intraprocessor communication. In *interprocessor* communication, two communicating tasks are located on different processors. This will always be the case if an algorithm creates one task per processor. In *intraprocessor* communication, two communicating tasks are located on the same processor. For simplicity, we assume that interprocessor and intraprocessor communication costs are comparable. Perhaps surprisingly, this assumption is not unreasonable in many multicomputers, unless intraprocessor communication is highly optimized. This is because the cost of the memory-to-memory copies and context switches performed in a typical implementation of intraprocessor communication is often comparable to the cost of an interprocessor communication. In other environments, such as Ethernet-connected workstations, intraprocessor communication is much faster.

In the idealized multicomputer architecture, the cost of sending a message between two tasks located on different processors can be represented by two parameters: the message startup time $t_s$, which is the time required to initiate the communication, and the transfer time per (typically four-byte) word $t_w$, which is determined by the physical bandwidth of the communication channel linking the source and destination processors. As illustrated in Figure 3.3, the time required to send a message of size $L$ words is then

$$T_{\text{msg}} = t_s + t_w L. \tag{3.1}$$

This idealized model of communication performance is adequate for many purposes but does break down in some situations. More detailed models are described in Section 3.7.

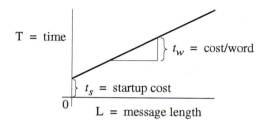

**Figure 3.3** Simple communication cost model: $T_{\mathrm{msg}} = t_s + t_w L$. In this plot of time versus message length, the slope of the line corresponds to the cost per word transferred and the $y$-intercept to the message startup cost.

Table 3.1 lists approximate values for $t_s$ and $t_w$ for some parallel computers. Because these values tend to change rapidly as hardware and systems software evolve, they should be verified before being used in performance models. Notice the considerable variation in both $t_s$ and $t_w$ values. Clearly, different computers have very different communication performance characteristics.

The values in Table 3.1 were obtained either from the literature or by fitting Equation 3.1 to execution times measured for a small test program that sends messages back and forth between two processors. Figure 3.4 presents some representative experimental data obtained with this program. These times are for a single round trip and hence are twice those given by Equation 3.1. The impact of startup and per-word costs on communication time is clearly visible. Notice the irregularities in both Ethernet and Fiber Distributed Data Interconnect (FDDI) times for small messages, and the periodic jumps in Paragon times. These are due to details of the communication protocols and buffer management strategies used in communication libraries. Nevertheless, we see that Equation 3.1 is a reasonably accurate representation of message costs, particularly for larger messages.

**Table 3.1** Approximate machine parameters for some parallel computers, in microseconds ($\mu$sec). Some of these data provided by T. Dunigan.

| Machine | $t_s$ | $t_w$ |
|---|---|---|
| IBM SP2 | 40 | 0.11 |
| Intel DELTA | 77 | 0.54 |
| Intel Paragon | 121 | 0.07 |
| Meiko CS-2 | 87 | 0.08 |
| nCUBE-2 | 154 | 2.4 |
| Thinking Machines CM-5 | 82 | 0.44 |
| Workstations on Ethernet | 1500 | 5.0 |
| Workstations on FDDI | 1150 | 1.1 |

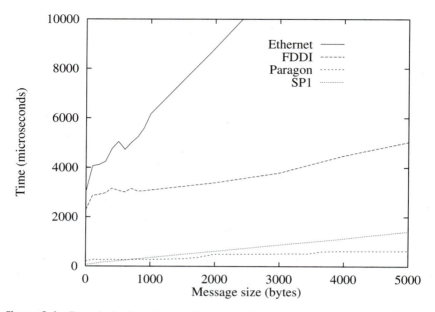

**Figure 3.4**   Round-trip time for a single message between two processors as a function of message length on Ethernet-connected workstations, FDDI-connected workstations, Intel Paragon, and IBM SP1. Data provided by W. Gropp.

Notice that both the $t_s$ and $t_w$ terms are required in Equation 3.1. Asymptotically (for large $L$) only the $t_w$ term is important; yet as $t_s$ is generally much larger than $t_w$, the $t_s$ term can dominate in applications that send mostly small messages.

The values in Table 3.1 represent "best achievable" performance and in general may be used as a lower bound on communication costs when estimating performance. Applications with less regular or structured communication patterns may perform less well. In addition, the values in Table 3.1 do not incorporate other costs such as buffer management associated with message passing. However, these additional costs are typically proportional to the number and size of messages communicated. Hence, it is generally possible, by fitting Equation 3.1 to empirical data, to obtain system- and algorithm-dependent values for $t_s$ and $t_w$ for which Equation 3.1 is valid for a large range of problem and machine sizes. This procedure is applied in several examples later in this chapter.

**Idle Time**   Both computation and communication times are specified explicitly in a parallel algorithm; hence, it is generally straightforward to determine their contribution to execution time. Idle time ($T_{\text{idle}}$) can be more difficult to determine, however, since it often depends on the order in which operations are performed.

A processor may be idle due to lack of computation or lack of data. In the first case, idle time may be avoided by using load-balancing techniques such as those introduced in Section 2.5.1. In the second case, the processor is idle while the computation and communication required to generate remote data are performed. This idle time can sometimes be

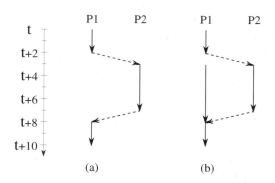

**Figure 3.5** Overlapping computation with communication. Solid lines represent computation and dashed lines represent communication operations. In both (a) and (b), processor P1 generates a request to processor P2 at time $t + 2$ and receives a reply at time $t + 8$. In both cases, the cost of actually sending the message is assumed to be 1 time unit. In (a), P1 has no other useful work to do while waiting for the reply and hence is idle for five time units after sending the message. In (b), P1 switches to another task as soon the request is generated. As this task requires five time units to complete, P1 is never idle.

avoided by structuring a program so that processors perform other computation or communication while waiting for remote data. This technique is referred to as *overlapping computation and communication*, since local computation is performed concurrently with remote communication and computation (Figure 3.5). Such overlapping can be achieved in two ways. A simple approach is to create multiple tasks on each processor. When one task blocks waiting for remote data, execution may be able to switch to another task for which data are already available. This approach has the advantage of simplicity but is efficient only if the cost of scheduling a new task is less than the idle time cost that is avoided. Alternatively, a single task can be structured so that requests for remote data are interleaved explicitly with other computation.

---

**EXAMPLE 3.1** (Finite Difference)    Throughout this chapter, we use a parallel finite difference algorithm similar to the atmosphere model considered in Section 2.6 to illustrate how performance models are developed and used. For simplicity, we assume a grid of size $N \times N \times Z$ points, where $Z$ is the number of points in the vertical dimension. Initially, we assume that this grid is decomposed in one horizontal dimension and partitioned among $P$ tasks, with each task responsible for a subgrid of size $N \times (N/P) \times Z$. Each task performs the same computation on each grid point and at each time step. Because the parallel algorithm does not replicate computation, we can model computation time in a single time step as

$$T_{\text{comp}} = t_c N^2 Z, \tag{3.2}$$

where $t_c$ is the average computation time at a single grid point.

As in Section 2.6, we consider a nine-point stencil, meaning that each task must exchange $2NZ$ data points with two neighboring tasks, for a total of two messages and $4NZ$ data. (We assume that each processor is allocated at least a $2 \times N$ subgrid; if not, communications will be required with more than two neighbors. Hence, the performance model that we develop does not apply on more than $N/2$ processors.) The total communication cost, summed over $P$ processors, is

$$T_{\text{comm}} = 2P\left(t_s + t_w 2NZ\right). \tag{3.3}$$

If $P$ divides $N$ and the amount of computation per grid point is a constant, idle time can be expected to be negligible in this example. In these circumstances, we can combine Equations 3.2 and 3.3 to obtain the following performance model:

$$
\begin{aligned}
T_{\text{1d finite diff.}} &= \frac{T_{\text{comp}} + T_{\text{comm}}}{P} \\
&= t_c \frac{N^2 Z}{P} + t_s 2 + t_w 4NZ.
\end{aligned}
\tag{3.4}
$$

## 3.3.2  Efficiency and Speedup

Execution time is not always the most convenient metric by which to evaluate parallel algorithm performance. As execution time tends to vary with problem size, execution times must be normalized when comparing algorithm performance at different problem sizes. Efficiency—the fraction of time that processors spend doing useful work—is a related metric that can sometimes provide a more convenient measure of parallel algorithm quality. It characterizes the effectiveness with which an algorithm uses the computational resources of a parallel computer in a way that is independent of problem size. We define *relative efficiency* as

$$E_{\text{relative}} = \frac{T_1}{PT_P}, \tag{3.5}$$

where $T_1$ is the execution time on one processor and $T_P$ is the time on $P$ processors. The related quantity *relative speedup*,

$$S_{\text{relative}} = PE, \tag{3.6}$$

is the factor by which execution time is reduced on $P$ processors.

The quantities defined by Equations 3.5 and 3.6 are called *relative* efficiency and speedup because they are defined with respect to the parallel algorithm executing on a single processor. They are useful when exploring the scalability of an algorithm but do not constitute an absolute figure of merit. For example, assume that we have a parallel algorithm that takes 10,000 seconds on 1 processor and 20 seconds on 1000 processors.

Another algorithm takes 1000 seconds on 1 processor and 5 seconds on 1000 processors. Clearly, the second algorithm is superior for $P$ in the range 1 to 1000. Yet it achieves a relative speedup of only 200, compared with 500 for the first algorithm.

When comparing two algorithms, it can be useful to have an algorithm-independent metric other than execution time. Hence, we define *absolute* efficiency and speedup, using as the baseline $T_1$ the uniprocessor time for the best-known algorithm. In many cases, this "best" algorithm will be the best-known uniprocessor (sequential) algorithm. From this point forward, we shall frequently use the terms efficiency and speedup without qualifying them as relative or absolute. However, the context will always make clear which is meant.

---

**EXAMPLE 3.2** (Efficiency of Finite Difference Algorithm)    In the finite difference algorithm, $T_1 = t_c N^2 Z$, and so from Equation 3.4 we have the following model for efficiency in the absence of load imbalances and when $P$ divides $N$:

$$E = \frac{t_c N^2 Z}{t_c N^2 Z + t_s 2P + t_w 4NZP}. \tag{3.7}$$

Because the uniprocessor algorithm is identical to the parallel algorithm when $P = 1$, this equation represents absolute efficiency.

---

## 3.4  Scalability Analysis

Performance models of the type developed in preceding sections are tools that we can use to explore and refine a parallel algorithm design. These models can be used without further refinement to perform *qualitative* analyses of performance. For example, from Equations 3.4 and 3.7 the following observations can be made about the finite difference algorithm:

- Efficiency decreases with increasing $P$, $t_s$, and $t_w$.
- Efficiency increases with increasing $N$, $Z$, and $t_c$.
- Execution time decreases with increasing $P$ but is bounded from below by the cost of exchanging two array slices.
- Execution time increases with increasing $N$, $Z$, $t_c$, $t_s$, and $t_w$.

These observations provide interesting insights into algorithm characteristics. However, they are not a sufficient basis for making design tradeoffs. This task requires quantitative results, which in turn require that we substitute machine-specific numeric values for the various parameters in performance models. In general, we seek to obtain these numeric values by empirical studies, as will be discussed in Section 3.5. Once augmented with empirical data, models can be used to answer questions such as the following.

- Does the algorithm meet design requirements (for execution time, memory requirements, etc.) on the target parallel computer?

- How adaptable is the algorithm? That is, how well does it adapt to increases in problem size and processor counts? How sensitive is it to machine parameters such as $t_s$ and $t_w$?
- How does the algorithm compare with other algorithms for the same problem? What difference in execution time can be expected from different algorithms?

It is important to remember that performance models are idealizations of more complex phenomena. Once an algorithm has been implemented, we are able to validate our models and hence increase our confidence in their quality. However, in the early stages of a design we must necessarily be cautious, especially if we are making quantitative predictions or if the target computer has an architecture very different from the idealized multicomputer.

### 3.4.1    Scalability with Fixed Problem Size

An important aspect of performance analysis is the study of how algorithm performance varies with parameters such as problem size, processor count, and message startup cost. In particular, we may evaluate the scalability of a parallel algorithm, that is, how effectively it can use an increased number of processors. One approach to quantifying scalability is to determine how execution time $T$ and efficiency $E$ vary with increasing processor count $P$ for a fixed problem size and machine parameters. This *fixed problem* analysis allows us to answer questions such as, What is the fastest I can solve problem $A$ on computer $X$? and What is the greatest number of processors I can utilize if I want to maintain an efficiency of 50 percent? The latter question may be of interest if a computer is shared and there is a charge for each processor used.

It is important to consider both $E$ and $T$ when evaluating scalability. While $E$ will generally decrease monotonically with $P$, $T$ may actually increase if the performance model includes a term proportional to a positive power of $P$. In such cases, it may not be productive to use more than some maximum number of processors for a particular problem size and choice of machine parameters.

---

**EXAMPLE 3.3**  (Scalability of Finite Difference)    Figure 3.6 illustrates fixed problem analysis applied to the finite difference algorithm (Equations 3.4 and 3.7). This figure plots $T$ and $E$ as a function of $P$ and $N$, using machine parameters characteristic of a relatively fine-grained multicomputer. The computation cost $t_c = 2$ $\mu$sec has been obtained by experiment, as will be described in Example 3.5. Recall that because the algorithm requires each task to have at least two grid columns, at most 64 processors can be used productively when $N = 128$ and 256 processors when $N = 512$. Later in the chapter, we shall see how these predictions compare with observed performance.

---

### 3.4.2    Scalability with Scaled Problem Size

Large parallel computers are frequently used not only to solve fixed-size problems faster, but also to solve larger problems. This observation encourages a different approach to the

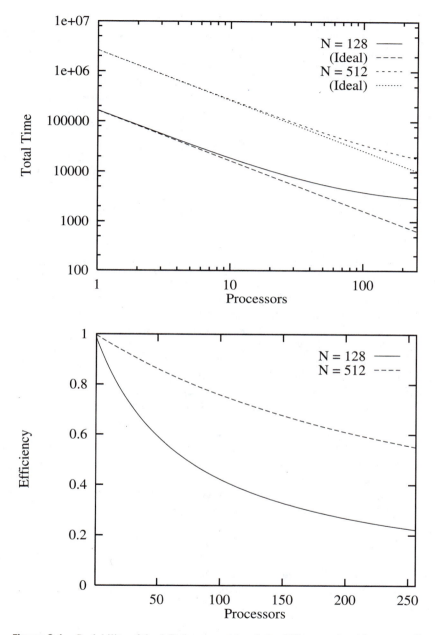

**Figure 3.6** Scalability of the 1-D decomposition finite difference algorithm, as predicted by Equations 3.4 and 3.7 when $t_c = 1$ $\mu$sec, $t_s = 100$ $\mu$sec, $t_w = 0.4$ $\mu$sec, and $Z = 10$: (a) execution time as a function of $P$; (b) efficiency as a function of $P$. Note that when $N = 128$, only 64 processors can be used productively.

analysis of algorithms called *scaled problem* analysis, whereby we consider not how $E$ varies with $P$, but how the amount of computation performed must scale with $P$ to keep $E$ constant. This function of $N$ is called an algorithm's *isoefficiency function* and can provide valuable insights into algorithm behavior. An algorithm with an isoefficiency function of $\mathcal{O}(P)$ is highly scalable, since the amount of computation needs to increase only linearly with respect to $P$ to keep efficiency constant. In contrast, an algorithm with a quadratic or exponential isoefficiency function would be poorly scalable.

Recall that efficiency $E$ is defined as the ratio between execution time on a single processor and total execution time summed over $P$ processors:

$$E = \frac{T_1}{T_{\text{comp}} + T_{\text{comm}} + T_{\text{idle}}}.$$

Hence, in order to maintain constant efficiency $E$, the following relation must hold for increasing $P$:

$$T_1 = E\left(T_{\text{comp}} + T_{\text{comm}} + T_{\text{idle}}\right).$$

That is, uniprocessor time must increase at the same rate as total parallel time or, equivalently, the amount of essential computation must increase at the same rate as overheads due to replicated computation, communication, and idle time.

Scaled problem analysis does not make sense for all problems. Real-time constraints, for example in weather forecasting, may require that computation be completed in a fixed amount of time. In other applications, scaling is not possible because of physical constraints on problem size. For example, in molecular modeling, the number of atoms in a molecule is fixed, as is the number of pixels in image-processing applications.

---

**EXAMPLE 3.4** (Isoefficiency of Finite Difference Algorithms)    We use isoefficiency analysis to examine the scalability of two parallel finite difference algorithms. Recall that the efficiency of an algorithm based on a 1-D decomposition of an $N \times N \times Z$ grid is given by Equation 3.7. For constant efficiency, a function of $P$, when substituted for $N$, must satisfy the following relation for increasing $P$ and constant $E$:

$$t_c N^2 Z \approx E(t_c N^2 Z + t_s 2P + t_w 4NZP).$$

The function $N = P$ satisfies this requirement, and yields the following relation, which is valid for all except small $P$, when the $t_s$ term becomes significant:

$$t_c Z \approx E\left(t_c Z + t_s \frac{2}{P} + t_w 4Z\right).$$

Because the finite difference computation operates on a square grid, scaling $N$ with $P$ causes the number of grid points and thus the amount of computation to scale as $P^2$. Hence, we say that the isoefficiency function for this algorithm is $\mathcal{O}(P^2)$, meaning that

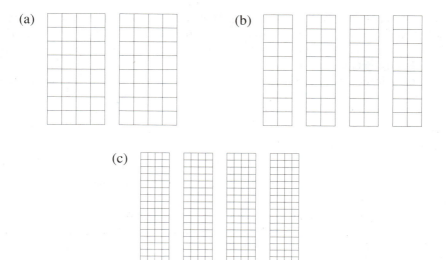

**Figure 3.7**  Scaling a finite difference algorithm based on a 1-D decomposition. In (a), $N = 8$ and $P = 2$. Each task has 32 grid points and must communicate with two neighbors. In (b), $P$ is doubled while $N$ stays the same. Total computation costs stay the same but communication costs double, so efficiency is reduced. In (c), both $P$ and $N$ are doubled, thereby increasing both computation costs and the $t_w$ component of communication costs by a factor of four; hence, efficiency remains the same.

the amount of computation must increase as the square of the number of processors in order for constant efficiency to be maintained. Figure 3.7 illustrates why this is so.

As a second example, consider a two-dimensional decomposition of the finite difference problem. Here, each task is responsible for $(N/\sqrt{P}) \times (N/\sqrt{P}) \times Z$ points and must exchange $2(N/\sqrt{P})Z$ points with each of four neighbors at each time step. Hence,

$$E = \frac{t_c N^2 Z}{t_c N^2 Z + t_s 4P + t_w 8N Z \sqrt{P}}. \tag{3.8}$$

For constant efficiency, a function of $P$, when substituted for $N$, must satisfy the following relation for increasing $P$:

$$t_c N^2 Z \approx E \left( t_c N^2 Z + t_s 4P + t_w 8N Z \sqrt{P} \right).$$

The function $N = \sqrt{P}$ meets this requirement and gives the following relation which is valid for all values of $P$:

$$t_c Z \approx E \left( t_c Z + t_s 4 + t_w 8Z \right).$$

Because total computation is again proportional to $N^2$, the isoefficiency function is $\mathcal{O}(P)$. This analysis shows that a 2-D decomposition is more scalable than a 1-D decomposition.

This example illustrates a general rule: Higher-dimensional decompositions tend to be more efficient than lower-dimensional decompositions. To understand why, consider Equations 3.7 and 3.8. While the 2-D decomposition sends slightly more messages (four instead of two), data volume is reduced by a factor of $\sqrt{P}$, from $\mathcal{O}(NP)$ to $\mathcal{O}(N\sqrt{P})$. Total communication costs are reduced unless $P$ and $N$ are small or $t_s$ is much larger than $t_w$.

### 3.4.3  Execution Profiles

If scalability analysis suggests that performance is poor on problem sizes and computers of interest, we can use models to identify likely sources of inefficiency and hence areas in which an algorithm can be improved.

Poor performance may be due to excessive replicated computation, idle time, message startups, data transfer costs, or some combination of these factors. An important first step when attempting to improve an algorithm is to identify which of these factors is dominant. We can do this by computing an expected *execution profile* for the algorithm, indicating the contributions of these different factors to execution time as a function of $N$ and/or $P$. This approach is illustrated in Figure 3.8 for the 1-D finite difference algorithm. The model predicts that when this algorithm is executed on a multicomputer with a single vertical layer ($Z = 1$), data transfer costs dominate execution time when $P$ is large; message startup costs are also significant. If the number of vertical levels is increased, message startup costs become negligible, and overall efficiency improves.

Cost information of this sort can be used to guide a redesign of an algorithm. Often, it may motivate us to reconsider decisions made earlier in the design process. For example, if replicated computation is reducing performance, then we may wish to reconsider an alternative algorithm, previously discarded, that avoids replicated computation at the expense of increased communication. Alternatively, high message startup costs may suggest further agglomeration so as to increase granularity. Similarly, if data transfer costs are high, we may seek to replicate computation or send more, smaller messages if doing so can reduce the total volume of data transferred.

## 3.5  Experimental Studies

Discussion in preceding sections has emphasized analytic modeling of performance. Yet parallel programming is first and foremost an experimental discipline. The flexibility and ease of modification of software on the one hand, and the complexity of parallel computer systems on the other, mean that approaches to parallel program design based entirely on theory are rarely cost effective. The role of modeling is most often to assist in what is essentially an experimental process, by guiding experiment and explaining results.

Experimental studies can be used in early design stages to determine values for parameters used in performance models, such as computation time per grid point, average depth of a search tree, message startup cost, and message transfer costs. They can also be used after programming begins, to compare observed and modeled performance.

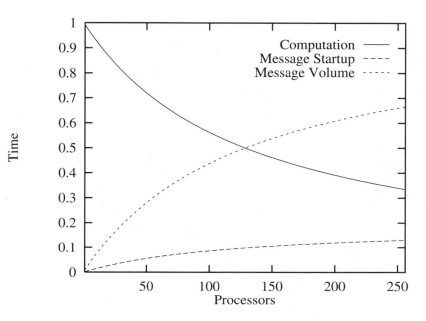

**Figure 3.8** Contributions of computation, message startup, and message transfer costs to total execution time in the 1-D finite difference algorithm, for $N = 512$, $Z = 1$, $t_s = 200$ $\mu$sec, $t_w = 0.8$ $\mu$sec, $t_c = 1$ $\mu$sec, and varying $P$. There is no replicated computation or idle time in this example.

Next we review several sometimes subtle issues that can arise during experimental studies.

### 3.5.1 Experimental Design

The first step in an experimental study is to *identify the data* that we wish to obtain. For example, when calibrating a performance model we may be interested in determining the execution time of a sequential version of our application as a function of problem size in order to determine $t_c$. Or, we may need to measure the execution time of a simple message-passing testbed program in order to determine $t_s$ and $t_w$.

Normally, experiments are performed for a range of data points—different problem sizes and/or processor counts. By maximizing the number of data points obtained, we reduce the impact of errors in individual measurements. When empirical data are used to evaluate the quality of an implementation, a range of data points also allows us to estimate the accuracy of the model and to identify regimes in which it is inadequate.

The next step in an experimental study is to *design the experiments* that will be used to obtain the required data. The critical issue here is to ensure that our experiments measure what we intend to measure. For example, if a program comprises an initialization step followed by a long series of iterations, and our performance model deals only with the cost of an iteration, then that is what we need to measure.

### 3.5.2  Obtaining and Validating Experimental Data

The principal challenge when performing experiments is to obtain accurate and reproducible results. Execution times can be obtained in various ways; which is best will depend on both our requirements and the facilities available on the target computer. A straightforward but potentially time-consuming approach is to incorporate code into our program that calls system timer routines to determine elapsed time. In principle, we should make these calls on every processor and then take the maximum time. However, we can often identify a reference processor that does not start or finish appreciably later or sooner than others, and measure times on this processor alone. Alternatively, we can use a profiling or tracing tool that obtains timing data automatically. We discuss specific tools in Chapter 9.

Experiments should always be repeated to verify that results are reproducible. Generally, results should not vary by more than a small amount—2 or 3 percent is a lot if one is trying to fine-tune algorithms. Possible causes of variation include the following.

- *A nondeterministic algorithm.* Programs may use random numbers or may explore a search space or allocate work to processors in a time-dependent manner (as in the search algorithm of Section 2.7). Nondeterminism due to random numbers can be controlled by using a reproducible parallel generator (Chapter 10). Nondeterminism due to time-dependent execution is more problematic. One solution is to perform a large number of trials. Another is to normalize execution times by dividing them by some measure of the amount of work done, such as search tree nodes visited.

- *An inaccurate timer.* The timer used to obtain execution times may have limited resolution or be inaccurate. If resolution is limited, we can improve accuracy by increasing execution time, for example by performing more iterations or by solving the same problem several times. If the timer is inaccurate, we need to find another way to determine execution times.

- *Startup and shutdown costs.* The time required for system management functions concerned with the acquisition of processors, loading of code, allocation of virtual memory, deallocation of processors, etc., can vary significantly according to the state of the system. Timings are often more accurate if these system-dependent components are excluded. Hence, we may start a timer after a program is loaded and stop it once a solution has been computed.

- *Interference from other programs.* On a nondedicated machine, other users may compete for shared resources such as processors, network bandwidth, and I/O bandwidth. Timings may also be perturbed by system functions such as accounting and backups that execute occasionally. Note that competition can occur even when processors are dedicated to our application. For example, a computer in which processors are connected in a 2-D mesh (Section 3.7.2) may be partitioned into disjoint submeshes. Yet I/O requests generated by programs executing in one submesh may need to traverse our submesh to reach I/O devices, thereby consuming bandwidth.

- *Contention.* On some computers, the time required for a communication operation can increase when several processors communicate at the same time. For example, an Ethernet-connected LAN can carry only one message at a time, and senders must back off and resend when messages collide. An unfortunate schedule can result in repeated resendings, thereby increasing execution time. In Section 3.7, we describe advanced modeling techniques that can account for some such effects.

- *Random resource allocation.* The operating system may use a random processor allocation strategy, which will affect execution times if communication costs depend on processor location in a network (see Section 3.7). If possible, the same allocation should be used for all experiments.

Studies of variability in experimental results can help us to identify sources of error or uncertainty in our measurements. However, even when results are reproducible, we still have no assurance that they are correct. Confidence in our results can be increased by measuring the same thing several different ways and verifying that the results of these redundant measurements are consistent. For example, in addition to measuring the time taken in individual program components, we can measure the total time for the entire program.

### 3.5.3  Fitting Data to Models

When experimental studies are performed for calibration purposes, we fit results to the function of interest to obtain values for unknown parameters. A fit can be performed graphically by plotting data points and estimating the fit. For example, if the function is

$$T_{\mathrm{msg}} = t_s + t_w L,$$

we can plot the data points $T_{\mathrm{msg}}(i)$ as a function of $L$ and draw a straight line that fits these points. The slope of this line will be $t_w$, and the intercept of the $T_{\mathrm{msg}}$ axis when $L = 0$ will be $t_s$.

Alternatively, and more accurately, we can perform a least-squares fit of the function with the data. (Mathematical packages such as Mathematica and Matlab incorporate fitting functions.) A least-squares fit involves a minimization of the sum of the squares of the differences between the observations, $\mathtt{obs}(i)$, and the corresponding function values, $\mathtt{f}(i)$:

$$\sum_i (\mathtt{obs}(i) - \mathtt{f}(i))^2.$$

For example, when fitting the function $T = t_c N^2 Z$ with observations of $T$ for different values of $N$ in order to determine the value $t_c$, we minimize

$$\sum_i \left(T(i) - t_c i^2 Z\right)^2.$$

When fitting to execution times for different numbers of processors, the method just described gives less weight to the (presumably smaller) times on larger numbers of processors. Yet these are typically the times of greatest interest. Hence, we can use a *scaled*

**Table 3.2**   Execution times in milliseconds for a single time step of the finite difference code on a Sun SPARC 2, with $Z = 10$.

| $N$ | $T_1$ | $T_2$ | $T_3$ | *Mean* |
|---|---|---|---|---|
| 2 | 0.477 | 0.471 | 0.479 | 0.476 |
| 4 | 1.75 | 1.73 | 1.73 | 1.74 |
| 8 | 6.62 | 6.63 | 6.68 | 6.64 |
| 16 | 26.9 | 26.9 | 26.4 | 26.7 |
| 32 | 112 | 112 | 112 | 112 |
| 64 | 459 | 459 | 460 | 459 |
| 128 | 1930 | 1929 | 1934 | 1931 |
| 256 | 7949 | 7873 | 7897 | 7906 |

least-squares fit in which the difference between observation and function value is scaled by the observation, as follows:

$$\sum_i \left( \frac{\text{obs}(i) - \text{f}(i)}{\text{obs}(i)} \right)^2 .$$

**EXAMPLE 3.5**  (Determining Computation Time ($t_c$))   We consider the problem of determining the computation cost per grid point in the finite difference problem. Recall that we have modeled this cost as follows (Equation 3.2):

$$T_{\text{comp}} = t_c N^2 Z.$$

In this equation, $t_c$ is the parameter that we wish to determine, and $N$ is a value that we can vary while measuring performance. (For simplicity, we keep $Z$ fixed.) Table 3.2 gives execution times measured on a Sun SPARC 2 workstation. Experiments were performed when the machine was idle but not in single-user mode; hence, there might have been a small amount of background activity. Each experiment was repeated three times so that we could study variability; the table also lists the means of each set of three values. The repeated experiments show little variation in total execution time.

Figure 3.9 shows simple and scaled least-squares fits of Equation 3.2 to the data in Table 3.2. The two fits correspond to $t_c$ values of 0.0120 msec and 0.0112 msec, respectively. The execution times predicted by the two models are shown in Table 3.3. As expected, the simple fit is more accurate for larger $N$, while the scaled fit is better for smaller $N$; both are good enough for most practical purposes. These results suggest that the hypothesized performance model, $T = t_c N^2 Z$, is an adequate characterization of finite difference computation time.

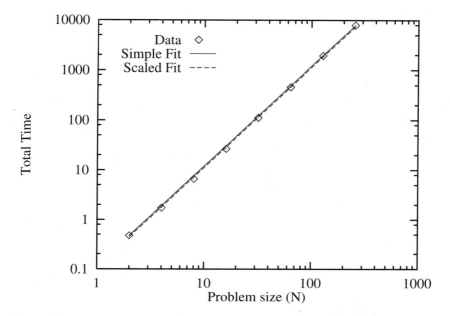

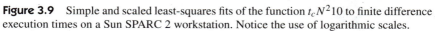

**Figure 3.9**   Simple and scaled least-squares fits of the function $t_c N^2 10$ to finite difference execution times on a Sun SPARC 2 workstation. Notice the use of logarithmic scales.

**Table 3.3**   Execution times predicted for finite difference code on Sun SPARC 2, with $Z = 10$ (milliseconds).

| | | Performance Model | |
| --- | --- | --- | --- |
| N | Observed | Simple | Scaled |
| 2 | 0.476 | 0.480 | 0.448 |
| 4 | 1.74 | 1.92 | 1.79 |
| 8 | 6.64 | 7.68 | 7.16 |
| 16 | 26.7 | 30.7 | 28.7 |
| 32 | 112 | 123 | 115 |
| 64 | 459 | 491 | 459 |
| 128 | 1931 | 1966 | 1835 |
| 256 | 7906 | 7864 | 7340 |

## 3.6    Evaluating Implementations

Performance models also play an important role after a design is complete, when we start to write programs. Comparisons of observed and predicted execution times can provide valuable information about both an algorithm and its implementation.

Even if considerable care is taken when designing and carrying out experiments, the idealized nature of our models means that observed and predicted execution times will seldom completely agree. Major discrepancies signify either that the model is incorrect or that the implementation is inadequate. In the first case, we can use the empirical results to determine where the model is deficient; this information in turn enables us to reassess the quantitative tradeoffs that we have used to justify design decisions. In the second case, we can use the model to identify areas in which the implementation can be improved.

When faced with a substantial difference between modeled and observed execution times, our first step should be to check both the performance model and our experimental design to verify not only that the model and experiments are correct but that they are measuring the same thing.

Our next step should be to obtain an execution profile of the parallel code. (In contrast to the execution profiles discussed in Section 3.4.3, this profile will be based on measured values.) The goal here is to obtain a more detailed view of program behavior, by measuring, for example, time spent in initialization, time spent in different phases of a computation, total idle time, and the total number and volume of messages communicated. Ideally, data will be obtained for a range of problem sizes and processor counts. Tables 3.4 and 3.5 show typical examples of execution profile data, in this case from a parallel computational chemistry code that incorporates the Fock matrix construction algorithm of Section 2.8 as a kernel. These data were obtained by using instrumentation inserted manually into the program.

Once we have obtained an execution profile, we can compare it with the performance model to identify deficiencies in either the model or the implementation. In the following sections, we list several potential problems that may be revealed in an execution profile.

### 3.6.1    Unaccounted-for Overhead

We first consider issues that may lead to observed execution times greater than predicted by a model. Most often, such a situation occurs because the performance model is incomplete: some aspect of an algorithm or its implementation was neglected as insignificant but proves in practice to contribute significantly to execution time.

- *Load imbalances.* An algorithm may suffer from computation or communication imbalances that were not considered in the performance model. These problems may be revealed by a study of how costs vary across processors.

- *Replicated computation.* Disparities between observed and predicted times can also signal deficiencies in the implementation. For example, we may have failed to parallelize some component, assuming that the cost of replicating its computation on every processor would be insignificant. On large numbers of processors, this as-

**Table 3.4**  A simple execution profile for a single step of a parallel computational chemistry code, here applied to a relatively small problem on an IBM SP computer. This code combines the Fock matrix construction algorithm of Chapter 2 ("fock") with additional components. The profile shows both the time spent in different parts of the program for varying processor counts and the total execution time. Scalability is reasonably good, although it is evident that the routine diag has not been parallelized. The init routine does not scale well, but this cost is less important because the code is normally run for many steps.

| Program Component | Number of Processors | | | | | |
|---|---|---|---|---|---|---|
| | 1 | 2 | 4 | 8 | 16 | 32 |
| le | 17.78 | 13.08 | 6.59 | 5.15 | 1.87 | 1.08 |
| fock | 3124.52 | 1588.35 | 816.00 | 420.04 | 213.29 | 109.80 |
| diag | 3.31 | 3.29 | 3.43 | 3.46 | 3.51 | 3.54 |
| mxm | 0.41 | 0.40 | 0.34 | 0.40 | 0.39 | 0.40 |
| dadd | 0 | 0.02 | 0.01 | 0.02 | 0.02 | 0.08 |
| zero | 0 | 0.02 | 0.01 | 0.02 | 0.02 | 0.06 |
| copy | 0 | 0.01 | 0.01 | 0.01 | 0.02 | 0.03 |
| init | 86.37 | 54.29 | 31.14 | 17.37 | 11.19 | 9.05 |
| other | 1.25 | 0.37 | 0.08 | 0.17 | 0.23 | 0.42 |
| Total | 3233.65 | 1659.85 | 857.64 | 446.69 | 230.57 | 124.47 |

sumption may not be valid. These sorts of problem can be detected by studying costs in different parts of a program and for varying numbers of processors.

- *Tool/algorithm mismatch.* The tools used to implement the algorithms may introduce inefficiencies. For example, we may have designed an algorithm that creates multiple tasks per processor so as to overlap computation and communication. Yet the programming language or library used to implement the algorithm may not implement tasks efficiently.

- *Competition for bandwidth.* Equation 3.1 may not be an adequate characterization of the communication network on which the program is executing. In particular, concurrent communications may compete for bandwidth, thereby increasing total communication costs. This issue is discussed in Section 3.7.

### 3.6.2  Speedup Anomalies

An implementation may execute faster than predicted by a performance model. If this effect becomes more marked as the number of processors increases, this phenomenon is termed a *speedup anomaly*—the observed speedup is greater than predicted. Sometimes, we may see a speedup that is greater than linear, or *superlinear*. Situations in which this can occur include the following:

**Table 3.5**   A more detailed execution profile for the parallel code of Table 3.4. This gives call frequencies and execution times for various communication routines on each processor. For brevity, only the first 6 of 16 processors are shown. Instrumentation overhead increases total time from the 230 seconds of Table 3.4 to around 241 seconds. The get, accum, and put routines read and write data in distributed global arrays. A get operation, which blocks waiting for a response to a remote request, takes around 1.7 milliseconds on average. Since each data transfer is relatively small, and the IBM SP's $t_w$ is low, this time must include substantial idle time that could perhaps be overlapped with local computation. The second major source of communication cost is the barrier operation, which is used to ensure that all updates to a global array have completed before reading begins. We may wish to examine the program to determine whether we really need 85 such operations per step.

| Program Component | Processor | | | | | |
|---|---|---|---|---|---|---|
| | 0 | 1 | 2 | 3 | 4 | 5 |
| *Counters:* | | | | | | |
| get | 9404 | 9837 | 5143 | 10237 | 10359 | 9948 |
| accum | 9398 | 9837 | 5143 | 10237 | 10359 | 9948 |
| put | 2502 | 2496 | 2496 | 2496 | 2496 | 2496 |
| barrier | 85 | 85 | 85 | 85 | 85 | 85 |
| zero | 8 | 8 | 8 | 8 | 8 | 8 |
| add | 4 | 4 | 4 | 4 | 4 | 4 |
| scale | 3 | 3 | 3 | 3 | 3 | 3 |
| gemm | 2 | 2 | 2 | 2 | 2 | 2 |
| *Timers:* | | | | | | |
| get | 17.483 | 17.336 | 10.848 | 18.095 | 18.773 | 18.039 |
| barrier | 5.403 | 7.001 | 4.742 | 2.409 | 4.049 | 4.342 |
| accum | 2.794 | 3.127 | 3.427 | 3.005 | 3.043 | 2.884 |
| put | 0.740 | 0.961 | 1.514 | 0.790 | 1.046 | 1.001 |
| gemm | 0.415 | 0.414 | 0.416 | 0.415 | 0.415 | 0.415 |
| zero | 0.062 | 0.069 | 0.069 | 0.069 | 0.068 | 0.068 |
| add | 0.034 | 0.034 | 0.030 | 0.033 | 0.033 | 0.033 |
| scale | 0.030 | 0.027 | 0.027 | 0.027 | 0.029 | 0.030 |
| Total | 241.648 | 241.467 | 241.440 | 241.466 | 241.447 | 241.450 |

- *Cache effects.* On most parallel computers, each processor has a small amount of fast memory (cache) and a larger amount of slower memory. When a problem is executed on a greater number of processors, more of its data can be placed in fast memory. As a result, total computation time ($T_{comp}$) will tend to decrease. If the reduction in $T_{comp}$ from this *cache effect* offsets increases in $T_{comm}$ and $T_{idle}$ resulting from the use of additional processors, then efficiency will be greater than 1 and speedup will be superlinear. Similarly, the increased physical memory available in a multiprocessor may reduce the cost of memory accesses by avoiding the need for virtual memory paging.

- *Search anomalies.* This phenomenon is encountered in some parallel search algorithms, such as the branch-and-bound search of Section 2.7. If a search tree contains solutions at varying depths, then multiple depth-first searches will, on average, explore fewer tree nodes before finding a solution than will a sequential depth-first search. Notice that in this case, the parallel algorithm executed is not the same as the sequential algorithm. In fact, the best uniprocessor algorithm may be one that pursues several searches concurrently.

---

**EXAMPLE 3.6** (Evaluating a Finite Difference Program)  We consider the behavior of an implementation of the 1-D finite difference algorithm. Figure 3.10 shows observed performance, performance predicted by Equation 3.4, and performance predicted by a refined model that we shall develop in the following. We present speedups rather than raw execution times in order to make results clearer for larger $P$. The predicted performance curves use machine parameter values obtained by a fitting process so as to take into account additional overheads not accounted for by the "best possible" parameter values of Table 3.1. A comparison of the two sets of parameter values ($t_s = 200$ $\mu$sec versus 77 $\mu$sec, $t_w = 2$ $\mu$sec versus 0.54 $\mu$sec) indicates that the finite difference implementation incurs significant overhead. This suggests that there may be opportunities for optimization.

Figure 3.10 shows that Equation 3.4 is inaccurate for $N = 512$ and larger values of $P$. The observed speedup does not increase continuously, as predicted, but in a stepwise fashion. This observation suggests that the model is incorrect in assuming that some aspect of program performance varies continuously with $P$. Examining Equation 3.4, we see that only computation cost depends on $P$; both the number of messages and message size per processor are constant and hence independent of $P$. The problem then becomes clear. Equation 3.4 assumes that each processor has $N/P$ columns of the grid. In reality, $P$ does not always divide $N$. More specifically, some tasks will be allocated $\lceil N/P \rceil NZ$ grid points and others $\lfloor N/P \rfloor NZ$ points. For example, if $N = 8$, $Z = 1$, and $P = 3$, some will have $3.8.1 = 24$ and others $2.8.1 = 16$ grid points. Hence, while total computation costs are as given by Equation 3.4, the maximum computation costs on any processor are as follows:

$$T_{\text{max comp}} = \left\lceil \frac{N}{P} \right\rceil NZ.$$

This uneven distribution of computation leads to idle time, since at each step processors with less computation will terminate before those with more. Total idle time is

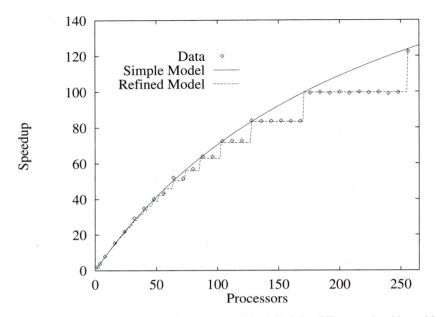

**Figure 3.10**   Speedup of an implementation of the 1-D finite difference algorithm with $N = 512$ and $Z = 10$ as measured on the Intel DELTA and as predicted by both a simple performance model that does not account for load imbalances and a more sophisticated model that does; both models assume $t_s = 200$ $\mu$sec and $t_w = 2$ $\mu$sec.

the difference between the maximum computation time and the mean computation times, multipled by the number of processors:

$$T_{\text{idle}} = \sum_{i=0}^{P-1} (T_{\text{max comp}} - T_{\text{comp}}^i)$$

$$= P T_{\text{max comp}} - T_{\text{comp}}.$$

Incorporating this idle time into Equation 3.4, we obtain the following more general performance model:

$$T = t_c N Z \left\lceil \frac{N}{P} \right\rceil + t_s 2 + t_w 4 N Z. \tag{3.9}$$

The second predicted performance curve in Figure 3.10 is obtained using this refined model. Notice that the two models are equivalent when $N$ is an integer multiple of $P$.

# 3.7  A Refined Communication Cost Model

Next we examine how the idealized communication cost model used in preceding sections can be extended to account for characteristics of realistic interconnection networks. We review a range of network architectures and develop a more detailed model of communication performance that takes into account the impact of competition for bandwidth on communication costs. This more detailed model is still idealized but can be significantly more accurate in some circumstances.

## 3.7.1  Competition for Bandwidth

In the idealized multicomputer architecture introduced in Chapter 1, the time required to send a message from one processor to another is independent of both processor location and the number of other processors that may be communicating at the same time. These assumptions are reflected in the communication cost model, Equation 3.1:

$$T_{\text{msg}} = t_s + t_w L.$$

While accurate for many algorithms and on many architectures, this model can break down if a computer's interconnection network has properties different from the ideal, particularly if an application generates many messages. In these cases, it is necessary to develop a more detailed model of the interconnection network.

Most interconnection networks use fewer than $N^2$ wires to connect $N$ processors. Hence, they must include routing nodes, or *switches*, to route messages from a source processor to a destination. A switching node may block or reroute messages when several messages require access to the same wire at the same time. The number of wires that must be traversed in order to get from one processor to another is termed the *distance* between those two processors. (The distance is equal to the number of switches plus one.) The maximum distance from any processor to any other processor is termed the *diameter* of the network. The distance between two processors and the length of the wires connecting them are not normally significant factors in determining performance, although networks with long wires may be more expensive to build. (Wire length can be important in networks extending over tens to thousands of kilometers, where the speed of light—about 5 $\mu$sec per kilometer in optical fiber—places a lower limit on communication latency.)

A factor that *can* have a significant impact on communication performance and which we study here in some depth is *competition for bandwidth*. Two processors may need to send data over the same wire at the same time. Typically, only one message can be transmitted simultaneously, so the other message will be delayed. However, for many practical purposes it suffices to think of the two processors as *sharing* the available bandwidth. Hence, we scale the data volume term of Equation 3.1 by $S$, the number of processors needing to send concurrently over the same wire:

$$T_{\text{msg bandwidth limited}} = t_s + t_w S L. \tag{3.10}$$

The scaling factor reflects the idea that the effective bandwidth available to each processor is $1/S$ of the true bandwidth.

Equation 3.10 does not account for additional contention costs that may be incurred if messages collide and must be retransmitted. (Network researchers have developed sophisticated simulation techniques to account for such effects.) However, experience shows that Equation 3.10 is sufficiently accurate for many practical purposes.

The impact of competition for bandwidth is most severe in algorithms that execute *synchronously*, that is, algorithms in which all processors are sending and receiving messages at approximately the same time and in which processors cannot proceed with other computation while awaiting messages. The finite difference problem and many other SPMD algorithms have this property. In algorithms such as the search and Fock matrix construction algorithms described in Chapter 2, processors execute asynchronously and are less likely to compete for bandwidth.

### 3.7.2   Interconnection Networks

The value $S$ in Equation 3.10 can depend on properties of both the parallel algorithm and the underlying interconnection network. In the following discussion, we use two examples to illustrate how the communication patterns of a particular algorithm can be analyzed to determine an approximate value for $S$ on different networks. We first consider properties of interconnection networks.

**Crossbar Switching Network**    A crossbar switch avoids competition for bandwidth by using $\mathcal{O}(N^2)$ switches to connect $N$ inputs to $N$ outputs (Figure 3.11). In this case, $S = 1$. Although highly nonscalable, crossbar switches are a popular mechanism for connecting small numbers of workstations, typically 20 or fewer. For example, the DEC GIGAswitch can connect up to 22 workstations. While larger crossbars can be constructed (for example, the Fujitsu VPP 500 uses a $224 \times 224$ crossbar to connect 224 processors), they are very expensive.

**Bus-based Networks**    In a bus-based network, processors share a single communication resource (the bus). A bus is a highly nonscalable architecture, because only one processor can communicate on the bus at a time. The competition factor $S$ is equal to the number of processors trying to communicate simultaneously.

Buses are commonly used in shared-memory parallel computers to communicate read and write requests to a shared global memory (Figure 3.12). In principle, the use of a global memory in a shared-memory computer simplifies parallel programming by making locality a nonissue. However, as discussed in Section 1.2.2, most shared-memory parallel computers introduce caches in an attempt to reduce bus traffic; hence, locality continues to be important.

**Ethernet**    The Ethernet network often used in LANs to connect workstations or personal computers at a departmental level is another example of a bus-based interconnect. As noted in Table 3.1, standard Ethernet can provide network bandwidths of up to about 1 Mbytes

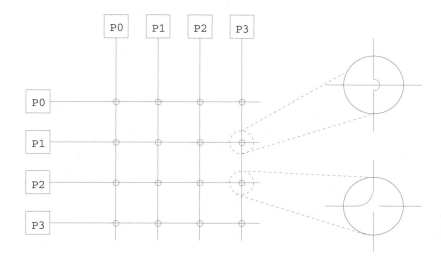

**Figure 3.11**   A 4×4 nonblocking crossbar, used here to connect 4 processors. On the right, two switching elements are expanded; the top one is set to pass messages through and the lower one to switch messages. Notice that each processor is depicted twice, and that any pair of processors can communicate without preventing other processor pairs from communicating.

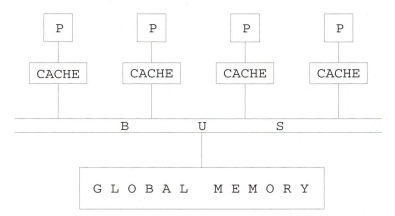

**Figure 3.12**   A bus-based interconnection network, here used to implement a shared-memory parallel computer. Each processor (P) is connected to the bus, which in turn is connected to the global memory. A cache associated with each processor stores recently accessed memory values, in an effort to reduce bus traffic.

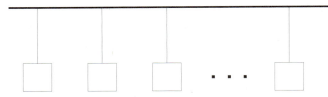

**Figure 3.13**    An Ethernet LAN. Multiple computers are connected to a single Ethernet cable, which acts as a communication bus, carrying a single signal at a time.

per second. All computers connected via an Ethernet share a single communication channel (Figure 3.13). A computer that needs to send must wait until the channel is idle, then send its message; if it detects a collision, it waits a while and then retransmits. Since a computer requires exclusive access to the entire channel when sending a message, any algorithm that requires more than one processor to communicate concurrently will suffer reduced effective bandwidth. Hence, the term $S$ in Equation 3.10 is, as in other bus-based networks, equal to the number of simultaneous senders. The impact of Ethernet bandwidth limitations on performance is illustrated in the examples that follow.

**Mesh Networks**    A mesh network can be thought of as a crossbar switch (Figure 3.11) in which processors are associated with switching elements rather than being placed on the edge of the mesh. In a mesh network of dimension $D$, each nonboundary processor is connected to $2D$ immediate neighbors. Connections typically consist of two wires, one in each direction. Two- and three-dimensional meshes are commonly used in parallel computing. They have the advantage over some more sophisticated networks that they can be constructed in three-dimensional space without long wires. In a 2-D mesh, a message is communicated from processor $(i, j)$ to processor $(k, l)$ in $|i - k| + |j - l|$ steps. One-, two- and three-dimensional cubic meshes of $P$ processors have diameters of $P - 1$, $2(\sqrt{P} - 1)$, and $3(\sqrt[3]{P} - 1)$ and contain $2(P - 1)$, $4(P - \sqrt{P})$, and $6(P - P^{2/3})$ wires, respectively. As illustrated in Figure 3.14, these diameters can be halved by extending a mesh with toroidal connections so that boundary processors are also connected with neighbors. However, the torus has two disadvantages. First, longer wires are needed for the end-around connections in the 3-D case. (The need for longer wires can be avoided in a 2-D torus by folding the mesh.) Second, a subset of a torus is not a torus, so the benefits of the toroidal connections are lost if a torus-connected computer is partitioned among several users.

Competition for bandwidth in a mesh network occurs when two or more processors attempt to send over the same wire at the same time (Figure 3.15). The analysis used to determine $S$ for a particular algorithm is illustrated in the examples that follow.

**Hypercube Network**    The hypercube network was introduced in Section 2.4.1. As in the mesh, processors in a hypercube network are associated with switching elements. A $d$-dimensional hypercube connects each of $2^d$ processors to $d$ other processors. A hypercube can be defined recursively as follows (Figure 3.16). A zero-dimensional hypercube is a single processor and a one-dimensional hypercube connects two zero-dimensional

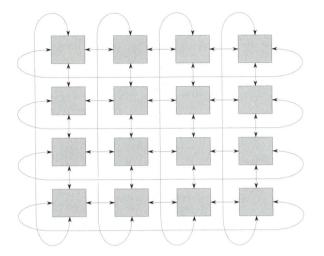

**Figure 3.14** A two-dimensional torus interconnection network. This is a 2-D mesh with end-around connections so that each processor is connected to four neighbors.

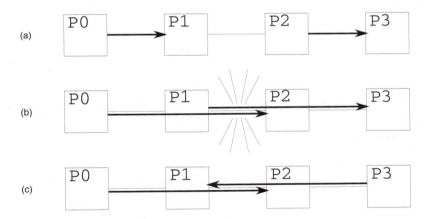

**Figure 3.15** Competition for bandwidth in a 1-D mesh. In (a), processors P0 and P1 communicate and P2 and P3 communicate. Because the two communications use different wires, both can proceed concurrently. In (b), processors P0 and P2 communicate and P1 and P3 communicate. The two communications must both traverse the wire connecting P1 and P2; hence, the two communications cannot proceed concurrently, and $S = 2$. In (c), processors P0 and P2 communicate and P3 and P1 communicate. Because each connection is bidirectional, the two communications can proceed concurrently.

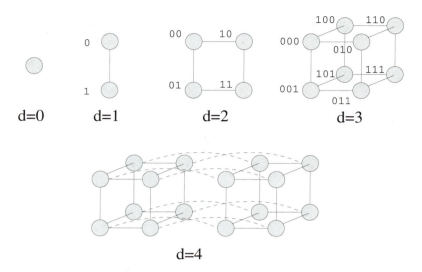

**Figure 3.16**   Hypercubes of dimension zero through four. The processors in the cubes of dimension 1, 2, and 3 are labeled with integers, here represented as binary numbers. Notice that two processors are neighbors in dimension $d$ if and only if their binary labels differ only in the $d$th place. Notice also that in a hypercube of dimension $d$, a message can be routed between any pair of processors in at most $d$ hops.

hypercubes. Generally, a hypercube of dimension $d + 1$ is constructed by connecting corresponding processors in two hypercubes of dimension $d$. As with the mesh, the competition-for-bandwidth factor $S$ is algorithm dependent, although the greater number of wires in the hypercube means that competition for bandwidth tends to occur less often.

The many interesting properties of hypercubes are beyond the scope of this book (but see Chapter 11). However, we note that when labeled as shown in Figure 3.16, two processors are connected if and only if the binary representation of their labels differs in a single position. We exploit this property when specifying algorithms that use the hypercube communication structure. Another important feature of a hypercube is that it contains a mesh: it may be considered a mesh with additional, long-distance connections. The additional connectivity reduces the diameter to $d$ and increases the number of available wires, particularly for nonlocal communication. A disadvantage of the hypercube interconnect from an engineering point of view is that it is more complex than the mesh. In particular, it requires more and longer wires, since a hypercube with dimension greater than three cannot be laid out in three-dimensional space so that wires connect only physically adjacent processors.

**Multistage Interconnection Networks**   In a multistage interconnection network (MIN), as in a crossbar, switching elements are distinct from processors. However, fewer than $\mathcal{O}(P^2)$ switches are used to connect $P$ processors. Instead, messages pass through a series of switch stages. Figure 3.17 illustrates two MINs, which are representatives of a general class of networks characterized by parameters $n$ and $k$. These networks are sometimes referred to as radix $k$, dimension $n$ butterflies, or $k$-ary $n$-flies. Either $n$ stages of $k^{n-1}$ $k \times k$

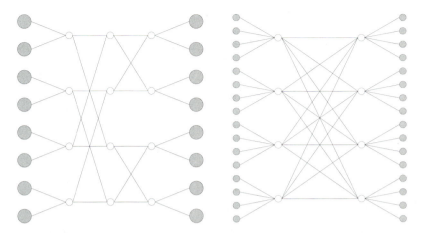

**Figure 3.17** Example multistage interconnection networks. Shaded circles represent processors and unshaded circles represent crossbar switches. The network on the left has $k = 2$ and $n = 3$; on the right, $k = 4$ and $n = 2$. The network can be constructed from unidirectional switches and links, in which case it is folded so that the processors on the left and right are the same. Alternatively, it can be constructed from bidirectional switches and links, in which case processors on the left and right are distinct.

unidirectional crossbar switches connect $P = k^n$ processors, or $n$ stages of $k^{n-1}$ $k \times k$ bidirectional crossbar switches connect $P = 2k^n$ processors. In the latter case, each link comprises two channels that carry data in opposite directions, and each crossbar switch can route data arriving on any of $2k$ inputs to any of $2k$ outputs. Notice that each stage of these networks connects $P$ inputs with $P$ outputs, although not every input is directly connected to every output in each stage.

In a unidirectional MIN, all messages must traverse the same number of wires, and so the cost of sending a message is independent of processor location. In effect, all processors are equidistant. In a bidirectional MIN, the number of wires traversed depends to some extent on processor location, although to a lesser extent than in a mesh or hypercube (Figure 3.18).

The fact that messages destined for different destinations may need to pass over the same wire means that MINs are not immune to competition for bandwidth. Nevertheless, a MIN connecting $P$ processors typically provides $P$ wires at each stage, so in principle we should be able to organize communications so that little competition occurs.

---

**EXAMPLE 3.7** (Competition for Bandwidth in Finite Difference)     In the first of two examples, we consider the impact of competition for bandwidth in an algorithm with a high degree of locality: the one-dimensional finite difference algorithm examined in preceding sections. Recall from Equation 3.3 that according to the idealized model of Equation 3.1, the per-processor communication costs for this algorithm are

$$T_{\text{ideal fd comm}} = t_s 2 + t_w 4NZ.$$

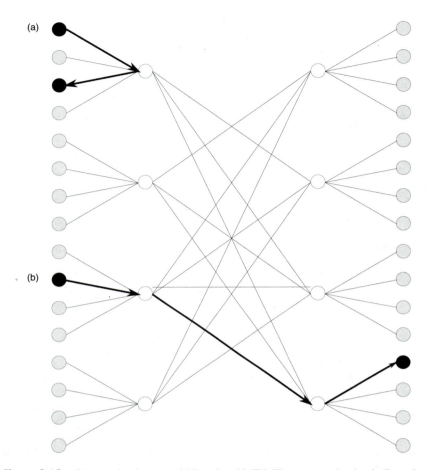

**Figure 3.18** Communications in a bidirectional MIN. The communication indicated at (a) involves processors connected to the same crossbar; it takes just two hops and passes through a single switch. The communication at (b) takes three hops and passes through two switches.

Competition for bandwidth is not an issue on a mesh or hypercube because the one-dimensional ring-based communication structure of the finite difference problem can be embedded in these networks using only nearest-neighbor connections. On a bus-based network, only one of the $P$ processors can communicate at one time; if we assume that in the communication phase of the algorithm, half the processors need to send at once (the other half are receiving), then $S = P/2$ and the communication volume term must be scaled by a factor of $P/2$, giving

$$T_{\text{bus fd comm}} = t_s 2 + t_w 2PNZ. \tag{3.11}$$

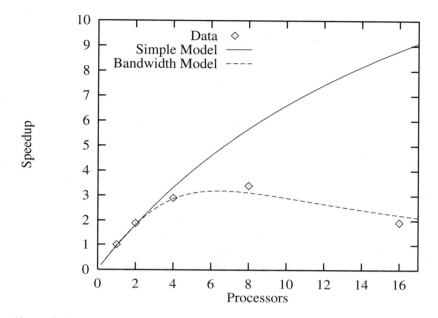

**Figure 3.19** Speedup of finite difference code with $N = 512$ and $Z = 5$ as measured on Ethernet-connected IBM RS6000 workstations and as predicted both by a simple performance model that does not take into account competition for bandwidth and by a more sophisticated model that does. Both models assume that $t_s = 1500$ $\mu$sec and $t_w = 5$ $\mu$sec.

Figure 3.19 illustrates both the large impact that bandwidth limitations can have on the performance of even a simple algorithm such as finite difference and the improved accuracy of the refined performance model. The figure shows performance measured on Ethernet-connected workstations and as predicted by Equations 3.3 and 3.11. We see that the more sophisticated model is reasonably accurate.

---

**EXAMPLE 3.8** (Competition for Bandwidth in Butterfly)    As a second example, we consider an algorithm in which $P$ tasks use the butterfly (or hypercube) communication structure illustrated in Figure 2.14 to perform $\log P$ exchanges of $N/P$ data. The summation algorithm described in Section 2.4.1 has this form. Other algorithms with similar characteristics are described in Chapter 11.

Per-processor communication costs associated with this algorithm are, in the absence of competition for bandwidth,

$$T_{\text{ideal butterfly comm}} = \log P \left( t_s + t_w \frac{N}{P} \right).$$

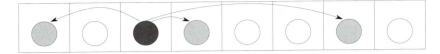

**Figure 3.20**  Execution of the butterfly summation algorithm on an eight-processor, one-dimensional mesh. Shading is used to highlight a single task and its communication partners, which are one, two, and four hops distant.

The algorithm can, of course, execute without competition for bandwidth on a crossbar switch. Somewhat less obviously, it can also execute without competition for bandwidth on a $P$-processor hypercube: Computation and communication can be organized so that each of the $\log P$ processors with which a processor must communicate is a neighbor on one of the hypercube links. On a bus-based network, only one processor can communicate at a time; hence, as in the finite difference algorithm considered in Example 3.7, we assume $S = P/2$ and from Equation 3.10 we have

$$T_{\text{bus butterfly comm}} = \log P \left( t_s + t_w \frac{N}{2} \right).$$

On a mesh, the limited number of wires becomes an issue. For example, on a one-dimensional mesh of $P$ processors, each processor generates messages that must traverse $1, 2, \ldots, 2^{p-1}$ hops in the $p$ steps of the algorithm (Figure 3.20). These messages travel a total of $P \sum_{i=0}^{p-1} 2^i = P(P-1)$ hops. This represents the number of wires to which each processor requires exclusive access during execution of the summation. As a one-dimensional bidirectional mesh provides only $2(P-1)$ wires, we see that the parallel algorithm cannot possibly proceed in less than $P/2$ steps rather than $\log P$ steps as supposed previously. In fact, it can proceed in $P/2$ steps only if we can define a communication schedule that keeps all wires busy all the time. Hence, the following model represents a lower bound on communication costs:

$$T_{\text{1d mesh butterfly comm}} \geq t_s \log P + t_w \frac{N}{2}.$$

Figure 3.21 compares observed speedups with those predicted by the simple and bandwidth-limited performance models on a one-dimensional mesh and on an Ethernet. These results are from an atmosphere modeling code that uses a parallel fast Fourier transform (FFT) to parallelize a numerical method called the spectral transform. The details of the numerical method are not important here; what is relevant is that at each step, the code must perform two butterfly communication operations (specifically, FFT) on a large array. Details of the two experiments are given in Table 3.6. (The $t_w$ term used on the DELTA is significantly smaller than in the finite difference code of Example 3.6; this reflects the fact that the communication code in the FFT implementation on the DELTA had been carefully optimized.)

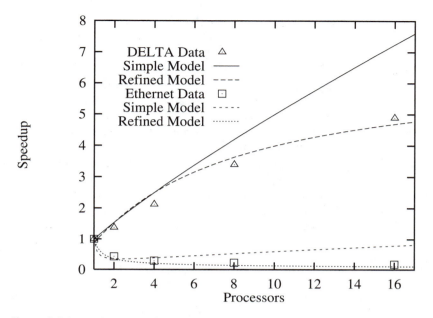

**Figure 3.21** Performance of parallel FFT in a spectral transform code on a one-dimensional mesh in Intel DELTA and on Ethernet-connected RS/6000 processors. The simple models do not take into account competition for bandwidth; the refined models do, and give a better fit to observed performance.

**Table 3.6** Parameters for butterfly performance study ($N$ in words, times in $\mu$sec).

| Machine | $T_1$ | $N$ | $t_s$ | $t_w$ |
|---|---|---|---|---|
| Intel DELTA | $8.5 \times 10^6$ | $1.7 \times 10^6$ | 200 | 0.6 |
| RS/6000 & Ethernet | $4.4 \times 10^6$ | $1.7 \times 10^6$ | 1500 | 5.0 |

## 3.8 Input/Output

An important determinant of performance in many parallel programs is the time required to move data between memory and secondary storage, that is, the time required for input/output (I/O). Applications with substantial I/O requirements include the following.

- *Checkpoints*. Many computations performed on parallel computers execute for extended periods. Periodic checkpointing of computation state is essential in order to reduce the cost of system failures. On large parallel computers, state can be large (many gigabytes).

- *Simulation data.* Scientific and engineering simulations that compute the time evolution of physical systems periodically save system state for subsequent visualization or analysis. Some simulations can generate very large amounts of data—hundreds of gigabytes or more in a single run.

- *Out-of-core computation.* Some programs must operate on data structures that are larger than available "core" memory. In principle, a virtual memory system can perform the necessary paging of data to and from disk. In practice, not all parallel computers provide virtual memory. Even when they do, application performance can often be enhanced by explicit management of data movement.

- *Data analysis.* Many applications involve the analysis of large amounts of data. For example, climate model output or data from weather satellites may be searched for "extreme events" such as high temperature values, a video database may be searched for specified images, and a database of credit card transactions may be searched for patterns of fraudulent use. These data analysis applications are particularly demanding from an I/O point of view, because relatively little computation is performed on each datum retrieved from disk.

It is difficult to provide a general discussion of parallel I/O because different parallel computers have radically different I/O architectures and hence parallel I/O mechanisms. However, we can make several points that have wide applicability.

We can often gain a reasonable understanding of the cost of an I/O operation by thinking of it as a communication from the processors that perform that operation to one or more disks. The cost of a disk I/O operation can be approximated by a startup cost and a per-word transfer cost in much the same way as an interprocessor communication. (However, the startup cost is typically much greater.) As in interprocessor communication, the keys to good performance are to maximize the utilization of available paths and to minimize startups.

If a computer has only a single disk or if multiple disks are connected to a single processor, little can be done to optimize I/O performance. However, in practice most parallel computers provide multiple paths from processors to disk, whether by providing distinct "I/O nodes" or by connecting disks directly to processors (Figure 3.22). On architectures of this sort, we seek to organize I/O operations so that multiple processors read and write concurrently, using multiple paths. Thus, centralized I/O strategies that cause data to pass through a single processor are unlikely to be efficient and are certainly not scalable.

In addition to maximizing concurrency in I/O operations, we need to be concerned about the number of distinct read or write requests required to transfer data between disk and processor memory. This can often have a greater impact on I/O performance than can the amount of data transferred. The number of I/O requests depends partly on how data are distributed on disk and in memory. The distribution in memory will presumably be determined by the application; the distribution on disk either will be under programmer control or will be selected by the file system. Data may sometimes be "striped" (scattered) across available disks so as to reduce the probability of many processors attempting to read from the same disk simultaneously.

If distributions on disk and in memory differ, then a large number of reads or writes may be required in order to achieve data transfer. This problem is analogous to what happens when transferring data structures between two parallel program components that

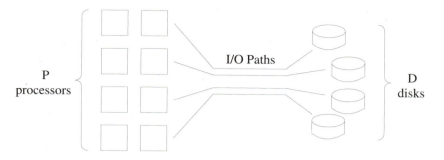

**Figure 3.22** I/O architecture of an idealized parallel computer. *P* processors are connected by multiple I/O channels to *D* disks.

require different distributions. As will be discussed in Chapter 4, at least two approaches are possible in this situation: we can modify one or both components to use different distributions, or we can explicitly redistribute data before or while transferring it. Because I/O requests tend to be more expensive than interprocessor communications, it is often better to perform an explicit redistribution of data in memory so as to minimize the number of I/O requests. This leads to a two-phase access strategy, in which the data distributions used on disk and in memory are decoupled. The merits of these various approaches can be explored analytically with performance models.

## 3.9  Case Study: Shortest-Path Algorithms

We conclude this chapter by using performance models to compare four different parallel algorithms for the all-pairs shortest-path problem. This is an important problem in graph theory and has applications in communications, transportation, and electronics problems. It is interesting because analysis shows that three of the four algorithms can be optimal in different circumstances, depending on tradeoffs between computation and communication costs.

The all-pairs shortest-path problem involves finding the shortest path between all pairs of vertices in a graph. A graph $G = (V, E)$ comprises a set $V$ of $N$ vertices, $\{v_i\}$, and a set $E \subseteq V \times V$ of edges connecting vertices in $V$. In a directed graph, each edge also has a direction, so edges $(v_i, v_j)$ and $(v_j, v_i)$, $i \neq j$, are distinct. A graph can be represented as an adjacency matrix $A$ in which each element $(i, j)$ represents the edge between element $i$ and $j$. $A_{ij} = 1$ if there is an edge $(v_i, v_j)$; otherwise, $A_{ij} = 0$ (Figure 3.23).

A *path* from vertex $v_i$ to vertex $v_j$ is a sequence of edges $(v_i, v_k), (v_k, v_l), \ldots, (v_m, v_j)$ from $E$ in which no vertex appears more than once. For example, $(1, 3), (3, 0)$ is a path from vertex 1 to vertex 0 in Figure 3.23. The shortest path between two vertices $v_i$ and $v_j$ in a graph is the path that has the fewest edges. The *single-source* shortest-path problem requires that we find the shortest path from a single vertex to all other vertices in a graph. The *all-pairs* shortest-path problem requires that we find the shortest path between all pairs of vertices in a graph. We consider the latter problem and present four different parallel algorithms, two based on a sequential shortest-path algorithm due to Floyd and two based

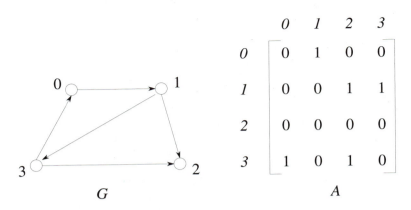

**Figure 3.23**    A simple directed graph, $G$, and its adjacency matrix, $A$.

on a sequential algorithm due to Dijkstra. All four algorithms take as input an $N \times N$ adjacency matrix $A$ and compute an $N \times N$ matrix $S$, with $S_{ij}$ the length of the shortest path from $v_i$ to $v_j$, or a distinguished value ($\infty$) if there is no path.

### 3.9.1    Floyd's Algorithm

Floyd's all-pairs shortest-path algorithm is given as Algorithm 3.1. It derives the matrix $S$ in $N$ steps, constructing at each step $k$ an intermediate matrix $I(k)$ containing the best-known shortest distance between each pair of nodes. Initially, each $I_{ij}(0)$ is set to the length of the edge $(v_i, v_j)$, if the edge exists, and to $\infty$ otherwise. The $k$th step of the algorithm considers each $I_{ij}$ in turn and determines whether the best-known path from $v_i$ to $v_j$ is longer than the combined lengths of the best-known paths from $v_i$ to $v_k$ and

```
procedure sequential_floyd
begin
    I_ij(0) = 0 if i = j
    I_ij(0) = length((v_i,v_j)) if edge exists and i ≠ j
    I_ij(0) = ∞ otherwise
    for k = 0 to N − 1
        for i = 0 to N − 1
            for j = 0 to N − 1
                I_ij(k+1) = min(I_ij(k), I_ik(k)+I_kj(k))
            endfor
        endfor
    endfor
    S = I(N)
end
```

**Algorithm 3.1**    Floyd's all-pairs shortest-path algorithm.

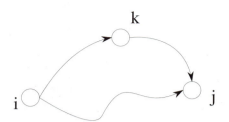

**Figure 3.24** The fundamental operation in Floyd's sequential shortest-path algorithm: Determine whether a path going from $v_i$ to $v_j$ via $v_k$ is shorter than the best-known path from $v_i$ to $v_j$.

from $v_k$ to $v_j$. If so, the entry $I_{ij}$ is updated to reflect the shorter path (Figure 3.24). This comparison operation is performed a total of $N^3$ times; hence, we can approximate the sequential cost of this algorithm as $t_c N^3$, where $t_c$ is the cost of a single comparison operation.

**Parallel Floyd 1** The first parallel Floyd algorithm is based on a one-dimensional, row-wise domain decomposition of the intermediate matrix $I$ and the output matrix $S$. Notice that this means the algorithm can use at most $N$ processors. Each task has one or more adjacent rows of $I$ and is responsible for performing computation on those rows. That is, it executes the following logic.

```
for k = 0 to N − 1
   for i = local_i_start to local_i_end
      for j = 0 to N − 1
         Iᵢⱼ(k + 1) = min(Iᵢⱼ(k), Iᵢₖ(k)+Iₖⱼ(k))
      endfor
   endfor
endfor
```

In the $k$th step, each task requires, in addition to its local data, the values $I_{k1}$, $I_{k2}$, ..., $I_{kN}$, that is, the $k$th row of $I$ (Figure 3.25). Hence, we specify that the task with this row broadcast it to all other tasks. This communication can be performed by using a tree structure in $\log P$ steps. Because there are $N$ such broadcasts and each message has size $N$, the cost is

$$T_{\text{Floyd 1}} = t_c \frac{N^3}{P} + N \log P (t_s + t_w N). \tag{3.12}$$

Notice that each task must serve as the "root" for at least one broadcast (assuming $P \leq N$). Rather than defining $P$ binary tree structures, it suffices to connect the $P$ tasks using a hypercube structure (Chapter 11), which has the useful property of allowing any node to broadcast to all other nodes in $\log P$ steps.

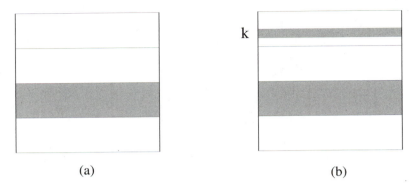

**Figure 3.25**  Parallel version of Floyd's algorithm based on a one-dimensional decomposition of the $I$ matrix. In (a), the data allocated to a single task are shaded: a contiguous block of rows. In (b), the data required by this task in the $k$th step of the algorithm are shaded: its own block and the $k$th row.

**Parallel Floyd 2**  An alternative parallel version of Floyd's algorithm uses a two-dimensional decomposition of the various matrices. This version allows the use of up to $N^2$ processors and requires that each task execute the following logic.

```
for k = 0 to N − 1
    for i = local_i_start to local_i_end
        for j = local_j_start to local_j_end
            I_ij(k + 1) = min(I_ij(k), I_ik(k)+I_kj(k))
        endfor
    endfor
endfor
```

In each step, each task requires, in addition to its local data, $N/\sqrt{P}$ values from two tasks located in the same row and column of the 2-D task array (Figure 3.26). Hence, communication requirements at the $k$th step can be structured as two broadcast operations: from the task in each row that possesses part of column $k$ to all other tasks in that row, and from the task in each column that possesses part of row $k$ to all other tasks in that column.

In each of $N$ steps, $N/\sqrt{P}$ values must be broadcast to the $\sqrt{P}$ tasks in each row and column, and the total cost is

$$
\begin{aligned}
T_{\text{Floyd 2}} &= t_c \frac{N^3}{P} + 2N \log \sqrt{P} \left( t_s + t_w \frac{N}{\sqrt{P}} \right) \\
&= t_c \frac{N^3}{P} + N \log P \left( t_s + t_w \frac{N}{\sqrt{P}} \right).
\end{aligned}
\tag{3.13}
$$

Notice that each task must serve as the "root" node for at least one broadcast to each task in the same row and column of the 2-D task array. These communication requirements can be satisfied by connecting tasks in the same row or column in a hypercube structure.

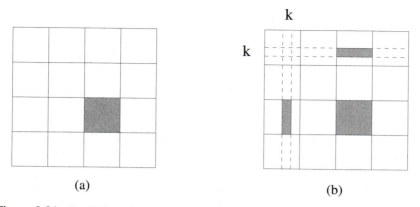

**Figure 3.26** Parallel version of Floyd's algorithm based on a two-dimensional decomposition of the $I$ matrix. In (a), the data allocated to a single task are shaded: a contiguous submatrix. In (b), the data required by this task in the $k$th step of the algorithm are shaded: its own block, and part of the $k$th row and column.

### 3.9.2 Dijkstra's Algorithm

Dijkstra's *single-source* shortest-path algorithm computes all shortest paths from a single vertex, $v_s$. It can also be used for the all-pairs shortest-path problem, by the simple expedient of applying it $N$ times—once to each vertex $v_0, \ldots, v_{N-1}$.

Dijkstra's sequential single-source algorithm is given as Algorithm 3.2. It maintains as $T$ the set of vertices for which shortest paths have not been found, and as $d_i$ the shortest known path from $v_s$ to vertex $v_i$. Initially, $T = V$ and all $d_i = \infty$. At each step of the algorithm, the vertex $v_m$ in $T$ with the smallest $d$ value is removed from $T$. Each

```
procedure sequential_dijkstra
begin
    d_s = 0
    d_i = ∞, for i ≠ s
    T = V
    for i = 0 to N − 1
        find v_m ∈ T with minimum d_m
        for each edge (v_m, v_t) with v_t ∈ T
            if (d_t > d_m + L_mt) then d_t = d_m + L_mt
        endfor
        T = T − v_m
    endfor
end
```

**Algorithm 3.2** Dijkstra's single-source shortest-path algorithm.

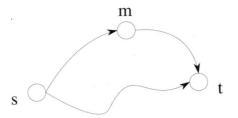

**Figure 3.27** The comparison operation performed in Dijkstra's single-source shortest-path algorithm. The best-known path from the source vertex $v_s$ to vertex $v_t$ is compared with the path that leads from $v_s$ to $v_m$ and then to $v_t$.

neighbor of $v_m$ in $T$ is examined to see whether a path through $v_m$ would be shorter than the currently best-known path (Figure 3.27).

An all-pairs algorithm executes Algorithm 3.2 $N$ times, once for each vertex. This involves $\mathcal{O}(N^3)$ comparisons and takes time $N^3 t_c F$, where $t_c$ is the cost of a single comparison in Floyd's algorithm and $F$ is a constant. Empirical studies show that $F \approx 1.6$; that is, Dijkstra's algorithm is slightly more expensive than Floyd's algorithm.

**Parallel Dijkstra 1**    The first parallel Dijkstra algorithm replicates the graph in each of $P$ tasks. Each task executes the sequential algorithm for $N/P$ vertices. This algorithm requires no communication but can utilize at most $N$ processors. Because the sequential Dijkstra algorithm is 1.6 times slower than the sequential Floyd algorithm, the parallel algorithm's execution time is

$$T_{\text{Dijkstra 1}} = t_c F \frac{N^3}{P}.$$

**Parallel Dijkstra 2**    The second parallel Dijkstra algorithm allows for the case when $P > N$. We define $N$ sets of $P/N$ tasks. Each set of tasks is given the entire graph and is responsible for computing shortest paths for a single vertex (Figure 3.28). Within each set of tasks, the vertices of the graph are partitioned. Hence, the operation

    Find $v_m \in T$ with minimum $d_m$

requires first a local computation to find the local vertex with minimum $d$ and second a reduction involving all $P/N$ tasks in the same set in order to determine the globally minimum $d_m$. The reduction can be achieved by using the butterfly communication structure of Section 2.4.1, in log $P/N$ steps. Hence, as the reduction is performed $N$ times and involves two values, the total cost of this algorithm is

$$T_{\text{Dijkstra 2}} = t_c F \frac{N^3}{P} + N \log \frac{P}{N} (t_s + 2t_w).$$

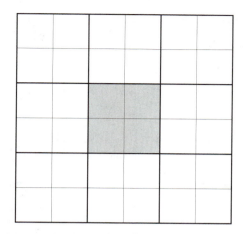

**Figure 3.28** The second parallel Dijkstra algorithm allocates $P/N$ tasks to each of $N$ instantiations of Dijkstra's single-source shortest-path algorithm. In this figure, $N = 9$ and $P = 36$, and one set of $P/N = 4$ tasks is shaded.

### 3.9.3 Shortest-Path Algorithms Summary

Table 3.7 summarizes the performance models developed for the four all-pairs shortest-path algorithms. Clearly, Floyd 2 will always be more efficient than Floyd 1. Both algorithms have the same computation costs and send the same number of messages, but Floyd 2 communicates considerably less data. On the other hand, Floyd 1 is easier to implement. Algorithms Dijkstra 1 and 2 will be more efficient than Floyd 2 in certain circumstances. For example, Dijkstra 1 is more efficient than Floyd 2 if $P \le N$ and

$$t_c(F - 1)\frac{N^3}{P} < t_s N \log P + t_w N^2 \frac{\log P}{\sqrt{P}}.$$

In addition to these factors, we must consider the fact that algorithms Dijkstra 1 and Dijkstra 2 replicate the graph $P$ and $P/N$ times, respectively. This replication may compromise the scalability of these algorithms. Also, the cost of replicating an originally distributed graph must be considered if (as is likely) the shortest-path algorithm forms part of a larger program in which the graph is represented as a distributed data structure.

**Table 3.7** Performance of four parallel shortest-path algorithms.

| Algorithm | $t_c$ | $t_s$ | $t_w$ | Maximum $P$ |
|-----------|-------|-------|-------|-------------|
| Floyd 1 | $N^3/P$ | $N \log P$ | $N^2 \log P$ | $N$ |
| Floyd 2 | $N^3/P$ | $N \log P$ | $N^2 \log P/\sqrt{P}$ | $N^2$ |
| Dijkstra 1 | $N^3 F/P$ | $0$ | $0$ | $N$ |
| Dijkstra 2 | $N^3 F/P$ | $N \log (P/N)$ | $2N \log (P/N)$ | $N^2$ |

Clearly, the choice of shortest-path algorithm for a particular problem will involve complex tradeoffs between flexibility, scalability, performance, and implementation complexity. The performance models developed in this case study provide a basis for evaluating these tradeoffs.

## 3.10    Summary

In this chapter, we have seen how to develop mathematical performance models that characterize the execution time, efficiency, and scalability of a parallel algorithm in terms of simple parameters such as problem size, number of processors, and communication parameters. We have also seen how these models can be used throughout the parallel program design and implementation cycle:

- Early in the design process, we characterize the computation and communication requirements of our parallel algorithms by building simple performance models. These models can be used to choose between algorithmic alternatives, to identify problem areas in the design, and to verify that algorithms meet performance requirements.

- Later in the design process, we refine our performance models and conduct simple experiments to determine unknown parameters (such as computation time or communication costs) or to validate assumptions. The refined models can be used to increase our confidence in the quality of our design before implementation.

- During implementation, we compare the performance of the parallel program with its performance model. Doing this can help both to identify implementation errors and to improve the quality of the model.

A performance model gives information about one aspect of an algorithm design: its expected parallel performance. We can use this information, when it is combined with estimates of implementation cost, etc., to make informed choices between design alternatives.

### Exercises

The exercises in this chapter are designed to provide experience in the development and use of performance models. When an exercise asks you to implement an algorithm, you should use one of the programming tools described in Part II.

1. Discuss the relative importance of the various performance metrics listed in Section 3.1 when designing a parallel floorplan optimization program for use in VLSI design.

2. Discuss the relative importance of the various performance metrics listed in Section 3.1 when designing a video server that uses a parallel computer to generate many hundreds of thousands of concurrent video streams. Each stream must be retrieved from disk, decoded, and output over a network.

3. The self-consistent field (SCF) method in computational chemistry involves two operations: Fock matrix construction and matrix diagonalization. Assuming that

diagonalization accounts for 0.5 per cent of total execution time on a uniprocessor computer, use Amdahl's law to determine the maximum speedup that can be obtained if only the Fock matrix construction operation is parallelized.

4. You are charged with designing a parallel SCF program. You estimate your Fock matrix construction algorithm to be 90 percent efficient on your target computer. You must choose between two parallel diagonalization algorithms, which on five hundred processors achieve speedups of 50 and 10, respectively. What overall efficiency do you expect to achieve with these two algorithms? If your time is as valuable as the computer's, and you expect the more efficient algorithm to take one hundred hours longer to program, for how many hours must you plan to use the parallel program if the more efficient algorithm is to be worthwhile?

5. Some people argue that in the future, processors will become essentially free as the cost of computers become dominated by the cost of storage and communication networks. Discuss how this situation may affect algorithm design and performance analysis.

6. Generate an execution profile similar to that in Figure 3.8 for an implementation of a parallel finite difference algorithm based on a 2-D decomposition. Under which circumstances will message startups contribute more to execution time than will data transfer costs?

7. Derive expressions that indicate when a 2-D decomposition of a finite difference computation on an $N \times N \times Z$ grid will be superior to a 1-D decomposition and when a 3-D decomposition will be superior to a 2-D decomposition. Are these conditions likely to apply in practice? Let $t_s = 1 \ \mu sec$, $t_w = 0.04 \ \mu sec$, $t_c = 1 \ \mu sec$, and $P = 1000$. For what values of $N$ does the use of a 3-D decomposition rather than a 2-D decomposition reduce execution time by more than 10 percent?

8. Adapt the analysis of Example 3.4 to consider 1-D and 2-D decompositions of a 2-D grid. Let $N = 1024$, and fix other parameters as in Exercise 7. For what values of $P$ does the use of a 2-D decomposition rather than a 1-D decomposition reduce execution time by more than 10 percent?

9. Implement a simple "ping-pong" program that bounces messages between a pair of processors. Measure performance as a function of message size on a workstation network and on one or more parallel computers. Fit your results to Equation 3.1 to obtain values for $t_s$ and $t_w$. Discuss the quality of your results and of the fit.

10. Develop a performance model for the program constructed in Exercise 5 in Chapter 2 that gives execution time as a function of $N$, $P$, $t_c$, $t_s$, and $t_w$. Perform empirical studies to determine values for $t_c$, $t_s$, and $t_w$ on different parallel computer systems. Use the results of these studies to evaluate the adequacy of your model.

11. Develop performance models for the parallel algorithms developed in Exercise 10 in Chapter 2. Compare these models with performance data obtained from implementations of these algorithms.

12. Determine the isoefficiency function for the program developed in Exercise 10. Verify this experimentally.

13. Use the "ping-pong" program of Exercise 9 to study the impact of bandwidth limitations on performance, by writing a program in which several pairs of processors perform exchanges concurrently. Measure execution times on a workstation network and on one or more parallel computers. Relate observed performance to Equation 3.10.

14. Implement the parallel summation algorithm of Section 2.4.1. Measure execution times as a function of problem size on a network of workstations and on one or more parallel computers. Relate observed performance to the performance models developed in this chapter.

15. Determine the isoefficiency function for the butterfly summation algorithm of Section 2.4.1, with and without bandwidth limitations.

16. Design a communication structure for the algorithm Floyd 2 discussed in Section 3.9.1.

17. Assume that a cyclic mapping is used in the atmosphere model of Section 2.6 to compensate for load imbalances. Develop an analytic expression for the additional communication cost associated with various block sizes and hence for the load imbalance that must exist for this approach to be worthwhile.

18. Implement a two-dimensional finite difference algorithm using a nine-point stencil. Use this program to verify experimentally the analysis of Exercise 17. Simulate load imbalance by calling a "work" function that performs different amounts of computation at different grid points.

19. Assume that $t_c = 1$, $t_s = 50$, and $t_w = 4$ $\mu$sec. Use the performance models summarized in Table 3.7 to determine the values of $N$ and $P$ for which the various shortest-path algorithms of Section 3.9 are optimal.

20. Assume that a graph represented by an adjacency matrix of size $N^2$ is distributed among $P$ tasks prior to the execution of the all-pairs shortest-path algorithm. Repeat the analysis of Exercise 19 but allow for the cost of data replication in the Dijkstra algorithms.

21. Extend the performance models developed for the shortest-path algorithms to take into account bandwidth limitations on a 1-D mesh architecture.

22. Implement algorithms Floyd 1 and Floyd 2, and compare their performance with that predicted by Equations 3.12 and 3.13. Account for any differences.

23. In so-called nondirect Fock matrix construction algorithms, the $N^4$ integrals of Equation 2.4 are cached on disk and reused at each step. Discuss the performance issues that may arise when developing a code of this sort.

24. The *bisection width* of a computer is the minimum number of wires that must be cut to divide the computer into two equal parts. Multiplying this by the channel bandwidth gives the *bisection bandwidth*. For example, the bisection bandwidth of a 1-D mesh with bidirectional connections is $2/t_w$. Determine the bisection bandwidth of a bus, 2-D mesh, 3-D mesh, and hypercube.

25. An array transpose operation reorganizes an array partitioned in one dimension so that it is partitioned in the second dimension (Figure 3.29). This can be achieved

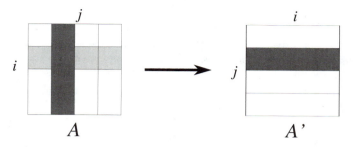

**Figure 3.29**    Parallel matrix transpose of a matrix $A$ decomposed by column, with $P = 4$. The components of the matrix allocated to a single task are shaded black, and the components required from other tasks are shaded gray.

in $P - 1$ steps, with each processor exchanging $1/P$ of its data with another processor in each step. Develop a performance model for this operation.

26. Equation 3.1 can be extended to account for the distance $D$ between originating and destination processors:

$$T = t_s + t_h D + t_w L. \tag{3.14}$$

The time per hop $t_h$ typically has magnitude comparable to $t_w$. Under what circumstances might the $t_h$ term be significant?

27. Develop a performance model for the matrix transpose algorithm on a 1-D mesh that takes into account per-hop costs, as specified by Equation 3.14. Assume that $t_h = 3t_w$ and $t_s = 25t_w$, and identify $P$ and $N$ values for which per-hop costs make a significant ($> 5$ percent) difference to execution time.

28. Demonstrate that the transpose algorithm's messages travel a total of $(P^3 - P)/3$ hops on a 1-D mesh. Use this information to refine the performance model of Exercise 25 to account for competition for bandwidth.

29. In the array transpose algorithm of Exercise 25, roughly half of the array must be moved from one half of the computer to the other. Hence, we can obtain a lower time bound by dividing the data volume by the bisection bandwidth. Compare this bound with times predicted by simple and bandwidth-limited performance models, on a bus, one-dimensional mesh, and two-dimensional mesh.

30. Implement the array transpose algorithm and study its performance. Compare your results to the performance models developed in preceding exercises.

## Chapter Notes

The observation commonly referred to as Amdahl's law was first formulated in [12]. Asymptotic analysis of parallel algorithms is discussed in many computer science texts, such as those by Akl [8], Leighton [187], and Smith [267]. Cook [64] discusses problems for which no efficient parallel algorithms have been discovered.

Many different approaches to performance modeling have been proposed, each appropriate for different purposes. See, for example, the papers by Culler et al. [67], Eager et al. [89], Flatt and Kennedy [97], Karp and Flatt [167], and Nussbaum and Agarwal [216]. Patel [224] discusses the modeling of shared-memory computers. The book by Kumar et al. [179] provides many example models and a more detailed treatment of the concept of isoefficiency. Gustafson et al. [129, 130] introduce the concept of scaled speedup. Singh, Hennessy, and Gupta [259], Sun and Ni [274], and Worley [297, 298] discuss various constraints on the scalability of parallel programs. Lai and Sahni [183] and Quinn and Deo [237] discuss speedup anomalies in search problems. Faber et al. [93] argue against the concept of superlinear speedup. Fromm et al. [115], Harrison and Patel [134], and Thomasian and Bay [284] use queuing models to study performance of parallel systems. Kleinrock [173] reviews techniques used for performance analysis of networks and discusses issues that arise in high-speed (gigabit/sec) WANs.

The chapter notes in Chapter 1 provide references on parallel computer architecture. Feng [94] provides a tutorial on interconnection networks. Hypercube networks have been used in a variety of multicomputers such as the Cosmic Cube [254], nCUBE-2 [212], Intel iPSC, and Thinking Machines CM2 [281]. The Intel DELTA and Intel Paragon [276] use two-dimensional mesh networks. The Cray T3D and MIT J machine [72] use a three-dimensional torus. Adams, Agrawal, and Siegel [2] survey multistage interconnection networks, and Harrison [133] discusses the analytic modeling of these networks. Various forms of multistage network have been used in the BBN Butterfly [31], NYU Ultracomputer [123], IBM RP3 [226], and IBM SP [271]. The IBM SP uses a bidirectional multistage network constructed from $4 \times 4$ crossbars (a modified 4-ary $n$-fly) similar to that illustrated in Figure 3.18. Seitz [253, 255] provides an introduction to multicomputers and their interconnection networks. Dally [69] discusses networks and the concept of bisection width, while Leighton [187] provides a more detailed and theoretical treatment. Dally and Seitz [70, 71] discuss routing techniques. The material in Example 3.8 is based on work by Foster and Worley [110]. Ethernet was designed by Metcalfe and Boggs [205]; Shoch, Dalal, and Redell [257] describe its evolution.

Miller and Katz [208], Foster, Henderson, and Stevens [103], and Pool et al. [229] discuss the I/O requirements of scientific and engineering applications. Del Rosario and Choudhary [76] discuss problems and prospects for parallel I/O. Henderson, Nickless, and Stevens [145] discuss application I/O requirements and describe a flexible I/O architecture for parallel computers. Plank and Li [228] discuss checkpointing. Bordawekar, del Rosario, and Choudhary [41] explain the utility of a two-phase I/O strategy. A special issue of the *Journal of Parallel and Distributed Computing* [60] discusses various aspects of parallel I/O, as do Aggarwal and Vitter [4] and Katz, Gibson, and Patterson [168]. DeWitt and Gray [79] discuss parallel database machines. Gibson [120] examines the design and performance analysis of redundant disk arrays (RAID disks). Hennessy and Patterson [134] provide a good description of I/O system performance analysis and design.

The parallel versions of Floyd's shortest-path algorithm [98] are due to Jenq and Sahni [158], while the parallel version of Dijkstra's single-source algorithm [80] is described by Paige and Kruskal [217]. Our analysis of these algorithms follows Kumar and Singh [182], who also present analyses that take into account bandwidth limitations on hypercube and two-dimensional mesh architectures. Bertsekas and Tsitsiklis [35] describe a pipelined variant of Floyd 2 that improves performance by allowing iterations to proceed concurrently, subject only to dataflow constraints. Aho, Hopcroft, and Ullman [7] and Cormen, Leiserson, and Rivest [65] provide good introductions to sequential graph algorithms. Quinn and Deo [236] and Das, Deo, and Prasad [73, 74] describe parallel graph algorithms. Ranka and Sahni's [238] book on parallel algorithms for image processing and pattern recognition includes relevant material.

The online version provides access here to additional information on performance analysis and the architecture and performance of parallel and distributed computer systems.

# 4  Putting Components Together

In previous chapters, we have focused on the problem of deriving efficient parallel algorithms for individual program components, such as search and finite difference computation. Yet complete programs may need to incorporate multiple parallel algorithms, each operating on different data structures and requiring different partitioning, communication, and mapping strategies for its efficient execution.

Experience shows that the complexity that tends to arise when constructing large programs can be controlled by the application of *modular design* techniques. The key idea is to encapsulate complex or changeable aspects of a design inside separate program components, or *modules*, with well-defined interfaces indicating how each module interacts with its environment. Complete programs are developed by plugging together, or *composing*, these modules. Modular design can increase reliability and reduce costs by making it easier to build programs, change programs to suit changing requirements, and reuse components in new programs.

Our goal in this chapter is to introduce some of the design issues that arise when developing large parallel programs. After studying this chapter, you should understand the basic principles and benefits of modular design. You should be familiar with the techniques used to apply modular design in parallel programs: what needs to be encapsulated in parallel program components, and the various ways in which components can be composed. You should also understand the performance issues that arise when composing parallel program components.

## 4.1  Modular Design Review

The basic idea underlying modular design is to organize a complex system (such as a large program, an electronic circuit, or a mechanical device) as a set of distinct components that can be developed independently and then plugged together. Although this may appear a simple idea, experience shows that the effectiveness of the technique depends critically on the manner in which systems are divided into components and the mechanisms used to plug components together. The following design principles are particularly relevant to parallel programming.

**Provide Simple Interfaces**  Simple interfaces reduce the number of interactions that must be considered when verifying that a system performs its intended function. Simple interfaces also make it easier to reuse components in different circumstances. Reuse is a major cost saver. Not only does it reduce time spent in coding, design, and testing, but it also allows development costs to be amortized over many projects. Numerous studies have shown that reusing software is by far the most effective technique for reducing software development costs.

As an example, a modular implementation of a climate modeling system (Figure 2.3) may define distinct modules concerned with atmosphere modeling, ocean modeling, etc. The interfaces to each module can comprise a small set of procedures that access boundary data, advance the simulation, and so on. Hence, there is no need for the user to become familiar with the implementation of the various modules, which collectively may comprise hundreds of procedures and tens of thousands of lines of code.

**Ensure that Modules Hide Information**    The benefits of modularity do not follow automatically from the act of subdividing a program. The way in which a program is decomposed can make an enormous difference to how easily the program can be implemented and modified. Experience shows that each module should encapsulate information that is not available to the rest of a program. This *information hiding* reduces the cost of subsequent design changes. For example, a module may encapsulate

- related functions that can benefit from a common implementation or that are used in many parts of a system,
- functionality that is likely to change during later design or deployment,
- aspects of a problem that are particularly complex, and/or
- code that is expected to be reused in other programs.

Notice that we do not say that a module should contain functions that are logically related because, for example, they solve the same part of a problem. This sort of decomposition does not normally facilitate maintenance or promote code reuse.

**Use Appropriate Tools**    While modular designs can in principle be implemented in any programming language, implementation is easier if the language supports information hiding by permitting the encapsulation of code and data structures. Fundamental mechanisms in this regard include the procedure (or subroutine or function) with its locally scoped variables and argument list, used to encapsulate code; the user-defined datatype, used to encapsulate data; and dynamic memory allocation, which allows subprograms to acquire storage without the involvement of the calling program. These features are supported by most modern languages (e.g., C++, Fortran 90, and Ada) but are lacking or rudimentary in some older languages (e.g., Fortran 77).

**Design Checklist**    The following design checklist can be used to evaluate the success of a modular design. As usual, each question should be answered in the affirmative.

1. Does the design identify clearly defined modules?
2. Does each module have a clearly defined purpose? (Can you summarize it in one sentence?)

3. Is each module's interface sufficiently abstract that you do not need to think about its implementation in order to understand it? Does it hide its implementation details from other modules?

4. Have you subdivided modules as far as usefully possible?

5. Have you verified that different modules do not replicate functionality?

6. Have you isolated those aspects of the design that are most hardware specific, complex, or otherwise likely to change?

---

**EXAMPLE 4.1** (Database Search)   We use a simple example to illustrate how information hiding considerations can influence design. To search a database for records matching a specified search pattern, we must read the database, search the database, and write any matching records found. One possible decomposition of this problem defines input, search, and output modules with the following interfaces.

```
input(in_file, database)
search(database, search_pattern, matches)
output(out_file, database, matches)
```

An examination of what must be done to read a database, perform a search, and so on could then lead us to define the procedures that comprise the input, search, and output modules.

This design provides simple interfaces. However, all three modules depend on the internal representation used for the database, and hence must be modified if this representation is changed. In addition, each module probably duplicates database access functions.

An alternative decomposition, driven by information hiding concerns, focuses on the internal representation of the database as something potentially complex, likely to change, and common to many components. Hence, this information is hidden in a single database module that provides operations such as the following.

```
read_record(file, id, record)
add_record(id, record, database)
get_record(id, record, database)
write_record(file, id, record)
```

The rest of the program can now be written without knowing anything about how the database is implemented. To change the internal representation of the database, we need simply to substitute a different implementation of the database module, which furthermore is ideally suited for reuse in other applications.

---

## 4.2   Modularity and Parallel Computing

The design principles reviewed in the preceding section apply directly to parallel programming. However, parallelism also introduces additional concerns. A sequential module encapsulates the code that implements the functions provided by the module's interface and the data structures accessed by those functions. In parallel programming, we need to consider not only code and data but also the tasks created by a module, the way in which data

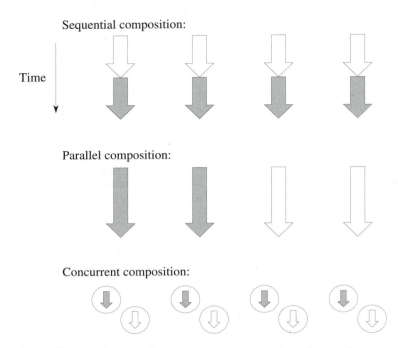

**Figure 4.1**   Three forms of parallel program composition. In each case, the program is shown executing on four processors, with each arrow representing a separate thread of control and shading denoting two different program components. In sequential composition, different program components execute in sequence on all processors. In parallel composition, different program components execute concurrently on different processors. In concurrent composition, different program components execute concurrently on the same processors.

structures are partitioned and mapped to processors, and internal communication structures. Probably the most fundamental issue is that of data distribution.

Another difference between sequential and parallel programming is that in the former, modules can be put together (composed) in just one way: sequentially. Execution of a program leads to a sequence of calls to functions defined in different modules. This is called *sequential composition* and can also be used in parallel programming, and indeed is fundamental to the SPMD programming model used in many parallel programs. However, we often need to compose program components in other ways (Figure 4.1). In *parallel composition*, different modules execute concurrently on disjoint sets of processors. This strategy can enhance modularity and improve scalability and locality. In *concurrent composition*, different modules execute concurrently on the same processors, with execution of a particular module enabled by the availability of data. Concurrent composition can both reduce design complexity and allow overlapping of computation and communication.

We distinguish between sequential, parallel, and concurrent composition both because they are different ways of thinking about programs and because not all parallel programming tools support all three compositional forms. Data-parallel languages (such as HPF) tend to support only sequential composition. Message-passing libraries (such as MPI) typically support both sequential and parallel composition but not concurrent composition. Other languages and libraries (such as CC++ and Fortran M) support all three forms of composition.

### 4.2.1  Data Distribution

In Chapters 2 and 3, we showed that the distribution of a program's data structures among tasks and processors (that is, the way in which data structures are partitioned and mapped) is an important aspect of parallel algorithm design. We also showed how to design data distributions that maximize performance and/or minimize software engineering costs.

Data distribution can become a more complex issue in programs constructed from several components. Simply choosing the optimal distribution for each component may result in different modules using different data distributions. For example, one module may output an array data structure distributed by columns, while another expects its input to be distributed by rows. If these two modules are to be composed, then either the modules themselves must be modified to use different distributions, or data must be explicitly redistributed as they are passed from one component to the other. These different solutions can have different performance characteristics and development costs.

Both performance tuning and program reuse are made easier if modules are designed to be *data distribution neutral*, that is, if they can deal with a variety of different data distributions. This neutrality can be achieved by specifying the distribution of a particular data structure as a runtime parameter or in the data structure itself. For example, the two modules referred to in the preceding paragraph could be defined to deal with arbitrary two-dimensional decompositions. The combined program could then utilize a decomposition by rows, a decomposition by columns, or (as a compromise) a two-dimensional decomposition.

Designing a module to be data distribution neutral is not necessarily easy. In some cases, different data distributions may call for quite different algorithms. This issue is explored in more detail in Section 4.6.

### 4.2.2  Sequential Composition

In a parallel program constructed using only sequential composition, each processor inevitably executes the same program, which in turn performs a series of calls to different program components. These program components may themselves communicate and synchronize, but they cannot create new tasks. Hence, the entire computation moves sequentially from one parallel operation to the next.

As an example, consider the following program, which could be executed by each task in an SPMD finite difference program.

```
while(not done) do
   finite_difference(localgrid, localmax)
   global_maximum(localmax, globmax)
   if(globmax < threshold) done = true
enddo
```

This program is structured as a sequential composition of two procedure calls and a conditional statement. At each step, each task first calls the `finite_difference` procedure to advance the simulation on its part of the finite difference grid. This updates `localgrid` and returns a local error estimate, `localmax`. Next, each task calls `global_maximum` to obtain a global maximum error, which is used to determine whether the simulation has converged. On a parallel computer, both the `finite_difference` and `global_maximum` routines must perform communication (to exchange the data required by the finite difference stencil and to compute the global maximum, respectively), but this activity is hidden from the rest of the program.

This example illustrates an important advantage of sequential composition and the SPMD model: the program executed by each process has a fairly straightforward sequential reading, and many sequential programming techniques can be used unchanged. For example, the procedures `finite_difference` and `global_maximum` can be defined in separate grid and reduction modules, both of which can encapsulate internal data structures (and communication structures).

A second advantage of sequential composition is that if different modules use the same data distribution, no data movement (and hence no communication) is required at module interfaces. For example, the top-level structure of an SPMD climate modeling system could be as follows. Procedures from ocean and atmosphere modules are called repeatedly in an interleaved fashion, with data generated by the ocean module being passed to the atmosphere module and vice versa. Communication is required only within the two components.

```
initialize_ocn(ocn_grid)
initialize_atm(atm_grid)
while(not done) do
   ocean(atm_grid, ocn_grid)
   atmosphere(ocn_grid, atm_grid, done)
enddo
```

As these examples show, a library intended for use in an SPMD programming environment can utilize an interface almost identical to that used in a comparable sequential library. The principal concerns are that library routines be able to deal with a variety of data distributions (that is, be data distribution neutral) and that parallel implementation details such as data structures and communication operations be hidden behind interfaces.

The simplicity of sequential composition and SPMD programming has stimulated some major parallel library development projects. One example, which we describe here to illustrate how data distribution neutral libraries are defined, is ScaLAPACK, a version of the popular LAPACK linear algebra library designed to execute on scalable parallel computers. ScaLAPACK supports a wide range of operations on dense and banded matrices, such as multiplication, transpose, and factorization. Its routines operate on data objects representing two-dimensional matrices decomposed by using a block cyclic distribution. The distribution of an array is specified by four parameters, $P$, $Q$, $r$, and $c$, where $P$ and $Q$ denote the number of processors and $r$ and $c$ the block size in each dimension (Figure 4.2). In principle, every routine can be called with any parameter values, so the programmer can experiment with alternative data distributions simply by changing parameters in a top-level program. This approach provides a high degree of mapping independence, in

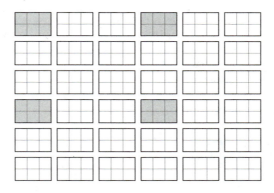

**Figure 4.2** A block cyclic distribution of a two-dimensional array of size $12 \times 18$ onto a processor array of size $3 \times 3$ ($P = Q = 3$) with a block size of $2 \times 3$ ($r = 2$, $c = 3$). Array elements mapped to processor $(0, 0)$ are shaded.

a manner evocative of the data distribution directives employed in the data-parallel language High Performance Fortran (HPF) (Chapter 7). In practice, certain limitations are placed on allowable parameter values so as to simplify the software. For example, the LU factorization routine requires that blocks be square. Internally, ScaLAPACK routines may incorporate multiple parallel algorithms and select between these algorithms based on distribution, problem size, and machine size. However, these details are hidden from the user. Program 4.1 illustrates the use of ScaLAPACK routines.

Not surprisingly, sequential composition also has limitations as a program structuring technique for parallel programs. We examine some of these limitations in the subsections that follow.

### 4.2.3 Parallel Composition

Parallel composition can be viewed as a generalization of the SPMD programming model in which different parts of a computer execute different programs. (It can also be thought of as a special case of concurrent composition in which concurrently executing tasks are required to execute on disjoint sets of processors.) A parallel composition specifies which program components are to execute in which parts of the computer and how these components are to exchange data.

In principle, any program expressed as a parallel composition can be converted to a sequential composition that interleaves the execution of the various program components appropriately. However, the use of parallel composition can enhance scalability and locality. For example, if two program components (such as the atmosphere and ocean model considered in the preceding section) can execute concurrently, then mapping them to disjoint sets of processors increases scalability by providing additional opportunities for parallel execution. If locality increases with granularity, then this parallel composition can also make more efficient use of cache, memory, and communication bandwidth than can a sequential composition of the same components. Parallel composition can also decrease total memory requirements by reducing the amount of code and data replicated on every processor.

```
// Declare virtual processor grid of size P×Q.
LaMatrix<pid> Procgrid(P,Q);

// Define distribution on Procgrid
LaSBSDecomp D(Procgrid, r);

// Create three distributed arrays using distribution D
LaSBSDistGenMat<double> A(M, N, D);
LaSBSDistGenMat<double> B(M, nb, D);
LaSBSDistGenMat<double> X(M, nb, D);

// Initialize input arrays
Initialize(A,B);

// Invoke solver to solve A.X=B
LaSolve(A, X, B);
```

**Program 4.1**    Example C++ code to invoke routines from a C++ version of ScaLAPACK called ScaLAPACK++. This code fragment creates three distributed arrays and applies a solver to solve A.X=B. The distributed arrays are declared to have a square block distribution (SBD) in which $r = c$. The array A has size M×N; the arrays B and X have size M × nb.

## 4.2.4  Concurrent Composition

Concurrent composition is the most general form of composition that we consider. A concurrent composition specifies the program components that are to execute concurrently, producer/consumer relationships between components, and the mapping of components to processors. Components then execute in a data-driven manner, meaning that they can be executed if the data that they require from other components are available. These ideas should be familiar from the discussion of the task/channel programming model in Chapter 1. In the terms of that model, a concurrent composition specifies a set of tasks, a set of channels connecting these tasks, and a mapping of tasks to processors.

Concurrent composition has both advantages and disadvantages relative to sequential and parallel composition. One important advantage is that it can facilitate information hiding and hence the development of modular programs. This is because the interfaces in a concurrent composition consist entirely of the channels connecting the various components. Internal implementation details concerning code, data structures, concurrency, and communication are hidden. Hence, program components can be designed and developed in isolation even when they need to execute on the same processors.

Concurrent composition can also simplify design by allowing decisions concerned with mapping and scheduling to be delayed or even avoided altogether. Because the semantics of a program specified by using concurrent composition are independent of how program components are mapped to processors, mapping decisions can be delayed until late in the design process, as recommended in Chapter 2. Because the execution schedule

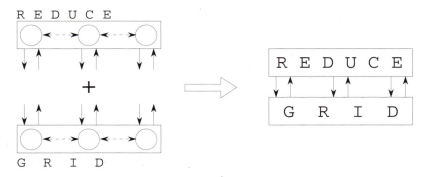

**Figure 4.3**  A finite difference program can be structured as a concurrent composition of `reduce` and `grid` components. The first of these components is designed to perform reductions, while the second performs finite difference computation. An array of channels defines the interface between the two components, which encapsulate internal task and channel structures. The two components may execute on the same or different processors.

is determined by the availability of data, execution order need not be specified explicitly by the programmer.

A disadvantage of concurrent composition in some environments is the cost of a data-driven execution model. While compilers and runtime systems can do much to reduce costs incurred when switching between tasks, these costs can be significant if task switches occur frequently.

---

**EXAMPLE 4.2** (Finite Difference Problem)    Figure 4.3 shows how the finite difference program can be constructed as a concurrent composition of `grid` and `reduce` components. The `grid` module might create a set of tasks specified as follows. The arguments `to_reduce` and `from_reduce` are ports referencing channels that can be used to send data to and receive data from the `reduce` module, respectively.

```
procedure grid(to_reduce, from_reduce)
begin
   while(not done) do                    ! Repeat for each step
      exchange_with_neighbors(grid)
      compute(grid, localmax)            ! Local computation
      send(to_reduce, localmax)          ! Dispatch request for reduction
      other_computation(grid)            ! More local computation
      receive(from_reduce, globmax)      ! Receive reduced value
      if(globmax < threshold) done = true
   enddo
end
```

At each step, this code performs some computation before sending a message requesting a reduction operation, and then performs other computation before receiving the result. The other computation can be overlapped with the communication required for the reduction.

---

### 4.2.5 Design Rules

We conclude this section with a set of design rules that can be used to determine how to compose modules and which sorts of interfaces to design.

1. Design modules to handle multiple data distributions. This feature can increase their reusability.
2. Incorporate data distribution information in data structures rather than in module interfaces. This approach simplifies interfaces and maximizes opportunities for code reuse.
3. Use sequential composition when designing for an SPMD programming system such as HPF or MPI.
4. Consider sequential composition when program components cannot execute concurrently or need to share a lot of data.
5. Consider concurrent composition if program components can execute concurrently, communication costs are high, and communication/computation overlap is possible.
6. Consider parallel composition if memory is at a premium or if intracomponent communication costs are greater than intercomponent communication costs.

## 4.3  Performance Analysis

When composing components to form programs, we also need to consider how to compose their performance models. For example, consider a program that combines two components $a$ and $b$ with performance models as follows:

$$T^a = T^a_{comp} + T^a_{comm} + T^a_{idle}$$
$$T^b = T^b_{comp} + T^b_{comm} + T^b_{idle}.$$

In the case of a sequential composition of $a$ and $b$ that does not require data redistribution, a performance model for the resulting program may sometimes be obtained simply by summing the components of $T^a$ and $T^b$:

$$T^{a+b} = T^a + T^b$$
$$= T^a_{comp} + T^b_{comp} + T^a_{comm} + T^b_{comm} + T^a_{idle} + T^b_{idle}.$$

In practice, the performance analysis of programs constructed from multiple modules is often complicated by the following factors. Fortunately, these complications can be accounted for by using the modeling techniques of Chapter 3.

*Increased computation.* Data transfer between modules can require computation, thereby increasing total computation costs. Less frequently, the merging of two modules will allow us to reduce computation costs by eliminating operations that are common to both components.

*Reduced idle time.* Recall that idle time represents time spent doing no useful work, either because a processor has completed its part of a computation early or because the processor is waiting for data. Idle time can be reduced in concurrent compositions if computation or communication in one module can proceed when other modules mapped to the same processors are idle.

*Increased communication.* Composition often introduces a need for additional communication. In sequential composition, communication may be required to redistribute data structures at component boundaries. In parallel composition, communication is required to move data between modules executing on different processors.

*Increased granularity.* Parallel composition tends to increase computation and communication granularity within composed components, because each executes within a subset of available processors. This effect can improve overall performance.

*Load imbalances.* Parallel composition can increase idle time if the computational resources allocated to different components do not allow the components to execute at equal rates. In this situation, one module will complete some phase of a computation before another and must then remain idle until the other module provides the data required to continue execution. This is a variant of the load-balancing problem discussed in Chapter 2.

## 4.4 Case Study: Convolution

In the remainder of this chapter, we apply the modular design techniques discussed in preceding sections in three case studies. We start with an example from image processing, which we use to study design tradeoffs that can arise when constructing parallel programs from several components. We consider the problem of applying a series of *convolution* operations to a sequence of images. Images, represented as arrays of size $N \times N$, are input in pairs on streams $A$ and $B$; convolution generates a new array of the same size that is output on stream $C$ (Figure 4.4). A single convolution operation involves the transformation of two input arrays using independent two-dimensional fast Fourier transforms (2-D FFTs), a pointwise multiplication of the two transformed arrays, and the transformation of the resulting array using an inverse 2-D FFT, thereby generating an output array. A 2-D FFT performs 1-D FFTs first on each row and then on each column of an array. A 1-D Fourier transform, $Y = \{y_k\}$, of a sequence of $N$ values, $X = \{x_j\}$, is given by

$$y_k = \sum_{j=0}^{N-1} x_j e^{2 \ \mathrm{i} jk/N},$$

where $\mathrm{i} = \sqrt{-1}$. The FFT exploits symmetry to perform this computation in $\log N$ steps, each involving $\mathcal{O}(N)$ operations.

### 4.4.1 Components

We first consider the three components from which the convolution algorithm is constructed: forward 2-D FFT, multiplication, and inverse 2-D FFT. The pointwise multiplication is the simplest: Its communication requirements are zero as long as the arrays on which it operates have the same data distribution.

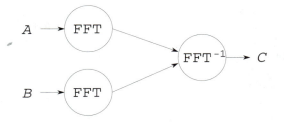

**Figure 4.4**  Dataflow diagram for an image-processing pipeline. Two streams of images, *A* and *B*, are passed through FFT modules and then into an inverse FFT module, which first multiplies them and then applies an inverse FFT.

A variety of parallel algorithms are possible for the forward and inverse 2-D FFTs. A fine-grained algorithm can exploit concurrency within the 1-D FFTs performed on individual rows and columns of the input array, at the cost of considerable communication. A more coarse-grained algorithm performs independent 1-D FFTs in parallel, thereby avoiding a need for communication within the 1-D FFTs, but requiring communication when moving from a row-based to a column-based decomposition. We consider two algorithms based on the latter strategy. The first processes the input image stream sequentially, performing row FFTs and then column FFTs on each image in turn. The second algorithm pipelines the image stream, performing column FFTs for one image in parallel with the row FFTs for the next (Figure 4.5). These two algorithms are in effect sequential and parallel compositions, respectively, of code fragments that perform 1-D FFTs on the rows and columns of a two-dimensional array.

The first parallel algorithm is termed the *transpose* algorithm, since it performs a series of one-dimensional transforms on *P* processors while the array is partitioned in one dimension, then transposes the array and performs transforms in the second dimension using the same processors. The transpose operation requires that each processor send one message of size $N^2/P^2$ to each of the $P-1$ other processors. Hence, total communication costs summed over *P* processors are

$$T_{\text{transpose fft}} = t_s P(P-1) + t_w N^2 \frac{P-1}{P}. \tag{4.1}$$

The second algorithm is termed the *pipeline* algorithm, since it partitions processors into two sets of size $P/2$ which perform FFTs on rows and columns, respectively. Each processor in the first set must communicate with each processor in the other set, for a total of $P^2/4$ messages. The entire array is communicated. Hence, total communication costs are

$$T_{\text{pipeline fft}} = t_s \frac{P^2}{4} + t_w N^2. \tag{4.2}$$

Notice that communication costs are not necessarily distributed equally among processors in the second algorithm, since the sending and receiving processors form distinct

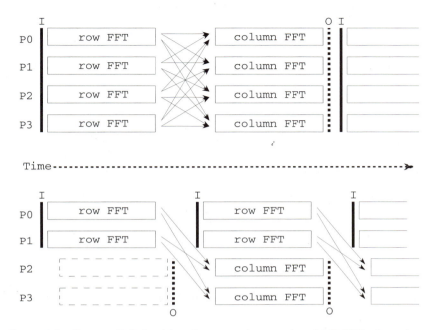

**Figure 4.5**   Two parallel algorithms for computing a series of 2-D FFTs. In each case, the activity on each of four processors (P0–3) is shown over time, with arrows denoting communication and I and O denoting input and output operations. The algorithm illustrated in the upper part of the figure is a sequential composition of program components that perform 1-D FFTs, first on rows and then on columns of each input 2-D array; all-to-all communication is required to transpose the array after performing row FFTs and before performing column FFTs. In the second algorithm, data flow from a first set of processors performing row FFTs (P0, P1) to a second set performing column FFTs (P2, P3). Communication is required to move data from P0 and P1 to P2 and P3.

groups. Nevertheless, Equations 4.1 and 4.2 give a rough idea of the relative performance of the two algorithms. The second algorithm sends significantly fewer messages and hence should be more efficient in situations in which message startup costs are dominant, for example, when $N$ and/or $t_w$ are small or when $P$ or $t_s$ are large. On the other hand, the first algorithm probably incurs lower data transfer costs and hence may be superior in other situations.

### 4.4.2   Composing Components

Having designed two alternative algorithms for the 2-D FFT, we now consider the parallel convolution algorithm proper. Its four components—two parallel 2-D FFTs, one matrix multiplication, and one inverse 2-D FFT(Figure 4.4)—can be combined using either sequential or parallel composition. If sequential composition is used, the parallel convolution algorithm can be represented as follows, with the fft and fft$^{-1}$ calls invoking the transpose 2-D parallel FFT.

```
for each image
    A' = fft(A)
    B' = fft(B)
    C' = A'.B'
    C = fft⁻¹(C')
endfor
```

If the input to this algorithm is decomposed appropriately (in one dimension, by rows), then because each FFT involves a transpose, total communication requirements are three times the cost of a single transpose:

$$T_{\text{sequential/transpose}} = 3 \left( t_s P(P-1) + t_w N^2 \frac{P-1}{P} \right).$$

Notice that because the forward FFT operates first on rows and then on columns, the inverse FFT must operate first on columns and then on rows, so as to avoid the need for an additional transpose operation between the forward and inverse FFTs.

If parallel composition is used, the three FFTs execute concurrently, each on one third of the available processors. (Because the multiplication involves $\mathcal{O}(N^2)$ rather than $\mathcal{O}(N^2 \log N)$ operations, we regard it as insignificant and compose it sequentially with the inverse FFT.) Communication costing $2(t_s(P/3) + t_w N^2)$ is required to move data from the processors handling the forward FFTs to the processors handling the inverse FFT.

The 2-D FFTs within the parallel composition can be implemented by using either the transpose or pipeline algorithms, yielding two algorithm variants. Costs are as specified by Equations 4.1 and 4.2, except that each algorithm is executed three times, with $P/3$ rather than $P$ processors involved in each execution. Combining these costs with the cost of the data movement between components, we obtain the following models.

$$T_{\text{parallel/transpose}} = t_s \left( P \left( \frac{P}{3} - 1 \right) + 2\frac{P}{3} \right) + t_w N^2 \left( 3\frac{P/3 - 1}{P/3} + 2 \right)$$

$$T_{\text{parallel/pipeline}} = t_s \left( \frac{P^2}{12} + 2\frac{P}{3} \right) + t_w N^2 (3 + 2).$$

The results of this brief analysis are summarized in Table 4.1. We see that the second and third algorithms perform fewer message startups but send more data. Hence, they can be expected to be more efficient on smaller problems and larger numbers of processors. This result can be confirmed experimentally, as illustrated in Figure 4.6. A flexible parallel program might incorporate all three algorithms and select the appropriate alternative at runtime. Of course, a programming tool that supports only sequential composition will allow only the first algorithm to be used.

**Table 4.1**   Approximate total message counts and data volumes for three parallel convolution algorithms, summed over $P$ processors and assuming that $P$ is reasonably large.

| Convolution | 2-D FFT | Messages | Data Volume |
|---|---|---|---|
| Sequential | Transpose | $3P^2$ | $3N^2$ |
| Parallel | Transpose | $(1/3)P^2$ | $5N^2$ |
| Parallel | Pipeline | $(1/12)P^2$ | $5N^2$ |

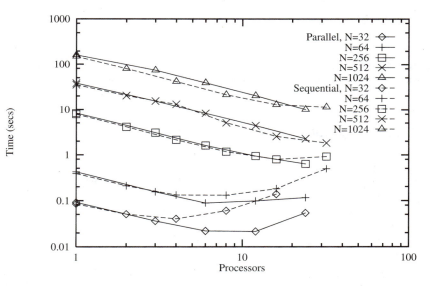

**Figure 4.6**   Performance of the sequential/transpose (Sequential) and parallel/transpose (Parallel) convolution algorithms on an IBM SP computer for different problem sizes and numbers of processors. The latter algorithm is more efficient for smaller problems and larger numbers of processors.

### 4.4.3   Convolution Problem Summary

The convolution problem illustrates the design tradeoffs that can arise when constructing even relatively simple parallel programs. These tradeoffs can arise at multiple levels. First, we must identify candidate parallel algorithms for the component modules: in this case, the 2-D FFT. Then, we must decide how to compose these building blocks so as to construct a complete parallel algorithm. Aspects of the complete design in turn influence the techniques used within components, requiring, for example, that we operate on columns before rows in the inverse FFT. The performance analysis must take into account all these design decisions.

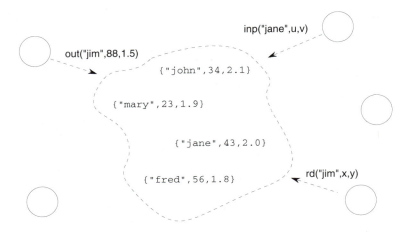

**Figure 4.7**  A tuple space, here used to contain personnel data. Tasks can generate asynchronous requests to read (`rd`), remove (`inp`), and add (`out`) tuples.

## 4.5  Case Study: Tuple Space

In the second case study, we illustrate how concurrent composition allows us to define reusable program components that support asynchronous operations on distributed sets. Various types of set can be defined, each distinguished by the particular operations that it supports. Here, we consider the example of the *tuple space*, which forms the basis for the Linda parallel programming language.

A tuple space is a collection of *tuples*—terms with a key and zero or more arguments. Five operations are supported: insert (`out`), blocking read (`rd`), nonblocking read (`rdp`), blocking read and delete (`in`), and nonblocking read and delete (`inp`). An element can be updated by first deleting it and then reinserting a modified version of it. The insert operation provides a key and values for a new tuple's arguments, while the read and the read/delete operations specify the key and arity (number of arguments) of the tuple that is to be retrieved. Duplicate tuples are supported, so the element retrieved by a read or delete operation is not necessarily uniquely determined by the key and arity provided. The predicate operations `inp` and `outp` are guaranteed to locate a matching tuple *if and only if* it can be shown that a matching tuple must have been added to tuple space before the request was generated and that this tuple could not have been removed before the request was processed. Figure 4.7 shows the tuple space in action.

The tuple space abstraction is a good candidate for encapsulation in a module. It is a useful structure with a well-defined interface and hence is both likely to be reused and easy to modularize. We may also wish to modify its implementation in order to optimize performance on different parallel computers. Hence, we define a tuple space module suitable for concurrent composition. This encapsulates the representation of the tuple space and provides an interface comprising an array of channels on which can be sent messages representing the various types of request.

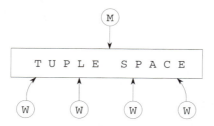

**Figure 4.8** A database search program constructed by the concurrent composition of a tuple space module, a manager task, and multiple worker tasks.

### 4.5.1 Application

We first illustrate the use of the tuple space module by showing how it can be used to implement a database search problem. We are given a file containing a set of search data, a target, and a routine that computes a numeric score for a single datum/target pair. We are required to identify the search datum that yields the highest score. This problem is prototypical of many database search problems. For example, the target may be a new genetic sequence and the database a collection of such sequences; in this case, a score is computed by a dynamic programming computation and reveals the degree to which two sequences are "related." Alternatively, the target may be a description of a physical process and the database a collection of alternative parameter values; a score is then obtained by simulating the process using a set of parameter values.

A straightforward solution to this programming problem is to create a single manager and a large number of workers, with all tasks having access to a shared tuple space (Figure 4.8). The logic executed by the manager and workers is summarized in Program 4.2. The manager makes a series of out requests to place the search data in the tuple space and then performs in operations to retrieve the results generated by workers. When all results have been retrieved, it signals the workers to terminate by placing stop tuples into tuple space, a technique known as a "poison pill." Each worker repeatedly removes a search datum from tuple space, compares it with the target, and puts the resulting score back in tuple space. Notice that this was essentially the technique used to parallelize the parameter study problem in Section 1.4.4. However, here we use a standard module (tuple space) in our solution—a good example of code reuse.

Notice that, because an in request blocks until a corresponding out request is processed by the tuple space, the order in which requests are generated by the manager and workers does not affect the result computed. In particular, workers can "run ahead" of the manager, generating in requests for which there are not yet any matching tuples.

### 4.5.2 Implementation

A variety of implementation strategies can be pursued for the tuple space module (Figure 4.9). One simple, although nonscalable, approach is to encapsulate the tuple space in a single task that maintains a set of tuples and a set of pending rd requests. Both sets can be represented by using hash tables. A hash function is applied to the key supplied with an

```
procedure manager
begin
  count = 0
  until end-of-file do
    read datum from file
    OUT("datum",datum)
    count = count+1
  enddo
  best = 0.0
  for i = 1 to count
    IN("score",value)
    if value > best then best = value
  endfor
  for i = 1 to numworkers
    OUT("datum","stop")
  endfor
end

procedure worker
begin
  IN("datum",datum)
  until datum = "stop" do
    value = compare(datum,target)
    OUT("score",value)
    IN("datum",datum)
  enddo
end
```

**Program 4.2**   Pseudo-code for master and worker tasks in a tuple-space solution to the database search problem.

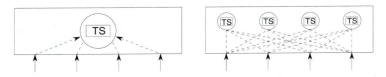

**Figure 4.9**   Two alternative implementation strategies for a tuple space module. The structure on the left uses a central server, while the structure on the right distributes the tuple space among multiple tasks using a hash function. Both structures provide the same interface, an array of channels.

out, rd, etc., operation, and the value returned is used to identify the hash bucket in which the associated element is stored.

The hashing approach is easily adapted to obtain a scalable parallel implementation. The first few bits of the hash value are used to determine the processor on which an item is located; the rest of the hash value locates the item within that processor. This strategy has the desirable property that no tuple space operation requires more than two communications: one to forward the request to the task in which the relevant tuple is located, and one to return a result. It also has the important attributes of being both highly concurrent and well balanced: if requests are generated in a distributed fashion and the hash function yields a balanced mapping of keys to processors, then $\mathcal{O}(P)$ accesses can proceed concurrently on $P$ processors.

## 4.6 Case Study: Matrix Multiplication

In our third case study, we use the example of matrix-matrix multiplication to illustrate issues that arise when developing data distribution neutral libraries. In particular, we consider the problem of developing a library to compute $C = A.B$, where $A$, $B$, and $C$ are dense matrices of size $N \times N$. (A *dense matrix* is a matrix in which most of the entries are nonzero.) This matrix-matrix multiplication involves $\mathcal{O}(N^3)$ operations, since for each element $C_{ij}$ of $C$, we must compute

$$C_{ij} = \sum_{k=0}^{N-1} A_{ik}.B_{kj}.$$

We wish a library that will allow each of the arrays $A$, $B$, and $C$ to be distributed over $P$ tasks in one of three ways: blocked by row, blocked by column, or blocked by row and column. This library may be defined with a subroutine interface suitable for sequential composition in an SPMD program or with a channel interface suitable for parallel or concurrent composition. The basic algorithmic issue remains the same: Does the library need to incorporate different algorithms for different distributions of $A$, $B$, and $C$, or should incoming data structures be converted to a standard distribution before calling a single algorithm?

### 4.6.1 Parallel Matrix-Matrix Multiplication

We start by examining algorithms for various distributions of $A$, $B$, and $C$. We first consider a one-dimensional, columnwise decomposition in which each task encapsulates corresponding columns from $A$, $B$, and $C$. One parallel algorithm makes each task responsible for all computation associated with its $C_{ij}$. As shown in Figure 4.10, each task requires all of matrix $A$ in order to compute its $C_{ij}$. $N^2/P$ data are required from each of $P - 1$ other tasks, giving the following per-processor communication cost:

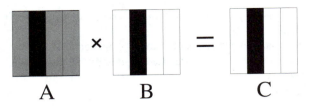

**Figure 4.10**  Matrix-matrix multiplication $A.B = C$ with matrices $A$, $B$, and $C$ decomposed in one dimension. The components of $A$, $B$, and $C$ allocated to a single task are shaded black. During execution, this task requires all of matrix $A$ (shown shaded gray).

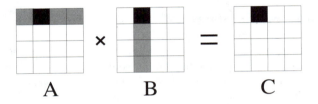

**Figure 4.11**  Matrix-matrix multiplication $A.B = C$ with matrices $A$, $B$, and $C$ decomposed in two dimensions. The components of $A$, $B$, and $C$ allocated to a single task are shaded black. During execution, this task requires corresponding rows and columns of matrix $A$ and $B$, respectively (shown shaded gray).

$$T_{\text{matrix-matrix 1d}} = (P - 1)\left(t_s + t_w\frac{N^2}{P}\right)$$

$$\approx t_s P + t_w N^2.$$

(4.3)

Note that as each task performs $\mathcal{O}(N^3/P)$ computation, if $N \approx P$, then the algorithm will have to transfer roughly one word of data for each multiplication and addition performed. Hence, the algorithm can be expected to be efficient only when $N$ is much larger than $P$ or the cost of computation is much larger than $t_w$.

Next, we consider a two-dimensional decomposition of $A$, $B$, and $C$. As in the one-dimensional algorithm, we assume that a task encapsulates corresponding elements of $A$, $B$, and $C$ and that each task is responsible for all computation associated with its $C_{ij}$. The computation of a single element $C_{ij}$ requires an entire row $A_{i*}$ and column $B_{*j}$ of $A$ and $B$, respectively. Hence, as shown in Figure 4.11, the computation performed within a single task requires the $A$ and $B$ submatrices allocated to tasks in the same row and column, respectively. This is a total of $\mathcal{O}(N^2/\sqrt{P})$ data, considerably less than in the one-dimensional algorithm.

To complete the second parallel algorithm, we need to design a strategy for com-

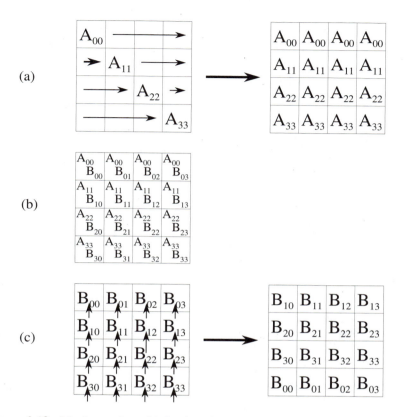

**Figure 4.12** Matrix-matrix multiplication algorithm based on two-dimensional decompositions. Each step involves three stages: (a) an $A$ submatrix is broadcast to other tasks in the same row; (b) local computation is performed; and (c) the $B$ submatrix is rotated upwards within each column.

municating the submatrices between tasks. One approach is for each task to execute the following logic (Figure 4.12):

```
set B' = B_local
for j=0 to √P − 2
    in each row i, the [(i + j) mod √P]th task broadcasts
        A' = A_local to the other tasks in the row
    accumulate A'.B'
    send B' to upward neighbor
endfor
```

Each of the $\sqrt{P} - 1$ steps in this algorithm involves a broadcast to $\sqrt{P} - 1$ tasks (for $A'$) and a nearest-neighbor communication (for $B'$). Both communications involve $N^2/P$ data. Because the broadcast can be accomplished in $\log \sqrt{P}$ steps using a tree structure,

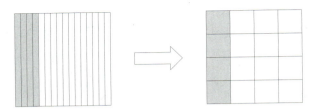

**Figure 4.13**   Reorganizing from a one-dimensional to a one-dimensional decomposition of a square matrix when $P = 16$. Shading indicates one set of four tasks that must exchange data during the reorganization.

the per-processor communication cost is

$$
\begin{aligned}
T_{\text{matrix-matrix 2d}} &= (\sqrt{P} - 1)\left(\frac{\log P}{2} + 1\right)\left(t_s + t_w \frac{N^2}{P}\right) \\
&\approx t_s \frac{\sqrt{P}\log P}{2} + t_w N^2 \frac{\log P}{2\sqrt{P}}.
\end{aligned}
\tag{4.4}
$$

Notice that because every task in each row must serve as the root of a broadcast tree, the total communication structure required for this algorithm combines a hypercube (butterfly) structure within each row of the two-dimensional task mesh and a ring within each column.

## 4.6.2   Redistribution Costs

Comparing Equations 4.3 with 4.4, we see that the two-dimensional decomposition yields the more efficient parallel algorithm. Does this mean that our parallel library should convert input arrays decomposed in one dimension to a two-dimensional decomposition before performing the matrix multiplication? To answer this question, we need to know the cost of the reorganization. The communication costs associated with the reorganization of a single array are as follows; each task exchanges data with $\sqrt{P} - 1$ other tasks, with each message having size $N^2/(P\sqrt{P})$ (Figure 4.13):

$$
\begin{aligned}
T_{\text{reorg 1d to 2d}} &= (\sqrt{P} - 1)\left(t_s + t_w \frac{N^2}{P\sqrt{P}}\right) \\
&\approx t_s \sqrt{P} + t_w \frac{N^2}{P}.
\end{aligned}
$$

If $A$, $B$, and $C$ are all decomposed in one dimension, we must perform three such conversions. This gives a worst-case total communication cost for reorganization and multiplication using the two-dimensional algorithm of

$$
T_{\text{mm 2d and reorg}} \approx t_s \sqrt{P}\left(3 + \frac{\log P}{2}\right) + t_w N^2\left(\frac{3}{P} + \frac{\log P}{2\sqrt{P}}\right).
$$

Comparing this expression with Equation 4.3, we see that the algorithm that reorganizes data structures to a 2-D decomposition before performing the multiplication will be more efficient than an algorithm that does not, when

$$t_s P + t_w N^2 > t_s \sqrt{P} \left( 3 + \frac{\log P}{2} \right) + t_w N^2 \left( \frac{3}{P} + \frac{\log P}{2\sqrt{P}} \right).$$

This condition holds for all except small $P$. Hence, we conclude that our parallel matrix multiply library should convert to a two-dimensional decomposition before performing computation, as follows.

```
procedure matrix_multiply(A, B, C)
begin
    if 1d_distributed(A) then reorg_to_2d(A)
    if 1d_distributed(B) then reorg_to_2d(B)
    2d_matrix_multiply(A, B, C)
    if 1d_distributed(C) then reorg_to_1d(C)
end
```

### 4.6.3 A Systolic Algorithm

We still have not said the last word about the ideal data distribution for matrix-matrix multiplication! An alternative algorithm allows the broadcast operations used in the preceding algorithm to be replaced with regular, nearest-neighbor ("systolic") communications. However, data must be distributed among tasks in a different fashion. As before, we assume that $A$, $B$, and $C$ are decomposed into $\sqrt{P} \times \sqrt{P}$ submatrices. Each task $(i, j)$ contains submatrices $A_{jk}$, $B_{ki}$, and $C_{ji}$, where $k = [(2\sqrt{P} - 1 - i - j) \bmod \sqrt{P}]$. This data layout is illustrated in Figure 4.14.

Computation proceeds in $\sqrt{P}$ steps. In each step, contributions to $C$ are accumulated in each task, after which values of $A$ move down and values of $B$ move right. The entire computation requires a total of $2(\sqrt{P} - 1)$ messages per task, each of size $N^2/P$, for a cost of

$$T_{\text{matrix}-\text{matrix systolic}} = 2(\sqrt{P} - 1) \left( t_s + t_w \frac{N^2}{P} \right).$$

Communication costs are less by a factor of about $(\log P)/4$ than in Equation 4.4. Again, this benefit must be weighed against the cost of converting matrices $A$, $B$, and $C$ into the layout required by this algorithm. This analysis is left as an exercise.

## 4.7 Summary

Modular design techniques are fundamental to good software engineering practice. In this chapter, we have shown how these techniques can be applied to the design of parallel programs. The major points are as follows:

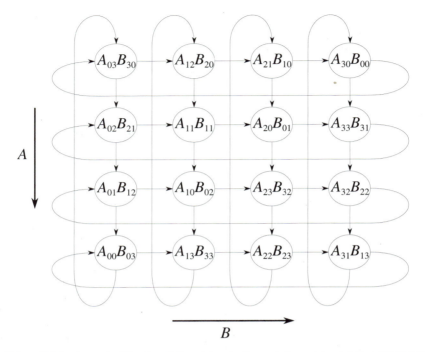

**Figure 4.14**   Layout of the *A* and *B* matrices in the systolic matrix-matrix multiplication algorithm for a 4 × 4 task mesh. The arrows show the direction of data movement during execution of the systolic algorithm.

1. The central tenets of modular design, such as simple interfaces and information hiding, apply in parallel programming just as in sequential programming.
2. Data distribution is an important implementation detail that, if abstracted out of a module interface, can facilitate code reuse.
3. It is useful to distinguish between sequential, parallel, and concurrent composition of parallel modules. Sequential composition is simple but inflexible. Parallel composition can be used to improve locality and scalability. Concurrent composition is the most general form.
4. Performance models can be composed, but care must be taken to account for communication costs at interfaces, overlapping of computation and communication, and other factors.

In Part II, we show how the modular design techniques introduced in this chapter can be applied when developing programs using a range of parallel programming tools.

# Exercises

1. Discuss ways in which modular design techniques are used in the design of an automobile engine, house, or suspension bridge.

2. Identify ways in which modularity ideas might apply to the management of an orchestra, educational institution, or company.

3. Develop analytic models for the maximum throughput (in requests processed per second) supported by the centralized and distributed tuple space implementations outlined in Section 4.5.

4. Using a language that supports concurrent composition, such as CC++ or Fortran M, implement centralized and distributed tuple space modules. Study the performance of these modules in a simple parameter study problem, and relate performance to the models of Exercise 3.

5. Discuss ways in which the database search algorithm of Section 4.5 could be modified to avoid the central bottleneck inherent in a single manager.

6. An alternative parallel algorithm for the 2-D FFT considered in Section 4.4.1 assumes a fixed 2-D decomposition of data structures; hence, communication is required within each 1-D FFT. Use a performance model to contrast this algorithm with those described in the text. Assume that the communication costs for a 1-D FFT algorithm operating on $N$ points on $P$ processors are $\log P(t_s + t_w(N/P))$.

7. A problem comprises two components, $A$ and $B$. $A$ can be solved in 1000 seconds on computer $C1$ and in 5000 seconds on computer $C2$; $B$ requires 4000 and 2000 seconds on $C1$ and $C2$, respectively. The two computers are connected by a 1000-km optical fiber link that can transfer data at 100 MB/sec with a latency of 10 msec. The two components can execute concurrently but must transfer 10 MB of data 10,000 times during execution. Is it cheapest (in terms of computational resources consumed) to solve the problem on computer $C1$, on computer $C2$, or on both computers together?

8. A problem similar to that of Exercise 7 is found to use fewer computational resources when run on the two networked computers than on either computer alone. Your public relations office proposes to promote this as an example of superlinear speedup. Do you agree?

9. A climate model consists of an atmosphere and ocean model. At each step, the models both perform a finite difference computation and exchange five 2-D arrays. Develop performance models for two alternative parallel implementations, based on sequential and parallel composition respectively. Discuss the relative performance of the two implementations.

10. Determine the problem size and processor count regimes in which each of the three convolution algorithms described in Example 4.4 would be faster, assuming machine parameters characteristic of (a) a multicomputer and (b) an Ethernet-connected LAN.

11. The performance analysis of the pipelined algorithms considered in Section 4.4 did not take into account idle time incurred when starting up and shutting down pipelines. Refine the performance models to account for these costs. How many images must be processed before efficiency reaches 95 percent of that predicted in the absence of these costs?

12. Execute by hand for $N = P = 4$ the matrix multiplication algorithm based on a 2-D decomposition described in Section 4.6.1.

13. A simpler variant of the multiplication algorithm for matrices decomposed in two dimensions uses a ring rather than a tree for the broadcast operations. Use performance models to compare the two algorithm variants. (Note that a broadcast can be performed on a $P$-node bidirectional ring in approximately $P/2$ steps.)

14. Extend the analysis and comparison of Exercise 13 to account for competition for bandwidth in a 2-D mesh architecture.

15. Develop a performance model for the systolic matrix multiplication algorithm of Section 4.6, and use this to identify regimes in which this algorithm is faster than the simpler algorithm based on regular 2-D decompositions. Account for data reorganization costs.

16. Another matrix multiplication algorithm collects the matrices that are to be multiplied on a single processor. Use performance models to identify regimes in which this algorithm might be competitive. Conduct empirical studies to validate your analytic results.

## Chapter Notes

The merits of modular design are described in landmark papers by Parnas [220, 221, 223] and Wirth [295]. The book by McConnell [198] provides an excellent survey of the software construction process. Booch [40] and Cox and Novobilski [66] provide good introductions to modularity and object-oriented programming. Milner [210], Hoare [154], and Chandy and Misra [54] provide abstract treatments of modularity and program composition in parallel programming. Foster and Taylor [107] explore the use of modular design techniques in concurrent logic programming. Mead and Conway [199] and Ullman [286] provide introductions to VLSI design, another area in which modular design techniques are used extensively.

Gropp and Smith emphasize the importance of data distribution neutrality in the design of SPMD libraries [127]. This principle is applied extensively in their Portable Extensible Tools for Scientific computing (PETSc) package. ScaLAPACK is described by Choi, Dongarra, and Walker [59], Dongarra and Walker [85], and Dongarra, van de Geign, and Walker [84]. Dongarra, Pozo, and Walker [83] describe the C++ interface. Other parallel SPMD libraries include Lemke and Quinlan's [188] P++ library for grid applications, Skjellum's [262] Multicomputer Toolbox, and Thinking Machine's [283] CMSSL. Skjellum et al. [265] discuss the use of the MPI message-passing standard to develop parallel libraries. A variety of other issues relating to parallel SPMD libraries are discussed in workshop proceedings edited by Skjellum [263, 264].

The tuple space module discussed in Section 4.5 forms the basis for the Linda parallel programming model of Carriero and Gelernter [47, 48, 49]. The tuple space used in Linda is more general than that described here. In particular, any field can be used as a key when retrieving tuples. The tuple space solution to the database search problem is based on a Linda program in [48]. The convolution problem and the performance results in Section 4.4 are taken from a paper by Foster et al. [101]. Foster and Worley [110] describe parallel algorithms for the fast Fourier transform.

The online version provides access here to additional information on modular programming, parallel program design, and parallel libraries.

# Tools

The second part of this book comprises five chapters that deal with the implementation of parallel programs. In parallel as in sequential programming, there are many different languages and programming tools, each suitable for different classes of problem. Because it would be neither feasible nor useful to describe them all, we restrict our attention to four systems—Compositional C++ (CC++), Fortran M (FM), High Performance Fortran (HPF), and the Message Passing Interface (MPI)—and explain how each can be used to implement designs developed using the techniques of Part I. We also describe, in Chapter 9, tools that aid in the collection and analysis of performance data.

Except where material is explicitly cross-referenced, each chapter in Part II is self-contained. Hence, it is quite feasible to base a practical study of parallel programming on just one of the four tools described here. However, while each of these tools is of broad utility, each also is most appropriate for different purposes, and we recommend that you become familiar with several systems.

CC++, described in Chapter 5, is a small set of extensions to C++. These extensions provide the programmer with explicit control over locality, concurrency, communication, and mapping and can be used to build libraries that implement tasks, channels, and other basic parallel programming abstractions. Designs developed using the techniques of Part I are easily expressed as CC++ programs.

FM, described in Chapter 6, is a small set of extensions to Fortran. These extensions provide explicit support for tasks and channels and hence can implement designs developed using the techniques of Part I directly. A distinguishing feature of FM is that programs can be guaranteed to be deterministic, meaning that two executions with the same input will produce the same output.

HPF, described in Chapter 7, is an example of a data-parallel language and has emerged as a de facto standard for scientific and engineering computation. Parallelism is expressed in terms of array operations—statements that apply to many elements of an array at once. Communication operations are inferred by the compiler, and need not be specified by the programmer.

MPI, described in Chapter 8, is a library of standard subroutines for sending and receiving messages and performing collective operations. Like HPF, MPI has emerged as a standard and hence supersedes earlier message-passing libraries such as PARMACS, p4, PVM, and Express.

When building parallel programs, our choice of tool will depend on the nature of the problem to be solved. HPF is particularly appropriate for numeric algorithms based on regular domain decompositions (for example, finite difference computations). CC++ and FM are better suited for applications involving dynamic task creation, irregular communication patterns, heterogeneous and irregular computation structures, and concurrent composition. They can also be used to build data-parallel libraries for regular problems. MPI is a lower-level approach to parallel programming than CC++, FM, or HPF and is particularly appropriate for algorithms with a regular SPMD structure.

CC++, FM, HPF, and MPI represent very different approaches to parallel programming. Nevertheless, we shall see that good design is independent of our choice of implementation language. The design techniques introduced in Part I apply regardless of language. Issues of concurrency, scalability, locality, and modularity must be addressed in any parallel program.

# Compositional C++

In this chapter, we describe Compositional C++ (CC++), a small set of extensions to C++ for parallel programming. CC++ provides constructs for specifying concurrent execution, for managing locality, and for communication. It allows parallel programs to be developed from simpler components using sequential, parallel, and concurrent composition. Hence, algorithms designed using the techniques described in Part I can be translated into CC++ programs in a straightforward manner.

Since the CC++ extensions are simple, we are able in this chapter to provide both a complete language description and a tutorial introduction to important programming techniques. We also provide a brief review of those C++ constructs used in this chapter, so as to make the presentation intelligible to readers familiar with C but not C++. In the process, we show how the language is used to implement various algorithms developed in Part I.

After studying this chapter, you should be able to write simple CC++ programs. You should know how to create tasks; how to implement structured, unstructured, and asynchronous communication patterns; and how to control the mapping of tasks to processors. You should also know both how to write deterministic programs and when it is useful to introduce nondeterministic constructs. Finally, you should understand how CC++ supports the development of modular programs, and you should know how to specify both sequential and parallel composition.

## 5.1 C++ Review

We first review some of the basic C++ constructs used in the rest of this chapter, so as to make subsequent material understandable to readers familiar with C but not C++. Readers familiar with C++ can skip this section.

With a few exceptions, C++ is a pure extension of ANSI C. Most valid ANSI C programs are also valid C++ programs. C++ extends C by adding strong typing and language support for data abstraction and object-oriented programming.

### 5.1.1 Strong Typing and Memory Management

ANSI standard C introduced function prototypes to the C language. A function prototype defines the type of each function argument and the function's return value (the function's *signature*). For example:

167

```
/* A forward declaration to a_function */
int a_function(float b, double c);

/* The definition of a_function */
int a_function(float b, double c) {
   /* Function body */
}
```

C++ requires that function prototypes be provided for all functions before they are used and enforces consistent function use between program files. Thus, it is possible to distinguish between functions that have the same name but different signatures. C++ uses this capability to allow function names to be *overloaded*. That is, more than one function can be defined with the same name; the compiler compares function call arguments with function signatures to determine which version to use.

In C programs, the library routines `malloc` and `free` are used for dynamic memory allocation. C++ defines two additional operators, `new` and `delete`, as illustrated in the following code fragments.

```
struct S {
   /* Structure body */
};

S *sPtr = new S;          /* Allocate instance of S */
delete sPtr;              /* Delete instance of S */

int *iPtr = new int[25];  /* Allocate array of integers */
delete [] iPtr;           /* Delete array of integers */
```

Notice that `new` is given a description of the type of the data object to be allocated; it returns a pointer to dynamically allocated data of that type. The `delete` operator is used to release dynamically allocated storage. The programmer must indicate when an array of objects is being deleted.

### 5.1.2  Classes

The most significant feature that C++ adds to C is the concept of classes. A class can be thought of as a generalization of a C structure. In C, a structure groups together data elements of various types under a single name; in C++, structures can also contain *member functions*. Like data elements of a C structure, member functions of a class can be accessed only through a reference to an object of the appropriate type. In C++, a class defines a scope in which names referring to functions and data can be defined. Classes can be introduced using the C keywords `struct` and `union` or the C++ keyword `class`.

Program 5.1 illustrates various features of the C++ class mechanism. This program defines a class named `Datum` containing a data member x, a member function `get_x`, and two constructor functions. (Notice the C++ single-line comments; anything after a double slash `//` is a comment.) These terms are defined in the following discussion.

The syntax `Datum::get_x()` is used to name a member function `get_x` of `Datum`. This name, called a *quantified name*, specifies that we are referring to a function defined in the scope of `Datum`. If we do not quantify the name, we are defining the *global* function

```
// Define a Datum class
class Datum {
public:
    int get_x();  // Public member functions
    Datum();
    Datum(int);
private:
    int x;          // Private variable
};

// A member function of Datum
int Datum::get_x() { return x; }

// Constructors for Datum
Datum::Datum() { x = 0; }
Datum::Datum(int arg_x) { x = arg_x; }

void test() {
    Datum a_datum;                      // Declare a datum
    Datum another_datum(23);            // Declare a second datum
    Datum *DatumPtr = new Datum(23);    // Allocate third datum
    int val = a_datum.get_x();          // Access x in first datum
    int val1 = DatumPtr->get_x();       // Access x in third datum
    delete DatumPtr;                    // Delete third datum
}
```

**Program 5.1** Example of a C++ class declaration. This code fragment declares a class Datum and defines a member function of this class (Datum::get_x) and two constructor functions (Datum::Datum). The function test illustrates the use of the class.

get_x(), which is a different function. Notice that within the definition of Datum::get_x() we can refer to the data member x directly, because x and get_x are defined in the same scope. We also could incorporate the definition for function get_x directly in the class definition, as follows.

```
public:
    int get_x() { return x; }
    .
    .
    .
```

The two member functions named Datum are *constructor functions* for the Datum class. A constructor has the same name as the class to which it applies and, if defined, is called whenever an object of the appropriate type is created. Constructor functions are used to perform initialization and can be overloaded.

The function test in Program 5.1 creates and uses three Datum objects, two of which are declared in the first two lines in the function body. Notice that the class name Datum can be used directly; in C we would have to write struct Datum. In the third line, the new operator is used to allocate the third Datum object.

Because constructors have been defined for Datum, they will be called whenever Datum objects are created. The constructor with no arguments, called a *default constructor*, is called when a_datum is created, thereby initializing the field x of a_datum to zero. The declaration of another_datum and the new operator both specify an integer argument and hence use the second constructor, thereby initializing the variable x to 23 in these two cases.

Recall that in C, the fields of a structure are accessed by using the dot operator (struct.fieldname), while the fields of a structure accessible via a pointer are accessed with the arrow operator (structptr->fieldname). As illustrated in the function test, these same mechanisms can be used to refer to the member functions of a C++ class.

The C++ class mechanism also supports *protection*. Members of a C++ class can be designated as being either public or private. A public class member can be used without restriction by any program that has a reference to an instance of a class. Public data members can be read or written, and public member functions may be called. In contrast, private members can be accessed only from within the class object. Private data members can be accessed only by a class member function, and private member functions can be called only from within another member function of the class. For example, the variable x in the Datum class is a private variable and hence can be accessed by the member function get_x but cannot be referenced directly as a_datum.x.

### 5.1.3   Inheritance

The final C++ feature described here is inheritance. As in C, a class or structure can be included as a member of another class, hence defining a *has-a* relationship between the two classes. In C++, inheritance is used to create an alternative relationship between classes, an *is-a* relationship. If a class D inherits from class B, then all public members of B are also members of D. We say that D is derived from B, and that D is a derived class while B is a base class. D includes all public members of B and may also include additional members, which are defined in the usual way. We can view D as being a specialized version of a B, hence the *is-a* relationship.

Program 5.2 illustrates the use of inheritance. The syntax for inheritance is to specify a list of base classes after the derived class name. The base class list is separated from the derived class name by a colon. The keywords public and private are associated with the base class names to specify whether the inherited members are to be public or private members of the derived class.

Members of the base class can be redefined in the derived class. For example, in Program 5.2 class D redefines func2. When func2 is called from an object of type B, we access the version of func2 defined in B. If func2 is called from an object of type D, we get the version of func2 defined in D.

In some situations, we may want a base class to call functions that are defined in a derived class. This facility is supported by a C++ mechanism called *virtual functions*. A function declared virtual in a base class can be defined in a derived class. This feature, which allows a programmer to specialize a generic base class for a specific application, is used in Section 5.8.2 to build a reusable parallel library.

```
class B {              // B is a base class
public:
    void base_func1();  // Public member functions, inherited
    void func2();       // by classes derived from B
};

class D : public B {   // D is derived from B
public:
    void func2();       // D redefines func2
};

void test() {
    B b;               // Create instance of B
    D d;               // Create instance of D
    d.base_func1();    // Call base_func1 defined in B
    b.func2();         // Call func2 defined in B
    d.func2();         // Call func2 defined in D
}
```

**Program 5.2** A program illustrating inheritance in C++. The class D is derived from the class B. The function `test` creates instances of these classes and calls the functions that they define.

## 5.2 CC++ Introduction

CC++ is a general-purpose parallel programming language comprising all of C++ plus six new keywords. It is a strict superset of the C++ language in that any valid C or C++ program that does not use a CC++ keyword is also a valid CC++ program. The CC++ extensions implement six basic abstractions:

1. The *processor object* is a mechanism for controlling locality. A computation may comprise one or more processor objects. Within a processor object, sequential C++ code can execute without modification. In particular, it can access local data structures. The keyword `global` identifies a processor object class, and the predefined class `proc_t` controls processor object placement.

2. The *global pointer*, identified by the type modifier `global`, is a mechanism for linking together processor objects. A global pointer must be used to access a data structure or to perform computation (using a remote procedure call, or RPC) in another processor object.

3. The *thread* is a mechanism for specifying concurrent execution. Threads are created independently from processor objects, and more than one thread can execute in a processor object. The `par`, `parfor`, and `spawn` statements create threads.

4. The *sync variable*, specified by the type modifier `sync`, is used to synchronize thread execution.

5. The *atomic function*, specified by the keyword `atomic`, is a mechanism used to control the interleaving of threads executing in the same processor object.

6. *Transfer functions*, with predefined type `CCVoid`, allow arbitrary data structures to be transferred between processor objects as arguments to remote procedure calls.

These abstractions provide the basic mechanisms required to specify concurrency, locality, communication, and mapping.

---

**EXAMPLE 5.1** (Bridge Construction)     Program 5.3 illustrates many CC++ features. It is an implementation of the bridge construction algorithm developed in Example 1.1. The program creates two tasks, `foundry` and `bridge`, and connects them with a channel. The channel is used to communicate a stream of integer values `1..100` from `foundry` to `bridge`, followed by the value –1 to signal termination.

While the concepts of task and channel are not supported directly in CC++, they can be implemented easily by using CC++ mechanisms. Hence, the main program creates two tasks by first using the `new` operator to create two processor objects and then using the `par` construct to create two threads, one per processor object. The two tasks engage in channel communication by invoking functions defined in a `Channel` class, which will be described in Section 5.11. A channel is declared in the main program and passed as an argument to `foundry` and `bridge`. These processes use access functions `get_out_port` and `get_in_port` to obtain pointers to out-port and in-port objects to which can be applied functions `send` and `receive`, respectively.

---

## 5.3 Concurrency

Next, we give a more complete description of CC++. The presentation is loosely structured according to the design methodology of Chapter 2. First, we describe how CC++ programs specify concurrent execution. Then, we explain how CC++ programs specify locality. Next, we explain how to specify various communication structures. Finally, we describe how CC++ programs specify mapping. Along the way, we also address the issues of modularity and determinism.

A CC++ program, like a C++ program, executes initially as a single thread of control (task). However, a CC++ program can use `par`, `parfor`, and `spawn` constructs to create additional threads. A parallel block is distinguished from an ordinary C++ block by the keyword `par`, as follows.

```
par {
        statement1;
        statement2;
        .
        .
        .
        statementN;
    }
```

```
// The Construction class is derived from the ChannelUser class.
global class Construction : public ChannelUser {
public:       // It has two public member functions
    void foundry(Channel, int);
    void bridge(Channel);
};

void Construction::foundry(Channel channel, int cnt) {
    // Extract outport from channel
    OutPort *out = (OutPort *) channel.get_out_port();
    // Send cnt values
    for (int i=1; i<=cnt; i++)
        out->send(i);     // Invoke method in OutPort class
    // Send end-of-channel value
    out->send(-1);
}

void Construction::bridge(Channel channel) {
    int val;
    // Extract inport from channel
    InPort *in = (InPort *) channel.get_in_port();
    // Receive values until end detected
    while ((val = in->receive()) != -1)
        printf("Got value %d\n",val);
}

void main(int argc, char *argv[]) {
    // Create new processor objects for foundry and bridge
    Construction *global foundry_pobj = new Construction;
    Construction *global bridge_pobj  = new Construction;
    // Create a channel
    Channel channel(foundry_pobj, bridge_pobj);
    // Run foundry and bridge, passing channel
    par {
      foundry_pobj->foundry(channel, 100);
      bridge_pobj ->bridge(channel);
    }
}
```

**Program 5.3**  CC++ implementation of bridge construction problem. The Channel class is defined later in the chapter.

A parallel block can include any legal CC++ statement except for variable declarations and statements that result in nonlocal changes in the flow of control, such as `return`.

Statements in a parallel block execute concurrently. For example, the following parallel block creates three concurrent threads: two `workers` and one `master`.

```
par {
    worker();
    worker();
    master();
}
```

A parallel block terminates when all its constituent statements terminate; execution then proceeds to the next executable statement. Thus, in the preceding parallel block, the thread that executed the parallel block proceeds to the next statement only when both the master and the workers have terminated.

A *parallel for-loop* creates multiple threads, all executing the same statements contained in the body of the for-loop. It is identical in form to the for-loop except that the keyword `parfor` replaces `for`. For example, the following code creates ten threads of control, each executing the function `myprocess`.

```
parfor (int i=0; i<10; i++) {
    myprocess(i);
}
```

Only the loop body of the `parfor` executes in parallel. Evaluation of the initialization, test, and update components of the statement follows normal sequential ordering. If the initialization section uses a locally declared variable (for example, `int i`), then each instance of the loop body has its own private copy of that variable.

CC++ parallel constructs can be nested arbitrarily. Hence, the following code creates ten `worker` threads and one `master`.

```
par {
    master();
    parfor (int i=0; i<10; i++)
        worker(i);
}
```

Finally, the `spawn` statement can be used to specify unstructured parallelism. This statement can be applied to a function to create a completely independent thread of control. The parent thread does not wait for the new thread to terminate execution, and cannot receive a return value from the called function. As we shall see in Section 5.10, one use for the `spawn` statement is to provide an efficient implementation of RPCs that do not require a return value.

## 5.4  Locality

In the task/channel programming model of Part I, the concepts of locality and concurrency are linked: a task is both a separate address space and a thread of control. In CC++, these two concepts are separated. Processor objects represent address spaces, and threads represent threads of control. Processor objects can exist independently of threads, and more than one thread can be mapped to a processor object.

### 5.4.1 Processor Objects

A processor object is defined by a C++ class declaration modified by the keyword global. A processor object is identical to a normal C++ class definition in all but two respects:

1. Names of C++ "global" variables and functions (that is, names with file scope) refer to unique objects within different instances of a processor object. Hence, there is no sharing between processor object instances.

2. Private members of a processor object need not be explicitly declared to be private. C++ "global" functions and variables are defined implicitly to be private members of the processor object in which they occur.

Processor object types can be inherited, and the usual C++ protection mechanisms apply, so private functions and data are accessible only from a processor object's member functions or from the member functions of derived objects. Hence, it is the member functions and data declared public that represent the processor object's interface.

For example, the following code from Program 5.3 creates a processor object class Construction with public member functions foundry and bridge. The class ChannelUser is specified as a base class and provides access to channel operations (Section 5.11).

```
global class Construction : public ChannelUser {
public:
    void foundry(Channel, int);
    void bridge(Channel);
};
```

### 5.4.2 Global Pointers

A *processor object* is a unit of locality, that is, an address space within which data accesses are regarded as local and hence cheap. A thread executing in a processor object can access data structures defined or allocated within that processor object directly, by using ordinary C++ pointers.

Processor objects are linked together using *global pointers*. A global pointer is like an ordinary C++ pointer except that it can refer to other processor objects or to data structures contained within other processor objects. It represents data that are potentially nonlocal and hence more expensive to access than data referenced by ordinary C++ pointers.

A global pointer is distinguished by the keyword global. For example:

```
float *global gpf;    // global pointer to a float
char * *global gppc;  // global pointer to pointer of type char
C *global gpC;        // global pointer to an object of type C
```

When the `new` statement is used to create an instance of a processor object, it returns a `global` pointer. For example, the statement

```
Construction *global foundry_pobj = new Construction;
```

from Program 5.3 creates a new processor object of type `Construction` and defines `foundry_pobj` to be a pointer to that object.

### 5.4.3    Thread Placement

By default, a CC++ thread executes in the same processor object as its parent. Computation is placed in another processor object via an RPC. A thread needs only a global pointer to another processor object to be able to invoke any of its public member functions. For example, in the following line from Program 5.3, `bridge_pobj` is a global pointer to the processor object on which the consumer is to execute, and `bridge` is a public member function of that object.

```
bridge_pobj->bridge();
```

Remote procedure calls are discussed in more detail in Section 5.5 below.

A single thread executing in a processor object implements what in Part I we termed a *task*. Many CC++ programs create exactly one thread per processor object, yielding computation structures like those described in Part I. We discuss situations in which it is useful to create more than one thread per processor object in Section 5.7.

---

**EXAMPLE 5.2** (Search I)    Program 5.4 uses processor objects and the `par` construct to implement a prototypical tree-structured computation. The program explores a binary tree recursively in the manner of Algorithm 1.1, creating a task (processor object + thread) for each tree node and returning the total number of leaf nodes that represent solutions. Notice the use of a parallel block to create the threads that search the two subtrees rooted at a nonleaf node. In this simple program, the tree is not represented by an explicit data structure; instead, a process's position in the tree is represented by an integer.

---

## 5.5    Communication

CC++ does not provide low-level primitives for directly sending and receiving data between threads. Instead, threads communicate by operating on shared data structures. For example, one thread may append items to a shared list structure, from which another thread removes items; this implements a form of channel communication. CC++ mechanisms can be used to implement a wide variety of such communication structures.

In this section, we first explain how global pointers are used to communicate data between processor objects. Then, we explain how sync variables and atomic functions are used to provide synchronization and mutual exclusion. Finally, we show how data transfer functions are used to communicate more complex data structures.

```
global class Tree { // Processor object: one member function
public:
    int search(int);
};

int Tree::search(int A) {
    int ls, rs;
    if(leaf(A)) {       // Leaf node: check whether a solution
        if solution(A)
            return(1);
        else
            return(0);
    }
    else {                  // Nonleaf node: explore subtrees
        Tree *global lobj = new Tree;
        Tree *global robj = new Tree;
        par {               // Create processes to search subtrees
            ls = lobj->search(left_child(A));
            rs = robj->search(right_child(A));
        }
        delete(lobj); delete(robj);
        return(ls+rs);
    }
}

void main(int argc, char *argv[]) {
    int total;
    // Create new processor object for search
    Tree *global searcher = new Tree;
    // Initiate search
    total = searcher->search(1);
    printf("There were %d solutions\n",total);
}
```

**Program 5.4** CC++ tree search program. The program uses two parallel constructs. The global keyword declares the processor object Tree and the par construct defines the parallel block that causes the two recursive calls to search to execute concurrently. Notice how two new processor objects (lobj, robj) are created for the recursive calls and then deleted when these calls complete.

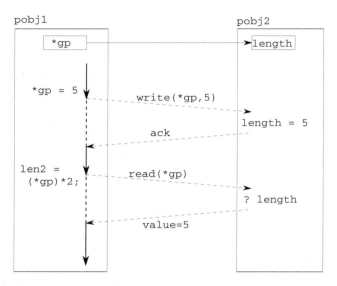

**Figure 5.1**    Remote read and write operations. At the top of the figure, we show a global pointer gp located in processor object pobj1 referencing an integer length in processor object pobj2. The rest of the figure is a timeline depicting the activity in these two processor objects as a thread in pobj1 first reads and then writes length. The thread in pobj1 is shown as a solid line when active and as a dashed line when suspended waiting for a remote operation. The diagonal dashed lines represent communications.

## 5.5.1  Remote Operations

CC++ global pointers are used in the same way as C++ local pointers; the only difference is that we use them to operate on data or to invoke functions that may be located in other processor objects. Hence, the following code fragment first assigns to and then reads from the remote location referenced by the global pointer gp.

```
global int *gp;
int len2;
*gp = 5;
len2 = (*gp) * 2;
```

As illustrated in Figure 5.1, these read and write operations result in communication.

If we invoke a member function of an object referenced by a global pointer, we perform what is called a remote procedure call (RPC). An RPC has the general form

```
<type> *global gp;
result = gp->p( ... )
```

where gp is a global pointer of an arbitrary <type>, p(...) is a call to a function defined in the object referenced by that global pointer, and result is a variable that will be set to the value returned by p(...). An RPC proceeds in three stages:

```
int length;           // Global variable: implicitly private

global class Length {
public:
    int read_len()              { return(length); }
    void write_len(int newval) { length = newval; }
};

// Test program: create and operate on datum objects
void test() {
    int len, len2;
    // Allocate new processor object
    Length *global lp = new Length;
    // Write the private variable length
    lp->write_len(5);
    // Read the private variable length
    len  = lp->read_len();
    len2 = len*2;
}
```

**Program 5.5** A CC++ implementation of a processor object with member functions supporting read and write operations on a private variable `length`, and a procedure `test` that uses these functions.

1. The arguments to the function p(...) are packed into a message, communicated to the remote processor object, and unpacked. The calling thread suspends execution.

2. A new thread is created in the remote processor object to execute the called function.

3. Upon termination of the remote function, the function return value is transferred back to the calling thread, which resumes execution.

Basic integer types (char, short, int, long, and the unsigned variants of these), floats, doubles, and global pointers can be transferred as RPC arguments or return values without any user intervention. Structures, regular pointers, and arrays can be transferred with the aid of transfer functions, to be discussed later in this section.

Program 5.5 uses RPCs to access a variable length located in another processor object; contrast this with the code fragment given at the beginning of this section, in which read and write operations were used for the same purpose. The communication that results is illustrated in Figure 5.2.

## 5.5.2 Synchronization

A producer thread can use an RPC to move data to a processor object in which a consumer thread is executing, hence effecting communication. However, we also require a mechanism for synchronizing the execution of these two threads, so that the consumer does

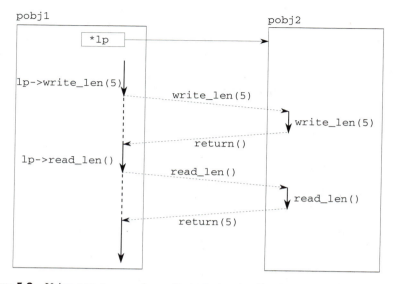

**Figure 5.2**   Using remote procedure calls to read and write a remote variable. At the top of the figure, we show a global pointer `lp` located in processor object `pobj1` referencing processor object `pobj2`. The rest of the figure is a timeline depicting the activity in these two processor objects as a thread in `pobj1` issues RPCs first to read and then to write the remote variable `length`. The thread in `pobj1` is shown as a vertical solid or dashed line when active or suspended, waiting for a remote operation; the diagonal dashed lines represent communications. The solid vertical lines in `pobj2` represent the threads created to execute the remote procedure calls.

not read the data before it is communicated by the producer. In the task/channel model of Part I, synchronization is achieved by making a consumer requiring data from a channel block until a producer makes data available. CC++ uses a different but analogous mechanism, the single assignment or *sync* variable (Figure 5.3). A sync variable is identified by the type modifier `sync`, which indicates that the variable has the following properties:

1. It initially has a special value, "undefined."

2. It can be assigned a value at most once, and once assigned is treated as a constant (ANSI C and C++ `const`).

3. An attempt to read an undefined variable causes the thread that performs the read to block until the variable is assigned a value.

We might think of a sync variable as an empty box with its interior coated with glue; an object cannot be removed once it has been placed inside.

Any regular C++ type can be declared `sync`, as can a CC++ global pointer. Hence, we can write the following.

```
sync int i;        // i is a sync integer
sync int *j;       // j is a pointer to a sync integer
int *sync k;       // k is a sync pointer to an integer
sync int *sync l;  // l is a sync pointer to a sync integer
```

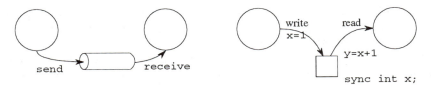

**Figure 5.3** Alternative synchronization mechanisms. On the left, the channel: a receiver blocks until a message is in the channel. On the right; the sync variable: a receiver blocks until the variable has a value.

We use the following code fragment to illustrate the use of sync variables. This code makes two concurrent RPCs to functions defined in Program 5.5: one to read the variable length and one to write that variable.

```
Length *global lp;
int val;
par {
    val = lp->read_len();
    lp->write_len(42);
}
```

What is the value of the variable val at the end of the parallel block? Because the read and write operations are not synchronized, the value is not known. If the read operation executes before the write, val will have some arbitrary value. (The Length class does not initialize the variable length.) If the execution order is reversed, val will have the value 42.

This nondeterminism can be avoided by modifying Program 5.5 to make the variable length a sync variable. That is, we change its definition to the following.

```
sync int length;
```

Execution order now does not matter: if read_len executes first, it will block until the variable length is assigned a value by write_len.

---

**EXAMPLE 5.3** (Channel Communication)    Global pointers and sync variables can be used to implement a variety of communication mechanisms. In this example, we use these constructs to implement a simple shared queue class. This class can be used to implement channel communication between two concurrently executing producer and consumer tasks: we simply allocate a queue object and provide both tasks with pointers to this object. We shall see in Section 5.11 how this Queue class can be encapsulated in the more convenient Channel class used in Program 5.3.

Recall that a channel is a message queue to which a sender can append a sequence of messages and from which a receiver can remove messages. The only synchronization constraint is that the receiver blocks when removing a message if the queue is empty. An obvious CC++ representation of a message queue is as a linked list, in which each entry contains a message plus a pointer to the next message. Program 5.6 takes this approach, defining a `Queue` class that maintains pointers to the head and tail of a message queue represented as a list of `IntQData` structures. The data structures manipulated by Program 5.6 are illustrated in Figure 5.4.

The `Queue` class provides `enqueue` and `dequeue` functions to add items to the tail of the queue and remove items from the head, respectively. The `sync` variable contained in the `IntQData` structure used to represent a linked list entry ensures synchronization between the enqueue and dequeue operations. The queue is initialized to be a single list element containing an undefined variable as its message.

The first action performed by `dequeue` is to read the message value associated with the first entry in the queue. This read operation will block if the queue is empty, providing the necessary synchronization. If the queue is not empty, the `dequeue` function will read the queue value, delete the list element, and advance the `head` pointer to the next list element. Similarly, the `enqueue` function first allocates a new list element and links it into the queue and then sets the `msg` field of the current tail list element. Notice that the order in which these two operations are performed is important. If performed in the opposite order,

```
tail->value = msg;
tail->next  = new IntQData;
```

then a dequeue function call blocked on the list element `tail->value` and enabled by the assignment `tail->value=msg` could read the pointer `tail->next` before it is set to reference a newly created element.

---

### 5.5.3  Mutual Exclusion

The `sync` variable allows us to synchronize the transfer of data from a producer to a consumer. In other situations, we may wish to allow two threads to operate on the same nonsync data structure while ensuring that they do not interfere with each other's execution. For example, the enqueue and dequeue operations of Example 5.3 allow a single sender and receiver to communicate by enqueuing to and dequeuing from a shared queue. What if we want multiple senders to be able to append messages to the same queue? We cannot allow two producers to make concurrent calls to enqueue, as an arbitrary interleaving of two enqueue calls could have bizarre results. What we need is a mechanism to ensure that only one message can be enqueued at a time.

This requirement is satisfied by CC++'s `atomic` keyword. Member functions of an object can be declared atomic. This declaration specifies that the execution of such a function will not be interleaved with the execution of any other atomic function of the same object. For example, to allow multiple producers to append to the same queue, we would declare the `enqueue` function to be `atomic`, as follows.

```
atomic void Queue::enqueue(int msg) {
    tail->next  = new IntQData;
    tail->value = msg;
    tail        = tail->next;
}
```

```
struct IntQData {           // A list element contains:
  sync int value;           //    sync variable (message), &
  struct IntQData *next;    //    pointer to next list element
};

class Queue {
public:
    void enqueue(int);
    int dequeue();
private:
    // Initialize: allocate single element
    void Queue() { head = tail = new IntQData; }
    IntQData *head, *tail;
};

void Queue::enqueue(int msg) {   // Enqueue a value:
    tail->next  = new IntQData;  //    allocate new element,
    tail->value = msg;           //    set message value, &
    tail        = tail->next;    //    advance tail pointer
}

int Queue::dequeue() {                  // Dequeue a value:
    int retval = head->value;           //    access message value,
    IntQData *newh = head->next;        // get next list item,
    delete head;                        //    delete old list head,
    head = newh;                        //    advance head pointer, &
    return retval;                      //    return message value
}
```

**Program 5.6**   The Queue class provides a constructor Queue() that initializes a queue, and enqueue and dequeue functions that add an element to a queue and remove an element from a queue, respectively. The IntQData structure incorporates a sync variable, used to synchronize enqueue and dequeue operations.

This ensures that even if multiple producers attempt to append to the same queue concurrently, the actual enqueue operations will occur in some sequential order and a valid queue will be generated.

### 5.5.4   Data Transfer Functions

In C++, declarations of the form

```
ostream& operator<<(ostream& v, const TYPE& obj_in);
istream& operator>>(istream& v, TYPE& obj_out);
```

in the class ios of the iostream library define infix operators << and >>, which can be used to write and read data of a specified TYPE to and from files. These operators are

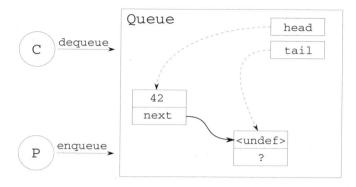

**Figure 5.4**  A message queue class, showing the internal representation of a queue as a linked list of `IntQData` structures (two are shown) with message values represented as sync values that are either defined (42) or undefined (`<undef>`). Producer and consumer tasks execute `enqueue` and `dequeue` operations, respectively.

predefined for simple types and can be provided by the programmer for more complex types. This facility enhances modularity by allowing a class definition to specify how its data structures should be read and written. A program can then read and write instances of that class without being aware of their internal structure.

CC++ uses an analogous mechanism for communicating data structures between processor objects. Associated with every CC++ datatype is a pair of *data transfer functions* that define how to transfer that type to another processor object. The function

```
CCVoid& operator<<(CCVoid&, const TYPE& obj_in);
```

defines how TYPE should be packaged for communication. It is called automatically by the compiler whenever an object of TYPE needs to be transferred to another processor object, that is, whenever an RPC call takes an argument of that type or returns a value of that type. Similarly, the function

```
CCVoid& operator>>(CCVoid&, TYPE& obj_out);
```

defines how TYPE should be unpackaged. It is called by the compiler whenever an object of TYPE is received from another processor object. Upon termination of this call, `obj_out` will be a copy of the `obj_in` used as the argument to the operator `<<` in the initial processor object.

The type CCVoid is a compiler-defined type analogous to the types `istream` and `ostream` used in the `iostream` library. Data transfer functions are generated automatically by the CC++ compiler for simple data types, but must be constructed by the programmer for local pointers, arrays, and structures that contain local pointers. For example, Program 5.7 shows both data transfer and `iostream` functions for a type DVector comprising a vector of doubles. These functions send (write) the vector length followed by the vector elements, and receive (read) these values in the same order. (The C++ qualifier `friend` names nonmember functions that can access a class's private variables.) Having defined

```
class DVector {
    int length;
    double *elements;
    friend CCVoid  & operator<<(CCVoid&, const DVector&);
    friend CCVoid  & operator>>(CCVoid&, DVector&);
    friend ostream & operator<<(ostream&, const DVector&);
    friend istream & operator>>(istream&, DVector&);
};

CCVoid& operator<<(CCVoid &v, const DVector &input) {
    v << input.length;             // Send length
    for (int i=0; i<input.length; i++)
        v << input.elements[i];    // Send element
    return v;
}

ostream& operator<<(ostream &v, const DVector &input) {
    v << input.length;             // Write length
    for (int i=0; i<input.length; i++)
        v << input.elements[i];    // Write element
    return v;
}

CCVoid& operator>>(CCVoid &v, DVector &output) {
    v >> output.length;            // Receive length
    output.elements = new double[output.length];
    for (int i=0; i<output.length; i++)
        v >> output.elements[i];   // Receive element
    return v;
}

istream& operator>>(istream &v, DVector &output) {
    v >> output.length;            // Read length
    output.elements = new double[output.length];
    for (int i=0; i<output.length; i++)
        v >> output.elements[i];   // Read element
    return v;
}
```

**Program 5.7**  Data transfer and iostream functions for a datatype DVector. After the class definition, we give first the output functions (for sending and writing) and then the input functions (for receiving and reading).

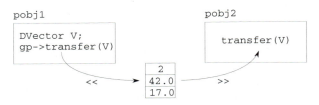

**Figure 5.5**   Using data transfer functions to communicate an instance of the user-defined type DVector between two processor objects. The global pointer gp is assumed to reference pobj2. The function << is used to package the data structure at the source, and the function >> is used to unpackage the data structure at the destination.

these data transfer functions, we can make an RPC with a DVector as an argument, as follows; the vector will be transferred correctly, as illustrated in Figure 5.5.

```
DVector V;
V.elements = new double[2];
V.length = 2;
V.elements[0] = 42.0; V.elements[1] = 17.0;
gp->transfer(V);
```

## 5.6   Asynchronous Communication

Recall that the need for asynchronous communication can arise when the tasks involved in a computation must access elements of a shared data structure in an unstructured manner (Section 2.3.4). This requirement can be satisfied in CC++ in three different ways:

1. The shared data structure can be encapsulated in a set of specialized *data tasks* to which read and write requests are directed by using channel operations.

2. The shared data structure can be distributed among the computation tasks. As discussed in Section 2.3.4, each computation task must then *poll* periodically for pending requests. For example, we can extend the Queue class of Program 5.6 to support a poll operation. The IntQData structure is augmented with a full/empty field, which is initialized to empty when a list element is created and set to full when a data value is placed in the list element. The poll function simply checks the status of this field in the list element at the head of the queue.

3. A third implementation approach exploits CC++'s RPC mechanism more directly. The shared data structure is distributed among the computation tasks. However, rather than sending a message on a channel, a task accesses data in another processor object by making an RPC to an appropriate member function. (The get_x function of Program 5.1 is a simple example of the sort of RPC we might write.)

The third approach is explored in a case study in Section 5.12.

## 5.7    Determinism

We noted in Section 1.3.1 that determinism can greatly simplify program development. CC++ does not provide any guarantees of deterministic execution: indeed, the basic execution model is highly nondeterministic, allowing as it does the interleaved execution of multiple threads in a single address space. Nevertheless, there are simple rules that, if followed, allow us to avoid unwanted deterministic interactions. In particular, a CC++ program is easily shown to be deterministic if it uses a task-based concurrency model (one thread per processor object) and if tasks interact only by using the channel library used in Program 5.3, with one sender and one receiver per channel.

While a task/channel model ensures determinism, there are also circumstances in which it is advantageous to use CC++ constructs in more flexible ways. For example:

1. Concurrent threads provide a mechanism for overlapping computation and communication. When one thread is suspended waiting for a communication, another thread can be executing. For example, the following code can perform computation while waiting for the remote datum, value.

   ```
   par {
       value = pobj->get_remote_value();
       perform_computation();
   }
   use_remote_value(value);
   ```

2. RPCs that read and write data structures in other processor objects can be used to implement a variety of asynchronous communication mechanisms; see, for example, Section 5.12.

3. On a shared-memory computer, threads created in the same processor object can execute in parallel (on different processors), communicating by reading and writing shared data rather than sending and receiving data. This shared-memory programming model (Section 1.3.2) can improve performance relative to channel-based communication by reducing data movement and copying.

These more general forms of concurrency and communication introduce the possibility of complex, nondeterministic interactions between concurrently executing threads. However, the risk of nondeterministic interactions can be reduced substantially by avoiding the use of global variables, by making shared data structures have the sync attribute, and by ensuring that accesses to nonsync shared data structures occur within atomic functions.

## 5.8    Mapping

A parallel program defined in terms of CC++ constructs can be executed on both uniprocessor and multiprocessor computers. In the latter case, a complete program must also specify how the processor objects created by a CC++ program are mapped to processors. Recall from Chapter 2 that this is an important part of parallel algorithm design.

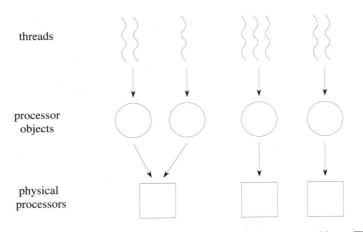

threads

processor
objects

physical
processors

**Figure 5.6**   Mapping in CC++. First, threads are mapped to processor objects. Then, processor objects are mapped to physical processors.

Mapping in CC++ is a two-stage process (Figure 5.6). First, threads are mapped to processor objects, and then processor objects are mapped to processors. The mapping of threads to processor objects can be one-to-one, in which case it is the mapping of processor objects to physical processors that is important. Alternatively, the mapping of processor objects to physical processors may be one-to-one, in which case it is the mapping of threads to processor objects that is important. If both mappings are one-to-one, then the mapping problem is straightforward.

An important aspect of the second mapping stage, processor object placement, is that it *influences performance but not correctness*. Hence, we can develop a program on a uniprocessor and then tune performance on a parallel computer by changing placement decisions. This is consistent with the design methodology of Chapter 2, in which mapping is the fourth and final stage of the design process. The first mapping stage, thread placement, has this property only if threads do not share data structures.

### 5.8.1   Processor Object Placement

By default, a newly created processor object is placed on the same processor as its creator. An alternative placement can be specified by using the *placement* argument to the new operator. In C++, this argument is used to position an object in memory space; in CC++, it can also be used to position a processor object in processor space. (It can also be used to specify where in a file system to find the code for a processor object; however, we do not discuss this facility here.) The location is specified by an implementation-dependent class named `proc_t`. The constructor functions `proc_t` and `node_t` defined in the CC++ library can be used to construct a placement structure with a specified processor name. These are used in the following code fragment, which creates a new processor object (of type `MyClass`) on a processor called `mymachine`.

```
MyClass *global G;
proc_t location(node_t("mymachine"));
G = new (location) MyClass;
```

The new statement creates a new processor object; the supplied `proc_t` object (`location`) specifies the machine name. To place the new processor object on a different processor, one need change only the second line of this code fragment, for example to the following.

```
proc_t location(node_t("yourmachine"));
```

As a further example, the following code creates 32 processor objects, placing each on a different processor of a multicomputer with nodes named sp#0, sp#1, ..., sp#31. Notice how `parfor` is used to create the different processor objects concurrently.

```
MyClass *global G[32];
parfor (int i=0; i<31; i++) {
    char node_name[256];
    sprintf(node_name,"sp#%d", i);
    proc_t location(node_t(node_name));
    G[i] = new (location) MyClass;
}
```

Although simple, this code represents bad programming practice, in that it embeds information about the environment in which the program is executing. A better approach is to encapsulate mapping decisions in a separate class, for example, the class `Mapping` defined in Program 5.8. This class encapsulates two private variables (P and `proc_names`) that represent the environment in which a program is to execute. The member function `initmap` is used to initialize these variables. Two additional member functions, `processor` and `random_p`, return a `proc_t` object representing the ith processor and a randomly-selected processor, respectively. Finally, two data transfer functions (omitted for brevity) package and unpackage the node list associated with a mapping object, allowing a mapping to be passed as an argument when creating a new processor object. The use of the `Mapping` class is illustrated in the following example.

---

**EXAMPLE 5.4** (Search II)   Recall that Program 5.4 explores a search tree in parallel by creating new threads to explore the subtrees rooted at each nonleaf node. Each thread executes in a new processor object. This program does not specify a mapping strategy for these processor objects. One strategy is to place each newly created processor object/thread pair on a processor selected at random. Program 5.9 uses the `Mapping` class of Program 5.8 to implement this behavior. There are three significant differences between this program and Program 5.4. First, a global `Mapping` object is defined and initialized at the beginning of `main` to contain the names of the processors on which the program is to execute. These names are read from a file. Second, a constructor is provided for the processor object class `Tree` that copies the `Mapping` object to each new processor object as it is created. Third, one of the processor object allocation calls in the `search` function is augmented with a call to `random_p`, which returns a `proc_t` structure on a randomly selected processor.

---

```
//  Mapping class encapsulates a list of processor names
class Mapping {
    friend CCVoid & operator<<(CCVoid &, const Mapping &);
    friend CCVoid & operator>>(CCVoid &, Mapping &);
public:
    proc_t processor(int);     // Access particular node
    proc_t random_p();         // Access random node
    void initmap(char **);     // Supply processor names
private:
    int P;                     // Number of processors
    char *proc_names[];        // Processor names
};

proc_t Mapping::processor(int i)
{ return(proc_t(node_t(proc_names[i%P]))); }

proc_t Mapping::random_p()
{ return processor(drand48()*((float) P)); }

//  Store list of processor names
void Mapping::initmap(char *plist[]) {
    P = 0;                     // First, count number of processors
    for (char **cPtr=plist; *cPtr!=0; cPtr++)
        P++;
    proc_names = plist; // Then store processor names
}
```

**Program 5.8**  The class Mapping encapsulates information about how to place a processor object on the ith of P processors named in the initmap call. The function processor returns a proc_t structure for a specified processor, while the function random_p returns a proc_t structure for a random processor. The two data transfer functions are omitted for brevity. The function drand48 is a standard random number generator.

### 5.8.2  Mapping Threads to Processor Objects

An alternative approach to mapping in CC++ is to create a fixed number of processor objects onto which threads are then placed. This approach is often used in SPMD computations, in which case a single thread is mapped to each processor object. Another important application is in situations where a computation creates a large number of lightweight threads that interact only via global pointers. We can map these threads to a static number of processor objects, hence avoiding the overhead of creating a new processor object when creating a new thread; as the threads do not share local data structures, the mapping of threads to processor objects does not influence the result computed.

Program 5.10 supports this general approach by defining a class POArray that can be used to create an array of processor objects of specified size and type. Each processor object is initialized to contain an array of pointers to the other processor objects, so that communication between the different processor objects can be achieved.

```
Mapping mapping;                          // Mapping information

global class Tree {
public:
    int search(int);                      // Search function
    Tree(Mapping m) { mapping = m; } // Initialization function
};

int Tree::search(int A) {
    int ls, rs;
    if (leaf(A)) {
        .
        .
        .
    }
    else {            // Create new processor objects
        Tree *global lobj = new Tree(mapping);
        Tree *global robj = new (mapping.random_p()) Tree(mapping);
        par {             // Create processes to search subtrees
            ls = lobj->search(left_child(A));
            rs = robj->search(right_child(A));
        }
        delete(lobj); delete(robj);
        return(ls+rs);
    }
}

void main(int argc, char *argv[]) {
    char *nodes[] = read_nodes();     // Read node information
    mapping.initmap(nodes);           // Initialize mapping
    Tree *global searcher = new Tree(mapping);
    int total = searcher->search(1);
    printf("There were %d solutions\n",total);
}
```

**Program 5.9** CC++ tree search program with mapping constructs. The second processor object allocation statement in the `search` function calls `random_p` to create the processor object on a randomly selected processor.

The class `POArray` provides an initialization function, `init`, that creates the processor objects. The arguments to this function specify the number and names of the processors on which processor objects are to be created. The `init` function first makes repeated calls to `create_pobj` to create an array of processor objects with type `POArrayNode`. It then initializes these processor objects by calling the function `init_pobj` with a copy of the `POArray` object (accessed by the C++ keyword `this`) as an argument.

We would like to be able to use `POArray` to create processor objects of arbitrary type. Hence, we use the keyword `virtual` and the notation `=0` to declare `create_pobj` and `init_pobj` to be *virtual functions*. This means that these functions can be defined in classes derived from the classes `POArrary` and `POArrayNode`, respectively. To create

```
class POArray {
    friend CCVoid & operator<<(CCVoid &, const POArray &);
    friend CCVoid & operator>>(CCVoid &, POArray &);
public:
    void init(int, char * []);
    virtual POArrayNode *global create_pobj(proc_t)=0;
    POArrayNode *global pobjs[];
    int posize;
};

global class POArrayNode {
    friend class POArray;
public:
    virtual void init_pobj(POArray &)=0;
    POArray *p_array;
};

void POArray::init(int sz, char *nodelist[]) {
    posize = sz;
    pobjs = new (POArrayNode *global)[posize];
    // Create new processor objects
    parfor (int i=0; i<posize; i++) {
        proc_t loc(node_t(nodelist[i]));
        pobjs[i] = create_pobj(loc);
    }
    // Copy processor object pointers to new processor objects
    parfor (int j=0; j<posize; j++)
        pobjs[j]->init_pobj(*this);
}
```

**Program 5.10**   The POArray class, used to create arrays of processor objects to which threads can be mapped subsequently. The C++ keyword this used in the last line is a pointer to the object in which it is called. For brevity, the data transfer functions are not provided.

an array of virtual functions of some type $T$, we simply derive new classes from POArray and POArrayNode and define the functions create_pobj and init_pobj in these classes to create and initialize new processor objects of type $T$. This mechanism is used in the following example and in Program 5.16, both of which use POArray for mapping.

---

**EXAMPLE 5.5** (Coupled Climate Model)   A coupled climate modeling system comprising an ocean model and an atmosphere model can be structured as a *parallel composition* of the two component models, in which each model executes on one half of P processors. This structure is implemented in Program 5.11. Mapping is achieved using the POArray class of Program 5.10. The class `AtmOcn` is derived from `POArray`. It extends it by defining the virtual function `create_pobj` used by `POArray` to create a processor object, as well as the functions `atmosphere` and `ocean` that implement the atmosphere and ocean models. Similarly, the processor object class `AtmOcnNode` is derived from `POArrayNode` and defines the virtual function `init_pobj` that initializes an ocean/atmosphere model processor object, as well as the functions `atm_proc` and `ocn_proc` that will be executed in each processor object. The `init_pobj` function creates a local instance of the `AtmOcn` object passed as an argument, hence providing each processor object with access to the other processor objects.

The main program first reads a list of processor names, `nodes`. Then, it creates two instances of the `AtmOcn` class (`atm` and `ocn`), and uses the member function `init` to create arrays of processor objects located on the lower P/2 and upper P/2 processors named in `nodes`, respectively. The `AtmOcn` objects are passed as arguments to the ocean and atmosphere model components, which use them to perform local mapping. The functions `atmosphere` and `ocean` initiate SPMD computation, placing a distinct instance of `atm_proc` (or `ocn_proc`) on each of the `posize` processor objects named in the `AtmOcn` object passed as an argument.

The advantage of the structure employed in Program 5.11 is that mapping decisions are specified separately from other aspects of program logic. As a result, the same program can be structured as a *concurrent composition*, in which the ocean and atmosphere models execute concurrently on the same processors, simply by changing the calls to `init` in the main program, as shown in Program 5.12.

## 5.9    Modularity

Example 5.5 showed how CC++ constructs can be used to implement parallel and concurrent composition. The basic ideas are straightforward: each component of a multicomponent program is implemented as a distinct task. Each such task is passed an array of `proc_t` objects representing its computational resources. The task creates a distinct set of processor objects and performs mapping and communication with respect to these `proc_t` objects and processor objects.

In this section, we discuss the techniques used to implement *sequential* composition in CC++ programs. Recall that in sequential composition, different program components execute in sequence on all processors (Section 4.2.2). These program components may themselves communicate and synchronize, but they cannot create new tasks. Hence, each process executes the same program, and the entire computation moves sequentially from one parallel operation to the next. This is the single program multiple data (SPMD) programming model discussed in Section 1.3.2.

A CC++ implementation of an SPMD program comprises two components. The *initialization* component creates the processor objects in which computation will be performed and the communication structures (such as channels) required by the program

```
global class AtmOcnNode : public POArrayNode {
public:
    void atm_proc(int);            // Computation routine
    void ocn_proc(int);            // Computation routine
    void init_pobj(POArray &ar)    // Initialization routine
        { p_array = new AtmOcn(ar); }
};

class AtmOcn : public POArray {
public:
    void atmosphere();
    void ocean();
    AtmOcn(const POArray & ar) : POArray(ar) {};
    POArrayNode *global create_pobj(proc_t locn)
        { return new (locn) AtmOcnNode; }
};

void AtmOcn::atmosphere() {
    parfor (int j=0; j<posize; j++)
        ((AtmOcnNode *global) pobjs[j])->atm_proc(j);
}

void atm_proc(int id) {
    // Main body of atmosphere model code
}

void main(int argc, char *argv[]) {
    int P = atoi(argv[1]);
    char *nodes[] = read_nodes();
    AtmOcn atm, ocn;
    atm.init(P/2, nodes);     // Assume P is even
    ocn.init(P/2, &nodes[P/2]);
    par {
        atm.atmosphere();
        ocn.ocean();
    }
}
```

**Program 5.11**  Mapping in an atmosphere/ocean model. The two models are placed on disjoint sets of P/2 processors. Resource allocation decisions are specified using the POArray class. The ocean function is similar to atmosphere, calling ocn_proc instead of atm_proc.

**Plate 1** The unbalanced coordinate bisection partitioning algorithm applied to a finite element mesh generated for a superconductivity simulation. *Image courtesy of P. Plassman.*

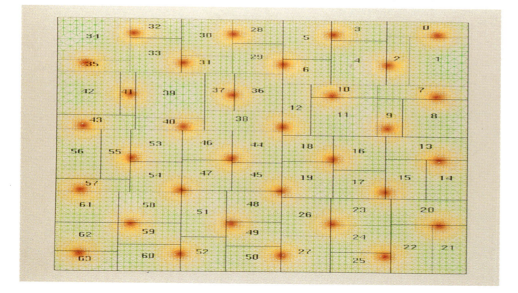

**Plate 2** The spectral bisection partitioning algorithm applied to a finite element mesh generated for an assembly part. *Image courtesy of Z. Johan.*

**Plate 3**  A dynamic, local load-balancing algorithm applied to a weather model. This shows the situation after grid points have migrated to compensate for a "hot spot" slightly to the left of the grid center. *Image courtesy of J. Michalakes.*

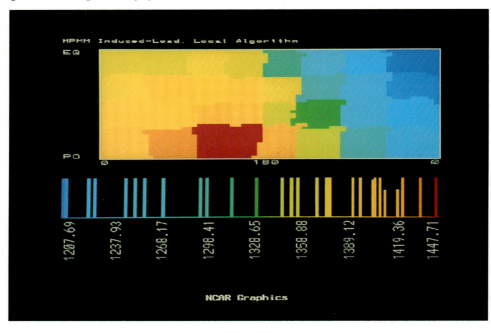

**Plate 4**  Potential temperature isosurface from a simulation of thunderstorm downdrafts, as described in the text. *Image courtesy of J. Anderson.*

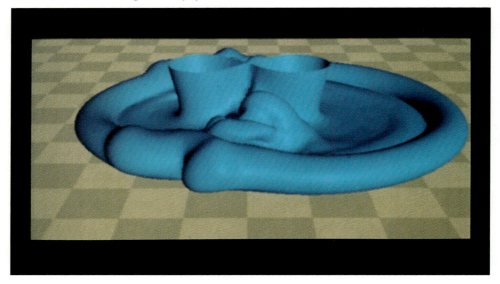

**Plate 5** Load distribution in an atmosphere model with a 64x128 grid. Each figure shows per-point computational load at a single time step, with the histogram giving relative frequency of different load values. The upper image shows a time step in which radiation time steps are performed, and the lower image an ordinary time step. Diurnal, land/ocean, and local variations are visible. *Images courtesy of J. Michalakes.*

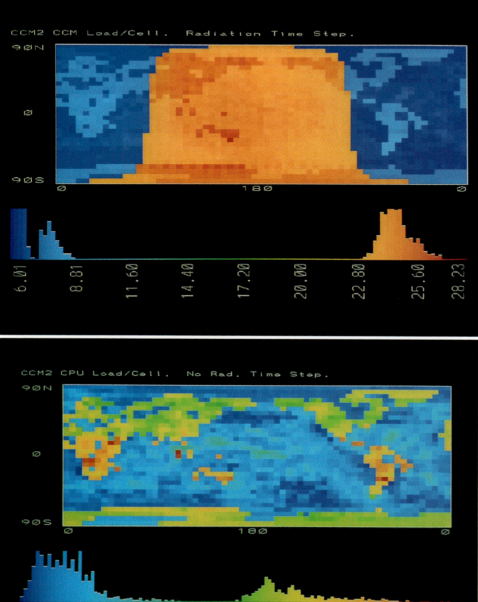

**Plate 6**  Molecular model for the active site region in the enzyme Malate Dehydrogenase, as described in the text. *Image courtesy of P. Bash.*

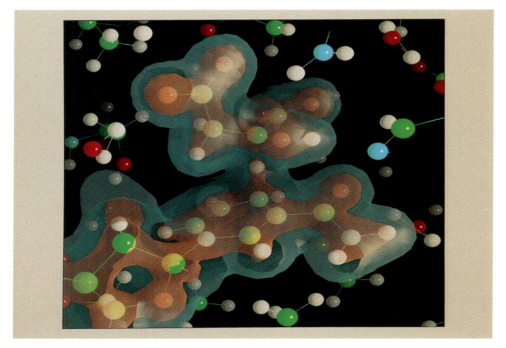

**Plate 7**  Profile data generated by the Gauge performance tool for a parallel atmospheric model running on 32 processors, showing per-processor communication volume and message counts and a three-dimensional profile in which color indicates time. Processors 24-31 are specialized I/O processors.

**Plate 8** Gantt chart and space-time graph for a parallel climate model executing on 64 processors, generated using the Paragraph performance tool.

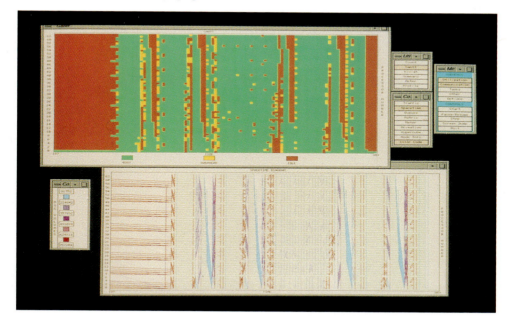

**Plate 9** Thinking Machine Corporation's PRISM performance tool, here applied to a Gaussian elimination algorithm. *Image courtesy of D. Reed.*

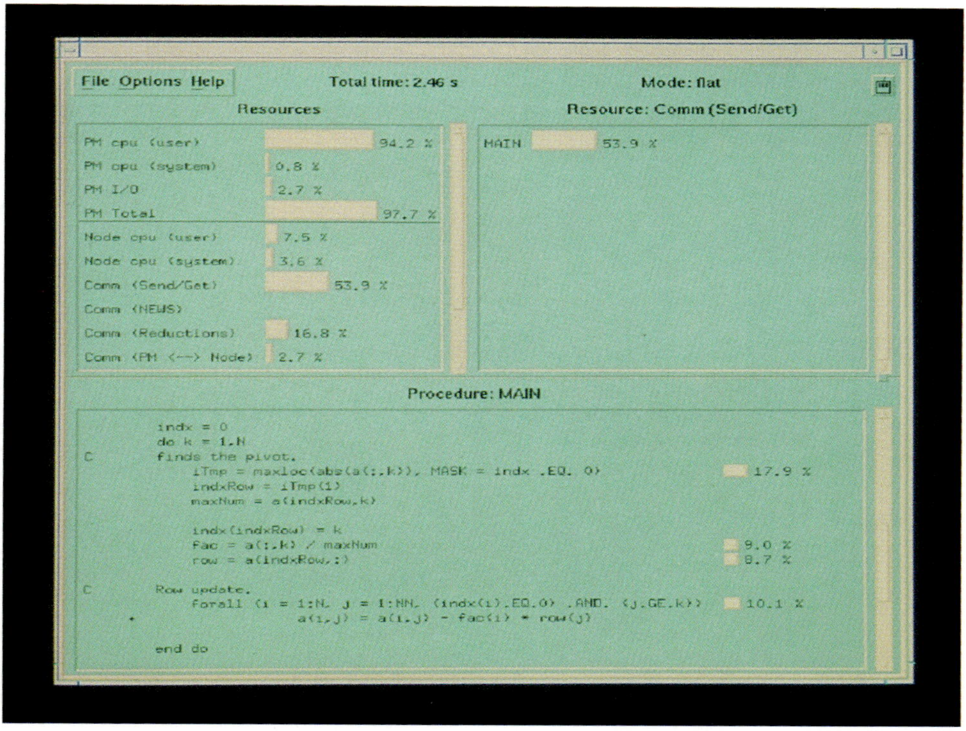

**Plate 10** Paragraph displays of instantaneous communication activity in a parallel climate model executing on 64 processors.

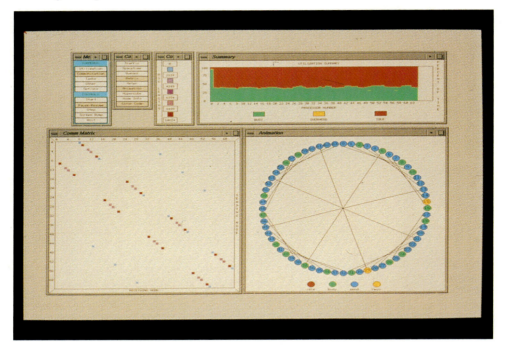

**Plate 11** Gantt chart, state duration histogram, and instantaneous state diagram for a search problem running on 16 processors, generated using Upshot. *Image courtesy of E. Lusk.*

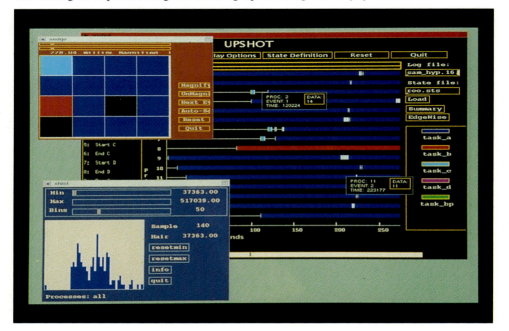

**Plate 12**   Gantt chart for a computational chemistry code executing on 8 processors of an IBM SP computer, generated using the Upshot performance tool. *Image courtesy of J. Tilson.*

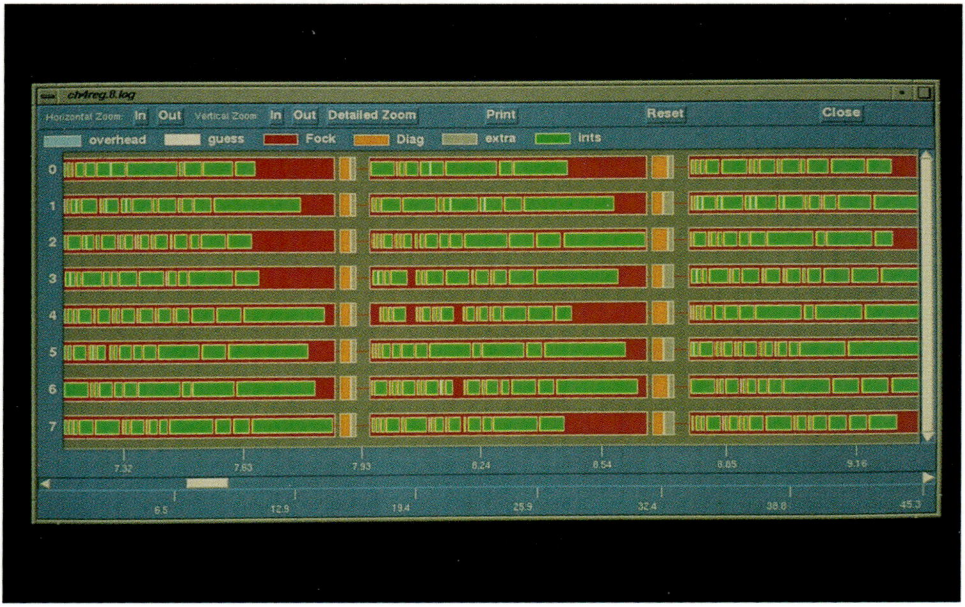

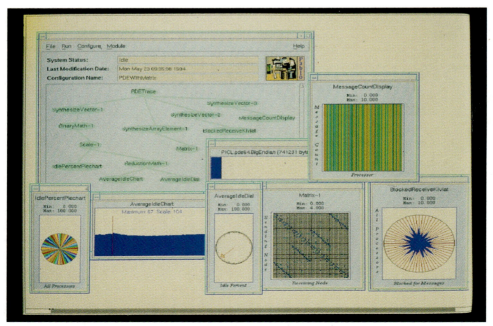

**Plate 13**   Pablo display of performance data collected from a numerical solver. *Image courtesy of D. Reed.*

**Plate 14**    Pablo virtual reality display of performance data. *Image courtesy of D. Reed.*

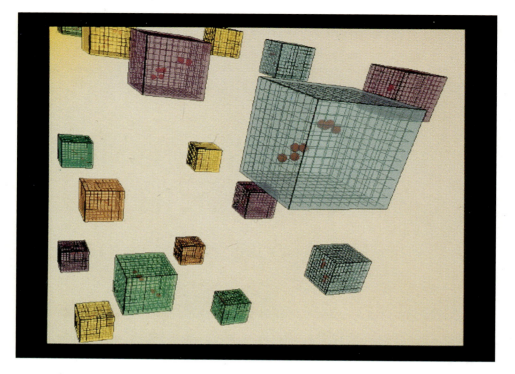

**Plate 15**    IBM's VT trace analysis tool.

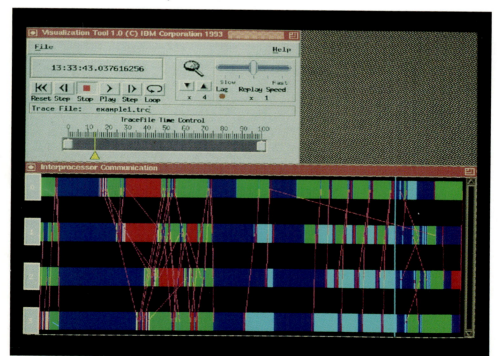

```
void main(int argc, char *argv[]) {
    int P = atoi(argv[1]);
    char *nodes[] = read_nodes();
    AtmOcn atm, ocn;
    atm.init(P, nodes);    // Only these lines
    ocn.init(P, nodes);    // are changed
    par {
        atm.atmosphere();
        ocn.ocean();
    }
}
```

**Program 5.12**   An alternative main program for the atmosphere/ocean model. This maps the two model components to the same processors.

components called in the sequential composition. The *execution* component performs the actual computation, using the structures created during the initialization phase. The execution component can be structured in two different ways (Figure 5.7). In the first approach, the top-level program is structured as a sequence of calls to routines that each use a `parfor` statement to create a thread on each processor object. In the second approach a single `parfor` statement creates a set of long-lived threads (one per processor object) that each make a sequence of calls to the various routines involved in the sequential composition. The first approach can lead to simpler programs, but the latter tends to be more efficient.

---

**EXAMPLE 5.6** (Finite Difference)    We apply the two approaches to the SPMD finite difference computation used to illustrate sequential composition in Section 4.2.2. This computation is structured as a sequence of calls to a finite difference routine that performs nearest-neighbor communication and a reduction routine used to detect termination; the latter routine performs global communication.

An implementation of this algorithm using the first approach is illustrated in Program 5.13. The execution component is structured as a while loop containing a sequential composition of parallel `finite_difference` and `global_maximum` routines. Concurrency and communication are encapsulated in these routines, which use `parfor` and other parallel constructs to create threads of control within the processor objects created in the initialization phase.

The second approach is illustrated in Program 5.14. Here, a single `parfor` statement creates one thread of control in each processor object. This thread makes a sequence of calls to routines that call local `finite_difference` and `global_maximum` routines. The resulting program is more complex but potentially more efficient, as it avoids the cost of repeatedly creating and destroying the threads used to perform the SPMD computation.

---

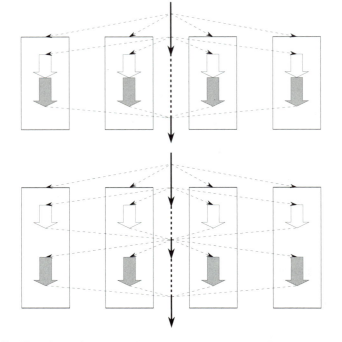

**Figure 5.7**   Two alternative approaches to the implementation of sequential composition in CC++. The two figures are timelines, with the parent thread shown as a solid dark line when active and a dashed dark line when suspended. In both cases, an initialization phase creates the four processor objects in which computation will occur. In the first approach, a set of long-lived threads is then created; each of these threads executes both components before terminating. In the second approach, control returns to the parent thread after the first component executes; the parent thread then creates a new set of threads for the second component.

## 5.10   Performance Issues

CC++ programs do not explicitly send and receive messages, but instead perform read and write operations on global pointers; make remote procedure calls; and use par, parfor, and spawn statements to create new threads of control. Nevertheless, the communication operations associated with a CC++ program can usually be determined easily. Normally, a read operation on a global pointer, a write operation on a global pointer, or an RPC all result in two communications: one to send the remote request and one to receive an acknowledgment or result. As noted in Chapter 3, the cost of each message can be specified with reasonable accuracy in terms of a startup cost and a per-word cost. It is necessary to distinguish between the communication costs incurred when communicating CC++ processes are located on different processors (*interprocessor* communication) or on the same processor (*intraprocessor* communication). Both these costs can depend significantly on

```
void finite_difference() {
    parfor (int i=0; i<P; i++)
        nodes[i]->finite_diff(i);
}

void main(int argc, char *argv[]) {
    int P = atoi(argv[1]);
    int done = FALSE;
    // Initialize, creating array of processor objects, nodes
    initialize(P);
    // Perform computation on processor objects
    while(!done) {
        finite_difference();
        glob_max = global_maximum();
        if(globmax < threshold) done = TRUE;
    }
}
```

**Program 5.13**   A code sketch of a CC++ implementation of an SPMD finite difference
code. Initialization creates processor objects and the global pointers needed for
communication; the while loop repeatedly calls the `finite_difference` routine
(shown) and a `global_maximum` routine (not shown) to perform computation.

```
// Each task in computation executes the same code
void node_execute() {
    while(!done) {
        finite_difference(localgrid, localmax);
        global_maximum(localmax, globmax);
        if(globmax < threshold) done = TRUE;
    }
}

void main(int argc, char *argv[]) {
    int P = atoi(argv[1]);
    // Initialize, creating array of processor objects, nodes
    initialize(P);
    // Initiate SPMD computation on processor objects
    parfor (int i=0; i<P; i++)
        nodes[i]->node_execute();
}
```

**Program 5.14**   A code sketch of an alternative CC++ implementation of an SPMD finite
difference code. In this version, each processor executes the `node_execute` routine,
which implements the SPMD computation.

implementation technology. Typically, interprocessor communication costs are similar to those in Table 3.1 in Chapter 3, and intraprocessor communication is cheaper. However, on some multicomputers with fast interprocessor communication and relatively low memory bandwidth, intraprocessor communication can actually be slower than interprocessor communication.

The following issues must also be considered when examining the performance of CC++ programs.

*Reading and writing global pointers.* Reading or writing a global pointer normally involves two communications: one to send the read or write request, and one to return a result and/or signal completion. Hence, global pointers must be used with caution, particularly on computers where communication is expensive. If a data structure is referenced often, it may be worthwhile to move that data structure to where it is used most often, or to replicate it. If a task requires many data items from the same processor object, it may be better to use an RPC to transfer all the required data in a single message.

*Remote procedure calls.* An RPC normally involves two communications: the first to transmit the procedure call and its data to the remote processor, and the second to signal completion and to return any result. In many situations, the return message is not required and hence represents overhead. This overhead can be avoided by using the spawn statement to create an asynchronous thread of control. For example, the performance of the following code from Program 5.15 below, which sends a value on a channel,

```
void send(int val) { inport->enqueue(val); }
```

can be improved in cases where one does not care when the send operation completes, by rewriting it to eliminate the reply, as follows.

```
void send(int val) { spawn inport->enqueue(val); }
```

*Fairness.* When two or more threads execute in the same processor object, CC++ guarantees that execution is fair: that is, that no thread that is not blocked waiting for data will be prevented indefinitely from executing. However, the time that a thread waits before executing can vary significantly depending on characteristics of both the application and a particular CC++ implementation. Hence, care must be taken if application performance depends on obtaining timely responses to remote requests.

*Remote operations.* As a general principle, operations involving global objects (processor object creation, RPC, etc.) are more expensive than operations involving only local objects. However, the cost of these operations can vary significantly from machine to machine. An RPC is typically less expensive than a processor object creation, and a remote read or write operation is typically less expensive than an RPC. The first processor object creation on a processor is often significantly more expensive than subsequent processor object creation operations on the same processor.

*Compiler optimization.* Because CC++ is a programming language rather than a library, a compiler may in some situations be able to reduce communication costs by eliminating replies, coalescing messages, or otherwise reorganizing a program to improve performance.

```
class Channel {
public:
   Channel(ChannelUser *global, ChannelUser *global);
   InPort  *global get_in_port()  { return in_port;  }
   OutPort *global get_out_port() { return out_port; }
private:
   InPort  *global in_port;
   OutPort *global out_port;
};
```

```
// Channel Member functions
Channel::Channel(ChannelUser *global out_pobj,
                 ChannelUser *global in_pobj) {
   in_port  = in_pobj->create_inport();
   out_port = out_pobj->create_outport(in_port);
}
```

```
global class ChannelUser {
public:
   OutPort *global create_outport(InPort *global ip)
      { return new OutPort(ip); }
   InPort  *global create_inport() { return new InPort; }
};
```

```
class InPort : Queue {
friend class OutPort; // Allow an OutPort to call enqueue
public:
   int receive() { return dequeue(); }
};
```

```
class OutPort {
public:
   OutPort(InPort *global iport) { inport = iport; }
   void send(int val) { inport->enqueue(val); }
private:
   InPort *global inport;
};
```

**Program 5.15**  Simple communication channel library. The `ChannelUser` class must be included as a base processor object class in programs wanting to use channels. The `InPort` class is derived from the `Queue` class presented earlier and provides a `receive` operation. The `OutPort` class provides a `send` operation.

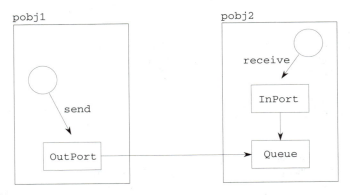

**Figure 5.8**    Data structures used in the CC++ channel library. In addition to a queue, a channel comprises an OutPort object and an InPort object used to encapsulate pointers to the queue. Processes apply send and receive operations to the outport and inport, respectively.

## 5.11    Case Study: Channel Library

In the first of two more substantial examples, we present an implementation of the channel library used in Program 5.3. This case study illustrates how CC++ can be used to develop libraries implementing particular programming paradigms: in this case, channel communication.

The channel library provides functions to create a channel, to extract pointers to inport and outport structures, and to send and receive messages. A channel is constructed from three basic data structures: the message queue itself and outport and inport objects used to contain pointers to the queue (Figure 5.8). The outport is created in the same processor object as the sender, while the inport and message queue are created in the same processor object as the receiver.

The implementation, Program 5.15, defines the processor object ChannelUser and the classes Channel, InPort, and OutPort. The processor object provides functions create_inport and create_outport that create the inport and outport associated with a channel; any program wanting to use the channel library must include this processor object as a base class. Recall that this was done when defining the processor object Construction in Program 5.3.

The Channel class provides three public member functions: the constructor Channel, which creates a new channel linking two specified processor objects; get_out_port, which returns a pointer to the channel's outport; and get_in_port, which returns a pointer to the channel's inport.

The InPort class is derived from the Queue class of Program 5.6. It adds to the functions already defined in that class a new function receive, which simply dequeues a message from the queue. Finally, the OutPort class encapsulates a global pointer and provides a send function that invokes an enqueue operation on the message queue referenced by this pointer.

```
global class FockNode : public POArrayNode {
public:
    void accumulate(int, DVector);   // Accumulate into array
    void fock_build();               // Computation routine
    void FockNode(int);              // Constructor
    void init_pobj(POArray &);       // Virtual function definition
private:
    double *da;                      // Local portion of arrays
    int blocksize;                   // Size of each block
    atomic void accum_local(int, DVector);
};

class Fock : public POArray {
public:
    Fock(int bs) { blocksize = bs; } // Constructor
    Fock(const POArray & ar) : POArray(ar) {};
    POArrayNode *global create_pobj(proc_t locn)
        { return new (proc) FockNode(blocksize); }
private:
    int blocksize;
};

void FockNode::init_pobj(POArray & ar) {
    p_array = new Fock(ar);
    p_array->blocksize = blocksize;
}

void FockNode::FockNode(int sz) {
    blocksize = sz;                  // Store block size
    da = new float[blocksize];       // Allocate array
    for (int i=0; i<blocksize; i++)  // Initialize array
        da[i] = 0.0;
}
```

**Program 5.16**   A CC++ implementation of a simple distributed-array class. The classes
Fock and FockNode provide functions to create a set of processor objects containing a
distributed array and to accumulate into elements of this array.

## 5.12   Case Study: Fock Matrix Construction

Our second case study illustrates the use of RPCs to implement asynchronous access to a
distributed data structure. Programs 5.16 and 5.17 sketch a CC++ implementation of the
parallel Fock matrix construction algorithm of Section 2.8. Recall that in this algorithm,
$P$ computation tasks must be able to read and write distributed arrays. The programs
presented here achieve this capability by distributing the arrays over a set of processor
objects. Computation threads, created one per processor object, operate on the distributed
array by invoking RPCs implementing operations such as accumulate and read.

```
void FockNode::accumulate(int index, DVector vec) {
    p_array->pobjs[index/blocksize]
            ->accum_local(index%blocksize, vec);
}


atomic void FockNode::accum_local(int idx, DVector vec) {
    for (int i=0; i<vec.length; i++)
        da[idx+i] += vec.elements[i];
}
```

**Program 5.17**  The `accumulate` member function of the `FockNode` class and the `accum_local` function used in its implementation.


The distributed array itself is implemented by the class `Fock` and the processor object class `FockNode`, presented in Program 5.16. These are derived from the classes `POArray` and `POArrayNode` of Program 5.10, much as in the climate model of Program 5.11, and provide definitions for the virtual functions `create_pobj` and `init_pobj`. The derived classes defined in Program 5.16 are used to create the array of processor objects within which computation will occur. The data structures that implement the distributed array are allocated within these same processor objects, with each of the `posize` processor objects being assigned `blocksize` array elements. Notice how the initialization function for `FockNode` allocates and initializes the elements of the distributed array.

For brevity, Program 5.16 implements only an `accumulate` operation. This function is defined in Program 5.17. Notice how it issues an RPC to a remote processor object (number `index/blocksize`) requesting an operation on a specified sequence of values. The function invoked by the RPC (`accum_local`) is an atomic function; this ensures that two concurrent accumulate operations do not produce meaningless results.

Having defined the classes `Fock` and `FockNode`, the implementation of the rest of the code is fairly straightforward. We first create and initialize $P$ processor objects of type `FockNode`, as follows.

```
Fock darray(1024);      // 1024 is block size
darray.init(P, nodes);  // P and nodes as usual
```

Then, we invoke on each processor object a task (`fock_build`) responsible for performing one component of the Fock matrix computation. Each such task makes repeated calls to `accumulate` to place the results of its computation into the distributed array.


## 5.13   Summary

In this chapter, we have learned about a programming language, CC++, that provides a small set of extensions to C++ for specifying concurrency, locality, communication, and mapping. CC++ does not support the task and channel abstractions of Part I directly, but its constructs can be used to build libraries that provide these abstractions. In keeping with

**Table 5.1** CC++ quick reference: the constructs described in this chapter, the section in which they are described, and programs that illustrate their use.

| Construct | Section | Illustrative Programs |
|-----------|---------|-----------------------|
| par | 5.3 | 5.3, 5.4, 5.11 |
| parfor | 5.3 | 5.10, 5.11, 5.13 |
| spawn | 5.3, 5.10 | |
| global | 5.4.1 | 5.3, 5.4, 5.5 |
| sync | 5.5.2 | 5.6 |
| atomic | 5.5.3 | 5.17 |
| proc_t | 5.8 | 5.8, 5.10, 5.11 |
| CCVoid | 5.5.4 | 5.7, 5.8 |

the design methodology of Chapter 2, CC++ allows mapping decisions to be changed independently of other aspects of a design. The performance modeling techniques of Chapter 3 and the modular design techniques of Chapter 4 also apply directly. Table 5.1 summarizes the language constructs that have been introduced.

The CC++ programs presented in this chapter tend to be more verbose than the equivalent Fortran M, High Performance Fortran, or Message Passing Interface programs to be presented in the chapters that follow. To a greater extent than these other systems, CC++ provides basic *mechanisms* that can be used to implement a variety of different parallel program structures. For example, we must implement a channel library in order to use channels in a CC++ program, and a processor object array library to create arrays of processor objects. Once these libraries have been written, however, they can be reused in many situations. This reuse is facilitated by the object-oriented features of C++.

## Exercises

1. Extend Program 5.4 to allow for nonbinary trees: that is, trees with an arbitrary number of subtrees rooted at each node.

2. Design and construct a CC++ implementation of the manager/worker structure used in the parameter study problem described in Section 1.4.4.

3. Design and construct a decentralized version of the manager/worker structure developed in Exercise 2. Design and carry out experiments to determine when each version is more efficient.

4. Design and implement a program that can be used to quantify CC++ processor object and thread creation costs, both within the same processor and on remote processors. Conduct experiments to measure these costs, and obtain estimates for $t_s$ and $t_w$.

5. Implement and instrument the channel library presented in Section 5.11, and use this code to measure CC++ communication costs on various parallel computers.

6. Modify the program developed in Exercise 5 to use `spawn` to implement the RPC used for a send operation, and conduct experiments to compare the performance of the two versions.

7. Complete Program 5.13, using the channel library of Section 5.11 to perform communication.

8. Complete Program 5.14, using the channel library of Section 5.11 to perform communication.

9. Design and carry out experiments to compare the performance of the programs developed in Exercises 7 and 8.

10. Use the `POArray` class of Program 5.10 to implement a version of Program 5.4 in which search tasks are implemented as threads mapped to a fixed number of processor objects.

11. Extend the program developed in Exercise 7 to provide a 2-D decomposition of principal data structures.

12. Extend the channel library presented in Section 5.11 to allow polling for pending messages.

13. Extend the channel library presented in Section 5.11 to provide a merger that allows multiple senders on a channel.

14. Implement a hypercube communication template (see Chapter 11). Use this template to implement simple reduction, vector reduction, and broadcast algorithms.

15. Construct a CC++ implementation of the tuple space module described in Section 4.5. Use this module to implement the database search problem described in that section.

## Chapter Notes

The C programming language was designed by Kernighan and Ritchie [170]. C++, which extends C in many respects, was designed by Stroustrup [92, 270]. A book by Barton and Nackman [29] provides an introduction to C++ for scientists and engineers. Objective C [66] is another object-oriented extension to C.

C* [281], Data-parallel C [136], and pC++ [38] are data-parallel C-based languages (see Chapter 7). COOL [50] and Mentat [125] are examples of parallel object-oriented languages. Concurrent C [117] and Concert C [19] are parallel C-based languages; the latter supports both remote procedure call and send/receive communication mechanisms. C-Linda [48] augments C with primitives for creating processes and for reading and writing a shared tuple space (Section 4.5).

CC++ was designed by Chandy and Kesselman [53]. The monograph *A Tutorial for CC++* [261] provides a tutorial and reference manual for the Caltech CC++ compiler. The sync or single-assignment variable has been used in a variety of parallel languages, notably Strand [107] and PCN [55, 105].

The online version provides access here to additional information on programming in CC++, including a public-domain compiler, a tutorial, and example programs.

# Fortran M

In this chapter, we describe Fortran M (FM), a small set of extensions to Fortran for parallel programming. In FM, tasks and channels are represented explicitly by means of language constructs. Hence, algorithms designed using the techniques discussed in Part I can be translated into programs in a straightforward manner.

Because Fortran M is a simple language, we are able in this chapter to provide both a complete language description and a tutorial introduction to important programming techniques. (Some familiarity with Fortran is assumed.) In the process, we show how the language is used to implement various algorithms developed in Part I.

After studying this chapter, you should be able to write simple FM programs. You should know how to create tasks and channels, how to implement structured, unstructured, and asynchronous communication patterns, and how to control the mapping of tasks to processors. You should also know both how to guarantee deterministic execution and when it is useful to introduce nondeterministic constructs. Finally, you should understand how FM supports the development of modular programs, and know how to specify both sequential and parallel composition.

## 6.1    FM Introduction

Fortran M provides language constructs for creating tasks and channels and for sending and receiving messages. It ensures that programs are deterministic if specialized constructs are not used, and it provides the encapsulation properties needed for modular programming. Its mapping constructs affect performance but not correctness, thereby allowing mapping decisions to be modified without changing other aspects of a design. These features make it particularly easy to translate algorithms designed using the techniques of Part I into executable FM programs.

FM is a small set of *extensions* to Fortran. Thus, any valid Fortran program is also a valid FM program. (There is one exception to this rule: the keyword COMMON must be renamed to PROCESS COMMON. However, FM compilers usually provide a flag that causes this renaming to be performed automatically.) The extensions are modeled whenever possible on existing Fortran concepts. Hence, tasks are defined in the same way as subroutines, communication operations have a syntax similar to Fortran I/O statements, and mapping is specified with respect to processor arrays.

The FM extensions are summarized in the following; detailed descriptions are provided in subsequent sections. In this chapter, FM extensions (and defined parameters) are typeset in UPPER CASE, and other program components in lower case.

1. A task is implemented as a process. A process definition has the same syntax as a subroutine, except that the keyword PROCESS is substituted for the keyword subroutine. Process common data are global to any subroutines called by that process but are not shared with other processes.

2. Single-producer, single-consumer channels and multiple-producer, single-consumer mergers are created with the executable statements CHANNEL and MERGER, respectively. These statements take new datatypes, called *inports* and *outports*, as arguments and define them to be references to the newly created communication structure.

3. Processes are created in *process blocks* and *process do-loops*, and can be passed inports and outports as arguments.

4. Statements are provided to SEND messages on outports, to RECEIVE messages on inports, and to close an outport (ENDCHANNEL). Messages can include port variables, thereby allowing a process to transfer to another process the right to send or receive messages on a channel or merger.

5. Mapping constructs can be used to specify that a program executes in a virtual processor array of specified size and shape, to locate a process within this processor array, or to specify that a process is to execute in a subset of this processor array.

6. For convenience, processes can be passed ordinary variables as arguments, as well as ports; these variables are copied on call and return, so as to ensure deterministic execution. Copying can be suppressed to improve performance.

The FM language design emphasizes support for *modularity*. Program components can be combined using sequential, parallel, or concurrent composition, as described in Chapter 4. In parallel and concurrent composition, the process serves as the basic building block. A process can encapsulate data, computation, concurrency, and communication; the ports and other variables passed as arguments define its interface to the rest of the program. The techniques used to implement sequential composition will be discussed in Section 6.9.

FM extensions can be defined for both the simpler and more established Fortran 77 and the more advanced Fortran 90. For the most part, we use Fortran 77 constructs in this chapter, except when Fortran 90 constructs are significantly more concise.

---

**EXAMPLE 6.1** (Bridge Construction)    Program 6.1 illustrates many FM features. This is an implementation of the bridge construction algorithm developed in Example 1.1. The program creates two processes, foundry and bridge, and connects them with a channel. The channel is used to communicate a stream of integer values 1..100 from foundry to bridge.

```
program fm_bridge_construction          ! Main program
INPORT (integer) pi                     ! Declare inport
OUTPORT (integer) po                    ! Declare output
CHANNEL(in=pi, out=po)                  ! Create channel
PROCESSES                               ! Create processes:
    PROCESSCALL foundry(100, po)        !   Two arguments
    PROCESSCALL bridge(pi)              !   One argument
ENDPROCESSES                            ! Block until done
end                                     ! End of program


PROCESS foundry(numgirders, po)         ! Process definition
integer numgirders                      ! Argument 1: integer
OUTPORT (integer) po                    ! Argument 2: outport
do i = 1, numgirders                    ! Repeatedly:
    SEND(po) i                          !   Send message
enddo                                   !
ENDCHANNEL(po)                          ! Terminate sequence
end                                     ! End of process


PROCESS bridge(pi)                      ! Process definition
INPORT (integer) pi                     ! Argument: inport
integer num, ioval                      ! Local variables
RECEIVE(port=pi, iostat=ioval) num      ! Receive message
do while(ioval .eq. 0)                  ! While not done:
    call use_girder(num)                !   Process message
    RECEIVE(port=pi, iostat=ioval) num  !   Receive message
enddo                                   !
end                                     ! End of process
```

**Program 6.1**    FM implementation of bridge construction problem.

This program comprises a main program and two process definitions. The main program creates a channel and instances of the processes foundry and bridge. It first declares two port variables, pi and po, that can be used to receive and send integer messages, respectively. The CHANNEL statement creates a channel and initializes pi and po to be references to this channel. The process block (PROCESSES/ENDPROCESSES) creates the two concurrent processes, passing the port variables as arguments.

The process definitions are distinguished by the PROCESS keyword. The foundry process uses the SEND statement to add a sequence of messages to the message queue associated with the channel referenced by po. The ENDCHANNEL statement terminates this sequence. The bridge process uses the RECEIVE statement to remove messages from this message queue until termination is detected.

## 6.2  Concurrency

We next give a more complete description of FM. The presentation is loosely structured according to the design methodology given in Chapter 2. First, we describe how FM programs define and create processes. Then, we explain how to specify various communication structures. Finally, we describe FM's mapping constructs. Along the way, we also address the issues of modularity and determinism.

### 6.2.1  Defining Processes

The first step in the development of an FM program is typically to define the tasks from which a computation will be constructed. As noted in Example 6.1, a task is implemented in FM as a process. A process definition has the same syntax as a subroutine except that the keyword PROCESS is used in place of subroutine, and common data are labeled PROCESS COMMON to emphasize that they are common only to the process and any subroutines that it calls. Processes cannot share common data.

A process definition also defines the process's interface to its environment. A process's dummy arguments (formal parameters) are a set of typed port variables. (For convenience, conventional argument passing is also permitted between a process and its parent. This feature is discussed in Section 6.7.) A port variable declaration has the general form

   *port_type* ( *data_type_list* ) *name_list*

The *port_type* is OUTPORT or INPORT and specifies whether the port is to be used to send or receive data, respectively. The *data_type_list* is a comma-separated list of type declarations and specifies the format of the messages that will be sent on the port, much as a subroutine's dummy argument declarations define the arguments that will be passed to the subroutine.

In Program 6.1, both pi and po are used to communicate messages comprising single integers. The following are examples of more complex message formats. In the second and third declaration, the names m and x have scope local to the port declaration. Notice how in the third declaration, the size of the array x is specified in the message.

```
INPORT (integer, real) p1          ! One integer, one real
INPORT (real x(128)) p2            ! Array of 128 reals
INPORT (integer m, real x(m)) p3   ! One integer (m); m reals
```

The value of a port variable is initially a distinguished value NULL and can be defined to be a reference to a channel by means of the CHANNEL, RECEIVE, MERGER, or MOVEPORT statements, to be defined in the following sections.

### 6.2.2  Creating Processes

Having defined one or more processes, we next construct a concurrent computation by creating instances of these processes. An FM program executes initially as a single process. This process can both execute sequential Fortran code and use process block and process do-loop constructs to create additional processes. A process block has the general form

```
PROCESSES
   statement_1
      ⋮
   statement_n
ENDPROCESSES
```

where $n \geq 0$ and the statements are process calls, process do-loops, and/or at most one subroutine call. A process call has the same syntax as a subroutine call except that the keyword PROCESSCALL is used in place of the keyword call.

Statements in a process block execute *concurrently*. For example, the following parallel block creates three concurrent processes: two workers and a single process_master.

```
PROCESSES
   PROCESSCALL worker(pi1)
   PROCESSCALL worker(pi2)
   PROCESSCALL process_master(po1,po2)
ENDPROCESSES
```

A process block terminates when all constituent statements terminate; execution then proceeds to the next executable statement. Thus, the parent process in this example proceeds to the statement after the parallel block only when both the the master and the workers have terminated execution.

A subroutine call in a parallel block allows the parent process to execute concurrently with the newly created processes. For example, the following variant of the preceding parallel block causes the current process to execute the subroutine subroutine_master concurrently with the two worker processes. Only two new processes are created, rather than three, and the subroutine can share common data with the calling process.

```
PROCESSES
   PROCESSCALL worker(pi1)
   PROCESSCALL worker(pi2)
   call subroutine_master(po1,po2)
ENDPROCESSES
```

A *process do-loop* creates multiple instances of the same process. It is identical in form to the do-loop except that the keyword PROCESSDO is used in place of the keyword do and the body can include only a process do-loop or a process call. For example, the following code creates ten instances of myprocess.

```
PROCESSDO i = 1,10
   PROCESSCALL myprocess
ENDPROCESSDO
```

Process do-loops can be nested inside both process do-loops and process blocks. Hence, the following code creates ten worker processes and one master.

```
PROCESSES
   PROCESSCALL master
   PROCESSDO i = 1,10
```

```
        PROCESSCALL worker
      ENDPROCESSDO
    ENDPROCESSES
```

## 6.3  Communication

FM processes, like the tasks introduced in Part I, cannot share data directly. Instead, they coordinate their execution and exchange data by sending and receiving messages on single-producer, single-consumer channels and multiple-producer, single-consumer mergers. Hence, the next step in program implementation after processes have been defined is to establish the channels and mergers needed for communication.

In this section, we focus on the constructs and techniques used to specify structured, "synchronous" communication operations (Section 2.3). In subsequent sections we examine both unstructured and asynchronous communication.

### 6.3.1  Creating Channels

The basic building block from which communication structures are constructed is the channel, created by executing the CHANNEL statement. This statement has the general form

    CHANNEL(in=*inport*, out=*outport*)

and both creates a new channel and defines *inport* and *outport* to be references to this channel, with *inport* able to receive messages and *outport* able to send messages. The two ports must be of the same type.

Optional iostat= and err= specifiers can be used to detect error conditions, as in Fortran file input/output statements. An err=*label* specifier causes execution to continue at the statement with the specified *label* if an error occurs while creating the channel. An iostat=*intval* specifier causes the integer variable *intval* to be set to zero if no error occurs and to a nonzero value otherwise. If neither err= nor iostat= specifiers are provided, an error causes the FM computation to terminate.

For succinctness, we use Fortran 90 *array sections* in the CHANNEL statement. An array section is like an array element but with a range rather than an index provided for one or more of its subscripts. A range is represented by a triplet with the following general form.

    *lower-bound* : *upper-bound* : *stride*

Bounds can be omitted if the corresponding bounds of the array are required; a stride of 1 is assumed if *stride* is omitted. See Figure 7.1 in Chapter 7 for examples of array sections.

Array sections provided in the in= and out= components of a CHANNEL statement must be *conformant*, that is, of the same size and shape. A channel is created for each pair of corresponding elements, as illustrated in Figure 6.1.

(a)
```
OUTPORT (integer) po(4)
INPORT  (integer) pi(4)
```

```
CHANNEL(out=po(:), in=pi(:))
```

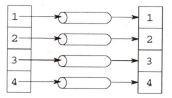

(b)
```
OUTPORT (integer) qo(4)
INPORT  (integer) qi(4)
```

```
CHANNEL(out=qo(2:4), in=qi(1:3))
CHANNEL(out=qo(1), in=qi(4))
```

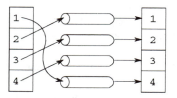

**Figure 6.1**   Array sections and the FM CHANNEL statement. In (a), a single statement creates four channels and, for $i = 1..4$, defines outport po$(i)$ and inport pi$(i)$ to reference the same channel. Hence, for example, a message sent on po(1) can be received on pi(1). In (b), two statements are used to define a "staggered" mapping of inports to outports, in which outport qo(mod$(i,4)$+1) and inport qi$(i)$ reference the same channel. Therefore, a message sent on qo(1) can be received on qi(4).

## 6.3.2   Sending Messages

A process sends a message by applying the SEND statement to an outport. Doing this adds the message to the message queue associated with the outport, with the outport declaration specifying the message format. For example, in the following code fragment the SEND statement sends a message consisting of the integer i followed by the first ten elements of the real array a.

```
OUTPORT (integer, real x(10)) po
⋮
SEND(po) i, a
```

A process sends a sequence of messages by repeated calls to SEND; it can also call ENDCHANNEL to send an end-of-channel (EOC) message. This usage is illustrated in Program 6.1, where the foundry process uses the SEND and ENDCHANNEL statements to send a total of 100 integer messages. ENDCHANNEL also sets the value of the outport variable to be NULL, thereby preventing further messages from being sent on that port.

Like Fortran's write and endfile statements, SEND and ENDCHANNEL are nonblocking (asynchronous); that is, they complete immediately. Variables named in a SEND statement can be modified in subsequent statements, without affecting the send operation.

An operation on an undefined port is treated as erroneous. Optional err= and iostat= specifiers (described in Section 6.3.1) can be included in SEND and ENDCHANNEL statements to indicate how to recover from this and other exceptional conditions.

### 6.3.3   Receiving Messages

A process receives a value by applying the RECEIVE statement to an inport. The inport declaration specifies the message format. For example, the bridge process in Program 6.1 makes repeated calls to the RECEIVE statement to receive a sequence of integer messages, detecting end-of-sequence by using the iostat specifier. A RECEIVE statement is blocking (synchronous); that is, it does not complete until data is available. Hence, a consumer process such as bridge cannot "run ahead" of the corresponding producer.

An array size can be included in a message, thereby allowing arrays of different sizes to be communicated on the same channel. For example, the following code fragment receives a message comprising the integer num followed by num real values. The incoming data are placed in array elements a(offset), a(offset+1), ..., a(offset+num-1).

```
INPORT (integer n, real x(n)) pi
integer num
real a(128)
RECEIVE(pi) num, a(offset)
```

An operation on an undefined port is treated as erroneous. A RECEIVE statement can include optional err= and iostat= specifiers to indicate how to recover from this and various exceptional conditions. In addition, an end=*label* specifier causes execution to continue at the statement with the specified *label* upon receipt of an end-of-channel message. This mechanism can be used to rewrite the bridge process of Program 6.1 as follows.

```
      PROCESS bridge(pi)              ! Process definition
      INPORT (integer) pi            ! Argument: inport
      integer num                    ! Local variable
      do while(.true.)               ! While not done:
         RECEIVE(port=pi, end=10) num !   Receive message
         call use_girder(num)        !   Process message
      enddo                          !
10    end                            ! End of process
```

```
program ring                              ! Main program
integer P                                 !
parameter (P=3)                           ! P processes
INPORT (real x(3)) pi(P)                  ! Inport declarations
OUTPORT (real x(3)) po(P)                 ! Outport declarations
CHANNEL(in=pi(1:P-1), out=po(2:P))        ! P-1 channels
CHANNEL(in=pi(P), out=po(1))              ! Pth channel
PROCESSDO i = 1,P                         ! Create processes
   PROCESSCALL ringnode(i, P, pi(i), po(i))
ENDPROCESSDO                              ! Block until done
end                                       ! End of program


PROCESS ringnode(i, p, left, right)       ! Code for single node
INPORT (real x(3)) left                   ! Inport (from left)
OUTPORT (real x(3)) right                 ! Outport (to right)
integer i, p                              !
real state(3), forces(3), msg(3)          ! Local variables
call initstate(i, state)                  ! Initialization
call copy(state, msg)                     !
call zero(forces)                         !
do j = 1, p-1                             ! Repeat P-1 times:
   SEND(right) msg                        !    Send to right
   RECEIVE(left) msg                      !    Receive from left
   call updateforces(msg, state, forces)  !    Compute
enddo                                     !
end                                       ! End of process
```

**Program 6.2**  FM implementation of ring pipeline.

---

**EXAMPLE 6.2** (Ring Pipeline)  Program 6.2 implements the ring-based pairwise interactions algorithm of Section 1.4.2. It comprises a main program and a process definition. The main program uses two channel statements to create P channels (Figure 6.1) and a process do-loop to create P processes. One inport and one outport are passed to each process as arguments, thereby connecting the processes in a unidirectional ring (Figure 6.2). The variables i and P are also passed to the processes as arguments; this capability is discussed in Section 6.7.

The ringnode process's four arguments are a unique identifier, the total number of processes, and an inport and outport referencing channels from one neighbor and to the other neighbor in the ring. The process first initializes its local state and then performs p-1 send-receive-compute steps before terminating.

---

**EXAMPLE 6.3** (Search)  Program 6.3 implements a prototypical tree-structured computation. The program explores a binary tree recursively in the manner of Algorithm 1.1, creating a task for each tree node and returning the total number of leaf nodes that represent

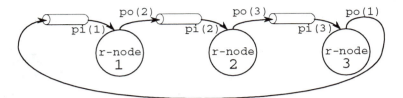

**Figure 6.2**   FM implementation of three-process ring pipeline showing channel connections.

solutions. In this simple program, the tree is not represented by an explicit data structure; instead, a process's position in the tree is represented by an integer.

The main program makes an initial call to the process `tree`. This process uses a process block to create recursively a set of $2n - 1$ ($n$ a power of 2) processes connected in a binary tree of depth $\log n$. Each process is connected to its parent by a channel; nonleaf processes also have channels from their two offspring. Notice the use of a subroutine call within a process block, as discussed in Section 6.2.2.

## 6.4   Unstructured Communication

In the preceding section, we saw how channels are used to implement regular communication structures such as a ring and a tree. Next, we examine the techniques used to implement *unstructured* communication algorithms in which the identity of communication partners changes during program execution (Section 2.3.3). These patterns require many-to-one and many-to-many communication structures, which can be implemented using FM's MERGER construct. They can also require the dynamic creation of channels during program execution.

### 6.4.1   Many-to-One Communication

FM's MERGER statement creates a first-in/first-out message queue, just as CHANNEL does. Unlike CHANNEL, however, it allows multiple outports to reference this queue and hence defines a many-to-one communication structure. Messages sent on any outport are appended to the queue, with the order of messages sent on each outport being preserved and any message sent on an outport eventually appearing in the queue. The MERGER statement has the general form

    MERGER(in=*inport*, out=*outport_specifier*)

where an *outport_specifier* can be a single outport, a comma-separated list of *outport_specifiers*, or an array section from an outport array. The statement creates a new merger and associates the named inport and outports with this merger. The inport and the outports must be of the same type. Optional `iostat=` and `err=` specifiers can be used to detect error conditions, as in the CHANNEL statement.

```
program fm_tree_example           ! Main program
INPORT (real) pi                  ! Inport
OUTPORT (real) po                 ! Outport
CHANNEL(in=pi, out=po)            ! Create channel
PROCESSES                         ! Create processes:
   PROCESSCALL root(pi)           !   Root of tree
   PROCESSCALL tree(0, 128, po)   !   Tree
ENDPROCESSES                      ! Block until done
end                               ! End of program


PROCESS tree(id, n, toparent)     ! Process definition
integer id                        ! Process identifier
integer n                         ! Number of processes
OUTPORT (real) toparent           ! Outport to parent
INPORT (real) li, ri              ! Ports for children
OUTPORT (real) lo, ro             ! Ports for children
if(n .gt. 1) then                 ! If not leaf:
   CHANNEL(in=li, out=lo)         !   Create channels
   CHANNEL(in=ri, out=ro)         !   for child processes
   PROCESSES                      !   Create children:
      PROCESSCALL tree(id, n/2, lo)      !     Left subtree
      PROCESSCALL tree(id+n/2, n/2, ro)  !     Right subtree
      call nonleaf(id, li, ri, toparent) !     Node
   ENDPROCESSES                   !
else                              ! If leaf:
   call leaf(id, toparent)        !   Create leaf process
endif                             !
end                               ! End of process
```

**Program 6.3**   FM formulation of a tree-structured computation.

The following code fragment implements a typical many-to-one communication structure. As illustrated in Figure 6.3, this uses a merger to connect four producer processes with a single consumer.

```
INPORT (integer) pi                ! Single inport
OUTPORT(integer) pos(4)            ! Four outports
MERGER(in=pi,out=pos(:))           ! Merger
PROCESSES                          !
   call consumer(pi)               ! Single consumer
   PROCESSDO i=1,4                 !
      PROCESSCALL producer(pos(i)) ! Four producers
   ENDPROCESSDO                    !
ENDPROCESSES                       !
```

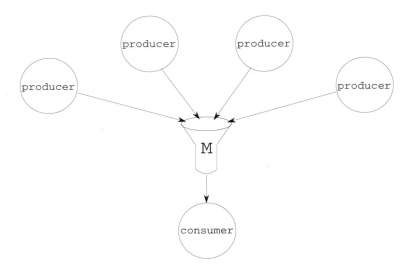

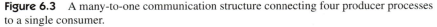

**Figure 6.3**   A many-to-one communication structure connecting four producer processes to a single consumer.

---

**EXAMPLE 6.4** (Manager/Worker)    As an additional example of many-to-one communication, we consider the manager/worker structure used in the parameter study problem described in Section 1.4.4. As illustrated in Figure 1.14, this structure comprises one manager task, one output task, and multiple workers. The FM implementation (Programs 6.4 and 6.5) comprises a main program and two process definitions. The `output` process definition is not shown.

The main program (Program 6.4) creates two mergers to implement the many-to-one communication structures connecting the workers to the manager and output tasks. It also creates NW channels to connect the manager to each worker.

Each worker (Program 6.5) repeatedly requests a task descriptor from the manager, waits to receive this task descriptor, and executes the task represented by the descriptor. A worker terminates when the channel from the manager is closed. The manager repeatedly receives and replies to requests for task descriptors until no more tasks remain. A request comprises the identifier of the requesting worker, an integer in the range 1..NW. The manager responds to the request by sending a new task descriptor (generated by the function `newtask`, and represented by a real number) on the appropriate channel. When all task descriptors have been allocated, the manager signals termination by closing the channels to the workers.

---

## 6.4.2    Many-to-Many Communication

A many-to-many communication structure allows multiple senders to communicate with multiple receivers. This structure is just a generalization of the many-to-one structure and

```
program fm_manager_worker                    ! Main program
integer NW                                   !
parameter(NW=31)                             !
INPORT (real) taskI(NW)                      ! Tasks: in
OUTPORT (real) taskO(NW)                     ! Tasks: out
INPORT (integer) reqI                        ! Task requests: in
OUTPORT (integer) reqO(NW)                   ! Task requests: out
INPORT (real) scoreI                         ! Scores: in
OUTPORT (real) scoreO(NW)                    ! Scores: out

CHANNEL(in=taskI(:), out=taskO(:))           ! Manager → workers
MERGER(in=reqI, out=reqO(:))                 ! Workers → manager
MERGER(in=scoreI, out=scoreO(:))             ! Workers → output

PROCESSES                                    ! Execute in parallel:
   call manager(reqI, taskO)                 !   one manager;
   PROCESSDO i=1,NW                          !   NW workers;
      PROCESSCALL worker(i, reqO(i), taskI(i), scoreO(i))
   ENDPROCESSDO                              !
   PROCESSCALL output(scoreI)                !   one output
ENDPROCESSES                                 !
end                                          ! End of program
```

**Program 6.4**   Top-level code for manager/worker problem.

can be implemented in a similar fashion, by using multiple mergers. The following code fragment implements a typical many-to-many structure. As illustrated in Figure 6.4, this code uses three mergers to connect four producer processes with three consumers. Each producer has an array of three outports; messages sent on outport $i$ are routed to consumer $i$. Each consumer has a single inport.

```
OUTPORT(integer) pos(3,4)                    ! 3 × 4 outports
INPORT (integer) pis(3)                      ! 3 inports
do i=1,3                                     ! 3 mergers
   MERGER(in=pis(i),out=pos(i,:))           !
enddo                                        !
PROCESSES                                    !
   PROCESSDO i=1,4                           !
      PROCESSCALL producer(pos(1,i))        ! 4 producers
   ENDPROCESSDO                              !
   PROCESSDO i=1,3                           !
      PROCESSCALL consumers(pis(i))         ! 3 consumers
   ENDPROCESSDO                              !
ENDPROCESSES                                 !
```

```
          PROCESS worker(myid,reqs,tasks,score)     ! Worker process
          integer myid                              ! Process identifier
          OUTPORT (integer) reqs                    ! Task request outport
          INPORT (real) tasks                       ! Task inport
          OUTPORT (real) score                      ! Score report port
          real best, task, val                      !
          real compute                              ! Real function
          best = 0.0                                ! Initial best score
          do while (.true.)                         ! Repeat until done:
             SEND(reqs) myid                        !   Send identifier
             RECEIVE(tasks,end=10) task             !   Wait for new task
             val = compute(task)                    !   Process task
             if(val .gt. best) best = val           !   Update score
          enddo                                     !
   10     continue                                  ! No more tasks
          SEND(score) best                          ! Report score
          end                                       ! End of worker

          PROCESS manager(reqs,tasks)               ! Manager process
          integer NW, NTASKS                        !
          parameter(NW=31, NTASKS=1000)             !
          INPORT (integer) reqs                     ! Inport from workers
          OUTPORT (real) tasks(NW)                  ! Outports to workers
          integer i, id                             !
          real nexttask                             ! Real function
          do i = 1, NTASKS                          ! Repeat for all tasks:
             RECEIVE(reqs) id                       !   Receive request
             SEND(tasks(id)) nexttask(i)            !   Send task
          enddo                                     !
          do i=1,NW                                 ! Signal each worker to
             ENDCHANNEL(tasks(i))                   ! end (close channel)
          enddo                                     !
          end                                       ! End of manager
```

**Program 6.5**   FM implementations of manager and worker processes.

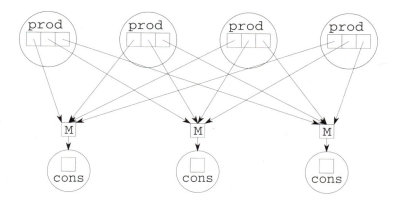

**Figure 6.4**  A many-to-many communication structure connecting four producer processes to three consumers. Each producer has an array of three outports, and each consumer has a single inport. Three mergers connect the outports with the inports.

### 6.4.3  Dynamic Channel Structures

Port variables can be incorporated in messages, hence transferring the ability to send or receive on a channel from one process to another. A port that is to be used to communicate port values must have an appropriate type. For example, the following declaration specifies that inport pi will be used to receive integer outports.

```
INPORT (OUTPORT (integer)) pi
```

A receive statement applied to this port must specify as an argument an integer outport variable into which the incoming port is to be placed. For example, the following code fragment first declares an integer outport variable qo and then receives an outport of the same type into that variable.

```
INPORT (OUTPORT (integer)) pi        ! Inport
OUTPORT (integer) qo                 ! Outport
RECEIVE(pi) qo                       ! Receive outport
```

Program 6.6 illustrates the transfer of ports in messages. This program implements a variant of the bridge construction program (Program 6.1) in which the bridge process makes explicit requests for data from the foundry process. Recall that in the original program, a stream of girders was communicated on a channel connecting foundry to bridge. In Program 6.6, things are reversed. A stream of requests is communicated on a channel connecting bridge to foundry. Each request comprises an outport that foundry uses to return a single data value to bridge. Hence, when bridge requires data, it creates a new channel, sends the outport to foundry, and waits for a reply on the input (Figure 6.5). This implements a *synchronous* communication protocol: the producer (foundry) produces data at the rate specified by the consumer (bridge) and hence cannot "run ahead" of the consumer.

In this example, it would perhaps be simpler to specify the desired behavior by using static "request" and "data" channels. With this structure, the producer sends a datum on

```
        program fm_bridge_construction_2      ! Main program
        INPORT (OUTPORT(integer)) pi          ! Declare inport
        OUTPORT (OUTPORT(integer)) po         ! Declare outport
        CHANNEL(in=pi, out=po)                ! Create channel
        PROCESSES                             ! Create processes
           PROCESSCALL foundry(pi)            !   Two arguments
           PROCESSCALL bridge(100,po)         !   One argument
        ENDPROCESSES                          ! Block until done
        end                                   ! End of program


        PROCESS foundry(pi)                   ! Process definition
        INPORT (OUTPORT (integer)) pi         ! Process argument
        OUTPORT (integer) qo                  ! Local variable
        num = 1                               ! Initialize count
        do while(.true.)                      ! Repeat:
           RECEIVE(pi, end=10) qo             !   Receive port
           SEND(qo) num                       !   Send on port
           num = num+1                        !   Increment count
        enddo                                 !
10      end                                   ! End of process


        PROCESS bridge(numgirders,po)         ! Process definition
        OUTPORT (OUTPORT (integer)) po        ! Process argument
        OUTPORT (integer) replyo              ! Local variable
        INPORT (integer) replyi               ! Local variable
        do i=1,numgirders                     ! Repeat:
           CHANNEL(in=replyi,out=replyo)      !   Create channel
           SEND(po) replyo                    !   Send outport
           RECEIVE(replyi) num                !   Receive value
           call use_girder(num)               !   Use value
        enddo                                 !
        ENDCHANNEL(po)                        ! Close channel
        end                                   ! End of process
```

**Program 6.6**   Using dynamic channels to implement synchronous communication.

the data channel each time it receives a request on the request channel. However, dynamic channels can be useful in more complex communication structures where a request must be routed through several intermediate steps before being serviced.

## 6.5   Asynchronous Communication

Recall that the need for asynchronous communication can arise when the tasks involved in a computation must access elements of a shared data structure in an unstructured manner

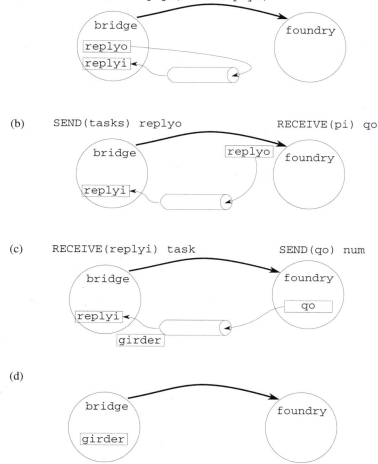

**Figure 6.5** Dynamic channel creation in the bridge construction problem. In (a), the bridge process creates a new channel. In (b), the new channel's outport is communicated to the foundry process. In (c), the new channel is used to return a datum (girder) to bridge. In (d), the communication is complete.

(Section 2.3.4). One implementation approach is to encapsulate the data structure in a set of specialized *data tasks* to which read and write requests can be directed. This approach is easily implemented using FM constructs: for example, the process structure illustrated in Figure 6.4 could be used to connect four computation tasks with three data tasks.

An alternative implementation approach is to distribute the shared data structure among the computation tasks. Individual computation tasks must then *poll* periodically for pending read and write requests. This approach is supported in FM by the PROBE statement, which allows a process to determine whether messages are pending on the channel or merger associated with an inport. This is a potentially nondeterministic operation, since the result returned by a PROBE statement can vary depending on the time at which it is executed. A PROBE statement has the general form

    PROBE(*inport*, empty=*logical*)

and sets the logical variable named by the empty specifier to true if the channel is empty (meaning a RECEIVE on the inport would block) and to false otherwise.

Optional iostat= and err= specifiers can be included in the control list; these are as in the Fortran inquire statement. Hence, applying a PROBE statement to an undefined port causes an integer variable named in an iostat specifier to be set to a nonzero value and causes execution to branch to a label provided in an err= specifier.

Knowledge about send operations is presumed to take a nonzero but finite time to become known to a process probing an inport. Hence, a probe of an inport that references a nonempty channel may signal true if a value was only recently communicated. However, if applied repeatedly without intervening receives, PROBE will eventually signal false and will then continue to do so until values are received.

The PROBE statement is useful whenever a process needs to interrupt local computation to handle communications that arrive at some unpredictable rate. For example, the following code might be used in an implementation of the branch-and-bound search algorithm of Section 2.7.

```
inport (T) requests             ! T an arbitrary type
logical eflag
do while (.true.)               ! Repeat:
    call advance_local_search   !   Compute
    PROBE(requests,empty=eflag) !   Poll for requests
    if(.not. eflag) call respond_to_requests
enddo
```

This code fragment alternates between advancing a local search and responding to requests for search problems from other processes.

The PROBE statement can also be used to receive data that arrive in a nondeterministic fashion from several sources. For example, Program 6.7 handles messages of types $T1$ and $T2$ received on ports data1 and data2, respectively. A disadvantage of this program is that if no messages are pending, it consumes resources by repeatedly probing the two channels. This busy waiting strategy is acceptable if no other computation can be performed on the processor on which this process is executing. In general, however, it is preferable to use a different technique. If $T1 = T2$, we can introduce a merger to combine the two message streams, as follows. The handlemsgs2 process then performs receive operations on its single inport, blocking until data are available.

```
MERGER(in=datai, out=data1o, out=data2o)
PROCESSES
    PROCESSCALL source1(data1o)
    PROCESSCALL source2(data2o)
    PROCESSCALL handlemsgs2(datai)
ENDPROCESSES
```

```
      PROCESS handlemsgs(data1,data2)              !
      INPORT (T1) data1                            ! Inport number 1
      INPORT (T2) data2                            ! Inport number 2
      logical empty1, empty2                       !
        :
        :
      do while(.true.)                             !
        PROBE(data1,empty=empty1)                  ! Look for data on 1
        if(.not. empty1) then                      ! If pending:
           RECEIVE(data1, end=10) val1             !   Receive message
           call handle_message1(val1)              !   and process it.
        endif                                      !
        PROBE(data2,empty=empty2)                  ! Look for data on 2
        if(.not. empty2) then                      ! If pending:
           RECEIVE(data2, end=10) val2             !   Receive message
           call handle_message2(val2)              !   and process it
        endif                                      !
      enddo                                        !
10    end                                          ! End of process
```

**Program 6.7**   Nondeterministic receive from two sources using PROBE.

## 6.6  Determinism

An important property of FM is that programs that do not use the nondeterministic constructs MERGER or PROBE can be guaranteed to be deterministic even if tasks and channels are created and deleted and channels are reconnected dynamically. The compiler and/or runtime system signal nondeterministic execution of programs that do not use nondeterministic constructs. As noted in Section 1.3.1, determinism can greatly simplify program development.

Individual FM processes execute deterministically. In addition, FM's send and receive operations maintain determinism as long as each channel has at most a single writer and a single reader. Hence, nondeterminism can arise only if an inport or outport is duplicated. This duplication would allow two or more processes to read or write the same channel, in which case the value retrieved from a channel with a receive operation would depend on the order in which different send and receive operations were executed. Situations in which this undesirable behavior could occur, and the FM mechanisms that avoid it, are as follows:

1. A port occurs more than once in a process block or process do-loop. The compiler and/or runtime system detects this and signals an error.

2. A port is communicated in a message and then used locally. The compiler generates code to invalidate a port that has been communicated. Hence, in the following code fragment the second send statement is erroneous and would be flagged as such either at compile time or at runtime.

```
OUTPORT (OUTPORT (real)) po        ! Interface port
OUTPORT (real) qo                  ! Other port
SEND(po) qo                        ! Send qo on po; invalidates qo
SEND(qo) x                         ! Try to send on qo; error!
```

3. A port occurs in an assignment statement. This situation is detected and flagged as an error by the compiler. The value of a port variable can be assigned to another port variable by using the MOVEPORT statement, but in this case the source port variable is invalidated. For example, the following code both sets p2 to the value of p1 and invalidates p1 by setting it to NULL.

```
INPORT (real) p1, p2               ! p1 and p2 are inports, type real
MOVEPORT(from=p1, to=p2)           ! Set p2 to p1; invalidate p1
```

## 6.7    Argument Passing

FM extends the basic task/channel model by allowing ordinary variables, as well as ports, to be passed as actual arguments in a process call. These values can be both read and modified inside the process, and updated values are available to the parent process when the process returns.

This capability is not essential: a value can always be passed to a process by defining a channel, sending the value on the outport, and passing the inport to the process as an argument. A similar strategy can be used to return a value from a process. However, normal argument passing often produces more concise and easy-to-understand programs. See Program 6.8 for a comparison of the two approaches.

### 6.7.1    Copying and Determinism

If unrestricted, argument passing could compromise determinism. The result computed by a program that passed the same variable to two processes could depend on the order in which those processes executed. For example, the following code fragments could be nondeterministic if a call to proc modifies the argument x and this variable is used in subsequent computation.

```
PROCESSDO i = 1,2                  PROCESSES
  PROCESSCALL proc(i,x)              PROCESSCALL proc(1,x)
ENDPROCESSDO                         PROCESSCALL proc(2,x)
                                   ENDPROCESSES
```

FM semantics ensure deterministic execution in these situations. Variables named as process arguments in a process block or do-loop are passed by value; that is, they are copied. In the case of arrays, the number of values copied is determined by the dummy argument declaration in the called process. Values are also copied back upon termination of the process block or do-loop, in textual and do-loop order. These copy operations ensure deterministic execution even when concurrent processes update the same value. Hence,

```
C   Main program                      C   Main program
    program args                          program channel
    integer num                           integer num
                                          INPORT (integer) numi
                                          OUTPORT (integer) numo
                                          CHANNEL(in=numi, out=numo)
    num = ...                             num = ...
                                          SEND(numo) num
    PROCESSCALL ap(num)                   PROCESSCALL cp(numi)
    end                                   end


C   Process ap                        C   Process cp
    PROCESS ap(num)                       PROCESS cp(numi)
                                          INPORT (integer) numi
    integer num                           integer num
                                          RECEIVE(numi) num
    call use(num)                         call use(num)
    end                                   end
```

**Program 6.8**   Argument passing vs. channels. The program on the left uses argument passing to pass the integer value num to the offspring process, which reads but does not write this value. The program on the right achieves the same effect using a channel.

these code fragments are deterministic even if proc does modify its argument. In both cases, the value computed by the process proc(2,x) is used to update x.

### 6.7.2 Avoiding Copying

Copying variables on process call and return can be expensive. Sometimes this copying is not necessary; for example, if a variable is only read by a process, not modified, then there is no need to copy it on return. We can provide INTENT declarations for dummy arguments to specify when copying is not to be performed. Three INTENT declarations are supported, as follows.

| | |
|---|---|
| INTENT(in) *var-list* | Copy on call only. |
| INTENT(out) *var-list* | Copy on return only. |
| INTENT(inout) *var-list* | (Default) Copy on call and return. |

We note that FM and Fortran 90 intent declarations have slightly different semantics. In a Fortran 90 subroutine, these declarations are assertions: intent(in) asserts that an argument is not written by the subroutine, and intent(out) asserts that the argument is not read. These assertions have no semantic content: a program with incorrect declarations is invalid. In contrast, INTENT declarations in an FM process have semantic content: they specify whether copying is to be performed, and they cannot be invalid.

---

**EXAMPLE 6.5** (Ring Pipeline)   We use a modified version of Program 6.2 to illustrate the use of INTENT declarations. Program 6.9 extends Program 6.2 by incorporating statements

```
        program ring                                  ! Main program
        integer P                                     !
        parameter (P=64)                              !
        :
        real input(3,P), output(3,P)                  ! I/O arrays
        call ring_read(input)                         ! Read input
        PROCESSDO i = 1,P                             ! Pass to processes
           PROCESSCALL ringnode(i, P, pi(i), po(i),
     $                       input(1,i), output(1,i))
        ENDPROCESSDO                                   !
        call ring_write(output)                       ! Write output
        end                                            ! End of program

        PROCESS ringnode(i, p, left, right, input, output)
        integer i, p                                  !
        real input(3), output(3)                      ! Data arguments
        INTENT(in) input                              ! Input only
        INTENT(out) output                            ! Output only
        :                                             ! Compute ...
        end                                           ! Return modified output
```

**Program 6.9**   Ring pipeline with INTENT declarations.

that read input data and write output data. The inport and outport declarations and the CHANNEL statements are as in Program 6.2 and are not shown here. The main program uses routines `ring_read` and `ring_write` to read and write two-dimensional arrays `input` and `output`, respectively. These arrays contain initial particle positions and final particle positions, respectively.

Argument passing is used to pass the appropriate components of these arrays to the subdomain processes, with INTENT declarations ensuring that `input` is copied only on call and `output` only on return (Figure 6.6). This centralized I/O strategy has the advantage of simplicity. A disadvantage on many computer systems is that it limits scalability, as the size of problem that can be solved is constrained by the need to fit the `input` and `output` arrays into a single processor's memory.

## 6.8  Mapping

Process blocks and do-loops define concurrent processes; channels and mergers define how these processes communicate and synchronize. A parallel program defined in terms of these constructs can be executed on both uniprocessor and multiprocessor computers. In the latter case, a complete program must also specify how processes are mapped to

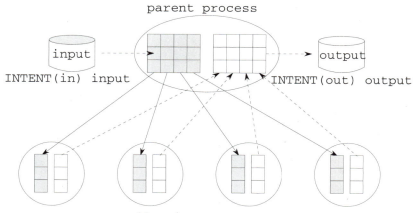

**Figure 6.6**   Argument passing and `INTENT` declarations in the ring pipeline program. The parent process reads the `input` array, which is of size $3 \times 4$, from a file and passes one column to each of four `ringnode` processes. The ring processes communicate among themselves and compute a column of the `output` array; upon termination, this array is copied back to the parent, which writes it to a file.

processors. Recall from Chapter 2 that this is an important part of parallel algorithm design.

FM provides three mapping constructs. The `PROCESSORS` declaration specifies the shape and dimension of a virtual processor array in which a program is assumed to execute, the `LOCATION` annotation maps processes to specified elements of this array, and the `SUBMACHINE` annotation specifies that a process should execute in a subset of the array. An important aspect of these constructs is that they *influence performance but not correctness*. Hence, we can develop a program on a uniprocessor and then tune performance on a parallel computer by changing mapping constructs. This is consistent with the PCAM design methodology discussed in Chapter 2, in which mapping is the fourth and final stage of the design process.

### 6.8.1   Virtual Computers

FM's process placement constructs are based on the concept of a *virtual computer*, a collection of virtual processors that may or may not have the same topology as the physical computer(s) on which a program executes. For consistency with Fortran concepts, an FM virtual computer is an $N$-dimensional array, and the constructs that control the placement of processes within this array are modeled on Fortran's array manipulation constructs.

The `PROCESSORS` declaration is used to specify the shape and size of the (implicit) processor array on which a process executes. This declaration is similar in form and function to the array `DIMENSION` statement. It has the general form

```
PROCESSORS(I₁, ... ,Iₙ)
```

PROCESSORS(16)

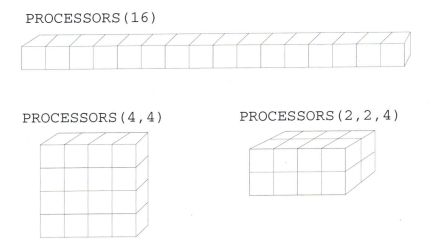

PROCESSORS(4,4)          PROCESSORS(2,2,4)

**Figure 6.7**   Three different PROCESSORS configurations, all involving 16 processors.

where $n \geq 0$ and the $I_j$ have the same form as the arguments to a DIMENSION statement. See Figure 6.7 for some examples.

The PROCESSORS declaration in the main (top-level) program specifies the shape and size of the virtual processor array on which that program is to execute. The mapping of these virtual processors to physical processors is specified at load time. This mapping may be achieved in different ways on different computers. Usually, there is a one-to-one mapping of virtual processors to physical processors. However, it can sometimes be useful to have more virtual processors than physical processors: for example, if a multicomputer program is being developed on one processor. The mapping of virtual processors to physical processors is not defined in FM, but is typically specified using a configuration file or command line arguments.

A PROCESSORS declaration in a process definition specifies the shape and size of the virtual processor array on which that particular process is to execute. As with a regular array passed as an argument, this processor array cannot be larger than that declared in its parent, but it can be smaller or of a different shape.

### 6.8.2   Process Placement

The LOCATION annotation is similar in form and function to an array reference. It has the general form

    LOCATION($I_1$, ... , $I_n$)

where $n \geq 0$ and the $I_j$ have the same form as the indices in an array reference, and specifies the processor on which the annotated process is to execute. The indices must not reference a processor array element that is outside the bounds specified by the PROCESSORS declaration provided in the process or subroutine in which the annotation occurs.

The following code fragment shows how the ring pipeline code of Program 6.2 might be extended to specify process placement. The PROCESSORS declaration indicates that this program is to execute in a virtual computer with P processors, while the LOCATION annotation placed on the process call specifies that each `ringnode` process is to execute on a separate virtual processor.

```
program ring                                 !
parameter(P=3)                               !
PROCESSORS(P)                                 ! Three virtual processors
  .                                           !
  .                                           !
PROCESSDO i = 1,P                             ! Each process on a processor
    PROCESSCALL ringnode(i, P, pi(i), po(i)) LOCATION(i)
ENDPROCESSDO                                   !
```

### 6.8.3  Submachines

A SUBMACHINE annotation is similar in form and function to an array section passed as an argument to a subroutine. It has the general form

```
SUBMACHINE(I₁, ... , Iₙ)
```

where $n \geq 0$ and the arguments $I_j$ have the same form as an array section and denote a set of processors in the current virtual computer. The annotated process executes in a new virtual computer comprising just these virtual processors. The PROCESSORS declaration in the process definition should agree in size and shape.

The SUBMACHINE annotation allows us to create "subcomputers," each comprising a subset of available processors, and hence to control resource allocation in programs comprising multiple components.

---

**EXAMPLE 6.6** (Coupled Climate Model)  A coupled climate modeling system comprising an ocean model and an atmosphere model can be structured as a *parallel composition* of the two component models. This organization is illustrated in Figure 6.8(a) and can be specified as follows.

```
parameter(P=4)
PROCESSORS(P,2*P)
  .
  .
PROCESSES
    PROCESSCALL atmosphere(...) SUBMACHINE(1:P, 1:P)
    PROCESSCALL ocean(...) SUBMACHINE(1:P, P+1:2*P)
ENDPROCESSES
```

The `ocean` and `atmosphere` processes are invoked in disjoint virtual computers of size P × P; hence, both process definitions should incorporate a declaration PROCESSORS(P,P). In some situations, it may be more efficient to structure the coupled model as

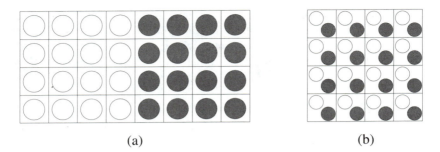

(a)                                                          (b)

**Figure 6.8**   Alternative mapping strategies in climate model. In (a), the two components are mapped to disjoint sets of $4 \times 4$ processors. In (b), they are mapped to the same processors.

a *concurrent composition* of the two components, as illustrated in Figure 6.8 (b). This effect can be achieved by changing the PROCESSORS declaration to PROCESSORS(P,P) and omitting the SUBMACHINE annotations. No change to the component programs is required.

---

**EXAMPLE 6.7**  (Search)   The following code fragment shows how virtual computers and the SUBMACHINE annotation can be used to control mapping in Program 6.3.

```
PROCESS tree(id, n, toparent)
PROCESSORS(n)                                ! Size of my computer
   :
PROCESSES                                    !   Create children
   PROCESSCALL tree(id, n/2, lo) SUBMACHINE(1:n/2)
   PROCESSCALL tree(id+n/2, n/2, ro) SUBMACHINE(1+n/2:n)
   call nonleaf(id, li, ri, toparent)
ENDPROCESSES
```

Recall that Program 6.3 creates a set of $2n - 1$ ($n$ a power of 2) processes connected in a binary tree of depth $\log n$. As illustrated in Figure 6.9, mapping can be achieved by using SUBMACHINE annotations to place processes located at the same depth in the tree on different processors (assuming that at least $n$ processors are available).

---

## 6.9   Modularity

Example 6.6 showed how FM constructs can be used to implement parallel and concurrent composition. The basic ideas are straightforward. A process (task) is defined for each component of a multicomponent program. These processes are then composed using a process block, with channels and/or mergers connecting ports in the different components. Mapping constructs control resource allocation and hence determine whether program components execute on the same or different processors.

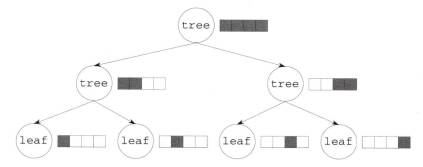

**Figure 6.9** Using submachines to control mapping in a tree-based algorithm executing on four processors. The figure shows both the nodes in the process tree (circles) and the virtual computer in which each process executes (the shaded portion of the original four-processor virtual computer).

In this section, we discuss the techniques used to implement *sequential* composition in FM programs. Recall that in sequential composition, different program components execute in sequence on all processors (Section 4.2.2). These program components may themselves communicate and synchronize, but they cannot create new tasks. Hence, each process executes the same program, and the entire computation moves sequentially from one parallel operation to the next. This is the SPMD programming model discussed in Section 1.3.2.

An FM implementation of an SPMD program comprises two components: initialization and execution. The *initialization* component creates the SPMD process structure and the communication structures (channels and mergers) required by the program components called in the sequential composition. The initialization typically comprises some channel and merger creation code followed by a process do-loop that creates one process per processor, with the appropriate ports passed as arguments.

The *execution* component implements the program executed by each process created by the process do-loop. This program comprises a sequence of calls to the program components involved in the sequential composition. These components can perform internal communication using the communication structure established during the setup phase of the computation.

The important point to understand about this structure is that once appropriate communication structures have been defined in the initialization phase, sequential composition can be used directly in the main body of the program, without any special constructs.

---

**EXAMPLE 6.8** (Sequential Composition)    We consider the SPMD finite difference computation used to illustrate sequential composition in Section 4.2.2. This computation is structured as a sequence of calls to a finite difference routine that performs nearest-neighbor communication and a reduction routine used to detect termination; the latter routine performs global communication. The basic logic executed by each process in this

```
        program fm_finite_diff                          ! Initialization code
        parameter(N=128, P=16, LogP=4)                  !
        INPORT (real x(N)) int(2,P)                     ! Inports: torus
        OUTPORT (real x(N)) outt(2,P)                   ! Outports: torus
        INPORT (real) inh(LogP, P)                      ! Inports: hypercube
        OUTPORT (real) outh(LogP, P)                    ! Outports: hypercube
C   Create nearest-neighbor channels
        CHANNEL(in=int(1,2:P), out=outt(2,1:P-1))
        CHANNEL(in=int(1,1), out=outt(2,P))             ! To left
        CHANNEL(in=int(2,1:P-1), out=outt(1,2:P))
        CHANNEL(in=int(2,P), out=outt(1,1))             ! To right
        do i = 1,P                                      ! Create hypercube channels
          do j = 1,LogP                                 !
            nbor = 1 + xor(i-1,2**(j-1))                !
            CHANNEL(in=inh(j,i), out=outh(j,nbor))
          enddo                                         !
        enddo                                           !
        PROCESSDO i = 1,P                               ! Create P processes
          PROCESSCALL node(int(1,i), outt(1,i), inh(1,i), outh(1,i))
        ENDPROCESSDO                                    !
        end                                             ! End of program
```

**Program 6.10**   Initialization code for FM finite difference program.

computation is as follows, where `localgrid` is the local component of the grid data structure.

```
        subroutine node
        real localgrid(N,N/P)
        while(.not. done) do
          call finite_difference(localgrid, localmax)
          call global_maximum(localmax, globmax)
          if(globmax .lt. threshold) done = .true.
        enddo
        end
```

Programs 6.10 and 6.11 implement the initialization and execution components of an FM implementation of this program. Because the program components invoked in the sequential composition perform both nearest-neighbor and hypercube communication, the initialization code first creates channels implementing these two communication structures. (The function `xor` is used as in Algorithm 11.1.) Then, a process do-loop creates P instances of the node process, passing each instance the appropriate ports.

The execution code comprises the process node, which calls first the procedure `finite_difference` and then the procedure `global_maximum`. These procedures use the ports passed as arguments to perform internal communication.

The various port variables passed as arguments in the execution component make for a rather clumsy program. The program can be made tidier by storing the ports in PROCESS COMMON with a series of MOVEPORT calls prior to calling user code. Each process can then execute the simpler code presented at the beginning of this example.

---

**EXAMPLE 6.9** (Message-passing Library)    The initialization code in Program 6.10 defined a separate communication structure for each component in the sequential composition. In this example, we present an alternative approach in which the initialization component of an SPMD program creates a single, general-purpose communication structure that can be used to perform any communication. In effect, we implement a message-passing library that provides similar functionality to the MPI library described in Chapter 8. We also use this example to show how port variables can be stored in PROCESS COMMON to simplify program interfaces.

Program 6.12 is a skeleton message-passing library that implements just simple send and receive functions. The main program first creates P mergers to implement a fully connected network, and then creates P node processes, passing each a single inport and P outports. The node process stashes the inport and outports in PROCESS COMMON and then calls the subroutine compute, which performs the actual computation. The PROCESS COMMON is defined as follows (file mp_stashed.com).

```
C    File "mp_stashed.com"
     PROCESS COMMON /stashed/ stashed_inp, stashed_outp
     INPORT (integer n, character x(n)) stashed_inp
     OUTPORT (integer n, character x(n)) stashed_outp(P)
```

This initialization code makes it possible for the rest of the program to call mp_send and mp_receive routines to send and receive messages to and from other processes.

---

## 6.10    Performance Issues

Because FM provides a direct implementation of the task/channel programming model, the performance analysis techniques developed in Chapter 3 can be applied directly to FM programs. Normally, a send on an outport results in a single communication. As noted in Chapter 3, the cost of each message can be specified with reasonable accuracy in terms of a startup cost and a per-word cost. It is necessary to distinguish between the communication costs incurred when communicating processes are located on different processors (*interprocessor* communication) or on the same processor (*intraprocessor* communication). Both these costs can depend significantly on implementation technology. Typically, interprocessor communication costs are similar to those in Table 3.1 in Chapter 3, and intraprocessor communication is cheaper. However, on some multicomputers with fast interprocessor communication and relatively low memory bandwidth, intraprocessor communication can actually be slower than interprocessor communication.

The following issues must also be considered when examining the performance of FM programs.

```
PROCESS node(int,outt,inh,outh)
INPORT (real x(N)) int(2)                    ! Inports: torus
OUTPORT (real x(N)) outt(2)                  ! Outports: torus
INPORT (real) inh(LogP)                      ! Inports: hypercube
OUTPORT (real) outh(LogP)                    ! Outports: hypercube
while(.not. done) do                         ! Repeat until done
    call finite_difference(localgrid, localmax, int, outt)
    call global_maximum(localmax, globmax, inh, outh)
    if(globmax .lt. threshold) done = .true.
enddo
end                                          ! End of node code


subroutine finite_difference(grid, max, int, outt)
INPORT (real x(N)) int(2)                    ! Inports: torus
OUTPORT (real x(N)) outt(2)                  ! Outports: torus
real grid(N,N/P), buff1(N), buff2(N)         !
SEND(outt(1)) grid(1,1)                       ! Send left
SEND(outt(2)) grid(1,N/P)                     ! Send right
RECEIVE(int(1)) buff1                         ! Receive left
RECEIVE(int(2)) buff2                         ! Receive right
max = update(grid, buff1, buff2)             ! Update grid
end                                          ! End of subroutine


subroutine global_maximum(local, global, inh, outh)
real local, global                           ! Input and output
INPORT (real) inh(LogP)                      ! Inports: hypercube
OUTPORT (real) outh(LogP)                     ! Outports: hypercube
work = local                                 ! Initial state
do i = 1, LogP                               ! For each neighbor:
    SEND(outh(i)) work                        !    Send state
    RECEIVE(inh(i)) newval                     !    Receive data
    work = max(work, newval)                  !    Update state
enddo                                        !
global = work                                ! Return state
end                                          ! End of subroutine
```

**Program 6.11**   Execution code for FM finite difference program. The first subroutine performs a simple finite difference computation, and the second performs a reduction using the hypercube algorithm of Chapter 2. For brevity, definitions for some variables and for parameters P, LogP, and N are omitted.

```
program mp_example                              ! Main program
parameter(P=16)                                 !
PROCESSORS(P)                                   !
INPORT (integer n, character x(n)) inp(P)
OUTPORT (integer n, character x(n)) outp(P, P)
do i = 1,P                                      !
   MERGER(in=inp(i),out=outp(i,:))              ! Fully connected
enddo                                           !
PROCESSDO i = 1,P                               ! Create nodes
   PROCESSCALL node(inp(i),outp(1,i)) LOCATION(i)
ENDPROCESSDO                                    !
end                                             ! End of program


PROCESS node(inp,outps)                         ! Single node code
parameter(P=16)                                 !
include "mp_stashed.com"                         ! PROCESS COMMON
INPORT (integer n, character x(n)) inp          !
OUTPORT (integer n, character x(n)) outp(P)
MOVEPORT(from=inp, to=stashed_inp)              ! Store inport
do i = 1,P                                       ! Store outports
   MOVEPORT(from=outp(i), to=stashed_outp(i))
enddo
call compute                                    ! Call program
end                                             ! End of process


subroutine mp_send(to, len, msg)                ! Send a message
parameter(P=16)                                 !
include "mp_stashed.com"                          ! PROCESS COMMON
character msg(len)                               !
SEND(stashed_outp(to)) len, msg                 !
end                                             ! End of send


subroutine mp_receive(len, msg)                 ! Receive a message
parameter(P=16)                                 !
include "mp_stashed.com"                          ! PROCESS COMMON
character msg(*)                                 !
RECEIVE(stashed_inp) len, msg                   !
end                                             ! End of receive
```

**Program 6.12**  A skeleton FM implementation of a general-purpose message-passing library.

*Process creation.* Process creation and deletion costs will only be a significant contributor to total execution time if a program creates and destroys many processes. These costs are influenced by the location of the created process (remote creation is typically more expensive than local creation) and by the number and size of process arguments (arguments must be copied upon call and return: see Section 6.7). In addition, a compiler may implement FM processes as heavyweight *Unix processes*, in which case process creation is relatively expensive, or as lightweight *threads*, in which case process creation is cheap.

*Fairness.* When two or more processes execute on the same processor, FM guarantees that execution is fair: that is, that no process that is not blocked waiting for data will be prevented indefinitely from executing. However, the time that a process waits before executing can vary significantly depending on characteristics of both the application and a particular FM implementation. Hence, care must be taken if application performance depends on obtaining timely responses to remote requests.

*Compiler optimization.* Because FM is a programming language rather than a library, a compiler may in some situations be able to reduce communication costs by coalescing messages or otherwise reorganizing a program to improve performance.

## 6.11    Case Study: Fock Matrix Construction

Programs 6.13 and 6.14 sketch an FM implementation of the parallel Fock matrix construction algorithm of Section 2.8. Recall that in this algorithm, $P$ computation tasks must be able to read and write two large distributed data structures. This capability is achieved by encapsulating these data structures in separate data tasks. Each computation task repeatedly generates requests for data values and then performs computation. The FM program implements computation and data tasks as compute and data processes, respectively, and connects these processes using a many-to-many communication structure, as illustrated in Figure 6.10. This structure uses P mergers to link P×P outports (To) with P inports (Ti). Each process is given an array of P outports, one connected to each merger. In Programs 6.13 and 6.14, P=128, and 1024 data values are allocated to P data tasks in a blocked fashion.

For brevity, the FM programs presented here implement only an accumulate operation. A compute process wanting to accumulate a value to address addr sends a message containing an offset (the integer mod(addr,ND)) and the value to be accumulated (a real) on outport number addr/ND. Notice that the compute and data processes are similar in structure to the manager and worker of Program 6.5.

## 6.12    Summary

In this chapter, we have discussed a programming language, Fortran M, that provides a direct and complete implementation of the task/channel programming model described in Part I. Fortran M incorporates language constructs for defining tasks and channels. In keeping with the design methodology discussed in Chapter 2, it allows mapping decisions to be changed independently of other design aspects. The performance modeling tech-

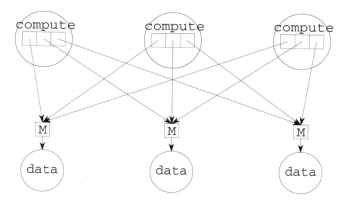

**Figure 6.10**    FM implementation of the Fock matrix problem, with P=3. Each of the P compute processes has an array of P outports connected via mergers with P data processes.

```
program simple_fm_fock                      ! Main program
parameter(P=128, N=1024, ND=N/P)            !
INPORT (integer, real) Ti(P)                !
OUTPORT (integer, real) To(P,P)             !
do i = 1,P                                  ! Mergers implement
   MERGER(in=Ti(i), out=To(i,:))            ! fully connected
enddo                                       ! network
PROCESSES                                   ! Create processes:
   PROCESSDO i=1,P                          !   P compute processes
      PROCESSCALL compute(To(1,i))          !
   ENDPROCESSDO                             !
   PROCESSDO i=1,P                          !   P data processes
      PROCESSCALL data(Ti(i))               !
   ENDPROCESSDO                             !
ENDPROCESSES                                !
end                                         ! End of program
```

**Program 6.13**    An FM solution to the Fock matrix construction problem: the main program.

niques given in Chapter 3 and the modular design techniques given in Chapter 4 also apply directly. Table 6.1 summarizes the language constructs that have been introduced.

## Exercises

1. Complete Programs 6.10 and 6.11. Modify each program to allow for fixed instead of periodic boundary conditions. Implement them on a parallel computer, and compare their performances with those predicted by the performance models developed in Chapter 3.

```
        PROCESS compute(outs)                    ! Compute process
        parameter(P=128, N=1024, ND=N/P)         !
        OUTPORT (integer, real) outs(0:P-1)
        integer addr, destnode, destaddr
        real value                               !
        :
        do i = 1,numtasks                        ! For each task ...
           addr = function1()                    ! Determine address
           value = function2()                   ! Determine value
           destnode = addr/ND                    ! Determine destination
           destaddr = mod(addr,ND)               ! and remote address
           SEND(outs(destnode)) destaddr, value
        enddo                                    !
        end                                      ! End of compute process

        PROCESS data(inp)                        ! Data process
        parameter(P=128, N=1024, ND=N/P)         !
        INPORT (integer, real) inp               !
        real array(0:ND-1)                       ! Local data
        integer address                          !
        real value                               !
        call initialize(array)                   ! Initialize data
        do while(.true.)                         ! Repeat:
           RECEIVE(inp,err=10) address, value
           call accumulate(address,value)        !   process request
        enddo                                    !
10      end                                      ! End of data process
```

**Program 6.14**  An FM solution to the Fock matrix construction problem: Process definitions.

2. Extend the programs developed in Exercise 1 to provide a 2-D decomposition of the principal data structures.

3. Complete Programs 6.4 and 6.5 and conduct experiments to study their performance.

4. A disadvantage of Program 6.4 is that a worker is idle while waiting for a task to arrive from the manager. This problem can be avoided by having the worker generate a request for the next task before processing the task just received. Write a variant of Program 6.4 based on this idea. Compare the performance of the two programs.

5. Design and implement a decentralized variant of the manager/worker structure described in Example 6.4. Design and carry out experiments to determine when this code is more efficient than the centralized code presented in the text.

**Table 6.1** FM quick reference: the constructs described in this chapter, with an outline of their syntax, the section in which they are described, and the programs that illustrate their use.

| Construct | Section | Illustrative Programs |
|---|---|---|
| PROCESS *name* | 6.2 | all |
| PROCESS COMMON | 6.2 | 6.12 |
| INPORT (*type*) *var* | 6.2.1 | all |
| OUTPORT (*type*) *var* | 6.2.1 | all |
| PROCESSES | 6.2.2 | 6.1, 6.4 |
| PROCESSDO | 6.2.2 | 6.2, 6.10, 6.4 |
| CHANNEL(in=*inport*,out=*outport*) | 6.3.1 | 6.1, 6.2, 6.5 |
| MERGER(in=*inport*,out=*outports*) | 6.4.1 | 6.4, 6.13 |
| SEND(*outport*) *values* | 6.3.2 | 6.1, 6.5, 6.14 |
| ENDCHANNEL(*outport*) | 6.3.2 | 6.1, 6.5 |
| RECEIVE(*inport*) *variables* | 6.3.3 | 6.1, 6.5, 6.7, 6.14 |
| MOVEPORT(from=*port*,to=*port*) | 6.2.1 | |
| PROBE(*inport*,empty=*logical*) | 6.5 | 6.7 |
| INTENT(*in-out-specifier*) *variables* | 6.7.2 | 6.9 |
| PROCESSORS(*dimensions*) | 6.8.1 | 6.3, 6.12 |
| LOCATION(*indices*) | 6.8.2 | 6.12 |
| SUBMACHINE(*array-section*) | 6.8.3 | 6.3 |

6. Write programs that can be used to quantify process creation and communication costs on a uniprocessor and on a networked or parallel computer system. Conduct experiments to measure these costs, and obtain estimates for $t_s$ and $t_w$.

7. Write programs that implement two-way communication (a) by using a pair of channels and (b) with a single channel and dynamically created reply channels. Compare the performance of the two programs on a parallel computer. Draw conclusions regarding the relative costs of the two mechanisms as implemented in your FM compiler.

8. Implement a variant of Programs 6.4 and 6.5 in which dynamically created reply channels, rather than a static network of reply channels, are used to return tasks to workers.

9. Extend Program 6.10 to use INTENT declarations to pass input and output arrays to and from subdomain processes.

10. Develop a program that receives data of different types from two sources, without busy waiting. *Hint*: Use additional channels to communicate type information.

11. Show how the functionality provided by the PROBE statement can be implemented

by using a merger. *Hint*: A process sends a distinguished message to itself when it wants to check for pending input.

12. Extend Program 6.13 to implement read requests.

13. Complete Program 6.12, extend it to support message tags (Chapter 8), and use the resulting program to implement the symmetric pairwise interactions algorithm of Section 1.4.2.

14. Using the code in Programs 6.10 and 6.11 as a basis, implement a hypercube communication template (see Chapter 11). Use this template to implement simple reduction, vector reduction, and broadcast algorithms.

15. Construct an FM implementation of the tuple space module described in Section 4.5. Use this module to implement the database search problem described in that section.

## Chapter Notes

Fortran was one of the first computer programming languages and, despite its age, continues to be widely used in science and engineering. An ongoing modernization process slowly introduces features found in more modern languages. The result is the ANSI standards Fortran 77 and Fortran 90 [300, 16]. The books by Metcalf and Reid [204], Adams et al. [3], and Brainerd, Goldberg, and Adams [43] provide good introductions to Fortran 90. Kerrigan [171] addresses the topic of migrating existing codes to Fortran 90. Chapter 7 reviews some Fortran 90 features.

Many parallel dialects of Fortran have been designed over the years. For example, Karp and Babb survey ten such dialects [165]. Most were designed for specifying concurrency in shared-memory computers and hence do not provide constructs for managing locality. Nor do they enforce determinism or modularity. Several recent language designs have emphasized data-parallel programming; these are discussed in Chapter 7, as is work on parallelizing compilers. Fortran M is distinguished by its support for task parallelism, deterministic execution, and modularity. Chandy and Foster provide both a language description and a more formal definition [102, 51], while the monograph *Programming in Fortran M* [106] provides a tutorial and reference manual for the Argonne Fortran M compiler.

The online version provides access here to additional information on programming in Fortran M, including a public-domain compiler, a tutorial, and example programs.

# 7 High Performance Fortran

The term *data parallelism* refers to the concurrency that is obtained when the same operation is applied to some or all elements of a data ensemble. A data-parallel program is a sequence of such operations. A parallel algorithm is obtained from a data-parallel program by applying domain decomposition techniques to the data structures operated on. Operations are then partitioned, often according to the "owner computes" rule, in which the processor that "owns" a value is responsible for updating that value. Typically, the programmer is responsible for specifying the domain decomposition, but the compiler partitions the computation automatically.

In this chapter, we introduce the key concepts of data-parallel programming and show how designs developed using the techniques discussed in Part I can be adapted for data-parallel execution. We base our presentation on the languages Fortran 90 (F90) and High Performance Fortran (HPF). Many of the ideas also apply to other data-parallel languages, such as C* and pC++. F90 provides constructs for specifying concurrent execution but not domain decomposition. HPF augments F90 with additional parallel constructs and data placement directives, which allow many HPF programs to be compiled with reasonable efficiency for a range of parallel computers.

After studying this chapter, you should know to write simple data-parallel programs using HPF. You should also understand how the design principles developed in Part I relate to data-parallel programs, and you should be able to evaluate the impact of HPF's data placement directives on performance. Finally, you should be able to determine when algorithms are suitable for data-parallel implementation.

## 7.1 Data Parallelism

We first provide a general introduction to data parallelism and data-parallel languages, focusing on concurrency, locality, and algorithm design.

### 7.1.1 Concurrency

Depending on the programming language used, the data ensembles operated on in a data-parallel program may be regular (e.g., an array) or irregular (e.g., a tree or sparse matrix). In F90 and HPF, the data structures operated on are arrays. In contrast, the data-parallel language pC++ allows programs to operate not only on arrays but also on trees, sets, and other more complex data structures.

Concurrency may be implicit or may be expressed by using explicit parallel constructs. For example, the F90 array assignment statement is an *explicitly* parallel construct; we write

```
A = B*C                          ! A, B, C are arrays
```

to specify that each element of array A is to be assigned the product of the corresponding elements of arrays B and C. This statement also implies *conformality*; that is, the three arrays have the same size and shape. In contrast, the following do-loop is *implicitly* parallel: a compiler may be able to detect that the various do-loop iterations are independent (meaning that one iteration does not write a variable read or written by another) and hence can be performed in parallel, but this detection requires some analysis.

```
do i = 1,m
   do j = 1,n
      A(i,j) = B(i,j)*C(i,j)
   enddo
enddo
```

A data-parallel program is a sequence of explicitly and implicitly parallel statements. On a distributed-memory parallel computer, compilation typically translates these statements into an SPMD program (Section 1.3.2), in which each processor executes the same code on a subset of the data structures. In many cases, the compiler can construct this program by first partitioning data structures into disjoint subdomains, one per processor, and then applying the *owner computes rule* to determine which operations should be performed on each processor. This rule states that the computation required to produce a datum is performed on the processor on which that datum is located. However, compilers can also use different techniques.

Compilation also introduces communication operations when computation mapped to one processor requires data mapped to another processor. As an example, consider the following program.

```
real y, s, X(100)                ! y, s scalars; X an array

X = X*y                          ! Multiply each X(i) by y
do i = 2,99
   X(i) = (X(i-1) + X(i+1))/2    ! Communication required
enddo
s = SUM(X)                       ! Communication required
```

The communication requirements of this program depend on how the variables X, y, and s are distributed over processors. If X is distributed while y and s are replicated, then the first assignment can proceed without communication, with each X(i) being computed by the processor that owns X(i). The second assignment (in the do-loop) requires communication: the processor computing X(i) requires the values of X(i-1) and X(i+1), which may be located on different processors. The summation also requires communication.

## 7.1.2 Locality

Data placement is an essential part of a data-parallel algorithm, since the mapping of data to processors determines the *locality* of data references and hence, to a large extent, the performance of a parallel program. For example, the simple array assignment A = B*C either can proceed without any communication or can require communication for every assignment, depending on whether corresponding elements of the arrays A, B, and C are located on the same or different processors.

Identifying the best distribution of the various data structures operated on by a data-parallel program is a global optimization problem and not generally tractable. Hence, data-parallel languages often provide the programmer with the ability to define how data structures are to be distributed. In HPF, the DISTRIBUTE directive fulfills this function. The statements

```
!HPF$ PROCESSORS pr(16)
      real X(1024)
!HPF$ DISTRIBUTE X(BLOCK) ONTO pr
```

indicate that the array X is to be distributed in a blocked fashion over 16 processors— processor 0 gets the first 1024/16 elements, processor 1 the second 1024/16 elements, and so on.

## 7.1.3 Design

The data-parallel programming model is both higher level and more restrictive than the task/channel model introduced in Part I. It is *higher level* in that the programmer is not required to specify communication structures explicitly: these are derived by a compiler from the domain decomposition specified by the programmer. It is *more restrictive* because not all algorithms can be specified in data-parallel terms. For these reasons, data parallelism, although important, is not a universal parallel programming paradigm.

Despite these differences between the task/channel and data-parallel programming models, the program design techniques developed in Part I are still applicable. Recall that we have decomposed the design process into partitioning, communication, agglomeration, and mapping phases. Data-parallel languages address the first phase directly, by providing implicit and explicit constructs that can be used to specify a very fine-grained partition of a computation, in which one task is created for each data element. As noted in Section 2.2, a key concern at this stage is to define a partition that identifies sufficient concurrency.

The PCAM design strategy of Chapter 2 requires that once we have developed a fine-grained partition, we determine communication requirements, agglomerate fine-grained tasks into larger tasks, and map tasks to processors. The beauty of the data-parallel approach is that the latter issues can be addressed at a particularly high level, by means of directives, rather than in terms of explicit communication and mapping operations. Directives indicate how arrays are to be aligned and distributed over processors and hence specify agglomeration and mapping. Communication operations are not specified explicitly by the programmer but are instead inferred by the compiler from the program.

The translation from fine-grained source program and directives to executable (typically SPMD) program is an automatic process that is performed by the data-parallel compiler. Nevertheless, the programmer must understand the essential characteristics of this translation in order to write efficient code and identify inefficient constructs. For example, an inappropriate choice of directives may lead to load imbalances or unnecessary communication. Alternatively, a data-parallel compiler may fail to recognize opportunities for concurrent execution. Generally, a data-parallel language compiler can be expected to generate reasonably efficient code when a program's communication structure is regular and local. Programs involving irregular and global communication patterns are less likely to be compiled efficiently. These and other performance issues are addressed in Section 7.7.

Finally, we note that the modular design techniques introduced in Chapter 4 apply to data-parallel programs. The issues involved are straightforward. Because data-parallel programs have sequential semantics, we need be concerned only with sequential composition of program components (Section 4.2.2). The primary concern in a parallel environment is the choice of data distributions in components that are to be composed. This issue is discussed in Section 7.5.

### 7.1.4   Data-Parallel Languages

In the remainder of this chapter, we first briefly introduce F90 and then describe HPF. Much of this material also applies to other data-parallel languages. The chapter notes provide pointers to relevant documentation.

F90 is a data-parallel programming language in its own right. Its array assignment statement and array intrinsic functions can be used to specify certain classes of data-parallel computations. Our main interest in F90, however, is that it forms the basis for HPF, which augments F90 with data distribution directives, a FORALL statement, the IN-DEPENDENT directive, and new intrinsics. Array assignment, the FORALL statement, and the INDEPENDENT directive are used to identify *concurrency* in an algorithm, while data distribution directives specify how data should be placed on physical processors and hence provide control over *locality*.

Although HPF defines only a small set of extensions to F90, it is nevertheless a complex language. The extensions have numerous variants and can interact with F90 constructs and with each other in a wide variety of ways. In the interests of succinctness and clarity, our presentation does not aim for completeness but rather seeks to present the essential ideas required to understand data-parallel programming and the HPF constructs required to write simple programs. These constructs are taken from the official *HPF subset*, which should in principle be supported by all HPF compilers.

## 7.2   Fortran 90

Fortran 90 (F90) is a complex language. It augments Fortran 77 (F77) with pointers, user-defined datatypes, modules, recursive subroutines, dynamic storage allocation, array operations, new intrinsic functions, and many other features. We focus here on those new features that are most relevant to parallel programming: the *array assignment statement* and the *array intrinsic functions*.

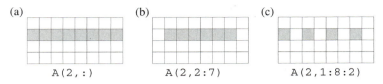

**Figure 7.1**   F90 array sections. The three examples show array sections comprising (a) all of row 2, (b) elements 2..7 of row 2, and (c) elements 1,3,5,7 of row 2, respectively.

### 7.2.1   Array Assignment Statement

F90 allows a variety of *scalar* operations—operations defined on single values—to be applied also to entire arrays. This feature causes the scalar operation to be applied to each element of the array. If an operation involves several values, all must be represented by *conformable* arrays, that is, scalar values or arrays of the same size and shape. The operation is performed on corresponding elements from each array. For example, consider the following scalar operation, which assigns the sum b+c to a.

```
integer a, b, c
a = b + c
```

In F90, we can apply the same operation to arrays A and B and scalar c, as follows. This assigns each element A(i,j) of A the sum B(i,j)+c.

```
integer A(10,10), B(10,10), c
A = B + c
```

In fact, all F90's unary and binary intrinsic operations can be applied to arrays, as the following examples show.

```
real A(10,20), B(10,20)
logical L(10,20)
A = A + 1.0          ! Adds 1.0 to each element of A
A = SQRT(A)          ! Computes square root of each element of A
L = A .EQ. B         ! Sets L(i,j) to .true. if A(i,j)=B(i,j);
                     ! and to .false. otherwise
```

A conformable *array section* can be substituted for an entire array in an array operation. An array section is represented by specifying a range for one or more subscripts. A range is represented by a triplet that has the following general form.

> *lower-bound* : *upper-bound* : *stride*

A stride of 1 is assumed if : *stride* is omitted, and bounds can be omitted if the corresponding bounds of the array are required. See Figure 7.1 for examples of array sections.

When operations are performed on arrays and array sections, corresponding elements are selected by position, not index. Hence, different array components do not need to have corresponding subscripts, and we can write the following code to compute the sum A(i)=B(i)+B(i+1) for $1 \le i \le 7$ (Figure 7.2).

```
A(1:7) = B(1:7) + B(2:8)
```

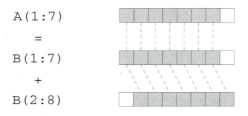

```
A(1:7)

    =

B(1:7)

    +

B(2:8)
```

**Figure 7.2**    Use of array sections to compute the sum $B(i)+B(i+1)$ for $1 \leq i \leq 7$.

**Table 7.1**    Selected F90 array intrinsic functions.

| Function | Return Value |
|---|---|
| MAXVAL(A) | Maximum value in A |
| MINVAL(A) | Minimum value in A |
| SUM(A) | Sum of elements of A |
| PRODUCT(A) | Product of elements of A |
| MAXLOC(ARRAY) | Indices of maximum value in A |
| MINLOC(ARRAY) | Indices of minimum value in A |
| MATMUL(A,B) | Matrix multiplication A*B |
| DOT_PRODUCT(A,B) | Vector dot product A.B |
| TRANSPOSE(A) | Transpose of A |
| CSHIFT(A,SHIFT,DIM) | Rotation of elements of A |

Finally, a masked array assignment uses the WHERE construct to restrict the array elements on which an assignment is performed. For example, the following statement replaces each nonzero element of X with its reciprocal (the F90 /= operator is equivalent to .NE. in F77).

```
WHERE(X /= 0) X = 1.0/X
```

## 7.2.2   Array Intrinsic Functions

All F90 intrinsic functions that apply to scalar values can also be applied to arrays, in which case the function is applied to each array element. For example, ABS(A) returns an array containing the absolute values of the elements of array A. In addition, F90 provides a number of *transformational* functions which return a scalar or array result that depends on the values of many elements of an array. Table 7.1 lists a representative selection of these functions.

MAXVAL, MINVAL, SUM, and PRODUCT perform a reduction operation (Section 2.3.2) on an array, returning a scalar value representing the maximum, minimum, sum, or product of the elements of the array, respectively. Hence, the following code sets the scalar variable s to the sum of the elements of the array X.

```
real s, X(100)
s = SUM(X)
```

The CSHIFT function performs a circular shift on an array, returning a new array of the same size and shape but with its elements in a different configuration. As illustrated in Figure 7.3, a call of the form

```
CSHIFT(A,s,d)
```

performs a circular shift on the elements of the array A, where the scalar or array s specifies the size and direction (left is positive) of the shift and the optional argument d indicates the dimension in which the shift is to be applied (it defaults to 1). This function is often used in expressions involving index expressions. For example, consider the following F77 loop.

```
real X(0:99), B(0:99)
do i = 0,99
   B(i) = ( X(mod(i+99,100) + X(mod(i+1,100)) )/2
enddo
```

This can be written in F90 as

```
real X(100), B(100), L(100), R(100)
L = CSHIFT(X,+1)
R = CSHIFT(X,-1)
B = ( L + R )/2
```

or simply as follows.

```
real X(100), B(100)
B = ( CSHIFT(X,+1) + CSHIFT(X,-1) )/2
```

In both cases, an array assignment sets the array B to the sum of two arrays: X shifted left one element, and X shifted right one element.

Although powerful, F90's array operations can be used to implement only a limited class of data-parallel algorithms. Consequently, F90 programs often incorporate code that, although implicitly parallel, must be executed sequentially if a compiler is unable to detect the implicit parallelism. For example, the following code zeroes the diagonal of an array. Although clearly a parallel operation, this cannot be expressed as such using the F90 array assignment statement.

```
do i = 1,100
   X(i,i) = 0.0
enddo
```

---

**EXAMPLE 7.1** (Finite Difference)     Program 7.1 illustrates F90's array assignment and array intrinsics. This program, for which both F77 and F90 versions are given, first applies a four-point finite difference stencil to the array X to obtain the array New and then computes the maximum difference between the two arrays. The F90 version uses an array assignment and the intrinsic functions ABS and MAXVAL.

---

(a)

| | | | | |
|---|---|---|---|---|
| 11 | 12 | 13 | 14 | 15 |
| 21 | 22 | 23 | 24 | 25 |
| 31 | 32 | 33 | 34 | 35 |
| 41 | 42 | 43 | 44 | 45 |

A =

CSHIFT(A,-1) →

| | | | | |
|---|---|---|---|---|
| 41 | 42 | 43 | 44 | 45 |
| 11 | 12 | 13 | 14 | 15 |
| 21 | 22 | 23 | 24 | 25 |
| 31 | 32 | 33 | 34 | 35 |

(b)

| | | | | |
|---|---|---|---|---|
| 11 | 12 | 13 | 14 | 15 |
| 21 | 22 | 23 | 24 | 25 |
| 31 | 32 | 33 | 34 | 35 |
| 41 | 42 | 43 | 44 | 45 |

A =

CSHIFT(A,-3,2) →

| | | | | |
|---|---|---|---|---|
| 13 | 14 | 15 | 11 | 12 |
| 23 | 24 | 25 | 21 | 22 |
| 33 | 34 | 35 | 31 | 32 |
| 43 | 44 | 45 | 41 | 42 |

**Figure 7.3**    The F90 CSHIFT function. In (a), a negative shift of one element is applied in dimension 1; in (b), a negative shift of three elements is applied in dimension 2.

## 7.3    Data Distribution

Array expressions specify concurrency but not locality. That is, they specify opportunities for parallel execution but not how these opportunities should be exploited so as to minimize communication costs on a parallel computer. HPF introduces *data distribution directives* to provide the programmer with control over locality. These directives work as follows. The PROCESSORS directive is used to specify the shape and size of an array of abstract processors. The ALIGN directive is used to align elements of different arrays with each other, indicating that they should be distributed in the same manner. The DISTRIBUTE directive is used to distribute an object (and any other objects that may be aligned with it) onto an abstract processor array. The mapping of abstract processors to physical processors is implementation dependent and is not specified in the language. The three directives are summarized in Figure 7.4.

Figure 7.5 illustrates the use of ALIGN and DISTRIBUTE. The two-phase mapping strategy reduces the number of changes needed to move from one machine to another. A different machine may necessitate a different partitioning strategy but is less likely to require changes to array alignments.

Data distribution directives can have a major impact on a program's performance but *do not affect the result computed*. In this sense, they are similar to FM mapping annotations. However, they have a more profound effect on program structure: they affect partitioning, agglomeration, and communication as well as mapping. As in FM, this orthogonality makes it possible to experiment with alternative parallel algorithms simply by changing directives.

Data distribution directives are *recommendations* to an HPF compiler, not instructions. The compiler does not have to obey them if, for example, it determines that performance can be improved by ignoring them.

```
C    F77 version:
     program f77_finite_difference
     real X(100,100), New(100,100)
     do i = 2,99
        do j = 2,99
           New(i,j) = (X(i-1, j) + X(i+1, j) +
     $                    X(i, j-1) + X(i, j+1) )/4
        enddo
     enddo
     diffmax = 0.0
     do i = 1,100
        do j = 1,100
           diff = abs(New(i,j)-X(i,j))
           if(diff .gt. diffmax) diffmax = diff
        enddo
     enddo
     end


C    F90 version:
     program f90_finite_difference
     real X(100,100), New(100,100)
     New(2:99,2:99) = (X(1:98, 2:99) + X(3:100, 2:99) +
     $                    X(2:99,1:98) + X(2:99, 3:100) )/4
     diffmax = MAXVAL(ABS(New-X))
     end
```

**Program 7.1**  F77 and F90 versions of a two-dimensional finite difference algorithm.

### 7.3.1  Processors

A PROCESSORS directive declares a named arrangement of abstract processors. For example, both of the following statements declare 32 abstract processors.

```
!HPF$ PROCESSORS P(32)
!HPF$ PROCESSORS Q(4,8)
```

Normally, one abstract processor is created for each physical processor, although an implementation could in principle use a smaller number of physical processors to implement the abstract processors. The mapping of abstract processors to physical processors is not specified in HPF and can vary according to the implementation.

### 7.3.2  Alignment

The ALIGN directive is used to specify array elements that should, if possible, be *collocated*—mapped to the same processor. Operations between aligned data objects are likely

```
!HPF$ PROCESSORS proc-name(dim1, ..., dimN)
```
*Declare an abstract processor array.*

    `proc-name`                   name of abstract processor array
    `dim1, ..., dimN`         size and shape of array

```
!HPF$ ALIGN array WITH target
```
*Align array with a target array.*

    `array`                      array to be aligned
    `target`                    array to be aligned to

```
!HPF$ DISTRIBUTE list-of-arrays [ONTO proc-name]
```
*Distribute array(s) onto processor array.*

    `list-of-arrays`          arrays to be distributed
    `proc-name`               abstract processor array

**Figure 7.4**   HPF data distribution directives.

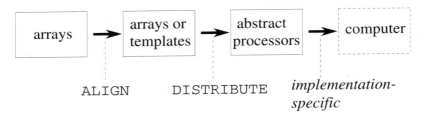

ALIGN         DISTRIBUTE     *implementation-specific*

**Figure 7.5**   HPF data allocation model. The mapping of data to abstract processors is performed in two phases: ALIGN is used to create a relationship between objects and DISTRIBUTE is used to partition onto processors both a specified object and any objects that are aligned with it.

to be more efficient than operations between objects that are not known to be aligned. An alignment directive has the general form

```
!HPF$ ALIGN array WITH target
```

which indicates that the specified `array` should be aligned with `target`. A list of subscripts associated with the array and target control the alignment. For example, the following code specifies a simple alignment of arrays B and C in which each B(i) is aligned with the corresponding C(i).

```
      real B(50), C(50)
!HPF$ ALIGN C(:) WITH B(:)
```

Dummy arguments can be used in ALIGN directives to name dimensions, integer expressions can be used to specify offsets, and * can be used to collapse dimensions. See

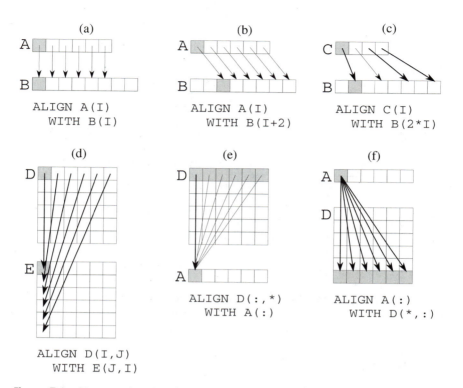

**Figure 7.6** Six examples of the HPF `ALIGN` statement, with arrows and shading used to associate representative aligned components in the two arrays being aligned. (a) A simple alignment of two one-dimensional arrays. (b) Alignment with an offset. (c) An alignment of a smaller array onto a larger. (d) Alignment with indices inverted (transpose). (e) Collapsing a dimension: aligning a two-dimensional array with a one-dimensional array. (f) Replicating data: aligning a one-dimensional array with a two-dimensional array.

Figure 7.6 for examples of the alignments that can be specified using these mechanisms. Notice that an `ALIGN` statement can be used to specify that elements of an array should be replicated over processors. This can improve efficiency if the array is read more often than it is written. For example, assume that the two-dimensional array `Y(N,N)` is to be distributed by columns so that each processor performs computation on one or more columns. If the computation performed at a single processor requires data from a one-dimensional array `X(N)` that is not updated during a computation, replicating `X` may be useful. This is accomplished by the following alignment directive

```
!HPF$ ALIGN X(j) WITH Y(*,j)
```

Care must be taken not to replicate arrays that are frequently updated, as considerable communication and/or redundant computation can result.

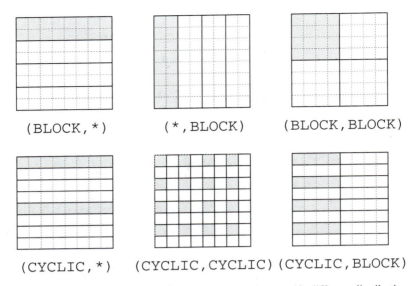

**Figure 7.7**   The HPF DISTRIBUTE statement, as used to specify different distributions of a two-dimensional array of size $8 \times 8$ onto four processors. The data mapped to processor 1 is shaded in each example.

### 7.3.3   Distribution

A DISTRIBUTE directive is used to indicate how data are to be partitioned among computer memories. It specifies, for each dimension of an array, a mapping of array indices to abstract processors in a processor arrangement. Each dimension of an array may be distributed in one of three ways.

| | |
|---|---|
| * | No distribution |
| BLOCK(n) | Block distribution (default: $n = N/P$) |
| CYCLIC(n) | Cyclic distribution (default: n=1) |

Let $N$ be the number of elements in an array dimension, and let $P$ be the number of processors. Then, as illustrated in Figure 7.7, a BLOCK distribution divides the indices in a dimension into contiguous, equal-sized blocks of size $N/P$, while a CYCLIC distribution maps every $P$th index to the same processor. The optional integer argument to BLOCK and CYCLIC specifies the number of elements in a block.

The ONTO specifier can be used to perform a distribution across a particular processor array. If no processor array is specified, one is chosen by the compiler. Hence, both DISTRIBUTE statements in the following code fragment are valid.

```
!HPF$ PROCESSORS p(32)
      real D(1024), E(1024)
!HPF$ DISTRIBUTE D(BLOCK)
!HPF$ DISTRIBUTE E(BLOCK) ONTO p
```

```
            program hpf_finite_difference
!HPF$  PROCESSORS pr(4)                    ! Running on 4 processors
       real X(100,100), New(100,100)   ! Data arrays
!HPF$  ALIGN New(:,:) WITH X(:,:)        ! Arrays decomposed in
!HPF$  DISTRIBUTE X(BLOCK,*) ONTO pr  ! one dimension.
       New(2:99,2:99) = (X(1:98, 2:99) + X(3:100, 2:99) +
      $                  X(2:99, 1:98) + X(2:99, 3:100))/4
       diffmax = MAXVAL(ABS(New-X))
       end
```

**Program 7.2**   HPF implementation of two-dimensional finite difference code.

A DISTRIBUTE directive applies not only to the named array but also to any arrays that are aligned with it. Thus, a DISTRIBUTE directive cannot be applied to an array that is aligned with another. For example, in the following code fragment the DISTRIBUTE directive specifies a mapping for all three arrays.

```
!HPF$  PROCESSORS p(20)
       real A(100,100), B(100,100), C(100,100)
!HPF$  ALIGN B(:,:) WITH A(:,:)
!HPF$  ALIGN C(i,j) WITH A(j,i)
!HPF$  DISTRIBUTE A(BLOCK,*) ONTO p
```

---

**EXAMPLE 7.2** (HPF Finite Difference)    Program 7.2 is an HPF version of Program 7.1. Notice that only three directives have been added: PROCESSORS, DISTRIBUTE, and ALIGN. These directives partition each of the two arrays by row, hence allocating 25 rows to each of four processors.

The following is an alternative set of directives that partitions the two arrays in two dimensions so that each processor has a block of size $50 \times 50$. Notice that only the directives need to be changed to specify this alternative algorithm.

```
!HPF$  PROCESSORS pr(2,2)
       real X(100,100), New(100,100)
!HPF$  ALIGN New(:,:) WITH X(:,:)
!HPF$  DISTRIBUTE X(BLOCK,BLOCK) ONTO pr
```

As discussed in Example 3.4, the two-dimensional decomposition is typically more efficient than the one-dimensional decomposition.

---

**EXAMPLE 7.3** (Pairwise Interactions)    Consider the following version of the pairwise interactions problem of Section 1.4.2. We must compute the total force $\text{force}_i$ acting on each of $N$ objects $x_i$. This is defined as follows, where $\text{force}_i$ and $x_i$ are both 3-vectors and the function $f$ computes the force between two objects:

$$\texttt{force}_i = \sum_{j=1}^{N} \texttt{f}(x_i, x_j) \quad (i \neq j).$$

An HPF formulation of this problem is presented in Program 7.3. This program is defined for an array of ten processors. The arrays Force, Tmp, and X are aligned and distributed blockwise. The $N(N-1)$ interactions are computed in $N-1$ steps, with the $i$th step computing interactions between each element $X_j$ and the element offset by $i$ in X. The CSHIFT operation is used to update a temporary array containing the offset values. This temporary array is shifted one element at each step. Each call to the function f computes $N$ interactions.

Naively, we might expect each of the CSHIFT operations to result in a communication operation. On many machines, it will be more efficient to block these communications so that data circulates among the ten processors in just nine communication steps, as described in Section 1.4.2. An HPF compiler would normally be expected to perform this optimization.

## 7.4　Concurrency

At this point, we have presented all the HPF features needed to write simple programs. Array assignment statements provide a mechanism for specifying fine-grained concurrency, while data distribution directives provide control over agglomeration and mapping.

The F90 array assignment statement provides a convenient and succinct notation for specifying data-parallel operations. However, it applies only to a limited set of such operations. For example, it requires that operands of right-hand-side expressions be conformant with (of the same shape as) the left-hand-side array. Two other HPF constructs allow an explicitly parallel representation of a wider range of data-parallel operations. These are the FORALL statement and the INDEPENDENT directive.

```
       program hpf_pairwise_interactions
       PROCESSORS pr(10)
       real X(3,1000), Force(3,1000), Tmp(3,1000)
!HPF$  ALIGN Force(:,:) WITH X(:,:)
!HPF$  ALIGN Tmp(:,:) WITH X(:,:)
!HPF$  DISTRIBUTE X(*, BLOCK) ONTO pr
       Force = 0.0
       Tmp = X
       do i = 1,999
          Tmp = CSHIFT(X,1)
          Force = Force + f(X,Tmp)
       enddo
       end
```

**Program 7.3**　HPF formulation of pairwise interactions problem.

### 7.4.1 The FORALL Statement

The FORALL statement allows for more general assignments to sections of an array. A FORALL statement has the general form

FORALL (*triplet*, ..., *triplet*, *mask*) *assignment*

where *assignment* is an arithmetic or pointer assignment and *triplet* has the general form

*subscript* = *lower-bound* : *upper-bound* : *stride*

(with : *stride* being optional) and specifies a set of indices.

The assignment statement is evaluated for those index values specified by the list of triplets that are not rejected by the optional *mask*. For example, the following statements set each element of X to the sum of its indices, zero the upper right triangle of Y, and zero the diagonal of Z, respectively.

```
FORALL (i=1:m, j=1,n)          X(i,j) = i+j
FORALL (i=1:n, j=1,n, i<j)     Y(i,j) = 0.0
FORALL (i=1:n)                 Z(i,i) = 0.0
```

A FORALL statement is evaluated as follows. First, the right-hand-side expression is evaluated for all index values; these evaluations can be performed in any order. Second, the assignments are performed, again in any order. To ensure determinism, a FORALL statement cannot assign to the same element of an array more than once. A compiler can attempt to detect that this requirement is violated but is not required to do so. Hence, the following statement is valid only if the array Index does not contain duplicate values.

```
FORALL (i=1:n) A(Index(i)) = B(i)
```

---

**EXAMPLE 7.4** (Use of FORALL)   The array assignment used to update the array New in Program 7.2 can also be expressed using FORALL, as follows.

```
      forall(i=2:99, j=2:99)
$       New(i,j) = (X(i-1, j) + X(i+1, j) +
$                   X(i, j-1) + X(i, j+1))/4
```

Of course, in this case there is no reason not to use an array assignment.

---

### 7.4.2 The INDEPENDENT Directive and Do-Loops

An HPF program can reveal additional opportunities for parallel execution by using the INDEPENDENT directive to assert that the iterations of a do-loop can be performed independently—that is, in any order or concurrently—without changing the result computed. In effect, this directive changes a do-loop from an implicitly parallel construct to an explicitly parallel construct.

The INDEPENDENT directive must immediately precede the do-loop to which it applies. In its simplest form, it has no additional argument and asserts simply that no iteration of the do-loop can affect any other iteration. (An iteration *I* affects an iteration *J* if *I* leads to an assignment to a value read by *J*.) For example, in the following code fragment the

assertion implies both that the array Index does not contain duplicate indices and that A
and B do not share storage, for example because of an equivalence statement.

```
!HPF$  INDEPENDENT
       do i=1,n
          A(Index(i)) = B(i)
       enddo
```

In the following code fragment, the directives indicate that the outer two loops are independent. The inner loop assigns elements of A repeatedly and hence is not independent.

```
!HPF$  INDEPENDENT
       do i=1,n1                      ! Loop over i independent
!HPF$     INDEPENDENT
          do j=1,n2                   ! Loop over j independent
             do k=1,n3                ! Inner loop not independent
                A(i,j) = A(i,j) + B(i,j,k)*C(i,j)
             enddo
          enddo
       enddo
```

An INDEPENDENT directive can also specify that the assertion would be correct *if* distinct storage were to be used for a specified set of variables for each iteration of the nested
do-loop. This is achieved by postfixing a NEW specifier, as in the following example. In this
code fragment, interleaved execution of different loop iterations would cause erroneous results if values of tmp1 and tmp2 computed in one iteration were used in another. The NEW
specifier ensures that this situation does not arise.

```
!HPF$  INDEPENDENT
       do i=1,n1
!HPF$     INDEPENDENT, NEW(tmp1,tmp2)
          do j=1,n2
             tmp1 = B(i,j) + C(i,j)
             tmp1 = B(i,j) - C(i,j)
             A(i,j) = tmp1*tmp2
          ENDDO
       ENDDO
```

---

**EXAMPLE 7.5** (Parallel Fast Fourier Transform)    A 2-D FFT applies a 1-D FFT operation
first to each row of a two-dimensional array and then to each column. The parallel algorithm discussed in Section 4.4 first distributes the array by rows (hence allowing the first
set of FFTs to proceed without communication) and then transposes the array before performing the second set of FFTs. The transpose involves considerable communication but
is frequently more efficient than an algorithm based on a static decomposition and parallel
FFTs. Program 7.4 implements the transpose algorithm. Notice the initial distribution of A
(blocked, by column) and the call to the transpose intrinsic. Notice also the use of the

```
          subroutine fft_2d(n, A)
!HPF$  PROCESSORS pr(24)
          complex A(n,n)
!HPF$  DISTRIBUTE A(*,BLOCK) ONTO pr
          call fft(n, A)
          A = transpose(A)
          call fft(n, A)
          end

C      One-dimensional FFT on 2-d array
          subroutine fft(n, A)
          complex A(n,n)
!HPF$  PROCESSORS pr(24)
!HPF$  DISTRIBUTE A(*,BLOCK) ONTO pr
!HPF$  INDEPENDENT
          do i = 1,n
             call rowfft(i, n, A)
          enddo
          end

C      One-dimensional FFT on 1 column of 2-d array
          subroutine rowfft(icol, n, A)
             ⋮
          end
```

**Program 7.4**  Two-dimensional fast Fourier transform using matrix transpose and INDEPENDENT directive.

INDEPENDENT directive to specify that the `rowfft` calls in the do-loop can proceed independently, even though each is passed the entire A array. This assertion is valid because each call to `rowfft` operates on a single column.

## 7.5  Dummy Arguments and Modularity

A large HPF program is typically constructed as a sequence of calls to subroutines and functions that implement different aspects of program logic. In the terminology used in Chapter 4, the program is a sequential composition of program components. As discussed in that chapter, one critical issue that arises when using sequential composition is the distribution of data structures that are shared by components.

Consider what happens when a subroutine is called in an HPF program. For a particular computer and problem size, there is presumably a distribution of that subroutine's dummy arguments and local variables that is optimal in the sense that it minimizes execution time in that subroutine. However, this optimal distribution may not correspond to the distribution specified in the calling program for variables passed as arguments. Hence, we have a choice of two different strategies at a subroutine interface. These strategies, and the HPF mechanisms that support them, are as follows.

1. We can ignore the distribution used in the calling program and specify a local distribution that must apply, even if it requires a (potentially expensive) remapping operation. For this purpose, we use the distribution directives DISTRIBUTE and ALIGN to specify the mapping of the dummy arguments.

2. We can use whatever data distribution is used in the calling program, even though it may not be locally optimal. For this purpose, we use the INHERIT directive.

As noted in Chapter 4, several tradeoffs must be evaluated when determining which strategy to adopt in a particular circumstance. The cost of the remapping inherent in strategy 1 should be weighed against the performance degradation that may occur if strategy 2 is used. Similarly, the effort required to optimize a subroutine for a particular distribution must be weighed against the subroutine's execution cost and frequency of use. These tradeoffs are more complex if a subroutine may be used in several contexts. In some cases, it may be worthwhile for a subroutine to incorporate different code for different distributions.

**Strategy 1: Remap Arguments**    Strategy 1 is straightforward to apply. Ordinary distribution directives are applied to dummy arguments. As for any other variable, these directives recommend that the requested distribution hold. Any necessary data movement is performed automatically when the subroutine or function is called. (In the absence of a DISTRIBUTE or ALIGN directive for a dummy argument, the compiler may choose to use any distribution or alignment.) Any redistribution is undone upon return from the subroutine, so any data movement costs introduced in this way are incurred twice. The exception to this rule are arguments used for input or output only, as specified by the use of the F90 intent directive.

Program 7.5 illustrates some of the issues involved in strategy 1. Arrays X and Y are distributed by rows and columns in the calling program, respectively, while the dummy argument Z of the subroutine fft is distributed by columns. Hence, the first call to fft requires that two matrix transpose operations be performed to convert from one distribution to the other—one upon entry to and one upon exit from the routine. In contrast, the second call to fft does not require any data movement because the array Y is already distributed appropriately.

**Strategy 2: Use Parent Mapping**    The second strategy is supported by the INHERIT directive, which, however, does not form part of the HPF subset because of the difficulty of generating code that can handle multiple distributions. For that reason, we do not consider this language feature in detail.

The following code fragment illustrates the use of INHERIT. This is an alternative version of the fft routine in Program 7.5. The INHERIT directive indicates that no remapping is to occur; hence, the two calls to fft in Program 7.5 will execute with (BLOCK,*) and (*,BLOCK) distribution, respectively.

```
      subroutine fft(n, Z)
      real Z(n,n)
        ⋮
!HPF$ INHERIT Z                          ! Z has parent mapping
        ⋮
      end
```

## 7.6  Other HPF Features

In this section, we discuss several miscellaneous aspects of HPF; we also list HPF features not covered in this book.

### 7.6.1  System Inquiry Intrinsic Functions

HPF introduces a small set of intrinsic functions in addition to those defined in F90. The two most relevant to parallel program design are the system inquiry functions NUMBER_OF_PROCESSORS and PROCESSORS_SHAPE. These functions allow a program to obtain information about the *number* of physical processors on which it executes and the *topology* connecting these processors. This information can be used to write programs that run efficiently on varying numbers of processors and processor configuration. The functions are modeled on the F90 inquiry functions SIZE and SHAPE, respectively, and provide a view of the underlying computer as a rectilinear, multidimensional processor array. A call to NUMBER_OF_PROCESSORS has the general form

```
          program main                   ! Main program
!HPF$     PROCESSORS pr(16)
          real X(128,128), Y(128,128)
!HPF$     DISTRIBUTE X(BLOCK,*), Y(*,BLOCK) ONTO pr
          call fft(128, X)               ! Needs redistribution
          call fft(128, Y)               ! Does not need redistribution
            ⋮
          end                            ! End of program


          subroutine fft(n, Z)           ! Subroutine FFT
          real Z(n,n)
            ⋮
!HPF$     DISTRIBUTE Z(*,BLOCK)
            ⋮
          end                            ! End of subroutine
```

**Program 7.5**  HPF code illustrating redistribution on procedure call.

32-Processor (4 × 8) Mesh-Connected Multicomputer:

```
PROCESSORS_SHAPE()        => /4, 8/
NUMBER_OF_PROCESSORS()    => 32
NUMBER_OF_PROCESSORS(1)   => 4
NUMBER_OF_PROCESSORS(2)   => 8
```

Uniprocessor Workstation:

```
PROCESSORS_SHAPE()        => / 1 /
NUMBER_OF_PROCESSORS()    => 1
```

**Figure 7.8**    Examples of values returned by HPF system inquiry intrinsic functions.

```
NUMBER_OF_PROCESSORS(dim)
```

where `dim` is an optional argument. A call to this function returns the number of processors in the underlying array or, if the optional argument is present, the size of this array along a specified dimension. A call to `PROCESSORS_SHAPE` has the following general form.

```
PROCESSORS_SHAPE()
```

It returns an array with rank (dimension) one and with size the rank of the underlying processor array. The $i$th element gives the size of the underlying array in its $i$th dimension.

The representation of a particular physical computer as a processor array is implementation dependent and not specified in HPF. Two representative examples are presented in Figure 7.8. System inquiry functions can be included in array declarations and HPF directives, hence permitting a program to declare abstract processor arrays that match available physical resources. For example, in the following code the first directive declares an abstract processor array P with size equal to the number of physical processors. The F90 inquiry function SIZE is then used to declare an integer array Q with size corresponding to the rank (dimension) of the physical processor array.

```
!HPF$ PROCESSORS P(NUMBER_OF_PROCESSORS())
      integer Q(SIZE(PROCESSORS_SHAPE()))
```

### 7.6.2  Storage and Sequence Association

Both F77 and F90 allow programmers to write programs that depend on a linear storage model, that is, a view of memory as linear, one dimensional, and sequentially addressed. This is the case if a program depends on *storage association*, using common or equivalence statements to align storage locations. (This might be done to reuse storage, for example.) It is also the case if a program relies on *sequence association*, for example, passing an array as an actual argument and then declaring the corresponding dummy argument to have a different size or shape.

Storage and sequence association are not natural concepts when data are distributed over multiple processors. If always enforced in an HPF compiler, they could compromise performance. Therefore, HPF states that by default, storage and sequence association are *not* supported. Hence, without the use of additional directives, it not possible to do the following:

1. Pass an array element as an actual argument to a subroutine, and declare the corresponding dummy argument to be an array.

2. Pass an array or array section as an actual argument to a subroutine, and declare the corresponding dummy argument to have a different size or shape.

3. Pass an assumed size array (an array declared with a dimension of *, for example, DIMENSION(32,*)) as as an actual argument.

4. Declare the same COMMON block to contain different variables in different parts of a program, or use the EQUIVALENCE statement except in certain restricted cases.

In order to support conversion of existing codes that rely on storage and sequence association to HPF, the SEQUENCE directive is provided to request that storage and sequence association be enabled for specified variables. Because this directive is intended only to support conversion of existing Fortran 77 codes and is not directly relevant to data-parallel programming, we do not discuss it further here.

### 7.6.3 HPF Features Not Covered

For simplicity, we have focused on a subset of the HPF language. In particular, we have described most of the *HPF subset*, which is a set of HPF constructs providing sufficient functionality to permit development of useful programs, while avoiding difficult implementation problems. Of necessity, numerous subtleties have been omitted in this brief description, and the following HPF features have not been covered at all.

1. *Templates.* The TEMPLATE directive allows a programmer to declare an abstract index space that can be distributed and used as an alignment target in the same way as an array can. This is useful when several arrays must be aligned relative to each other, but there is no need to define a single array that spans the entire index space of interest.

2. *Mapping inquiry intrinsic functions.* These functions allow a program to determine the actual mapping of an array to processors. They are useful when the extrinsic function facility (described in item 7 of this list) is used to call non-HPF subprograms.

3. FORALL *construct.* This more general form of the FORALL statement can control multiple assignments, masked array assignments, and nested FORALL statements and constructs. This construct broadens the range of algorithms that can be expressed using FORALL.

4. PURE *procedures.* A function or subroutine declared to be PURE can be called in FORALL statements. A PURE function causes no side effects; that is, it does not perform I/O or modify dummy arguments or global data. A PURE subroutine may modify arguments but not global variables. This facility broadens the range of algorithms that can be expressed using the FORALL statement, for example by allowing the same function to be applied to each row or column of an array.

5. *Dynamic data distribution.* The executable directives REDISTRIBUTE and RE-ALIGN can be used to modify the distribution and alignment of a data structure if

that data structure is declared to have attribute DYNAMIC. The HPF compiler and runtime system perform any data movement that may be required. This facility makes it easier to use different distributions in different parts of a computation, as discussed in Section 7.5.

6. *Computational library.* For each reduction operation in F90 (e.g., SUM and MAX-VAL), HPF provides corresponding combining scatter, parallel prefix, and parallel suffix operations (e.g., SUM_SCATTER, SUM_PREFIX, and SUM_SUFFIX). Functions for sorting and for counting bits in an integer array are also provided. This computational library broadens the set of global operations available to the programmer. (The combining scatter operations allow elements of one array to be *scattered* to the elements of another array, under the control of index arrays. A *parallel prefix* using an operation $\mathcal{O}$ of a sequence X yields a sequence Y of the same size, with each element $Y(j) = \mathcal{O}_{i=1}^{j}(X_i)$. That is, each element is a function of the preceding elements. A *parallel suffix* is the same as a parallel prefix except that each element is a function of the elements that follow it rather than those that precede it.)

7. *Extrinsic functions.* HPF programs can call non-HPF procedures as extrinsic procedures. The non-HPF procedure is invoked on every processor, and the local components of distributed arrays named in the interface are passed as arguments. This facility can be used to invoke MIMD procedures developed with message-passing systems such as MPI.

## 7.7   Performance Issues

The performance of an HPF program depends not only on the skill of the programmer but also on the capabilities of the compiler, which in effect generates the actual parallel program from a high-level specification provided by the programmer. The structure and hence the performance of this program may not be intuitively obvious to the programmer. However, a good HPF compiler should provide feedback identifying hard-to-parallelize components, and of course intuition can be developed with experience.

Two major obstacles impact the efficient execution of an HPF program: sequential bottlenecks and excessive communication costs. In the following sections, we first examine the compilation process and then discuss these two obstacles in turn.

### 7.7.1   HPF Compilation

Compilers for HPF and related languages generally proceed roughly as follows. Data decomposition statements are analyzed to determine the decomposition of each array in a program. Computation is then partitioned across processors, typically (but not always) using the owner-computes rule. This process allows nonlocal references, and hence communication requirements, to be identified. Communication operations are then optimized. In particular, an attempt is made to move messages out of loops so as to reduce communication costs.

```
      program compiler_output
      real New(100,25), X(100,0:26)
      real difflocal, diffmax
      my_p = mynode()                              ! my_p in range 0..3
C     Exchange data with neighbors
      call stencil_exchange_1d(X, my_p, 4, 100, 25, 1)
      lb = max((my_p*25)+1,2)-(my_p*25)
      ub = min((my_p+1)*25,99)-(my_p*25)
      New(2:99,1:25) = (X(1:98,lb:ub) + X(3:100,lb:ub) +
      $    X(2:99,lb-1:ub-1) + X(2:99,lb+1:ub+1))/4
      difflocal = maxval(abs(New(2:99,1:25)-X(2:99,1:25)))
C     Perform reduction to obtain diffmax
      call reduce_real("max", difflocal, diffmax)
      end
```

**Program 7.6**  The code that might be generated by an HPF compiler for Program 7.2.

As an illustration of how an HPF compiler operates, Program 7.6 gives the code that might be generated for Program 7.2. Recall that Program 7.2 implements a parallel algorithm based on a one-dimensional decomposition of a two-dimensional finite-difference problem and executes on four processors. The generated code is a mixture of F90 statements and calls to library routines that perform communication operations. In this example, two such routines are called: `stencil_exchange_1d` and `reduce_real`. The first routine exchanges data with the processors handling neighboring parts of the finite difference grid, and the second performs the reduction operation required to compute a maximum difference. These routines account for the communication requirements of the program.

In this example, communication costs are easy to determine. The nearest-neighbor exchange will send two messages having a total size of 200 words; the reduction will generate $\log 4 = 2$ communications, each of size one word. Hence, total costs are $t_s 4 + t_w$ 202. As in addition, this program decomposes computation evenly across processors, it can be expected to execute with reasonable efficiency.

### 7.7.2  Sequential Bottlenecks

A *sequential bottleneck* occurs when a code fragment does not incorporate sufficient parallelism or when parallelism exists (in the sense that data dependencies do not prevent concurrent execution) but cannot be detected by the compiler. In either case, the code fragment cannot be executed in parallel. Sequential bottlenecks of this sort may not be serious if a program is intended to execute on only a small number of processors, but they inevitably reduce a program's scalability. More precisely, if some fraction $1/s$ of a program's total execution time executes sequentially, then Amdahl's law applies, and the maximum possible speedup that can be achieved on a parallel computer is $s$ (Section 3.2.1).

An HPF compiler should provide information about constructs that it was unable to parallelize. The programmer may then be able to restructure the code in question to enable parallelization.

### 7.7.3    Communication Costs

We next discuss a number of issues that affect the communication performance of HPF programs.

*Intrinsics.* Many F90 and HPF intrinsic functions combine data from entire arrays (Table 7.1) and hence involve considerable communication if the arrays to which they are applied are distributed. For example, operations such as MAXVAL and SUM perform array reductions which, as noted in Chapter 2, can be performed in $\log P$ steps on $P$ processors, for a total communication cost of $\log P(t_s + t_w)$. This cost is independent of the size of the arrays to be reduced. In contrast, the cost of a TRANSPOSE or MATMUL operation depends on both the size and distribution of the operation's arguments. Other operations such as DOT_PRODUCT involve communication only if their arguments are not aligned.

*Array operations.* Array assignments and FORALL statements can result in communication if, in order to compute some array element A(i), they require data values (e.g., B(j)) that are not on the same processor. Program 7.6 showed one example: the references X(i,j-1) and X(i,j+1) resulted in communication. The CSHIFT operation is another common source of communication.

Cyclic distributions will often result in more communication than will block distributions. However, by scattering the computational grid over available processors, they can produce better load balance in some applications. (Recall that this strategy was discussed in Section 2.5.1.)

To help you develop intuition regarding communication costs, we present in Figure 7.9 the communication requirements associated with a number of different FORALL statements for three arrays A, B, and C distributed as follows.

```
!HPF$ PROCESSORS pr(3)
      integer A(8), B(8), C(8)
!HPF$ ALIGN B(:) WITH A(:)
!HPF$ DISTRIBUTE A(BLOCK) ONTO pr
!HPF$ DISTRIBUTE C(CYCLIC) ONTO pr
```

*Different mappings.* Even simple operations performed on nonaligned arrays can result in communication. For example, the assignment A=B can require considerable communication if arrays A and B have different distributions. The cost of this sort of communication must be weighed against the cost of converting to a common distribution before performing the operation.

*Procedure boundaries.* As discussed in Sections 4.2.1 and 7.5, switching from one decomposition of an array to another at a procedure boundary can result in considerable communication. Although the precise amount of communication required depends on the decomposition, the total cost summed over $P$ processors of moving between decompositions of an $M \times N$ array will often be approximately $t_s P^2 + t_w SMN$, where $S$ is the size of an array element in four-byte words. This cost arises because, generally, each of the $P$

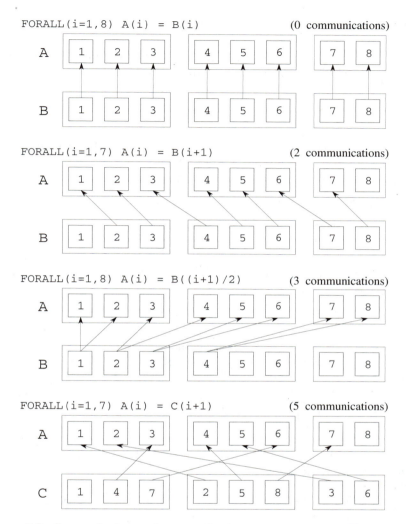

**Figure 7.9** Communication requirements of various FORALL statements. The arrays A and B are aligned and distributed in a blocked fashion on three processors, while the array C is distributed in a cyclic fashion.

processors must communicate with every other processor, and each $M.N$ array element must be communicated.

*Compiler optimization.* A good HPF compiler does not compile a program statement by statement. Instead, it seeks to reduce communication costs by combining communication operations and otherwise reorganizing program statements. In addition, it may choose to use data distributions different from those recommended by the programmer. Hence, it is always necessary to verify analytic results using instrumentation data.

## 7.8   Case Study: Gaussian Elimination

To further illustrate the use of HPF, we present a slightly more complex example. The problem considered is the Gaussian elimination method used to solve a system of linear equations

$$Ax = b,$$

where $A$ is a known matrix of size $N \times N$, $x$ is the required solution vector, and $b$ is a known vector of size $N$. This example is often used in discussions of HPF as it shows the benefits of cyclic distributions. The method proceeds in two stages:

1. *Gaussian elimination.* The original system of equations is reduced to an upper triangular form

$$Ux = y,$$

   where $U$ is a matrix of size $N \times N$ in which all elements below the diagonal are zero, and diagonal elements have the value 1.

2. *Back substitution.* The new system of equations is solved to obtain the values of $x$.

The Gaussian elimination stage of the algorithm comprises $N - 1$ steps. In the basic algorithm, the $i$th step eliminates nonzero subdiagonal elements in column $i$ by subtracting the $i$th row from each row $j$ in the range $[i + 1, n]$, in each case scaling the $i$th row by the factor $A_{ji}/A_{ii}$ so as to make the element $A_{ji}$ zero. Hence, the algorithm sweeps down the matrix from the top left corner to the bottom right corner, leaving zero subdiagonal elements behind it (Figure 7.10).

For numerical stability, this basic algorithm is modified so that instead of stepping through rows in order, it selects in step $i$ the row in the range $[i, n]$ with the largest element in column $i$. This row (called the *pivot*) is swapped with row $i$ prior to performing the subtractions.

Program 7.7 is an HPF implementation of this algorithm. For efficiency, this program maintains the vector $b$ in the $N + 1$th column of the array $A$. The first do-loop implements Gaussian elimination. The MAXLOC intrinsic is used to identify the pivot row. Rather than performing an explicit swap with row $i$, an indirection array called indx is used to keep track of the actual indices of selected rows. This array is updated once the pivot is identified. The next statement computes the N scale factors; notice that the computation can be performed with a single array assignment. Finally, the FORALL statement performs the subtractions. The mask ensures that the subtraction is performed only for rows that have not been previously selected as pivots (Indx(j).EQ.0). Once the do-loop is complete, a second FORALL is used to reorganize the matrix into upper triangular form.

The last four lines of the program perform the back substitution. In reverse order from $N$ to 1, each element $x_i$ of the solution is computed and then substituted into $A$ to simplify the matrix.

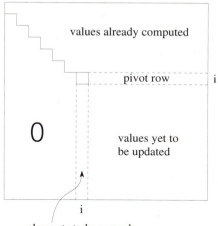

values already computed

pivot row     i

0     values yet to
be updated

i

elements to be zeroed

**Figure 7.10**   The $i$th step of the Gaussian elimination algorithm in which nonzero subdiagonal elements in column $i$ are eliminated by subtracting appropriate multiples of the pivot row.

Before developing data distribution directives for this program, let us determine how much concurrency it exposes and what data dependencies may lead to communication. We can think of the data-parallel program as specifying a fine-grained partition comprising $N \times N$ tasks, each responsible for a single element of $A$. (These tasks characterize the computation that would be associated with data elements by the owner-computes rule.) As illustrated in Figure 7.11, each of the $N - 1$ steps of the elimination algorithm involves five principal steps, as follows:

1. The MAXLOC statement involves a reduction operation by the $N$ tasks in the $i$th column.

2. The maximum value identified by the reduction (max_indx) must be broadcast within the $i$th column, since it is required for the computation of scale factors.

3. The computation of scale factors (the array Fac) requires $N$ independent operations, one in each task in the $i$th column.

4. A scale factor (Fac(j)) and a pivot row value (Row(k)) must be broadcast within each column and row, respectively, since they are required for the update.

5. The FORALL statement involves $\mathcal{O}(N^2)$ independent operations, one per task.

Studying this algorithm, we see that it has two interesting attributes. First, there is little locality in communication beyond the fact that broadcasts and reductions are performed in rows and columns. Second, computation tends to be clustered: in each step, much of the computation is performed by tasks in a single row and column (before the FORALL) and in the bottom right-hand corner (the FORALL). These attributes can be exploited when developing data distribution directives to complete the parallel algorithm.

```
      subroutine gauss(n, A, x)
      integer n
      real A(n,n+1)
      real X(n), Fac(n), Row(n+1)
      integer Indx(n), Itmp(1)
      integer i, j, k, max_indx
      real maxval

      Indx = 0                                    ! Initialize mask array
      do i = 1,n                                  ! Repeat for each column
C     Find pivot
      Itmp = MAXLOC(ABS(A(:,i)), MASK=Indx .EQ. 0)
      max_indx = Itmp(1)                          ! Extract pivot index
      Indx(max_indx) = i                          ! Update indirection array
      Fac = A(:,i)/A(max_indx,i)                  ! Scale factors for column
      Row = A(max_indx,:)                         ! Extract pivot row
C     Row update
      FORALL (j=1:n, k=i:n+1, Indx(j).EQ.0)
   $         A(j,k) = A(j,k) - Fac(j) * Row(k)
      enddo

      FORALL (j=1:n) A(Indx(j),:) = A(j,:)        ! Row exchange

      do j = n, 1, -1                             ! Back substitution
         X(j) = A(j,n+1) / A(j,j)
         A(1:j-1, n+1) = A(1:j-1, n+1) - A(1:j-1,j)*X(j)
      enddo
      end
```

**Program 7.7**   HPF implementation of Gaussian elimination.

In many grid-based problems, we prefer to use a BLOCK distribution of the principal data structures because it reduces communication requirements by enhancing locality. However, in the Gaussian elimination problem, a BLOCK distribution has no communication advantages; furthermore, it causes many processors to be idle, particularly in the later stages of computation. In contrast, a CYCLIC distribution scatters computation over many processors and hence reduces idle time. Therefore, we could use the following data distribution directives.

```
!HPF$ ALIGN Row(j) WITH A(1,j)
!HPF$ ALIGN X(i) WITH A(i,N+1)
!HPF$ DISTRIBUTE A(*,CYCLIC)
```

Of course, the number of processors that can be used efficiently by this one-dimensional decomposition is limited. An alternative formulation, more efficient on large numbers of processors, decomposes A in two dimensions. This can be specified as follows.

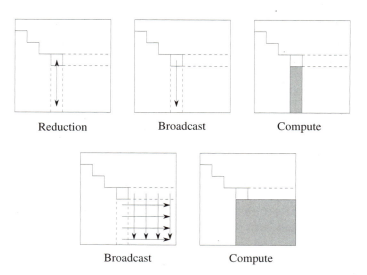

Reduction          Broadcast          Compute

Broadcast          Compute

**Figure 7.11**   Communication and computation in the various phases of the HPF Gaussian elimination algorithm. Arrows represent communication, and shading indicates tasks involved in computation in each phase. The five phases are described in Section 7.8.

```
!HPF$  ALIGN Row(j) WITH A(1,j)
!HPF$  ALIGN X(i) WITH A(i,N+1)
!HPF$  DISTRIBUTE A(CYCLIC,CYCLIC)
```

## 7.9   Summary

In this chapter, we have presented fundamental concepts of data-parallel programming and illustrated the application of these concepts in the programming languages Fortran 90 and High Performance Fortran. The eight HPF constructs described in this chapter are summarized in Table 7.2. These are in addition to the F90 array language described in Section 7.2.

F90's array language and HPF's data distribution directives and related constructs provide a powerful notation for data-parallel computations in science and engineering. Their chief features are as follows:

1. An array language comprising array assignments, array intrinsics, and (in HPF) FORALL and INDEPENDENT constructs is used to reveal the fine-grained concurrency inherent in data-parallel operations on arrays.

2. Data distribution directives are introduced to provide the programmer with control over partitioning, agglomeration, and mapping (and hence locality).

3. An HPF compiler translates this high-level specification into an executable program by generating the communication code implied by a particular set of data-parallel operations and data distribution directives.

**Table 7.2**   HPF quick reference: the HPF constructs described in this chapter, the figure in which each is defined, the section in which each is described, and the programs that illustrate the use of each.

| HPF Construct | Figure | Section | Programs |
|---|---|---|---|
| !HPF$ PROCESSORS | 7.4 | 7.3.1 | 7.2, 7.3 |
| !HPF$ ALIGN | 7.4 | 7.3.2 | 7.2, 7.3 |
| !HPF$ DISTRIBUTE | 7.4 | 7.3.3 | 7.2, 7.3 |
| FORALL | | 7.4.1 | 7.7 |
| !HPF$ INDEPENDENT | | 7.4.2 | 7.4 |
| NUMBER_OF_PROCESSORS | | 7.6.1 | |
| PROCESSORS_SHAPE | | 7.6.1 | |
| !HPF$ SEQUENCE | | 7.6.2 | |

The most attractive feature of the data-parallel approach as exemplified in HPF is that the compiler takes on the job of generating communication code. This has two advantages. First, it allows the programmer to focus on the tasks of identifying opportunities for concurrent execution and determining efficient partition, agglomeration, and mapping strategies. Second, it simplifies the task of exploring alternative parallel algorithms; in principle, only data distribution directives need be changed.

A problematic feature of HPF is the limited range of parallel algorithms that can be expressed in HPF *and* compiled efficiently for large parallel computers. However, the range of problems for which HPF is an appropriate tool can be expected to grow as compiler technology improves.

## Exercises

1. Write an HPF program to multiply two matrices $A$ and $B$ of size $N \times N$. (Do not use the MATMUL intrinsic!) Estimate the communication costs associated with this program if $A$ and $B$ are distributed blockwise in a single dimension or blockwise in two dimensions.

2. Compare the performance of your matrix multiplication program with that of the MATMUL intrinsic. Explain any differences.

3. Complete Program 7.2 and study its performance as a function of $N$ and $P$ on one or more networked or parallel computers. Modify the program to use a two-dimensional data decomposition, and repeat these performance experiments. Use performance models to interpret your results.

4. Compare the performance of the programs developed in Exercise 3 with equivalent CC++, FM, or MPI programs. Account for any differences.

5. Complete Program 7.3 and study its performance on one or more parallel computers as a function of problem size $N$ and number of processors $P$. Compare with the performance obtained by a CC++, FM, or MPI implementation of this algorithm, as described in Section 1.4.2. Explain any performance differences.

6. Develop an HPF implementation of the symmetric pairwise interactions algorithm of Section 1.4.2. Compare its performance with an equivalent CC++, Fortran M, or MPI program. Explain any differences.

7. Learn about the data-parallel languages Data-parallel C and pC++, and use one of these languages to implement the finite-difference and pairwise interactions programs presented in this chapter.

8. Develop a performance model for the HPF Gaussian elimination program of Section 7.8, assuming a one-dimensional cyclic decomposition of the array A. Compare your model with observed execution times on a parallel computer. Account for any differences that you see.

9. Develop a performance model for the HPF Gaussian elimination program of Section 7.8, assuming a two-dimensional cyclic decomposition of the array A. Is it more efficient to maintain one or multiple copies of the one-dimensional arrays Row and X? Explain.

10. Study the performance of the HPF global operations for different data sizes and numbers of processors. What can you infer from your results about the algorithms used to implement these operations?

11. Develop an HPF implementation of the convolution algorithm described in Section 4.4.

## Chapter Notes

Early data-parallel programming notations included Kali [200], CM Fortran [282], Fortran D [112], and Vienna Fortran [56]. Other data-parallel languages include *Lisp [281], C* [281], Data-parallel C [136, 137], pC++ [38], NESL [37], and DINO [247]. In a rather different approach, several projects have explored the use of C++ class libraries to encapsulate data-parallel operations on data objects such as arrays [83, 188].

The compilation of HPF and related languages requires specialized analysis and optimization techniques. Hiranandani et al. [152] and Zima and Chapman [303] provide a good introduction to these topics; see also papers by Albert, Lukas, and Steele [10], Bozkus et al. [42], Callahan and Kennedy [45], Rogers and Pingali [245], and Zima, Bast, and Gerndt [302] and the monographs by Banerjee [27] and Wolfe [296].

The description of F90 and HPF provided here is necessarily brief. See Chapter 6 for F90 references. Loveman [193] provides more information on both the HPF language and the process by which it was designed. The HPF Language Specification prepared by the HPF Forum provides a comprehensive, although sometimes impenetrable, description of the language [149]. The book by Koelbel et al. [176] presents essentially the same information but in a more readable form, and also provides a useful introduction to F90.

Extensions to the data-parallel programming model that would allow its application to a wider range of problems is an active area of research. Chapman, Mehrotra, and Zima [57] propose a range of extensions. Saltz, Berryman, and Wu [251] and Agrawal, Sussman, and Saltz [6] describe techniques for irregular problems. Subhlok et al. [273] generate pipeline parallelism automatically from HPF code augmented with additional directives. Foster [100] discusses issues relating to the integration of task parallelism. Chandy et al. [52] address the integration of HPF and Fortran M.

The online version provides access here to additional information on programming in High Performance Fortran, including a specification, information about compilers, and example programs.

# 8 Message Passing Interface

In the message-passing library approach to parallel programming, a collection of processes executes programs written in a standard sequential language augmented with calls to a library of functions for sending and receiving messages. In this chapter, we introduce the key concepts of message-passing programming and show how designs developed using the techniques discussed in Part I can be adapted for message-passing execution. For concreteness, we base our presentation on the Message Passing Interface (MPI), the de facto message-passing standard. However, the basic techniques discussed are applicable to other such systems, including p4, PVM, Express, and PARMACS.

MPI is a complex system. In its entirety, it comprises 129 functions, many of which have numerous parameters or variants. As our goal is to convey the essential concepts of message-passing programming, not to provide a comprehensive MPI reference manual, we focus here on a set of 24 functions and ignore some of the more esoteric features. These 24 functions provide more than adequate support for a wide range of applications.

After studying this chapter, you should understand the essential features of the message-passing programming model and its realization in MPI, and you should be able to write simple MPI programs. In particular, you should understand how MPI implements local, global, and asynchronous communications. You should also be familiar with the mechanisms that MPI provides to support the development of modular programs and the sequential and parallel composition of program components.

## 8.1 The MPI Programming Model

In the MPI programming model, a computation comprises one or more processes that communicate by calling library routines to send and receive messages to other processes. In most MPI implementations, a fixed set of processes is created at program initialization, and one process is created per processor. However, these processes may execute different programs. Hence, the MPI programming model is sometimes referred to as *multiple program multiple data* (MPMD) to distinguish it from the SPMD model in which every processor executes the same program.

Because the number of processes in an MPI computation is normally fixed, our focus in this chapter is on the mechanisms used to communicate data between processes. Processes can use *point-to-point* communication operations to send a message from one named process to another; these operations can be used to implement local and unstructured communications. A group of processes can call *collective* communication operations to perform commonly used global operations such as summation and broadcast. MPI's ability to *probe* for messages supports asynchronous communication. Probably MPI's most important feature from a software engineering viewpoint is its support for modular programming. A mechanism called a *communicator* allows the MPI programmer to define modules that encapsulate internal communication structures. In the terminology used in Chapter 4, these modules can be combined by both sequential and parallel composition.

Most parallel algorithms designed using the techniques of Part I are readily implemented using MPI. Algorithms that create just one task per processor can be implemented directly, with point-to-point or collective communication routines used to meet communication requirements. Algorithms that create tasks in a dynamic fashion or that rely on the concurrent execution of several tasks on a processor must be further refined to permit an MPI implementation. For example, consider the first branch-and-bound search algorithm developed in Section 2.7, which creates a tree of "search" tasks dynamically. This algorithm cannot be implemented directly in MPI; however, as discussed in Chapter 2, it can be refined to obtain an algorithm that creates a fixed set of worker processes that exchange messages representing tree nodes to be searched. The resulting SPMD algorithm can be implemented as an MPI program. Algorithms that are not easily modified in this way are better implemented using alternative technologies.

## 8.2  MPI Basics

Although MPI is a complex and multifaceted system, we can solve a wide range of problems using just six of its functions! We introduce MPI by describing these six functions, which initiate and terminate a computation, identify processes, and send and receive messages:

| | |
|---|---|
| MPI_INIT | Initiate an MPI computation. |
| MPI_FINALIZE | Terminate a computation. |
| MPI_COMM_SIZE | Determine number of processes. |
| MPI_COMM_RANK | Determine my process identifier. |
| MPI_SEND | Send a message. |
| MPI_RECV | Receive a message. |

Function parameters are detailed in Figure 8.1. In this and subsequent figures, the labels IN, OUT, and INOUT indicate whether the function uses but does not modify the parameter (IN), does not use but may update the parameter (OUT), or both uses and updates the parameter (INOUT).

All but the first two calls take a communicator handle as an argument. A communicator identifies the process group and context with respect to which the operation is to be performed. As explained later in this chapter, communicators provide a mechanism for identifying process subsets during development of modular programs and for ensuring that messages intended for different purposes are not confused. For now, it suffices to provide

MPI_INIT(int *argc, char ***argv)
*Initiate a computation.*

> argc, argv are required only in the C language binding,
> > where they are the main program's arguments.

MPI_FINALIZE()
*Shut down a computation.*

MPI_COMM_SIZE(comm, size)
*Determine the number of processes in a computation.*

| | | |
|---|---|---|
| IN | comm | communicator (handle) |
| OUT | size | number of processes in the group of comm (integer) |

MPI_COMM_RANK(comm, pid)
*Determine the identifier of the current process.*

| | | |
|---|---|---|
| IN | comm | communicator (handle) |
| OUT | pid | process id in the group of comm (integer) |

MPI_SEND(buf, count, datatype, dest, tag, comm)
*Send a message.*

| | | |
|---|---|---|
| IN | buf | address of send buffer (choice) |
| IN | count | number of elements to send (integer $\geq 0$) |
| IN | datatype | datatype of send buffer elements (handle) |
| IN | dest | process id of destination process (integer) |
| IN | tag | message tag (integer) |
| IN | comm | communicator (handle) |

MPI_RECV(buf, count, datatype, source, tag, comm, status)
*Receive a message.*

| | | |
|---|---|---|
| OUT | buf | address of receive buffer (choice) |
| IN | count | size of receive buffer, in elements (integer $\geq 0$) |
| IN | datatype | datatype of receive buffer elements (handle) |
| IN | source | process id of source process, or MPI_ANY_SOURCE (integer) |
| IN | tag | message tag, or MPI_ANY_TAG (integer) |
| IN | comm | communicator (handle) |
| OUT | status | status object (status) |

**Figure 8.1**   Basic MPI. These six functions suffice to write a wide range of parallel programs. The arguments are characterized as having mode IN or OUT and as having type integer, choice, handle, or status. These terms are explained in the text.

the default value `MPI_COMM_WORLD`, which identifies *all* processes involved in a computation. Other arguments have type integer, datatype handle, or status. These datatypes are explained in the following.

The functions `MPI_INIT` and `MPI_FINALIZE` are used to initiate and shut down an MPI computation, respectively. `MPI_INIT` must be called before any other MPI function and must be called exactly once per process. No further MPI functions can be called after `MPI_FINALIZE`.

The functions `MPI_COMM_SIZE` and `MPI_COMM_RANK` determine the number of processes in the current computation and the integer identifier assigned to the current process, respectively. (The processes in a process group are identified with unique, contiguous integers numbered from 0.) For example, consider the following program. This is not written in any particular language: we shall see in the next section how to call MPI routines from Fortran and C.

```
program main
begin
  MPI_INIT()                              Initiate computation
  MPI_COMM_SIZE(MPI_COMM_WORLD, count)    Find # of processes
  MPI_COMM_RANK(MPI_COMM_WORLD, myid)     Find my id
  print("I am", myid, "of", count)        Print message
  MPI_FINALIZE()                          Shut down
end
```

The MPI standard does not specify how a parallel computation is started. However, a typical mechanism could be a command line argument indicating the number of processes that are to be created: for example, `myprog -n 4`, where `myprog` is the name of the executable. Additional arguments might be used to specify processor names in a networked environment or executable names in an MPMD computation.

If the above program is executed by four processes, we will obtain something like the following output. The order in which the output appears is not defined; however, we assume here that the output from individual print statements is not interleaved.

```
I am 1 of 4
I am 3 of 4
I am 0 of 4
I am 2 of 4
```

Finally, we consider the functions `MPI_SEND` and `MPI_RECV`, which are used to send and receive messages, respectively. A call to `MPI_SEND` has the general form

```
MPI_SEND(buf, count, datatype, dest, tag, comm)
```

and specifies that a message containing `count` elements of the specified `datatype` starting at address `buf` is to be sent to the process with identifier `dest`. As will be explained in greater detail subsequently, this message is associated with an envelope comprising the specified `tag`, the source process's identifier, and the specified communicator (`comm`).

A call to `MPI_RECV` has the general form

```
MPI_RECV(buf, count, datatype, source, tag, comm, status)
```

and attempts to receive a message that has an envelope corresponding to the specified `tag`, `source`, and `comm`, blocking until such a message is available. When the message arrives, elements of the specified `datatype` are placed into the buffer at address `buf`. This buffer is guaranteed to be large enough to contain at least `count` elements. The `status` variable can be used subsequently to inquire about the size, tag, and source of the received message (Section 8.4).

Program 8.1 illustrates the use of the six basic calls. This is an implementation of the bridge construction algorithm developed in Example 1.1. The program is designed to be executed by two processes. The first process calls a procedure `foundry` and the second calls `bridge`, effectively creating two different tasks. The first process makes a series of `MPI_SEND` calls to communicate 100 integer messages to the second process, terminating the sequence by sending a negative number. The second process receives these messages using `MPI_RECV`.

### 8.2.1 Language Bindings

Much of the discussion in this chapter will be language independent; that is, the functions described can be used in C, Fortran, or any other language for which an MPI library has been defined. Only when we present example programs will a particular language be used. In that case, programs will be presented using the syntax of either the Fortran or C language binding. Different language bindings have slightly different syntaxes that reflect a language's peculiarities. Sources of syntactic difference include the function names themselves, the mechanism used for return codes, the representation of the handles used to access specialized MPI data structures such as communicators, and the implementation of the `status` datatype returned by `MPI_RECV`. The use of handles hides the internal representation of MPI data structures.

**C Language Binding**    In the C language binding, function names are as in the MPI definition but with only the `MPI` prefix and the first letter of the function name in upper case. Status values are returned as integer return codes. The return code for successful completion is `MPI_SUCCESS`; a set of error codes is also defined. Compile-time constants are all in upper case and are defined in the file `mpi.h`, which must be included in any program that makes MPI calls. Handles are represented by special defined types, defined in `mpi.h`. These will be introduced as needed in the following discussion. Function parameters with type IN are passed by value, while parameters with type OUT and INOUT are passed by reference (that is, as pointers). A `status` variable has type `MPI_Status` and is a structure with fields `status.MPI_SOURCE` and `status.MPI_TAG` containing source and tag information. Finally, an MPI datatype is defined for each C datatype: `MPI_CHAR`, `MPI_INT`, `MPI_LONG`, `MPI_UNSIGNED_CHAR`, `MPI_UNSIGNED`, `MPI_UNSIGNED_LONG`, `MPI_FLOAT`, `MPI_DOUBLE`, `MPI_LONG_DOUBLE`, etc.

**Fortran Language Binding**    In the Fortran language binding, function names are in upper case. Function return codes are represented by an additional integer argument. The return code for successful completion is `MPI_SUCCESS`; a set of error codes is also defined. Compile-time constants are all in upper case and are defined in the file `mpif.h`,

```
program main
begin
  MPI_INIT()                              Initialize
  MPI_COMM_SIZE(MPI_COMM_WORLD, count)
  if count != 2 then exit                 Must be just 2 processes
  MPI_COMM_RANK(MPI_COMM_WORLD, myid)
  if myid = 0 then                        I am process 0:
    foundry(100)                            Execute foundry
  else                                    I am process 1:
    bridge()                                Execute bridge
  endif
  MPI_FINALIZE()                          Shut down
end

procedure foundry(numgirders)            Code for process 0
begin
  for i = 1 to numgirders                Send messages
    MPI_SEND(i, 1, MPI_INT, 1, 0, MPI_COMM_WORLD)
  endfor
  i = -1                                 Send shutdown message
  MPI_SEND(i, 1, MPI_INT, 1, 0, MPI_COMM_WORLD)
end

procedure bridge                         Code for process 1
begin
  MPI_RECV(msg, 1, MPI_INT, 0, 0, MPI_COMM_WORLD, status)
  while msg != -1 do                     Receive messages
    use_girder(msg)                      Use message
    MPI_RECV(msg, 1, MPI_INT, 0, 0, MPI_COMM_WORLD, status)
  enddo
end
```

**Program 8.1**   MPI implementation of bridge construction problem. This program is designed to be executed by two processes.

which must be included in any program that makes MPI calls. All handles have type IN-
TEGER. A status variable is an array of integers of size MPI_STATUS_SIZE, with the
constants MPI_SOURCE and MPI_TAG indexing the source and tag fields, respectively. Finally, an MPI datatype is defined for each Fortran datatype: MPI_INTEGER, MPI_REAL,
MPI_DOUBLE_PRECISION, MPI_COMPLEX, MPI_LOGICAL, MPI_CHARACTER, etc.

**EXAMPLE 8.1** (Pairwise Interactions)   The pairwise interactions algorithm discussed in
Section 1.4.2 illustrates the two language bindings. Recall that in this algorithm, $T$ tasks

```
#include "mpi.h"                                    /* Include file */

main(int argc, char *argv[]) {                      /* Main program */
    int myid, np, ierr, lnbr, rnbr;
    real x[300], buff[300], forces[300];
    MPI_Status status;

    ierr = MPI_Init(&argc, &argv);                  /* Initialize */
    if(ierr != MPI_SUCCESS) {                       /* Check return code */
       fprintf(stderr,"MPI initialization error\n");
       exit(1);
    }
    MPI_Comm_size(MPI_COMM_WORLD, &np);             /* Number of procs */
    MPI_Comm_rank(MPI_COMM_WORLD, &myid);           /* My process id */
    lnbr = (myid+np-1)%np;                          /* Id of left neighbor */
    rnbr = (myid+1)%np;                             /* Id of right nbr */

    initialize(x, buff, forces);

    for (i=0; i<np-1; i++) {                        /* Circulate messages */
       MPI_Send(buff, 300, MPI_FLOAT, rnbr, 0, MPI_COMM_WORLD);
       MPI_Recv(buff, 300, MPI_FLOAT, lnbr, 0, MPI_COMM_WORLD,
                &status);
       update_forces(x, buff, forces);
    }

    print_forces(myid, forces);                     /* Print result */
    MPI_Finalize();                                 /* Shutdown */
}
```

**Program 8.2**  MPI pairwise interactions program (C version).

($T$ an odd number) are connected in a ring. Each task is responsible for computing interactions involving $N$ data. Data are circulated around the ring in $T - 1$ phases, with interactions computed at each phase. Programs 8.2 and 8.3 are C and Fortran versions of an MPI implementation, respectively.

The number of processes created is specified when the program is invoked. Each process is responsible for 100 objects, and each object is represented by three floating-point values, so the various work arrays have size 300. As each process executes the same program, the first few lines are used to determine the total number of processes involved in the computation (np), the process's identifier (myid), and the identify of the process's neighbors in the ring (lnbr, rnbr). The computation then proceeds as described in Section 1.4.2 but with messages sent to numbered processes rather than on channels.

```
program pairwise_interactions            ! Main program
include "mpif.h"                          ! Include file
real x(3,100), buff(3,100), forces(3,100)
integer lnbr, rnbr, status(MPI_STATUS_SIZE), ierr, myid, np

call MPI_INIT(ierr)                       ! Initialize
if(ierr .ne. MPI_SUCCESS) then            ! Check return code
   print *,"MPI initialization error"
   stop 1
endif
call MPI_COMM_SIZE(MPI_COMM_WORLD, np, ierr)   ! No. of processes
call MPI_COMM_RANK(MPI_COMM_WORLD, myid, ierr) ! My process id
lnbr = mod(myid+np-1, np)                 ! Id of left neighbor
rnbr = mod(myid+1, np)                    ! Id of right nbr

call initialize(x, buff, forces)

do i = 1,np-1                             ! Circulate messages
   call MPI_SEND(buff, 300, MPI_REAL, rnbr, 0, MPI_COMM_WORLD,
$                ierr)
   call MPI_RECV(buff, 300, MPI_REAL, lnbr, 0, MPI_COMM_WORLD,
$                status, ierr)
   call update_forces(x, buff, forces)
enddo

call print_forces(myid, forces)          ! Print result
call MPI_FINALIZE(ierr)                   ! Shutdown
end                                       ! End of program
```

**Program 8.3**   MPI pairwise interactions program (Fortran version).

## 8.2.2   Determinism

Before proceeding to more sophisticated aspects of MPI, we consider the important topic of determinism. Message-passing programming models are by default nondeterministic: the arrival order of messages sent from two processes, A and B, to a third process, C, is not defined. (However, MPI *does* guarantee that two messages sent from one process, A, to another process, B, will arrive in the order sent.) It is the programmer's responsibility to ensure that a computation is deterministic when (as is usually the case) this is required.

In the task/channel programming model, determinism is guaranteed by defining separate channels for different communications and by ensuring that each channel has a single writer and a single reader. Hence, a process C can distinguish messages received from A or B as they arrive on separate channels. MPI does not support channels directly, but it does provide similar mechanisms. In particular, it allows a receive operation to specify a source, tag, and/or context. (Recall that these data constitute a message's envelope.) We consider the first two of these mechanisms in this section.

The *source* specifier in the MPI_RECV function allows the programmer to specify that a message is to be received either from a single named process (specified by its integer process identifier) or from any process (specified by the special value MPI_ANY_SOURCE). The latter option allows a process to receive data from any source; this is sometimes useful. However, the former is preferable because it eliminates errors due to messages arriving in time-dependent order.

Message *tags* provide a further mechanism for distinguishing between different messages. A sending process must associate an integer tag with a message. This is achieved via the tag field in the MPI_SEND call. (This tag has always been set to 0 in the examples presented so far.) A receiving process can then specify that it wishes to receive messages either with a specified tag or with any tag (MPI_ANY_TAG). Again, the former option is preferable because it reduces the possibility of error.

---

**EXAMPLE 8.2** (Nondeterministic Program)    To illustrate the importance of source specifiers and tags, we examine a program that fails to use them and that, consequently, suffers from nondeterminism. Program 8.4 is part of an MPI implementation of the symmetric pairwise interaction algorithm of Section 1.4.2. Recall that in this algorithm, messages are communicated only half way around the ring (in $T/2 - 1$ steps, if the number of tasks $T$ is odd), with interactions accumulated both in processes and in messages. As in Example 8.1, we assume 100 objects, so the arrays to be communicated in this phase have size 100.3.2=600. In a final step, each message (with size 100.3=300) is returned to its originating process. Hence, each process sends and receives $T/2 - 1$ *data* messages and one *result* message.

Program 8.4 specifies neither sources nor tags in its MPI_RECV calls. Consequently, a result message arriving before the final data message may be received as if it were a data message, thereby resulting in an incorrect computation. Determinism can be achieved by specifying either a source processor or a tag in the receive calls. It is good practice to use *both* mechanisms. In effect, each "channel" in the original design is then represented by a unique (source, destination, tag) triple.

---

## 8.3    Global Operations

As explained in Chapter 2, parallel algorithms often call for coordinated communication operations involving multiple processes. For example, all processes may need to cooperate to transpose a distributed matrix or to sum a set of numbers distributed one per process. Clearly, these global operations can be implemented by a programmer using the send and receive functions introduced in Section 8.2. For convenience, and to permit optimized implementations, MPI also provides a suite of specialized *collective communication* functions that perform commonly used operations of this type. These functions include the following.

```
main(int argc, char *argv[]) {
   int rnbr, rdest, myid, np;
   float buff[600];
   MPI_Status status;
   ⋮
   ⋮
   MPI_Comm_rank(MPI_COMM_WORLD, &myid);
   MPI_Comm_size(MPI_COMM_WORLD, &np);
   rnbr = (myid+1)%np;
   rdest = (myid+np/2+1)%np;
   ⋮
   /* Circulate data around ring */
   for (i=0; i<np/2; i++) {
      MPI_Send(buff, 600, MPI_FLOAT, rnbr, 1, MPI_COMM_WORLD);
      MPI_Recv(buff, 600, MPI_FLOAT, MPI_ANY_SOURCE, MPI_ANY_TAG,
         MPI_COMM_WORLD, &status);
      ⋮
      ⋮
   }
   /* Return accumulated data to source */
   MPI_Send(buff, 300, MPI_FLOAT, rdest, 2, MPI_COMM_WORLD);
   MPI_Recv(buff, 300, MPI_FLOAT, MPI_ANY_SOURCE, MPI_ANY_TAG,
      MPI_COMM_WORLD, &status);
   ⋮
   ⋮
}
```

**Program 8.4**  Part of a potentially nondeterministic MPI solution to the symmetric pairwise interactions problem. Notice the use of MPI_ANY_SOURCE and MPI_ANY_TAG in the MPI_RECV calls.

- Barrier: Synchronizes all processes.
- Broadcast: Sends data from one process to all processes.
- Gather: Gathers data from all processes to one process.
- Scatter: Scatters data from one process to all processes.
- Reduction operations: Sums, multiplies, etc., distributed data.

These operations are summarized in Figure 8.2. All are executed collectively, meaning that each process in a process group calls the communication routine with the same parameters.

### 8.3.1  Barrier

MPI_BARRIER is used to synchronize execution of a group of processes. No process returns from this function until all processes have called it. A barrier is a simple way of separating two phases of a computation to ensure that messages generated in the two phases do not

```
MPI_BARRIER(comm)
```
*Global synchronization.*
> IN    comm        communicator (handle)

```
MPI_BCAST(inbuf, incnt, intype, root, comm)
```
*Broadcast data from root to all processes.*
> INOUT inbuf      address of input buffer, or output buffer at root (choice)
> IN    incnt      number of elements in input buffer (integer)
> IN    intype     datatype of input buffer elements (handle)
> IN    root       process id of root process (integer)
> IN    comm       communicator (handle)

```
MPI_GATHER(inbuf, incnt, intype, outbuf, outcnt, outtype,
           root, comm)
MPI_SCATTER(inbuf, incnt, intype, outbuf, outcnt, outtype,
           root, comm)
```
*Collective data movement functions.*
> IN    inbuf      address of input buffer (choice)
> IN    incnt      number of elements sent to each (integer)
> IN    intype     datatype of input buffer elements (handle)
> OUT   outbuf     address of output buffer (choice)
> IN    outcnt     number of elements received from each (integer)
> IN    outtype    datatype of output buffer elements (handle)
> IN    root       process id of root process (integer)
> IN    comm       communicator (handle)

```
MPI_REDUCE(inbuf, outbuf, count, type, op, root, comm)
MPI_ALLREDUCE(inbuf, outbuf, count, type, op, comm)
```
*Collective reduction functions.*
> IN    inbuf      address of input buffer (choice)
> OUT   outbuf     address of output buffer (choice)
> IN    count      number of elements in input buffer (integer)
> IN    type       datatype of input buffer elements (handle)
> IN    op         operation; see text for list (handle)
> IN    root       process id of root process (integer)
> IN    comm       communicator (handle)

**Figure 8.2**   MPI global communication functions.

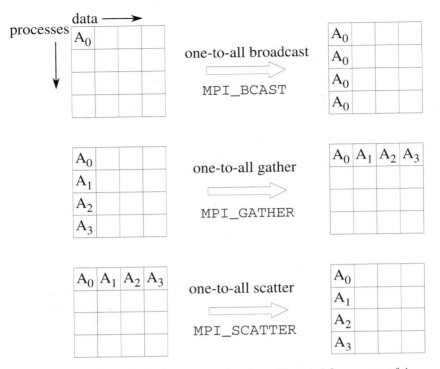

**Figure 8.3**   MPI collective data movement functions, illustrated for a group of 4 processes. In each set of 16 boxes, each row represents data locations in a different process. Thus, in the one-to-all broadcast, the data $A_0$ is initially located just in process 0; after the call, it is replicated in all processes. In each case, both `incnt` and `outcnt` are 1, meaning that each message comprises a single data element.

intermingle. For example, a call to `MPI_BARRIER` could be inserted before the second send operation in Program 8.4 to ensure deterministic execution. Of course, in this example as in many others, the need for an explicit barrier can be avoided by the appropriate use of tags, source specifiers, and/or contexts.

### 8.3.2   Data Movement

`MPI_BCAST`, `MPI_GATHER`, and `MPI_SCATTER` are collective *data movement* routines, in which all processes interact with a distinguished `root` process to broadcast, gather, or scatter data, respectively. The operation of these functions is illustrated in Figure 8.3. In each case, the first three arguments specify the location (`inbuf`) and type (`intype`) of the data to be communicated and the number of elements to be sent to each destination (`incnt`). Other arguments specify the location and type of the result (`outbuf`, `outtype`) and the number of elements to be received from each source (`outcnt`).

MPI_BCAST implements a one-to-all *broadcast* operation whereby a single named process (root) sends the same data to all other processes; each process receives these data from the root process. At the time of call, the data are located in inbuf in process root and consist of incnt data items of a specified intype. After the call, the data are replicated in inbuf in all processes. As inbuf is used for input at the root and for output in other processes, it has type INOUT.

MPI_GATHER implements an all-to-one *gather* operation. All processes (including the root process) send data located in inbuf to root. This process places the data in contiguous nonoverlapping locations in outbuf, with the data from process $i$ preceding that from process $i + 1$. Hence, the outbuf in the root process must be $P$ times larger than inbuf, where $P$ is the number of processes participating in the operation. The outbuf in processes other than the root is ignored.

MPI_SCATTER implements a one-to-all *scatter* operation; it is the reverse of MPI_GATHER. A specified root process sends data to all processes, sending the $i$th portion of its inbuf to process $i$; each process receives data from root in outbuf. Hence, the inbuf in the root process must be $P$ times larger than outbuf. Notice the subtle difference between this function and MPI_BCAST: while in MPI_BCAST every process receives the *same* value from the root process, in MPI_SCATTER every process receives a *different* value.

### 8.3.3  Reduction Operations

The functions MPI_REDUCE and MPI_ALLREDUCE implement reduction operations. They combine the values provided in the input buffer of each process, using a specified operation op, and return the combined value either to the output buffer of the single root process (in the case of MPI_REDUCE) or to the output buffer of all processes (MPI_ALLREDUCE). The operation is applied pointwise to each of the count values provided by each process. All operations return count values with the same datatype as the operands. Valid operations include maximum and minimum (MPI_MAX and MPI_MIN); sum and product (MPI_SUM and MPI_PROD); logical and, or, and exclusive or (MPI_LAND, MPI_LOR, and MPI_LXOR); and bitwise and, or, and exclusive or (MPI_BAND, MPI_BOR, and MPI_BXOR).

As an example, the following call would be used to compute the minimum of two sets of $P$ values, where $P$ is the number of processes involved in the reduction.

```
MPI_REDUCE(inbuf, outbuf, 2, MPI_INT, MPI_MIN, 0, MPI_COMM_WORLD)
```

After the reduction, outbuf[0] in process 0 contains the minimum of the first element in each input buffer (min(inbuf[0])); similarly, outbuf[1] contains min(inbuf[1]). The operation of this and other calls to MPI reduction functions are illustrated in Figure 8.4.

---

**EXAMPLE 8.3** (Finite Difference)   Once again we consider a finite difference problem, this time to illustrate the use of global operations. The algorithm considered requires both nearest-neighbor communication (to exchange boundary values) and global communication (to detect termination). Similar problems have previously been discussed in Chapter 2.

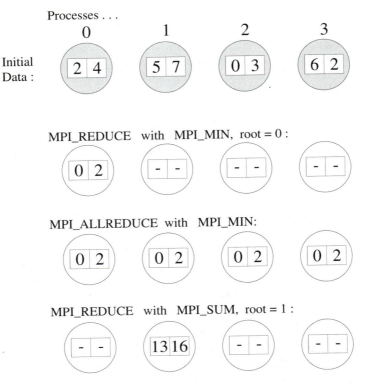

**Figure 8.4**    Applications of `MPI_REDUCE` and `MPI_ALLREDUCE`. The first line shows the send buffers (of size 2) in each of four processes; subsequent lines show the output buffers in each process following four different global communication calls.

The MPI implementation given in Program 8.5 is for a one-dimensional decomposition of a one-dimensional problem in which each process has two neighbors. It uses `MPI_SEND` and `MPI_RECV` for nearest-neighbor communication and four MPI global communication routines, for a total of five distinct communication operations. These are summarized as follows and are illustrated in Figure 8.5:

1. `MPI_BCAST` to broadcast the problem size parameter (`size`) from process 0 to all np processes;

2. `MPI_SCATTER` to distribute an input array (`work`) from process 0 to other processes, so that each process receives `size/np` elements;

3. `MPI_SEND` and `MPI_RECV` for exchange of data (a single floating-point number) with neighbors;

4. `MPI_ALLREDUCE` to determine the maximum of a set of `localerr` values computed at the different processes and to distribute this maximum value to each process; and

5. `MPI_GATHER` to accumulate an output array at process 0.

```
main(int argc, char *argv[]) {
    MPI_Comm com = MPI_COMM_WORLD;
    MPI_Init(&argc, &argv);
    MPI_Comm_size(com, &np);
    MPI_Comm_rank(com, &me);
    if (me == 0) {                          /* Read problem size at process 0 */
        read_problem_size(&size);
        buff[0] = size;
    }
    /* Global broadcast propagates this data to all processes */
    MPI_Bcast(buff, 1, MPI_INT, 0, com);
    /* Extract problem size from buff; allocate space for local data */
    lsize = buff[0]/np;
    local = malloc(lsize+2);
    /* Read input data at process 0; then distribute to processes */
    if (me == 0) { work = malloc(size); read_array(work); }
    MPI_Scatter(work, lsize, MPI_FLOAT, local+1, lsize,
            MPI_FLOAT, 0, com);
    lnbr = (me+np-1)%np;                     /* Determine my neighbors in ring */
    rnbr = (me+1)%np;
    globalerr = 99999.0;
    while (globalerr > 0.1) {               /* Repeat until termination */
        /* Exchange boundary values with neighbors */
        ls = local+lsize;
        MPI_Send(local+1, 1, MPI_FLOAT, lnbr, 10, com);
        MPI_Recv(local, 1, MPI_FLOAT, rnbr, 10, com, &status);
        MPI_Send(ls, 1, MPI_FLOAT, rnbr, 20, com);
        MPI_Recv(ls+1, 1, MPI_FLOAT, lnbr, 20, com, &status);
        compute(local);
        localerr = maxerror(local);         /* Determine local error */
        /* Find maximum local error, and replicate in each process */
        MPI_Allreduce(&localerr, &globalerr, 1, MPI_FLOAT,
            MPI_MAX, com);
    }
    /* Collect results at process 0 */
    MPI_Gather(local+1, lsize, MPI_FLOAT, work, lsize,
            MPI_FLOAT, 0, com);
    if (me == 0) { write_array(work); free(work); }
    MPI_Finalize();
}
```

**Program 8.5**  Outline of an MPI finite difference algorithm.

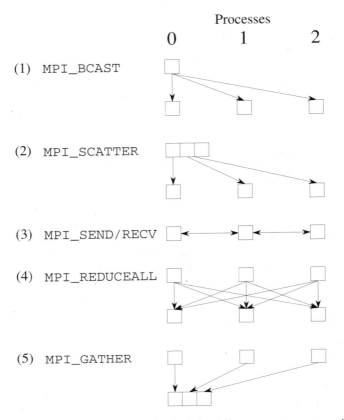

**Figure 8.5** Communication performed in the finite difference program, assuming three processes. Each column represents a processor; each subfigure shows data movement in a single phase. The five phases illustrated are (1) broadcast, (2) scatter, (3) nearest-neighbor exchange, (4) reduction, and (5) gather.

The use of scatter and gather operations to transfer input and output data is particularly simple and convenient. Note, however, that their use in this example is inherently nonscalable. As we solve larger problems, storage limitations will eventually prevent us from accumulating all input and output data in a single process. In addition, the associated communication costs may be prohibitive.

## 8.4  Asynchronous Communication

Recall from Chapter 2 that the need for asynchronous communication can arise when a computation must access elements of a shared data structure in an unstructured manner. One implementation approach is to encapsulate the data structure in a set of specialized

```
MPI_IPROBE(source, tag, comm, flag, status)
```
*Poll for a pending message.*

| | | |
|---|---|---|
| IN | source | id of source process, or MPI_ANY_SOURCE (integer) |
| IN | tag | message tag, or MPI_ANY_TAG (integer) |
| IN | comm | communicator (handle) |
| OUT | flag | (logical/Boolean) |
| OUT | status | status object (status) |

```
MPI_PROBE(source, tag, comm, status)
```
*Return when message is pending.*

| | | |
|---|---|---|
| IN | source | id of source process, or MPI_ANY_SOURCE (integer) |
| IN | tag | message tag, or MPI_ANY_TAG (integer) |
| IN | comm | communicator (handle) |
| OUT | status | status object (status) |

```
MPI_GET_COUNT(status, datatype, count)
```
*Determine size of a message.*

| | | |
|---|---|---|
| IN | status | status variable from receive (status) |
| IN | datatype | datatype of receive buffer elements (handle) |
| OUT | count | number of data elements in message (integer) |

**Figure 8.6**   MPI inquiry and probe operations.

data tasks to which read and write requests can be directed. This approach is not typically efficient in MPI, however, because of its MPMD programming model.

As noted in Section 2.3.4, an alternative implementation approach is to distribute the shared data structure among the computational processes, which must then poll periodically for pending read and write requests. This technique is supported by the MPI_IPROBE function, which is described in this section along with the related functions MPI_PROBE and MPI_GET_COUNT. The three functions are summarized in Figure 8.6.

The MPI_IPROBE function checks for the existence of pending messages without receiving them, thereby allowing us to write programs that interleave local computation with the processing of incoming messages. A call to MPI_IPROBE has the general form

```
MPI_IPROBE(source, tag, comm, flag, status)
```

and sets a Boolean argument flag to indicate whether a message that matches the specified source, tag, and communicator is available. If an appropriate message is available, flag is set to true; otherwise, it is set to false. The message can then be received by using MPI_RECV. The receive call must specify the same source, tag, and communicator; otherwise, a different message may be received.

Related to MPI_IPROBE is the function MPI_PROBE, which blocks until a message of the specified source, tag, and communicator is available and then returns and sets its status argument. The MPI_PROBE function is used to receive messages for which we have incomplete information.

The `status` argument constructed by an `MPI_RECV` call, an `MPI_PROBE` call, or a successful `MPI_IPROBE` call can be used to determine the (pending) message's source, tag, and size. The inquiry function `MPI_GET_COUNT` yields the length of a message just received. Its first two (input) parameters are a `status` object set by a previous probe or `MPI_RECV` call and the `datatype` of the elements to be received, while the third (output) parameter is an integer used to return the number of elements received (Figure 8.6). Other information about the received message can be obtained directly from the `status` object. In the C language binding, this object is a structure with fields `MPI_SOURCE` and `MPI_TAG`. Thus, `status.MPI_SOURCE` and `status.MPI_TAG` contain the source and tag of the message just received. In Fortran, the `status` object is an array of size `MPI_STATUS_SIZE`, and the constants `MPI_SOURCE` and `MPI_TAG` are the indices of the array elements containing the source and tag information. Thus, `status(MPI_SOURCE)` and `status(MPI_TAG)` contain the source and tag of the message just received.

The following code fragment uses these functions to receive a message from an unknown source and containing an unknown number of integers. It first detects arrival of the message using `MPI_PROBE`. Then, it determines the message source and uses `MPI_GET_COUNT` to determine the message size. Finally, it allocates a buffer of the appropriate size and receives the message.

```
int count, *buf, source;
MPI_Probe(MPI_ANY_SOURCE, 0, comm, &status);
source = status.MPI_SOURCE;
MPI_Get_count(status, MPI_INT, &count);
buf = malloc(count*sizeof(int));
MPI_Recv(buf, count, MPI_INT, source, 0, comm, &status);
```

---

**EXAMPLE 8.4** (Fock Matrix Construction)    The Fock matrix construction algorithm of Section 2.8 allocates to each processor a data task, which manages part of the D and F matrices, and a computation task, which generates requests for matrix elements. The two tasks execute concurrently, with the data task responding to requests for data and the computation task performing computation. Briefly, the two tasks are defined as follows.

```
/* Data task */                    /* Computation task */
while(done != TRUE) {              while(done != TRUE) {
   receive(request);                  identify_next_task();
   reply_to(request);                 generate_requests();
}                                      process_replies();
                                   }
```

A polling version of this program integrates the functions of the database and computation tasks into a single process, which alternates between checking for pending data requests and performing computation. This integration can be achieved as in Program 8.6. The program uses the `MPI_IPROBE` function to determine whether database messages are pending. If they are, these messages are processed before further computation is performed.

For simplicity, the procedure `process_request` deals with a single type of request: a read operation on a single array element. A process receiving such a request determines

```
main(int argc, char *argv[]) {
   MPI_Status status;
   int flag, done = FALSE;
   MPI_Init(&argc, &argv);
   while(done != TRUE) {                    /* Repeat until done */
      MPI_Iprobe(MPI_ANY_SOURCE, 0, MPI_COMM_WORLD,
                  &flag, &status);
      while (flag == TRUE) {                /* Receive pending messages */
         process_request(status);
         MPI_Iprobe(MPI_ANY_SOURCE, 0, MPI_COMM_WORLD,
                     &flag, &status);
      }
      identify_next_task();                 /* Execute next task ... */
      generate_requests();                  /* sending requests to */
      process_replies();                    /* other tasks */
   }
   MPI_Terminate();                         /* Shutdown */
}

process_request(MPI_Status status) {
   int address;
   float value;
   int source = status.MPI_SOURCE;
   MPI_Recv(&address, 1, MPI_INT, source, 0,
            MPI_COMM_WORLD, &status);
   value = data[address];
   MPI_Send(&value, 1, MPI_FLOAT, source, 5, MPI_COMM_WORLD);
}
```

**Program 8.6** Outline of an MPI implementation of Fock matrix problem using MPI_IPROBE, MPI_GET_COUNT, and the status argument.

the source of the message, retrieves the requested value, and returns the value to the source process.

## 8.5 Modularity

In Chapter 4, we distinguished three general forms of composition that can be used for the modular construction of parallel programs: sequential, parallel, and concurrent. Recall that in sequential composition, two program components execute in sequence on the same set of processors. In parallel composition, two program components execute concurrently on disjoint sets of processors. In concurrent composition, two program components execute on potentially nondisjoint sets of processors.

MPI supports modular programming via its communicator mechanism, which provides the information hiding needed when building modular programs, by allowing the specification of program components that encapsulate internal communication operations and that provide a local name space for processes. In this section, we show how communicators can be used to implement various forms of sequential and parallel composition. MPI's MPMD programming model means that the full generality of concurrent composition is not generally available.

An MPI communication operation always specifies a communicator. This identifies the process group that is engaged in the communication operation and the context in which the communication occurs. As we shall see, process groups allow a subset of processes to communicate among themselves using local process identifiers and to perform collective communication operations without involving other processes. The context forms part of the envelope associated with a message. A receive operation can receive a message only if the message was sent in the same context. Hence, if two routines use different contexts for their internal communication, there can be no danger of their communications being confused.

In preceding sections, all communication operations have used the default communicator MPI_COMM_WORLD, which incorporates all processes involved in an MPI computation and defines a default context. We now describe four functions that allow communicators to be used in more flexible ways. These functions, and their roles in modular design, are as follows.

1. MPI_COMM_DUP. A program may create a new communicator comprising the same process group but a new context to ensure that communications performed for different purposes are not confused. This mechanism supports sequential composition.

2. MPI_COMM_SPLIT. A program may create a new communicator comprising just a subset of a given group of processes. These processes can then communicate among themselves without fear of conflict with other concurrent computations. This mechanism supports parallel composition.

3. MPI_INTERCOMM_CREATE. A program may construct an *intercommunicator*, which links processes in two groups. This mechanism supports parallel composition.

4. MPI_COMM_FREE. This function can be used to release a communicator created using the preceding three functions.

The four functions are summarized in Figure 8.7; their arguments and the ways they are called are described next.

## 8.5.1    Creating Communicators

As discussed in Section 8.2.2, message tags provide a mechanism for distinguishing between messages used for different purposes. However, they do not provide a sufficient basis for modular design. For example, consider an application that calls a library routine implementing (for example) an array transpose operation. It is important to ensure that the

```
MPI_COMM_DUP(comm, newcomm)
```
*Create new communicator: same group, new context.*

| | | |
|---|---|---|
| IN | comm | communicator (handle) |
| OUT | newcomm | communicator (handle) |

```
MPI_COMM_SPLIT(comm, color, key, newcomm)
```
*Partition group into disjoint subgroups.*

| | | |
|---|---|---|
| IN | comm | communicator (handle) |
| IN | color | subgroup control (integer) |
| IN | key | process id control (integer) |
| OUT | newcomm | communicator (handle) |

```
MPI_INTERCOMM_CREATE(comm, leader, peer, rleader, tag, inter)
```
*Create an intercommunicator.*

| | | |
|---|---|---|
| IN | comm | local intracommunicator (handle) |
| IN | leader | local leader (integer) |
| IN | peer | peer intracommunicator (handle) |
| IN | rleader | process id of remote leader in peer (integer) |
| IN | tag | tag for communicator set up (integer) |
| OUT | inter | new intercommunicator (handle) |

```
MPI_COMM_FREE(comm)
```
*Destroy a communicator.*

| | | |
|---|---|---|
| IN | comm | communicator (handle) |

**Figure 8.7**    MPI communicator functions.

message tags used in the library are distinct from those used in the rest of the application (Figure 8.8). Yet the user of a library routine may not know the tags the library uses; indeed, tag values may be computed on the fly.

Communicators provide a solution to this problem. A call of the form

```
MPI_COMM_DUP(comm, newcomm)
```

creates a new communicator newcomm comprising the same processes as comm but with a new context. This new communicator can be passed as an argument to the library routine, as in the following code, which calls transpose to transpose an array A.

```
integer comm, newcomm, ierr            ! Handles are integers
  ⋮

call MPI_COMM_DUP(comm, newcomm, ierr)  ! Create new context
call transpose(newcomm, A)              ! Pass to library
call MPI_COMM_FREE(newcomm, ierr)       ! Free new context
```

The transpose routine itself will be defined to use the communicator newcomm in all communication operations, thereby ensuring that communications performed within this routine cannot be confused with communications performed outside.

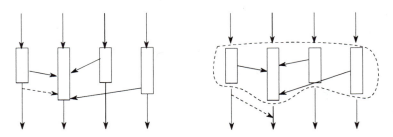

**Figure 8.8**   Errors can occur in a sequential composition of two parallel program
components (e.g., an application program and a parallel library) if the two components
use the same message tags. The figure on the left shows how this can occur. Each of the
four vertical lines represents a single thread of control (process) in an SPMD program. All
call an SPMD library, which are represented by the boxes. One process finishes sooner
than the others, and a message that this process generates during subsequent computation
(the dashed arrow) is intercepted by the library. The figure on the right shows how this
problem is avoided by using contexts: the library communicates using a distinct tag space,
which cannot be penetrated by other messages.

### 8.5.2   Partitioning Processes

Recall that we use the term *parallel composition* to denote the parallel execution of two
or more program components on disjoint sets of processors (Section 4.2). One approach
to the implementation of parallel composition is to create tasks dynamically and to place
newly created tasks on different processors. This *task-parallel* approach is taken in CC++
and Fortran M, for example. In MPMD programs, parallel composition is implemented
differently. As illustrated in Figure 8.9, available processes are partitioned into disjoint
sets, with each set executing the appropriate program. This partitioning is achieved by
using the function MPI_COMM_SPLIT. A call of the form

```
MPI_COMM_SPLIT(comm, color, key, newcomm)
```

creates one or more new communicators. This function is a collective communication operation, meaning that it must be executed by each process in the process group associated
with comm. A new communicator is created for each unique value of color other than
the defined constant MPI_UNDEFINED. Each new communicator comprises those processes
that specified its value of color in the MPI_COMM_SPLIT call. These processes are assigned identifiers within the new communicator starting from zero, with order determined
by the value of key or, in the event of ties, by the identifier in the old communicator. Thus,
a call of the form

```
MPI_COMM_SPLIT(comm, 0, 0, newcomm)
```

in which all processes specify the same color and key, is equivalent to a call

```
MPI_COMM_DUP(comm, newcomm)
```

That is, both calls create a new communicator containing all the processes in the old

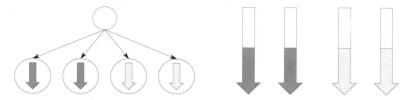

**Figure 8.9**   Different views of parallel composition. On the left is the task-parallel view, in which new tasks are created dynamically to execute two different program components. Four tasks are created: two perform one computation (dark shading) and two another (light shading). On the right is the MPMD view. Here, a fixed set of processes (represented by vertical arrows) change character, for example, by calling different subroutines.

communicator `comm`. In contrast, the following code creates three new communicators if `comm` contains at least three processes.

```
MPI_Comm comm, newcomm;
int myid, color;
MPI_Comm_rank(comm, &myid);
color = myid%3;
MPI_Comm_split(comm, color, myid, &newcomm);
```

For example, if `comm` contains eight processes, then processes 0, 3, and 6 form a new communicator of size three, as do processes 1, 4, and 7, while processes 2 and 5 form a new communicator of size two (Figure 8.10).

As a final example, the following code fragment creates a new communicator (`newcomm`) containing at most eight processes. Processes with identifiers greater than eight in communicator `comm` call `MPI_COMM_SPLIT` with `newid=MPI_UNDEFINED` and hence are not part of the new communicator.

```
MPI_Comm comm, newcomm;
int myid, color;
MPI_Comm_rank(comm, &myid);
if (myid < 8)                    /* Select first 8 processes */
   color = 1;
else                             /* Others are not in group */
   color = MPI_UNDEFINED;
MPI_Comm_split(comm, color, myid, &newcomm);
```

### 8.5.3   Communicating between Groups

A communicator returned by `MPI_COMM_SPLIT` can be used to communicate within a group of processes. Hence, it is called an *intracommunicator*. (The default communicator, `MPI_COMM_WORLD`, is an intracommunicator.) It is also possible to create an *intercommu-nicator* that can be used to communicate between process groups. An intercommunicator that connects two groups $A$ and $B$ containing $N_A$ and $N_B$ processes, respectively, allows processes in group $A$ to communicate with processes $0..N_B - 1$ in group $B$ by using MPI

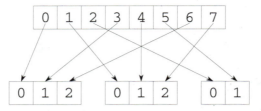

**Figure 8.10** Using `MPI_COMM_SPLIT` to form new communicators. The first communicator is a group of eight processes. Setting color to `myid%3` and calling `MPI_COMM_SPLIT(comm, color, myid, newcomm)` split this into three disjoint process groups.

send and receive calls (collective operations are not supported). Similarly, processes in group $B$ can communicate with processes $0..N_A - 1$ in group $A$.

An intercommunicator is created by a collective call executed in the two groups that are to be connected. In making this call, the processes in the two groups must each supply a local intracommunicator that identifies the processes involved in their group. They must also agree on the identifier of a "leader" process in each group and a parent communicator that contains all the processes in both groups, via which the connection can be established. The default communicator `MPI_COMM_WORLD` can always be used for this purpose. The collective call has the general form

```
MPI_INTERCOMM_CREATE(comm, local_leader, peercomm,
                     remote_leader, tag, intercomm)
```

where `comm` is an intracommunicator in the local group and `local_leader` is the identifier of the nominated leader process within this group. (It does not matter which process is chosen as the leader; however, all participants in the collective operation must nominate the same process.) The parent communicator is specified by `peercomm`, while `remote_leader` is the identifier of the other group's leader process *within the parent communicator*. The two other arguments are (1) a "safe" tag that the two groups' leader processes can use to communicate within the parent communicator's context without confusion with other communications and (2) the new intercommunicator `intercomm`.

Program 8.7 illustrates these ideas. It first uses `MPI_COMM_SPLIT` to split available processes into two disjoint groups. Even-numbered processes are in one group; odd-numbered processes are in a second. Calls to `MPI_COMM_RANK` are used to determine the values of the variables `myid` and `newid`, which represent each process's identifier in the original communicator and the appropriate new communicator, respectively. In this example, `newid=myid/2`. Then, the `MPI_INTERCOMM_CREATE` call defines an intercommunicator that links the two groups (Figure 8.11). Process 0 within each group are selected as the two leaders; these processes correspond to processes 0 and 1 within the original group, respectively. Once the intercommunicator is created, each process in the first group sends a message to the corresponding process in the second group. Finally, the new communicators created by the program are deleted.

```
      integer comm, intercomm, ierr, status(MPI_STATUS_SIZE)
C     For simplicity, we require an even number of processes
      call MPI_COMM_SIZE(MPI_COMM_WORLD, count, ierr)
      if(mod(count,2) .ne. 0) stop
C     Split processes into two groups: odd and even numbered
      call MPI_COMM_RANK(MPI_COMM_WORLD, myid, ierr)
      call MPI_COMM_SPLIT(MPI_COMM_WORLD, mod(myid,2), myid,
     $      comm, ierr)
C     Determine process id in new group
      call MPI_COMM_RANK(comm, newid, ierr)
      if(mod(myid,2) .eq. 0) then
C         Group 0: create intercommunicator and send message
C         Arguments: 0=local leader; 1=remote leader; 99=tag
          call MPI_INTERCOMM_CREATE(comm, 0, MPI_COMM_WORLD, 1, 99,
     $          intercomm, ierr)
          call MPI_SEND(msg, 1, type, newid, 0, intercomm, ierr)
      else
C         Group 1: create intercommunicator and receive message
C         Note that remote leader has id 0 in MPI_COMM_WORLD
          call MPI_INTERCOMM_CREATE(comm, 0, MPI_COMM_WORLD, 0, 99,
     $          intercomm, ierr)
          call MPI_RECV(msg, 1, type, newid, 0, intercomm,
     $          status, ierr)
      endif
C     Free communicators created during this operation
      call MPI_COMM_FREE(intercomm, ierr)
      call MPI_COMM_FREE(comm, ierr)
```

**Program 8.7**   An MPI program illustrating creation and use of an intercommunicator.

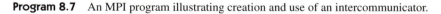
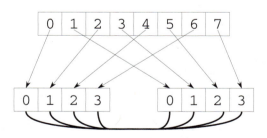

**Figure 8.11**   Establishing an intercommunicator between two process groups. At the top is an original group of eight processes; this is MPI_COMM_WORLD. An MPI_COMM_SPLIT call creates two process groups, each containing four processes. Then, an MPI_INTERCOMM_CREATE call creates an intercommunicator between the two groups.

## 8.6    Other MPI Features

In this section, we discuss MPI's derived datatype mechanism. We also list MPI features not covered in this book.

### 8.6.1    Derived Datatypes

In earlier sections of this chapter, MPI routines have been used to communicate *simple* datatypes, such as integers and reals, or arrays of these types. The final set of MPI functions that we describe implements *derived types*, a mechanism allowing noncontiguous data elements to be grouped together in a message. This mechanism permits us to avoid data copy operations. Without it, the sending of a row of a two-dimensional array stored by columns would require that these noncontiguous elements be copied into a buffer before being sent.

Three sets of functions are applied for manipulating derived types. Derived datatypes are constructed by applying *constructor* functions to simple or derived types; we describe three constructor functions MPI_TYPE_CONTIGUOUS, MPI_TYPE_VECTOR, and MPI_TYPE_INDEXED. The *commit* function, MPI_TYPE_COMMIT, must be applied to a derived type before it can be used in a communication operation. Finally, the *free* function, MPI_TYPE_FREE, should be applied to a derived type after use, in order to reclaim storage. These functions are summarized in Figure 8.12.

The constructor MPI_TYPE_CONTIGUOUS is used to define a type comprising one or more contiguous data elements. A call of the form

```
MPI_TYPE_CONTIGUOUS(count, oldtype, newtype)
```

defines a derived type newtype comprising count consecutive occurrences of datatype oldtype. For example, the sequence of calls

```
      call MPI_TYPE_CONTIGUOUS(10, MPI_REAL, tenrealtype, ierr)
      call MPI_TYPE_COMMIT(tenrealtype, ierr)
      call MPI_SEND(data, 1, tenrealtype, dest, tag,
     $            MPI_COMM_WORLD, ierr)
      call MPI_TYPE_FREE(tenrealtype, ierr)
```

is equivalent to the following single call.

```
      call MPI_SEND(data, 10, MPI_REAL, dest, tag,
     $            MPI_COMM_WORLD, ierr)
```

Both code fragments send a sequence of ten contiguous real values at location data to process dest.

The constructor MPI_TYPE_VECTOR is used to define a type comprising one or more blocks of data elements separated by a constant stride in an array. A call of the form

```
MPI_TYPE_VECTOR(count, blocklen, stride, oldtype, newtype)
```

defines a derived type newtype comprising count consecutive blocks of data elements with datatype oldtype, with  each block containing blocklen data elements, and the start of successive blocks separated by stride data elements. For example, the sequence of calls

```
MPI_TYPE_CONTIGUOUS(count, oldtype, newtype)
```
*Construct datatype from contiguous elements.*
| IN | count | number of elements (integer ≥0) |
| IN | oldtype | input datatype (handle) |
| OUT | newtype | output datatype (handle) |

```
MPI_TYPE_VECTOR(count, blocklen, stride, oldtype, newtype)
```
*Construct datatype from blocks separated by stride.*
| IN | count | number of elements (integer ≥0) |
| IN | blocklen | elements in a block (integer ≥0) |
| IN | stride | elements between start of each block (integer) |
| IN | oldtype | input datatype (handle) |
| OUT | newtype | output datatype (handle) |

```
MPI_TYPE_INDEXED(count, blocklens, indices, oldtype, newtype)
```
*Construct datatype with variable indices and sizes.*
| IN | count | number of blocks (integer ≥0) |
| IN | blocklens | elements in each block (array of integer ≥0) |
| IN | indices | displacements for each block (array of integer) |
| IN | oldtype | input datatype (handle) |
| OUT | newtype | output datatype (handle) |

```
MPI_TYPE_COMMIT(type)
```
*Commit datatype so that it can be used in communication.*
| INOUT | type | datatype to be committed (handle) |

```
MPI_TYPE_FREE(type)
```
*Free a derived datatype.*
| INOUT | type | datatype to be freed (handle) |

**Figure 8.12**   MPI derived datatype functions.

```
float data[1024];
MPI_Datatype floattype;
MPI_Type_vector(10, 1, 32, MPI_FLOAT, &floattype);
MPI_Type_commit(&floattype);
MPI_Send(data, 1, floattype, dest, tag, MPI_COMM_WORLD);
MPI_Type_free(&floattype);
```

is equivalent to the following code.

```
float data[1024], buff[10];
for (i=0; i<10; i++) buff[i] = data[i*32];
MPI_Send(buff, 10, MPI_FLOAT, dest, tag, MPI_COMM_WORLD);
```

Both send ten floating-point numbers from locations data[0], data[32], . . ., etc.

**EXAMPLE 8.5** (Finite Difference Stencil)    Program 8.8 uses derived types to communicate the north and south rows and the west and east columns of a $4 \times 6$ Fortran array. As illustrated in Figure 8.13, a column of this array is stored in contiguous locations and can be accessed by using a contiguous derived type. On the other hand, row $i$ of this array (comprising elements array($i$,1), ($i$,2), ..., ($i$,6)) is located in elements $i$, $i+4$, ..., $i+20$. Because these elements are not stored in contiguous locations, a call to MPI_TYPE_VECTOR is used to define the appropriate type, rowtype.

Program 8.8 frees the derived types that it defines immediately after they are used. In practice, a type might be reused many times before being freed.

```
        integer coltype, rowtype, comm, ierr
C       The derived type coltype is 4 contiguous reals.
        call MPI_TYPE_CONTIGUOUS(4, MPI_REAL, coltype, ierr)
        call MPI_TYPE_COMMIT(coltype, ierr)
C       The derived type rowtype is 6 reals, located 4 apart.
        call MPI_TYPE_VECTOR(6, 1, 4, MPI_REAL, rowtype, ierr)
        call MPI_TYPE_COMMIT(rowtype, ierr)
        :
        call MPI_SEND(array(1,1), 1, coltype, west, 0, comm, ierr)
        call MPI_SEND(array(1,6), 1, coltype, east, 0, comm, ierr)
        call MPI_SEND(array(1,1), 1, rowtype, north, 0, comm, ierr)
        call MPI_SEND(array(4,1), 1, rowtype, south, 0, comm, ierr)
        :
        call MPI_TYPE_FREE(rowtype, ierr)
        call MPI_TYPE_FREE(coltype, ierr)
```

**Program 8.8**    Using derived types to communicate a finite difference stencil. The variables west, east, north, and south refer to the process's neighbors.

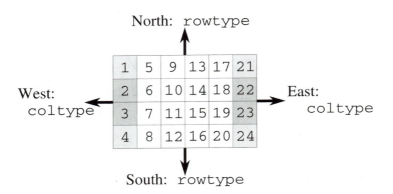

**Figure 8.13**    A $4 \times 6$ finite difference grid. Areas to be sent to west, east, north, and south neighbors are highlighted.

The third constructor, MPI_TYPE_INDEXED, is used to define a type comprising one or more blocks of a primitive or previously defined datatype, where block lengths and the displacements between blocks are specified in arrays. A call of the form

```
MPI_TYPE_INDEXED(count, lengths, indices, oldtype, newtype)
```

defines a derived type newtype comprising count consecutive blocks of data elements with datatype oldtype, with block *i* having a displacement of indices(*i*) data elements and containing lengths(*i*) data elements.

---

**EXAMPLE 8.6** (Fock Matrix Problem)   In Example 8.4 and Program 8.6, we developed an implementation for a Fock matrix task that receives read requests containing the address of a single data value. A more realistic program might support messages comprising len/2 indices followed by len/2 block lengths. The MPI_TYPE_INDEXED constructor can then be used to return the required values, as follows.

```
      call MPI_TYPE_INDEXED(len/2, inbuf(len/2+1), inbuf(1),
$                           MPI_REAL, focktype, ierr)
      call MPI_TYPE_COMMIT(focktype, ierr);
      call MPI_SEND(data, 1, focktype, source, MPI_COMM_WORLD, ierr)
      call MPI_TYPE_FREE(focktype, ierr)
```

An alternative approach that does not use the constructor is to accumulate the values that are to be returned in a buffer. The relative efficiency of the two approaches depends on several factors, including the amount of data to be transferred and the capabilities of the computer used to execute the program.

---

### 8.6.2  MPI Features Not Covered

For simplicity, we have focused on a subset of MPI in this chapter. Of necessity, numerous subtleties have been omitted in this brief description. Also, the following MPI features have not been covered.

1. *Heterogeneous types*. Different datatypes can be encapsulated in a single derived type, thereby allowing communication of heterogeneous messages. In addition, data can be sent in "raw" format, without data conversion in heterogeneous networks.

2. *Environmental inquiry.* A program can obtain information about the environment in which it is running, including information that can be used to tune algorithm performance.

3. *Additional global operations*. These operations support all-to-all communication and variable-sized contributions from different processes. Additional reduction operations can be used to determine the location of minimum and maximum values and to perform reductions with user-defined functions.

4. *Specialized communication modes*. These modes include synchronous communication, which causes the sender to block until the corresponding receive operation has begun; buffered communication, which allows the programmer to allocate

buffers so as to ensure that system resources are not exhausted during communications; and nonblocking communication, which can be more efficient on computers that allow user computation to be overlapped with some of the sending of a message.

## 8.7   Performance Issues

The performance analysis techniques developed in Chapter 3 can be applied directly to MPI programs. We discuss some relevant costs here.

An MPI_SEND/MPI_RECV pair communicates a single message. The cost of this communication can be modeled with Equation 3.1. The cost of the blocking MPI_PROBE operation will normally be similar to that of an ordinary receive. The cost of the nonblocking MPI_IPROBE operation can vary significantly according to implementation: in some implementations it may be negligible, while in others it can be higher than an ordinary receive.

The performance of global operations is less straightforward to analyze, as their execution can involve considerable internal communication. Implementations of these functions can normally be expected to use efficient communication algorithms, such as the hypercube algorithms described in Chapter 11. In the absence of bandwidth limitations, these allow a barrier to complete in $\log P$ steps on $P$ processors, a broadcast of $N$ words to proceed in time $\log P(t_s + t_w N)$ if $N$ is small and in time $2(t_s \log P + t_w N)$ if $N$ is large, and so on. The costs associated with these algorithms are summarized in Table 8.1. Remember that on many architectures, bandwidth limitations can increase actual costs, especially for larger messages (Section 3.7).

The MPI_COMM_DUP, MPI_COMM_SPLIT, and MPI_COMM_FREE operations should not normally involve communication. The cost of the MPI_INTERCOMM_CREATE operation is implementation dependent, but will normally involve at least one communication operation. The cost of the MPI_INIT and MPI_FINALIZE operations is implementation dependent and can be high. However, these functions are called once only in a program execution. Other functions can normally be expected to execute without communication and with little local computation.

**Table 8.1**   Communication costs associated with various MPI global operations when implemented using hypercube communication algorithms on the idealized multicomputer architecture. The term $t_{op}$ represents the cost of a single reduction operation.

| Operation | Cost (small $N$) | Cost (large $N$) |
|---|---|---|
| MPI_BARRIER | $t_s \log P$ | $t_s \log P$ |
| MPI_BCAST | $\log P(t_s + t_w N)$ | $2(t_s \log P + t_w N)$ |
| MPI_SCATTER | $t_s \log P + t_w N$ | $t_s \log P + t_w N$ |
| MPI_GATHER | $t_s \log P + t_w N$ | $t_s \log P + t_w N$ |
| MPI_REDUCE | $\log P(t_s + (t_w + t_{op})N)$ | $t_s 2 \log P + (t_w 2 + t_{op})N$ |
| MPI_ALLREDUCE | $\log P(t_s + (t_w + t_{op})N)$ | $t_s 2 \log P + (t_w 2 + t_{op})N$ |

## 8.8   Case Study: Earth System Model

We conclude by showing how the earth system model introduced in Chapter 2 can be constructed in a modular fashion by using MPI communicators. In particular, we consider a hypothetical model constructed as a parallel composition of atmosphere, ocean, and graphics components. The atmosphere and ocean models execute concurrently and exchange data periodically; in addition, the atmosphere model sends data periodically to the graphics component, which performs data reduction and rendering functions and outputs high-quality graphics. We allocate the same number of processes to each component; this approach is unlikely to be efficient in practice, but simplifies the presentation.

Program 8.9 implements this modular structure (Figure 8.14). The first two lines partition available processes into the three equal-sized, disjoint process groups that will be used to execute the three components. The code following the "if" statement establishes intercommunicators that link the atmosphere model with the ocean and graphics components, and initiates execution of the three components. Part of the ocean model code is shown also. This performs a reduction within the ocean model processes by using MPI_ALLREDUCE and the intracommunicator comm. Then, it exchanges data with corresponding processes in the atmosphere model by using the intercommunicator atm_ocn.

## 8.9   Summary

This chapter has described the message-passing library approach to parallel programming and has shown how parallel algorithm designs developed using the techniques from Part I can be translated into message-passing programs. It has also provided a tutorial introduction to the MPI message-passing standard. Table 8.2 summarizes the MPI routines described in this chapter; Tables 8.3 and 8.4 summarize the C and Fortran language bindings, respectively, for these functions and give the types of each function's arguments.

The principal features of the message-passing programming model as realized in MPI are as follows.

1. A computation consists of a (typically fixed) set of heavyweight processes, each with a unique identifier (integers 0 .. P–1).

2. Processes interact by exchanging typed messages, by engaging in collective communication operations, or by probing for pending messages.

3. Modularity is supported via communicators, which allow subprograms to encapsulate communication operations and to be combined in sequential and parallel compositions.

4. Algorithms developed using the techniques set out in Part I can be expressed directly if they do not create tasks dynamically or place multiple tasks on a processor.

5. Algorithms that *do* create tasks dynamically or place multiple tasks on a processor can require substantial refinement before they can be implemented in MPI.

6. Determinism is not guaranteed but can be achieved with careful programming.

```
      integer comm, atm_ocn, atm_gra
C     Generate three intracommunicators: 1/3 of processes each.
      call MPI_COMM_RANK(MPI_COMM_WORLD, myid, ierr)
      call MPI_COMM_SPLIT(MPI_COMM_WORLD, myid/3, myid, comm,
     $                    ierr)
C     Create intercommunicators and invoke three components.
      if (myid/3 .eq. 0) then
         call MPI_INTERCOMM_CREATE(comm, 0, MPI_COMM_WORLD, 1, 99,
     $                             atm_ocn, ierr)
         call ocean(comm, atm_ocn)
      else if (myid/3 .eq. 1) then
         call MPI_INTERCOMM_CREATE(comm, 0, MPI_COMM_WORLD, 0, 99,
     $                             atm_ocn, ierr)
         call MPI_INTERCOMM_CREATE(comm, 0, MPI_COMM_WORLD, 2, 88,
     $                             atm_gra, ierr)
         call atmosphere(comm, atm_ocn, atm_gra)
      else if (myid/3 .eq. 2) then
         call MPI_INTERCOMM_CREATE(comm, 0, MPI_COMM_WORLD, 1, 88,
     $                             atm_gra, ierr)
         call graphics(comm, atm_gra)
      endif


C     Ocean model component
      subroutine ocean(comm, atm_ocn)
      integer comm                    ! Intracommunicator for internal use
      integer atm_ocn                 ! Intercommunicator with atmosphere
      :
C     Perform reduction operation over ocean model processes
      call MPI_ALLREDUCE(local, global, 1, type, op, comm, ierr)
      :
C     Exchange data with corresponding process in atmosphere model
      call MPI_COMM_RANK(comm, myid, ierr)
      call MPI_SEND(buf, size, type, myid, tag, atm_ocn, ierr)
      call MPI_RECV(buf, size, type, myid, tag, atm_ocn, status,
     $             ierr)
      :
      end
```

**Program 8.9**  Use of intercommunicators in an earth system model.

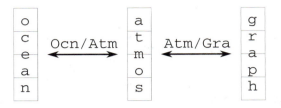

**Figure 8.14** Communicators and intercommunicators in an earth system model. Available processes are partitioned into three disjoint groups, each with its own communicator used for internal communication. Intercommunicators allow the atmosphere model to communicate with the ocean model and graphics model.

**Table 8.2** MPI quick reference: the functions included in the MPI subset, the figure in which each is defined, the section in which each is described, and the programs that illustrate their use.

| MPI Function | Figure | Section | Illustrative Programs |
|---|---|---|---|
| MPI_INIT | 8.1 | 8.2 | 8.1, 8.2, 8.3, etc. |
| MPI_FINALIZE | 8.1 | 8.2 | 8.1, 8.2, 8.3, etc. |
| MPI_COMM_SIZE | 8.1 | 8.2 | 8.1, 8.2, 8.3, etc. |
| MPI_COMM_RANK | 8.1 | 8.2 | 8.1, 8.2, 8.3, etc. |
| MPI_SEND | 8.1 | 8.2 | 8.1, 8.2, 8.3, etc. |
| MPI_RECV | 8.1 | 8.2 | 8.1, 8.2, 8.3, etc. |
| MPI_BARRIER | 8.2 | 8.3.1 | |
| MPI_BCAST | 8.2 | 8.3.2 | 8.5 |
| MPI_GATHER | 8.2 | 8.3.2 | 8.5 |
| MPI_SCATTER | 8.2 | 8.3.2 | 8.5 |
| MPI_REDUCE | 8.2 | 8.3.3 | |
| MPI_ALLREDUCE | 8.2 | 8.3.3 | 8.5 |
| MPI_IPROBE | 8.6 | 8.4 | 8.6 |
| MPI_PROBE | 8.6 | 8.4 | |
| MPI_GET_COUNT | 8.6 | 8.4 | 8.6 |
| MPI_COMM_DUP | 8.7 | 8.5.1 | |
| MPI_COMM_SPLIT | 8.7 | 8.5.2 | 8.7, 8.9 |
| MPI_INTERCOMM_CREATE | 8.7 | 8.5.3 | 8.7, 8.9 |
| MPI_COMM_FREE | 8.7 | 8.5.1 | 8.7 |
| MPI_TYPE_CONTIGUOUS | 8.12 | 8.6.1 | 8.8 |
| MPI_TYPE_VECTOR | 8.12 | 8.6.1 | 8.8 |
| MPI_TYPE_INDEXED | 8.12 | 8.6.1 | |
| MPI_TYPE_COMMIT | 8.12 | 8.6.1 | 8.8 |
| MPI_TYPE_FREE | 8.12 | 8.6.1 | 8.8 |

**Table 8.3**   MPI quick reference: C language binding.

```
int MPI_Init(int *argc, char ***argv)
int MPI_Finalize()
int MPI_Comm_size(MPI_Comm comm, int *size)
int MPI_Comm_rank(MPI_Comm comm, int *rank)
int MPI_Send(void *buf, int count, MPI_Datatype datatype,
        int dest, int tag, MPI_Comm comm)
int MPI_Recv(void *buf, int count, MPI_Datatype datatype,
        int source, int tag, MPI_Comm comm, MPI_Status *status)

int MPI_Barrier(MPI_Comm comm)
int MPI_Bcast(void *buf, int count, MPI_Datatype datatype,
        int root, MPI_Comm comm)
int MPI_Gather(void *inbuf, int incnt, MPI_Datatype intype,
        void *outbuf, int outcnt, MPI_Datatype outtype,
        int root, MPI_Comm comm)
int MPI_Scatter(void *inbuf, int incnt, MPI_Datatype intype,
        void *outbuf, int outcnt, MPI_Datatype outtype,
        int root, MPI_Comm comm)
int MPI_Reduce(void *inbuf, void *outbuf, int count,
        MPI_Datatype type, MPI_Op op, int root, MPI_Comm comm)
int MPI_Allreduce(void *inbuf, void *outbuf, int count,
        MPI_Datatype type, MPI_Op op, MPI_Comm comm)

int MPI_Iprobe(int source, int tag, MPI_Comm comm, int *flag,
        MPI_Status *status)
int MPI_Probe(int source, int tag, MPI_Comm comm,
        MPI_Status *status)
int MPI_Get_count(MPI_Status status, MPI_datatype type, int *count)

int MPI_Comm_dup(MPI_Comm comm, MPI_comm *newcomm)
int MPI_Comm_split(MPI_Comm comm, int color, int key, MPI_comm *newcomm)
int MPI_Intercomm_create(MPI_Comm comm, int leader1,
        MPI_Comm peer, int leader2, int tag, MPI_Comm *inter)
int MPI_Comm_free(MPI_Comm *comm)

int MPI_Type_contiguous(int count, MPI_Datatype oldtype,
        MPI_Datatype *newtype)
int MPI_Type_vector(int count, int blocklen, int stride,
        MPI_Datatype oldtype, MPI_Datatype *newtype)
int MPI_Type_indexed(int count, int *blocklens, int *indices,
        MPI_Datatype oldtype, MPI_Datatype *newtype)
int MPI_Type_commit(MPI_Datatype *datatype)
int MPI_Type_free(MPI_Datatype *datatype)
```

**Table 8.4** MPI quick reference: Fortran language binding. For brevity, we adopt the convention that arguments with an I prefix have type INTEGER unless specified otherwise. The ISTATUS argument is always an integer array of size MPI_STATUS_SIZE.

```
MPI_INIT(IERR)
MPI_FINALIZE(IERR)
MPI_COMM_SIZE(ICOMM, ISIZE, IERR)
MPI_COMM_RANK(ICOMM, IRANK, IERR)
MPI_SEND(BUF, ICOUNT, ITYPE, IDEST, ITAG, ICOMM, IERR)
       <type> BUF(*)
MPI_RECV(BUF, ICOUNT, ITYPE, ISOURCE, ITAG, ICOMM, ISTATUS, IERR)
       <type> BUF(*)

MPI_BARRIER(ICOMM, IERR)
MPI_BCAST(BUF, ICOUNT, ITYPE, IROOT, ICOMM, IERR)
       <type> BUF(*)
MPI_GATHER(INBUF, INCNT, INTYPE, OUTBUF, IOUTCNT, IOUTTYPE,
       IROOT, ICOMM, IERR)
       <type> INBUF(*), OUTBUF(*)
MPI_SCATTER(INBUF, INCNT, INTYPE, OUTBUF, IOUTCNT, IOUTTYPE,
       IROOT, ICOMM, IERR)
       <type> INBUF(*), OUTBUF(*)
MPI_REDUCE(INBUF, OUTBUF, ICOUNT, ITYPE, IOP, IROOT, ICOMM, IERR)
       <type> INBUF(*), OUTBUF(*)
MPI_ALLREDUCE(INBUF, OUTBUF, ICOUNT, ITYPE, IOP, ICOMM, IERR)
       <type> INBUF(*), OUTBUF(*)

MPI_IPROBE(ISOURCE, ITAG, ICOMM, FLAG, ISTATUS, IERR)
       LOGICAL FLAG
MPI_PROBE(ISOURCE, ITAG, ICOMM, ISTATUS, IERR)
MPI_GET_COUNT(ISTATUS, ITYPE, ICOUNT, IERR)

MPI_COMM_DUP(ICOMM, INEWCOMM, IERR)
MPI_COMM_SPLIT(ICOMM, ICOLOR, IKEY, INEWCOMM, IERR)
MPI_INTERCOMM_CREATE(ICOMM, ILEADER1, IPEER, ILEADER2,
       ITAG, INTERCOMM, IERR)
MPI_COMM_FREE(ICOMM, IERR)

MPI_TYPE_CONTIGUOUS(ICOUNT, IOLDTYPE, INEWTYPE, IERR)
MPI_TYPE_VECTOR(ICOUNT, IBLOCKLEN, ISTRIDE, IOLDTYPE,
       INEWTYPE, IERR)
MPI_TYPE_INDEXED(ICOUNT, IBLOCKLENS, INDICES, IOLDTYPE,
       INEWTYPE, IERR)
       INTEGER IBLOCKLENS(*), INDICES(*)
MPI_TYPE_COMMIT(ITYPE, IERR)
MPI_TYPE_FREE(ITYPE, IERR)
```

## Exercises

1. Devise an execution sequence for five processes such that Program 8.4 yields an incorrect result because of an out-of-order message.

2. Write an MPI program in which two processes exchange a message of size $N$ words a large number of times. Use this program to measure communication bandwidth as a function of $N$ on one or more networked or parallel computers, and hence obtain estimates for $t_s$ and $t_w$.

3. Compare the performance of the program developed in Exercise 2 with an equivalent CC++ or FM program.

4. Implement a two-dimensional finite difference algorithm using MPI. Measure performance on one or more parallel computers, and use performance models to explain your results.

5. Compare the performance of the program developed in Exercise 4 with an equivalent CC++, FM, or HPF programs. Account for any differences.

6. Study the performance of the MPI global operations for different data sizes and numbers of processes. What can you infer from your results about the algorithms used to implement these operations?

7. Implement the vector reduction algorithm of Section 11.2 by using MPI point-to-point communication algorithms. Compare the performance of your implementation with that of MPI_ALLREDUCE for a range of processor counts and problem sizes. Explain any differences.

8. Use MPI to implement a two-dimensional array transpose in which an array of size $N \times N$ is decomposed over $P$ processes ($P$ dividing $N$), with each process having $N/P$ rows before the transpose and $N/P$ columns after. Compare its performance with that predicted by the performance models presented in Chapter 3.

9. Use MPI to implement a three-dimensional array transpose in which an array of size $N \times N \times N$ is decomposed over $P^2$ processes. Each processor has $(N/P) \times (N/P)$ $x/y$ columns before the transpose, the same number of $x/z$ columns after the first transpose, and the same number of $y/z$ columns after the second transpose. Use an algorithm similar to that developed in Exercise 8 as a building block.

10. Construct an MPI implementation of the parallel parameter study algorithm described in Section 1.4.4. Use a single manager process to both allocate tasks and collect results. Represent tasks by integers and results by real numbers, and have each worker perform a random amount of computation per task.

11. Study the performance of the program developed in Exercise 10 for a variety of processor counts and problem costs. At what point does the central manager become a bottleneck?

12. Modify the program developed in Exercise 10 to use a decentralized scheduling

structure. Design and carry out experiments to determine when this code is more efficient.

13. Construct an MPI implementation of the parallel/transpose and parallel/pipeline convolution algorithms of Section 4.4, using intercommunicators to structure the program. Compare the performance of the two algorithms, and account for any differences.

14. Develop a variant of Program 8.8 that implements the nine-point finite difference stencil of Figure 2.22.

15. Complete Program 8.6, adding support for an accumulate operation and incorporating dummy implementations of routines such as `identify_next_task`.

16. Use MPI to implement a hypercube communication template (see Chapter 11). Use this template to implement simple reduction, vector reduction, and broadcast algorithms.

## Chapter Notes

Message-passing functions were incorporated in specialized libraries developed for early distributed-memory computers such as the Cosmic Cube [254], iPSC [227], and nCUBE [211]. Subsequent developments emphasized portability across different computers and explored the functionality required in message-passing systems. Systems such as Express [219], p4 [44, 194], PICL [118], PARMACS [143, 144], and PVM [275] all run on a variety of homogeneous and heterogeneous systems. Each focused on a different set of issues, with the commercially supported Express and PARMACS systems providing the most extensive functionality, p4 integrating shared-memory support, PICL incorporating instrumentation, and PVM permitting dynamic process creation. A special issue of *Parallel Computing* includes articles on many of these systems [196].

An unfortunate consequence of this exploration was that although various vendor-supplied and portable systems provided similar functionality, syntactic differences and numerous minor incompatibilities made it difficult to port applications from one computer to another. This situation was resolved in 1993 with the formation of the Message Passing Interface Forum, a consortium of industrial, academic, and governmental organizations interested in standardization [203]. This group produced the MPI specification in early 1994. MPI incorporates ideas developed previously in a range of systems, notably p4, Express, PICL, and PARMACS. An important innovation is the use of communicators to support modular design. This feature builds on ideas previously explored in Zipcode [266], CHIMP [90, 91], and research systems at IBM Yorktown [24, 25].

The presentation of MPI provided in this chapter is intended to be self-contained. Nevertheless, space constraints have prevented inclusion of its more complex features. The MPI standard provides a detailed technical description [202]. Gropp, Lusk, and Skjellum [126] provide an excellent, more accessible tutorial text that includes not only a description of MPI but also material on the development of SPMD libraries and on MPI implementation.

The online version provides access here to additional information on programming in MPI, including public domain implementations, a tutorial, and example programs.

# Performance Tools

In Chapter 3, we emphasized the importance of using empirical data at each stage of the parallel program design and implementation process, in order to calibrate and validate performance models and implementations. However, we did not address the topic of how to collect or analyze these data. Clearly, a stopwatch is not enough. In this chapter, we survey the various sorts of performance data that may be of interest and describe tools that can assist in the tasks of gathering, analyzing, and interpreting these data.

A discussion of tools for gathering and analyzing performance data is difficult because few standards exist. The various public domain and commercial tools take different approaches, use different performance data file formats, and provide different display technologies. Nevertheless, we can identify basic principles that apply to most existing tools, and can illustrate these principles by describing several popular systems.

We emphasize that performance measurement is not an end in itself but is useful only in the context of a performance analysis methodology such as that described in Chapter 3. Hence, we do not repeat material from Chapter 3 here but base our presentation on the assumption that performance models have been developed and are guiding the data collection and analysis process, thereby allowing us to pose performance questions, identify performance data of interest, and isolate and correct performance problems.

After studying this chapter, you should be familiar with the basic ideas of data collection, data reduction, and data visualization. You should understand the difference between profiles, counts, and execution traces and the role each plays in performance analysis. You should also be familiar with a number of popular performance analysis tools.

## 9.1 Performance Analysis

We distinguish three basic steps in the performance analysis process: data collection, data transformation, and data visualization. *Data collection* is the process by which data about program performance are obtained from an executing program. Data are normally collected in a file, either during or after execution, although in some situations they may be presented to the user in real time. Three basic data collection techniques can be distinguished:

- *Profiles* record the amount of time spent in different parts of a program. This information, though minimal, is often invaluable for highlighting performance problems. Profiles typically are gathered automatically.

- *Counters* record either frequencies of events or cumulative times. The insertion of counters may require some programmer intervention.

- *Event traces* record each occurrence of various specified events, thus typically producing a large amount of data. Traces can be produced either automatically or with programmer intervention.

The raw data produced by profiles, counters, or traces are rarely in the form required to answer performance questions. Hence, *data transformations* are applied, often with the goal of reducing total data volume. Transformations can be used to determine mean values or other higher-order statistics or to extract profile and counter data from traces. For example, a profile recording the time spent in each subroutine on each processor might be transformed to determine the mean time spent in each subroutine on each processor, and the standard deviation from this mean. Similarly, a trace can be processed to produce a histogram giving the distribution of message sizes. Each of the various performance tools described in subsequent sections incorporates some set of built-in transformations; more specialized transformation can also be coded by the programmer.

Parallel performance data are inherently multidimensional, consisting of execution times, communication costs, and so on, for multiple program components, on different processors, and for different problem sizes. Although data reduction techniques can be used in some situations to compress performance data to scalar values, it is often necessary to be able to explore the raw multidimensional data. As is well known in computational science and engineering, this process can benefit enormously from the use of *data visualization* techniques. Both conventional and more specialized display techniques can be applied to performance data.

As we shall see, a wide variety of data collection, transformation, and visualization tools are available. When selecting a tool for a particular task, the following issues should be considered:

1. *Accuracy.* In general, performance data obtained using sampling techniques are less accurate than data obtained by using counters or timers. In the case of timers, the accuracy of the clock must be taken into account.

2. *Simplicity.* The best tools in many circumstances are those that collect data automatically, with little or no programmer intervention, and that provide convenient analysis capabilities.

3. *Flexibility.* A flexible tool can be extended easily to collect additional performance data or to provide different views of the same data. Flexibility and simplicity are often opposing requirements.

4. *Intrusiveness.* Unless a computer provides hardware support, performance data collection inevitably introduces some overhead. We need to be aware of this overhead and account for it when analyzing data.

5. *Abstraction.* A good performance tool allows data to be examined at a level of abstraction appropriate for the programming model of the parallel program. For example, when analyzing an execution trace from a message-passing program, we probably wish to see individual messages, particularly if they can be related to send and receive statements in the source program. However, this presentation is probably *not* appropriate when studying a data-parallel program, even if compilation generates a message-passing program. Instead, we would like to see communication costs related to data-parallel program statements.

## 9.2 Data Collection

Next, we examine in more detail the techniques used to collect performance data. We consider in turn profiling, counters, and event traces, focusing in each case on the principles involved. Individual tools are described in Section 9.4.

### 9.2.1 Profiles

The concept of a profile should be familiar from sequential computing. Typically, a profile shows the amount of time spent in different program components. This information is often obtained by sampling techniques, which are simple but not necessarily highly accurate. The value of the program counter is determined at fixed intervals and used to construct a histogram of execution frequencies. These frequences are then combined with compiler symbol table information to estimate the amount of time spent in different parts of a program. This profile data may be collected on a per-processor basis and may be able to identify idle time and communication time as well as execution time.

Profiles have two important advantages. They can be obtained automatically, at relatively low cost, and they can provide a high-level view of program behavior that allows the programmer to identify problematic program components without generating huge amounts of data. (In general, the amount of data associated with a profile is both small and independent of execution time.) Therefore, a profile should be the first technique considered when seeking to understand the performance of a parallel program.

A profile can be used in numerous ways. For example, a single profile on a moderate number of processors can help identify the program components that are taking the most time and that hence may require further investigation. Similarly, profiles performed for a range of processor counts and problem sizes can identify components that do not scale.

Profiles also have limitations. In particular, they do not incorporate temporal aspects of program execution. For example, consider a program in which every processor sends to each other processor in turn. If all processors send to processor 0, then to processor 1, and so on, overall performance may be poor. This behavior would not be revealed in a profile, as every processor would be shown to communicate the same amount of data.

Profilers are available on most parallel computers but vary widely in their functionality and sophistication. The most basic do little more than collect sequential profile data on each processor; the most sophisticated provide various mechanisms for reducing this data, displaying it, and relating it to source code. Because efficient profiling requires the assistance of a compiler and runtime system, most profiling tools are vendor supplied and machine specific.

### 9.2.2  Counters

As its name suggests, a counter is a storage location that can be incremented each time a specified event occurs. Counters can be used to record the number of procedure calls, total number of messages, total message volume, or the number of messages sent between each pair of processors. Counts may be generated by compiler-generated code, by code incorporated in communication libraries, or by user-inserted calls to counter routines.

Counters complement profilers by providing information that is not easily obtainable using sampling techniques. For example, they can provide the total number and volume of messages, information that can be combined with communication time data from a profile to determine the efficiency of communication operations.

A useful variant of a counter is an *interval timer*, a timer used to determine the length of time spent executing a particular piece of code. This information can be accumulated in a counter to provide an accurate determination of the total time spent executing that program component. A disadvantage of interval timers is that the logic required to obtain a timer value can be expensive.

The use of counters and interval timers in a computational chemistry code was illustrated in Section 3.6: see in particular Tables 3.4 and 3.5.

### 9.2.3  Traces

An execution trace is the most detailed and low-level approach to performance data collection. Trace-based systems typically generate log files containing time-stamped event records representing significant occurrences in a program's execution, such as calling a procedure or sending a message. Trace records may include information such as the type of event and the procedure name or destination task, and can be generated either automatically or under programmer control. Table 9.1 shows an example of trace records.

Trace-based approaches support a particularly broad study of program behavior. They can be used to examine causal relationships between communications, to localize sources of idle time, and to identify temporary hot spots. For example, an execution trace could be used to determine that all processors are sending to the same processor at the same time. An execution trace can also be postprocessed to obtain profile, count, and interval timer information; to compute higher-order statistics such as the means and variances of these values; and to obtain other data such as mean message queue length in a message-passing system.

The disadvantages of trace-based approaches stem primarily from the huge volume of data that can be generated. Particularly when a program is executing on large numbers of processors, it is easy to generate tens, hundreds, or even thousands of megabytes of data. (For example, if a 20-byte record is logged for every message on a 128-processor system, then assuming messages are sent at the rate of one every 10 milliseconds, trace data will be generated at 256 kilobytes per second, or about 1 gigabyte per hour.) This large data

**Table 9.1**   Trace records generated by the Portable Instrumented Communication Library. The various records contain information regarding the type of event, the processor number involved, a time stamp, and other information. Clearly, these records are not meant to be interpreted by humans.

| Trace Record | Description |
|---|---|
| 11  0  1553  2  0  1078 | Timer data |
| 6  0  2237  2  1  1  8 | Receive |
| 11  0  2237  2  0  1078 | Timer data |
| 11  0  2500  2  0  1341 | Timer data |
| 4  0  3186  2  3  2  12 | Send |
| 11  0  3186  2  0  1341 | Timer data |
| 11  0  3502  2  0  1656 | Timer data |
| 4  0  3672  2  4  2  12 | Send |
| 11  0  3672  2  0  1656 | Timer data |

volume has three unwelcome consequences. First, the logging of this data tends to perturb performance, thereby leading to what is called the *probe effect* in which the measuring of performance data changes their characteristics. Second, the sheer volume of data makes postprocessing difficult. Frequently, sophisticated analysis is required to extract relevant information. Third, the programmer, in order to combat the problems caused by volume, may have to spend considerable effort tuning the data collection process so that only relevant events are recorded while the phenomenon of interest is retained. Tracing then becomes a labor-intensive process. For these reasons, tracing should be used with care and only if other data collection techniques are not available or do not provide sufficient information.

Many parallel programming tools provide some automatic tracing capabilities, for example by generating a trace record for every message generated or received. These capabilities are invoked by linking with a specialized version of a communication library and/or by a runtime flag. Mechanisms for generating user-defined events may also be provided.

In principle, event traces can be interpreted in various ways by using different tools. A stumbling block here is a lack of standards for event log records. One proposed standard is the Pablo Self Describing Data Format (SDDF) designed at the University of Illinois. As illustrated in Figure 9.1, this associates an integer event type with a record description that specifies a type and name for each field.

### 9.2.4  Summary of Data Collection Tools

A broad spectrum of data collection mechanisms can be used to obtain information about parallel program performance. In general, those requiring the least programmer intervention are also the least intrusive and provide the highest-level, least-detailed view of program behavior; those providing greater detail are progressively more intrusive and demand

```
#105:
// "description" "Procedure Exit Trace Record"
"Procedure Exit Trace" {
    // "Time" "Timestamp"
    int "Timestamp"
    // "ID" "Event ID"
    int "Event Identifier"
    // "Node" "Processor Number"
    int "Processor Number"
    // "Procedure" "Procedure Index"
    int "Procedure Index"
    // "Inclusive Duration" "Inclusive Procedure Duration"
    int "Inclusive Duration"
    // "Exclusive Duration" "Exclusive Procedure Duration"
    int "Exclusive Duration"
};;
```

**Figure 9.1**    An example of the Pablo Self Describing Data Format. The data record `"Procedure Exit Trace"` has an event type of 105 and six data fields, all integers.

more programmer effort. Hence, for maximum programmer efficiency, the process of collecting and interpreting performance data should proceed in a staged manner, as follows.

1. Use profile and count information to obtain any parameter values needed to complete performance models.

2. Measure execution times for a range of processor counts and problem sizes, and compare these results with values predicted by performance models.

3. If observed and modeled performance differ significantly, use profile and count information to verify the basic assumptions underlying your model. For example, check that message counts and volumes match your predictions, and check for load imbalances and replicated computation (Section 3.6).

4. If there are still unexplained aspects of program performance, incorporate simple tracing (or enable automatic tracing capabilities), and study performance on a few processors. Increase the number of processors as your understanding improves.

Of course, the actual path followed to obtain performance data will also depend on the functionality provided in a particular parallel programming system.

## 9.3   Data Transformation and Visualization

Data transformation and visualization tools transform raw data collected during program execution to yield data and images more easily understood by the programmer. In this section, we provide a general discussion of transformation and display techniques, indicating which are useful for which purposes. In the next section, we present examples of specific tools and describe specific transformations and display formats.

### 9.3.1   Profile and Counts

A typical profile provides information about the time spent in each procedure on each processor, the number of times each procedure is called, the number of messages generated on each processor, the volume of these messages, and so forth. Data reduction techniques can be used to reduce this multidimensional data to a smaller number of dimensions, and various forms of display can be used to visualize both the original and the reduced data.

Zero-dimensional (scalar) data are of course trivial to display, consisting of a single number: total computation time, total number of messages, mean message size, and so forth. However, numbers of this sort provide relatively little insight into program behavior. For example, we may notice that total communication volume is greater than expected. This observation may stimulate us to ask several questions. Is the additional communication concentrated in a subset of the processors? Is it concentrated in a single procedure? In which phase of the computation does it occur? More data are required if we are to answer these questions.

The histogram is often a convenient display format for one-dimensional data. If the number of processors is large, the size of a histogram can be reduced by binning, in which case histogram bars represent the number of processors (or procedures or whatever) that have computation time in a specified range. Two-dimensional data can be displayed using color and a two-dimensional matrix. For example, in Plates 7 and 8 color is used, respectively, to indicate execution time per procedure per processor, and communication volume between pairs of processors.

### 9.3.2   Traces

Trace data can often be reduced to one, two, or three dimensions and then displayed using the histogram techniques described in Section 9.3.1. For example, we can plot communication volume or efficiency as a function of time, or plot histograms of trace values. Other forms of display can provide more detailed views of temporal dependencies between different processors and program components by sacrificing scalability and abstraction for detail. We describe just two displays of this sort; others are illustrated in later sections.

The *Gantt chart* is a horizontal bar chart in which each bar represents the status of each processor as a function of time (Plates 8 and 12). Bars can simply represent status (computing, communicating, or idling) and/or indicate the program component or procedure that is executing on each processor at a particular time. A Gantt chart can highlight unexpected dependencies between program components. Note that dependencies inferred from these sorts of displays are valid only if the computer and performance tool that we are using ensure that times recorded for events occurring on different processors are consistent. This will generally be the case if we use the performance tools described in this chapter, as these all incorporate appropriate clock synchronization logic.

If we augment a Gantt chart by drawing lines to connect corresponding send and receive events on different processors, we obtain a *space-time diagram*, illustrated in the lower part of Plate 8. A space-time diagram can make it easier to infer temporal dependencies, because it is often possible to identify the specific communication event for which a processor is waiting and hence idle.

### 9.3.3  Data-Parallel Languages

In data-parallel languages such as HPF and pC++, performance analysis is simplified by the fact that each processor typically executes the same program. On the other hand, the semantic gap between parallel program and executable code is particularly high. Apparently innocuous assignment statements can cause large amounts of communication if distributions do not match, while a compiler may restructure code to eliminate other communication operations that the programmer may assume will occur. Similarly, the mapping of computation to processors may not be obvious to the programmer. Therefore, low-level information about computation and communication tends to have only limited value.

Performance tools for data-parallel languages can both take advantage of the SPMD nature of data-parallel computation and overcome the semantic gap by relating performance data to the program statements concerned. For example, they can label the source code with communication costs or can color data arrays to indicate the computation costs and communication volumes associated with each element. These forms of display can involve a considerable degree of compiler assistance and/or postprocessing, since in many cases the executed code has been transformed out of recognition. This approach is illustrated in Plate 9, which shows a communication summary produced by Thinking Machine's Prism performance tool. The program illustrated is the Gaussian elimination code used as a case study in Chapter 7. The plate indicates sources of communication in a data-parallel Fortran program and the relative cost of each communication operation.

## 9.4  Tools

Next, we describe a number of both public-domain and commercial performance tools, explaining how each is used to collect and display performance data. While the tools exhibit important differences, there are also many similarities, and frequently our choice of tool will be driven more by availability than by the features provided.

### 9.4.1  Paragraph

Paragraph is a portable trace analysis and visualization package developed at Oak Ridge National Laboratory for message-passing programs. It was originally developed to analyze traces generated by a message-passing library called the Portable Instrumented Communication Library (PICL) but can in principle be used to examine any trace that complies to its format. Like many message-passing systems, PICL can be instructed to generate execution traces automatically, without programmer intervention.

Paragraph is an interactive tool. Having specified a trace file, the user instructs Paragraph to construct various displays concerning processor utilization, communication, and the like. The trace files consumed by Paragraph include, by default, time-stamped events for every communication operation performed by a parallel program. Paragraph performs on-the-fly data reduction to generate the required images. Users also can record events that log the start and end of user-defined "tasks."

Paragraph's *processor utilization* displays allow the user to distinguish time spent computing, communicating, and idling. Communication time represents time spent in system communication routines, while idle time represents time spent waiting for messages. These displays can be used to identify load imbalances and code components that suffer from excessive communication and idle time costs. Some of these displays are shown in Plate 8, which shows a Gantt chart (top part) and a space time diagram (bottom part) for a parallel climate model executing on 64 Intel DELTA processors. In the space-time diagram, the color of the lines representing communications indicates the size of the message being transferred. The climate model is a complex program with multiple phases. Initially, only processor 0 is active. Subsequently, the model alternates between computation and communication phases. Some of the communication phases involve substantial idle time, which should be the subject of further investigation.

*Communication* displays can be used both to obtain more detailed information on communication volumes and communication patterns and to study causal relationships, for example between communication patterns and idle time. Plate 10 shows some of these displays, applied here to the trace data set of Plate 8. The communication matrix on the left and the circle on the right both show instantaneous communication patterns. The colors in the communication matrix indicate communication volume, as defined by the scale above the matrix. Most matrix entries are on the diagonal, which indicates mostly nearest-neighbor communication. Another display in the top right presents cumulative data on processor utilization.

A disadvantage of Paragraph is that the relationship between performance data and program source is not always clear. This problem can be overcome in part by explicitly logging events that record the start and end of "tasks" corresponding to different phases of a program's execution. Paragraph provides task Gantt and task histogram displays to examine this information.

Of the portable tools described here, Paragraph is probably the simplest to install and use. Because it operates on automatically generated traces, it can be used with little programmer intervention. Paragraph displays are particularly intuitive, although the inability to scroll within display windows can be frustrating.

### 9.4.2  Upshot

Upshot is a trace analysis and visualization package developed at Argonne National Laboratory for message-passing programs. It can be used to analyze traces from a variety of message-passing systems: in particular, trace events can be generated automatically by using an instrumented version of MPI. Alternatively, the programmer can insert event logging calls manually.

Upshot's display tools are designed for the visualization and analysis of state data derived from logged events. A state is defined by a starting and ending event. (For example, an instrumented collective communication routine can generate two separate events on each processor to indicate when the processor entered and exited the routine.) The Upshot Gantt chart display shows the state of each processor as a function of time. States can be nested, thereby allowing multiple levels of detail to be captured in a single display. States can be defined either in an input file or interactively during visualization. A histogramming facility allows the use of histograms to summarize information about state duration (Plate 11).

Plate 12 illustrates the use of nested states within Upshot. This is a trace generated from a computational chemistry code that alternates between Fock matrix construction (Section 2.8) and matrix diagonalization, with the former taking most of the time. Each Fock matrix construction operation (red) involves multiple integral computations (green). A substantial load imbalance is apparent—some processors complete their final set of integrals much later than do others. The display makes it apparent why this load imbalance occurs. Integrals are being allocated in a demand-driven fashion by a central scheduler to ensure equitable distribution of work; however, smaller integrals are being allocated before larger ones. Reversing the allocation order improves performance.

Upshot provides fewer displays than does Paragraph, but has some nice features. The ability to scroll and zoom its displays is particularly useful.

### 9.4.3  Pablo

The Pablo system developed at the University of Illinois is the most ambitious (and complex) of the performance tools described here. It provides a variety of mechanisms for collecting, transforming, and visualizing data and is designed to be extensible, so that the programmer can incorporate new data formats, data collection mechanisms, data reduction modules, and displays. Predefined and user-defined data reduction modules and displays can be combined in a mix-and-match fashion by using a graphical editor. Pablo is as much a performance tool toolkit as it is a performance tool proper and has been used to develop performance tools for both message-passing and data-parallel programs.

A source code instrumentation interface facilitates the insertion of user-specified instrumentation into programs. In addition, Pablo calls can be incorporated into communication libraries or compilers to generate trace files automatically. When logging an event, Pablo can be requested to invoke a user-defined event handler that may perform on-the-fly data reduction. For example, a user-defined handler can compute communication statistics rather than logging every message or can combine procedure entry and exit events to determine procedure execution times. This very general mechanism provides great flexibility. A disadvantage is that the overhead associated with logging an event is greater than in other, less general systems.

A novel feature of Pablo is its support for automatic *throttling* of event data generation. The user can specify a threshold data rate for each type of event. If events are generated at a greater rate, event recording is disabled or replaced by periodic logging of event counts, thereby enabling a variety of events to be logged without the danger that one will unexpectedly swamp the system.

Pablo provides a variety of data reduction and display modules that can be plugged together to form specialized data analysis and visualization networks. For example, most displays provided by Paragraph can be constructed using Pablo modules. This feature is illustrated in Plate 13, which shows a variety of Paragraph-like displays and the Pablo network used to generate them. As noted earlier, Pablo uses its own SDDF.

An interesting feature of the Pablo environment is its support for novel "display" technologies, such as sound and immersive virtual environments. Sound appears to be particularly effective for alerting the user to unusual events, while immersive virtual environments can be used to display higher-dimensional data, as illustrated in Plate 14. In this plate, each cube represents a different performance metric, and the spheres within the cubes represent processors moving within a three-dimensional metric space. While both approaches are still experimental at present, they are suggestive of future directions.

### 9.4.4 Gauge

The Gauge performance tool developed at the California Institute of Technology is distinguished by its focus on profiles and counters rather than execution traces. The Gauge display tool allows the user to examine a multidimensional performance data set in a variety of ways, collapsing along different dimensions and computing various higher-order statistics. For example, a three-dimensional view of an execution profile uses color to indicate execution time per processor and per routine; corresponding two-dimensional displays provide histograms for time per routine summed over all processors or for time per processor for all routines. Idle time is also measured on a per-processor basis and associated with program components by determining which task is enabled by arrival of a message. Some of these displays are illustrated in Plate 7.

### 9.4.5 ParAide

The ParAide system developed by Intel's Supercomputer Systems Division is specialized for the Paragon parallel computer. It incorporates a variety of different tools. Modified versions of the standard Unix `prof` and `gprof` tools provide profiling on a per-node basis. An enhanced version of Paragraph provides various data reduction and display mechanisms. The System Performance Visualization system uses displays specialized for the Paragon's two-dimensional mesh architecture to show data collected by hardware performance monitors. These provide detailed low-level information regarding the utilization of the processor, communication network, and memory bus. This fine level of detail is made possible by hardware and operating system support in the Paragon computer.

### 9.4.6 IBM's Parallel Environment

The IBM AIX Parallel Environment is specialized for IBM computers, in particular the SP multicomputer. It incorporates a variety of different tools. A variant of the standard Unix `prof` and `gprof` commands can be used to generate and process multiple profile files, one per task involved in a computation. The Visualization Tool (VT) can be used to display a variety of different trace data. Three types of trace data are supported, as follows:

1. A communication record represents a low-level communication event, such as a send, receive, or call to a global (collective) communication routine.

2. A system statistics record samples low-level statistics such as CPU utilization, disk traffic, and virtual memory statistics. The sampling rate can be selected by the programmer.

3. An application marker record is generated manually by a programmer and may be used to delineate distinct stages in a program's execution.

Communication trace records and system statistics are generated automatically, although the programmer can turn them on and off and can control their frequency.

VT displays are similar to those provided by Paragraph in many respects, but they give the programmer greater flexibility in how data are displayed and can deal with a wider range of data. Plate 15 shows one display, in this case a space-time diagram.

### 9.4.7 AIMS

The Automated Instrumentation and Monitoring System (AIMS) developed at the NASA Ames Research Center provides both instrumentation tools and a variety of trace visualization mechanisms for message-passing programs. Users can either specify trace events manually or request AIMS to log communication events and procedure calls automatically. The resulting traces can be visualized by using the AIMS View Kernel (VK), Pablo, or Paragraph. A strength of AIMS is its tight integration with a source code browser that allows the user both to mark code blocks for tracing and to relate communication events with source code. For example, the user can click on a line representing a communication in a space-time diagram to identify the corresponding communication operation in the source code. AIMS also provides statistical analysis functions that can be used to determine average resource utilization and message latencies.

### 9.4.8  Custom Tools

We conclude this section by noting that while general-purpose tools have the advantage of being easy to use, custom performance tools can also be valuable, particularly in understanding the performance of a complex parallel program. Extensible tools such as Pablo can be useful in this regard. So can text manipulation systems such as awk and PERL, statistical packages such as Mathematica and Matlab, and general-purpose graphics packages such as AVS.

As an example of this approach, Plate 5 shows an image generated by a tool developed specifically to help understand load imbalances in a parallel climate model. This tool collects timing data by using interval timers and counters inserted manually into the parallel climate model. The data are postprocessed to compensate for timer overhead and are then displayed by using a general-purpose graphics package. Sequences of such images provide insights into how computational load varies over time, and have motivated the design of load-balancing algorithms.

## 9.5  Summary

As discussed in Sections 3.5 and 3.6, parallel programming is an experimental discipline. An analytic performance model is an idealization of program behavior that must be validated by comparison with empirical results. This validation process can reveal deficiencies in both the model and the parallel program. Performance analysis is most effective when guided by an understanding rooted in analytic models, and models are most accurate when calibrated with empirical data.

Because performance data tend to be complex and multidimensional, performance tools are a vital part of any parallel programming toolkit. In this chapter, we have introduced basic techniques and surveyed popular tools for collecting, transforming, and analyzing performance data. At the data collection level, we distinguished between profiles, counters, and event traces. Each approach has a role to play in performance analysis: profile and counter data are easier to obtain and to analyze, while traces can show fine detail. At the data transformation and visualization levels, we have emphasized the importance of data reduction techniques that are able to reduce raw performance data to more meaningful and manageable quantities, and data visualization tools that can facilitate the navigation of large multidimensional data sets.

## Exercises

1. Use one or more performance tools to obtain and analyze performance data from programs developed by using tools described in earlier chapters. Relate observed performance to analytic models and explain any disparities.

2. Devise and carry out experiments to quantify the overhead of data collection in the performance tool(s) used in Exercise 1.

3. Explain why reversing the order in which integrals are allocated can be expected to improve performance in the computational chemistry code discussed in Section 9.4.2 and illustrated in Plate 12.

## Chapter Notes

Cheng [58] surveys parallel programming tools, including tools for performance data collection and analysis. Reed [240] provides both a useful review of techniques for parallel performance analysis and an introduction to Pablo. Reed et al. [241] provide a more detailed description of Pablo, including its sound and virtual reality displays. Herrarte and Lusk [148] describe Upshot. Heath and Etheridge [139] describe Paragraph, and Heath [138] presents case studies showing how it is used to tune parallel program performance. Kesselman [104, 172] provides a detailed description of Gauge; while originally developed for the parallel languages Strand and PCN, a general-purpose implementation is under development. Ries et al. [244] describe Intel's ParAide system. Yan et al. [301] describe AIMS.

Graham et al. [124] describe the sampling approach to profiling sequential programs. Lamport [185] discusses clock synchronization algorithms. Tufte [285] provides a wonderful introduction to the visual presentation of multidimensional data.

Other systems not described here include Cray Research's MPP Apprentice, which provides integrated performance analysis, optimization, and prediction capabilities; Thinking Machines's Prism system, which provides specialized analysis capabilities for data-parallel programs; Parasoft's Express message-passing system, which provides execution profiling, communication profiling, and event trace analysis mechanisms; Applied Parallel Research's HPF profiler; and the IPS-2 system from University of Wisconsin Madison [207]. Other systems are described in a conference proceedings edited by Haring and Kotsis [132].

The online version provides access here to additional information on performance tools, including public domain implementations, documentation, tutorials, and examples of performance tool output.

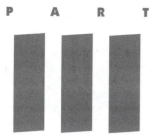

# Resources

In Parts I and II of this book, we have described the fundamental concepts and tools required to design and build parallel programs. In the process, we have also introduced a number of important algorithms, communication structures, and problem-solving techniques that can serve as building blocks in our programs. In Part III, we add to this set of building blocks. The goal is not to be in any way comprehensive, but instead simply to indicate the range of parallel algorithms that have been developed and to provide pointers to other information sources.

Hence, Chapter 10 introduces the important topic of parallel random numbers. Chapter 11 surveys parallel algorithms based on an important communication structure, the hypercube. Chapter 12 provides additional bibliographical material. And, Chapter 13 describes how to access *Designing and Building Parallel Programs (Online)*.

# 10

# Random Numbers

Random numbers are used in computing to simulate apparently random processes in the external world or to sample large parameter spaces. Well-known sequential techniques exist for generating, in a deterministic fashion, number sequences largely indistinguishable from true random sequences. The deterministic nature of these techniques is important because it provides for reproducibility in computations.

On parallel computers, random number generation becomes more complicated because many concurrently executing tasks may require access to random numbers. Generally, efficiency concerns will require that we generate these numbers in a distributed fashion; nevertheless, we wish to preserve randomness and reproducibility. In this chapter, we introduce these issues by showing how one commonly used sequential technique can be adapted to meet these potentially conflicting requirements.

## 10.1 Sequential Random Numbers

Although the casinos at Monte Carlo are, one hopes, based on random phenomena, true random numbers are rarely used in computing. Not only would such numbers be difficult to generate reliably, but also the lack of reproducibility would make the validation of programs that use them extremely difficult. Instead, computers invariably use *pseudo-random* numbers: finite sequences generated by a deterministic process but indistinguishable, by some set of statistical tests, from a random sequence. (In the following, we use the term random to mean pseudo-random.) The statistical methods used to validate random sequences are an important topic of research, but beyond the scope of this book. See the chapter notes for further reading on this subject.

Methods for generating a *sequence* of random numbers have been extensively studied and are well understood. A function called a *generator* is defined that, when applied to a number, yields the next number in the sequence. For example, the *linear congruential* generators considered in this chapter have the general form

$$X_{k+1} = (aX_k + c) \bmod m, \tag{10.1}$$

where $X_k$ is the $k$th element of the sequence and $X_0$, $a$, $c$, and $m$ define the generator. Random numbers in the range [0,1] are then obtained by dividing $X_k$ by $m$.

As numbers are taken from a finite set (for example, integers between 1 and $2^{31}$), any generator will eventually repeat itself. The length of the repeated cycle is called the *period* of the generator. A good generator is one with a long period and no discernible correlation between elements of the sequence.

The parameters $X_0$, $a$, $c$, and $m$ in the linear congruential generator are chosen to make the sequence look as random as possible. Common choices for these values are

$$X_0 = \text{any positive integer}$$
$$a = 16807$$
$$m = 2^{31} - 1 \text{ (or some other large prime)} \tag{10.2}$$
$$c = 0.$$

This generator has period $m - 1$, that is, $2^{31} - 2$ for $m = 2^{31} - 1$. Other common choices are

$$X_0 = \text{any positive odd integer}$$
$$a = 8z + 5 \text{ ($z$ any integer)}$$
$$m = 2^e \text{ ($e$ a positive integer)} \tag{10.3}$$
$$c = 0,$$

in which case the period of the generator is $m/4 = 2^{e-2}$. A typical choice for $m$ in this case is the word size of the machine on which we are executing. See the references in the chapter notes for sources of appropriate values for $a$, $c$, and $m$.

A fundamental property of Equation 10.1 is that if $c = 0$, then

$$X_{k+n} = (a^n X_k) \bmod m.$$

That is, the $(k + n)$th element of the sequence is related to the $k$th in the same way as is the $(k + 1)$th, albeit with a different value for $a$. We shall exploit this property when developing parallel generators.

## 10.2  Parallel Random Numbers

We can distinguish three general approaches to the generation of random numbers on parallel computers: centralized, replicated, and distributed. In the *centralized* approach, a sequential generator is encapsulated in a task from which other tasks request random numbers. This avoids the problem of generating multiple independent random sequences, but is unlikely to provide good performance. Furthermore, it makes reproducibility hard to achieve: the response to a request depends on when it arrives at the generator, and hence the result computed by a program can vary from one run to the next.

In the *replicated* approach, multiple instances of the same generator are created (for example, one per task). Each generator uses either the same seed or a unique seed, derived, for example, from a task identifier. Clearly, sequences generated in this fashion are not guaranteed to be independent and, indeed, can suffer from serious correlation problems. However, the approach has the advantages of efficiency and ease of implementation and should be used when appropriate.

In the *distributed* approach, responsibility for generating a single sequence is partitioned among many generators, which can then be parceled out to different tasks. The generators are all derived from a single generator; hence, the analysis of the statistical properties of the distributed generator is simplified. As only distributed generators are at all difficult to implement on parallel computers, we focus on this topic in the rest of this chapter.

## 10.3  Distributed Random Generators

The techniques described here for constructing distributed random number generators are based on an adaptation of the linear congruential algorithm called the *random tree* method. We first show how this method can be applied to a single generator to construct a tree of generators in a deterministic and reproducible fashion. This facility is particularly valuable in computations that create and destroy tasks dynamically during program execution.

### 10.3.1  The Random Tree Method

The random tree method employs two linear congruential generators, $L$ and $R$, that differ only in the values used for $a$.

$$L_{k+1} = a_L L_k \bmod m$$
$$R_{k+1} = a_R R_k \bmod m$$

Application of the left generator $L$ to a seed $L_0$ generates one random sequence; application of the right generator $R$ to the same seed generates a different sequence. By applying the right generator to elements of the left generator's sequence (or vice versa), a tree of random numbers can be generated. By convention, the right generator $R$ is used to generate random values for use in computation, while the left generator $L$ is applied to values computed by $R$ to obtain the starting points $R^0$, $R^1$, etc., for new right sequences (Figure 10.1).

The strength of the random tree method is that it can be used to generate new random sequences in a reproducible and noncentralized fashion. This is valuable, for example, in applications in which new tasks and hence new random generators must be created dynamically. Before creating a new task, a parent task uses the left generator to construct a new right generator, which it passes to its new offspring. The new task uses this right generator to generate the random numbers required for its computation. If it in turn must generate a new task, it can apply the left generator to its latest random value to obtain a new random seed.

A deficiency of the random tree method as described here is that there is no guarantee that different right sequences will not overlap. The period of $R$ is usually chosen to be

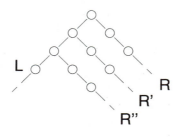

**Figure 10.1**    The random tree method. Two generators are used to construct a tree of random numbers. The right generator is applied to elements of the sequence $L$ generated by the left generator to generate new sequences $R$, $R'$, $R''$, etc.

near to $m$. because this maximizes the quality of the random numbers obtained by using the generator. Hence, the starting points $R^i$ returned by the left generator are likely to be different points in the same sequence, in which case we can think of $L$ as selecting random starting points in the sequence constructed by $R$. If two starting points happen to be close to each other, the two right sequences that are generated will be highly correlated.

## 10.3.2    The Leapfrog Method

In some circumstances, we may know that a program requires a fixed number of generators. (For example, we may require one generator for each task in a domain decomposition algorithm.) In this case, a variant of the random tree method called the *leapfrog* method can be used to generate sequences that can be guaranteed not to overlap for a certain period.

Let $n$ be the number of sequences required. Then we define $a_L$ and $a_R$ as $a$ and $a^n$, respectively, so that we have

$$L_{k+1} = a L_k \bmod m$$
$$R_{k+1} = a^n R_k \bmod m.$$

Then, we create $n$ different right generators $R^0..R^{n-1}$ by taking the first $n$ elements of $L$ as their starting values. The name "leapfrog method" refers to the fact that the $i$th sequence $R^i$ consists of $L_i$ and every $n$th subsequent element of the sequence generated by $L$ (Figure 10.2). As this method partitions the elements of $L$, each subsequence has a period of at least $P/n$, where $P$ is the period of $L$. (If $n$ divides $P$, then the period of a subsequence is exactly $P/n$.) In addition, the $n$ subsequences are disjoint for their first $P/n$ elements.

The generator for the $r$th subsequence, $R^r$, is defined by $a^n$ and $R_0^r = L_r$. We can compute these values as follows. We first compute $a^r$ and $a^n$; these computations can be performed in $\mathcal{O}(\log n)$ time by taking advantage of the identity

$$a^{2k} \bmod m = ((a^k \bmod m)^2) \bmod m.$$

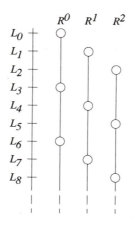

**Figure 10.2** The leapfrog method with $n = 3$. Each of the three right generators selects a disjoint subsequence of the sequence constructed by the left generator's sequence.

We then compute members of the sequence $R^r$ as follows, to obtain $n$ generators, each defined by a triple $(R_0^r, a^n, m)$, for $0 \le r < n$.

$$R_0^r = (a^r L_0) \bmod m$$
$$R_{i+1}^r = (a^n R_i^r) \bmod m$$

The leapfrog method can be applied recursively: the subsequence corresponding to a generator $(R_0^r, a^n, m)$ can be further subdivided by a second application of the leapfrog method. Doing this can be useful when random numbers are required at several levels in a task hierarchy. However, the periods of the resulting sequences become shorter, and their statistical properties are less certain.

### 10.3.3 Modified Leapfrog

In other situations, we may know the maximum number, $n$, of random values needed in a subsequence but not the number of subsequences required. In this case, a variant of the leapfrog method can be used in which the roles of $L$ and $R$ are reversed so that the elements of subsequence $i$ are the contiguous elements $L_{in}..L_{(i+1)n-1}$ (Figure 10.3), as follows:

$$L_{k+1} = a^n L_k \bmod m$$
$$R_{k+1} = a R_k \bmod m.$$

It is not a good idea to choose $n$ as a power of two, as this can lead to serious long-term correlations.

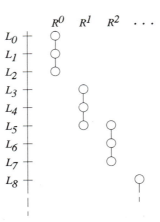

**Figure 10.3**  Modified leapfrog with $n = 3$. Each subsequence contains three contiguous numbers from the main sequence.

## 10.4  Summary

In this chapter, we have shown how one commonly used sequential random number generator, the linear congruential method, can be adapted for parallel execution. This example shows how parallel computation can introduce new issues even in apparently simple problems. In the case of random numbers, these issues include reproducibility, scalability, the preservation of randomness, and the greater number of random values consumed when executing on many processors.

### Exercises

1. An application running on $10^3$ processors consumes $10^5$ random numbers per second per processor. For how long can the application execute before it exhausts all available numbers, assuming that the leapfrog method is applied to the linear congruential generator of Equation 10.3 on a 32-bit machine? A 64-bit machine?

2. A Monte Carlo simulation must perform $10^7$ independent trials. How many random numbers can be employed in each trial without duplication, assuming that the modified leapfrog method is applied to the linear congruential generator of Equation 10.1 on a 32-bit machine? A 64 bit machine?

3. Monte Carlo integration techniques are sometimes used to compute integrals of high dimension. They approximate the $r$-dimensional integral

$$I = \int_0^1 f(\mathbf{x})d^r x$$

of a function $f$ as

$$I \approx \frac{1}{N} \sum_{i=0}^{N-1} f(\mathbf{x}_i),$$

where each $\mathbf{x}_i$ is an $r$-vector of random values. Design and implement a parallel algorithm for this method, and use it to compute the one-dimensional integral

$$\pi = 4 \int_0^1 \frac{dx}{1 + x^2}.$$

Measure and account for the performance of the parallel program as a function of $N$ and P.

## Chapter Notes

Knuth [175] provides a wealth of material on random number generation, including a table of appropriate values for $a$ and $m$ and tests that can be used to determine the quality of a particular generator. See in particular the table on page 102. Anderson [13] provides a more up-to-date survey of random number generation algorithms. He includes a short but useful section on parallel computers and provides numerous references. The random tree method was first described by Frederickson et al. [114].

Random numbers are used extensively in the Monte Carlo method, in which a large, statistically valid sequence of "samples" is used to compute properties of mathematical functions or physical processes. Koonin [177] provides a good introduction to the computational issues associated with Monte Carlo methods on sequential computers, and Kalos [163] provides a more detailed discussion.

The online version provides access here to additional information on random number generation on parallel computers.

# 11 Hypercube Algorithms

I n Chapter 2, we pointed out that the communication requirements of a reduction operation can be structured as a series of pairwise exchanges, one with each neighbor in a *hypercube* (butterfly) structure. This structure allows a computation requiring all-to-all communication among $P$ tasks to be performed in just $\log P$ steps, rather than $P$ steps as might be expected from a superficial analysis.

It turns out that the hypercube structure can be used to implement many other parallel algorithms requiring all-to-all communication; that is, algorithms in which each task must communicate with every other task. In this chapter, we review three such algorithms: vector reduction, matrix transposition, and sorting. The purpose of this discussion is both to describe some useful algorithms and to introduce the concept of a parallel algorithm *template*. A template is a basic program form that a programmer can augment with application-specific information to implement a particular parallel algorithm. The hypercube communication structure described in this chapter is one of the most useful templates in parallel computing.

After studying this chapter, you should have a good understanding of the hypercube communication structure and how it is used to implement all-to-all communication in parallel algorithms. You should also be familiar with the concept of a template and the role templates play in parallel algorithm design and programming.

## 11.1 The Hypercube Template

Recall from Section 3.7.2 that a hypercube connects each of $P$ tasks ($P$ a power of 2) to $\log P$ other tasks (Figure 3.16). The template considered in this chapter uses this communication structure in an SPMD fashion, with each task executing Algorithm 11.1. A local `state` variable is first set to be the supplied input data. Computation then proceeds in $\log P$ steps. In each step, each task first exchanges its local `state` with one of its neighbors in the hypercube and then combines the `message` received from the neighbor with `state` to generate a new `state`. The output of the computation is the `state` generated in the final step.

In Algorithm 11.1, the XOR function denotes an exclusive or operation and is used to identify neighbors. (Exclusive or is defined as follows: 0 XOR 0=0, 0 XOR 1=1, 1 XOR 0=1, 1 XOR 1=0.) As noted in Section 3.7.2, the hypercube has the property that the

```
procedure hypercube(myid, input, logp, output)
begin
    state = input                    ! Local state = input
    for i = 0 to logp-1              ! Repeat logp times
        dest = myid XOR 2^i          ! Determine comm partner
        send state to dest           ! Exchange data
        receive message from dest    !
        state = OP(state,message)    ! Perform operation
    endfor                           !
    output = state                   ! Output = final state
end
```

**Algorithm 11.1**   The hypercube communication template. This program is executed by each task in a hypercube communication structure, with `logp` denoting the size of the hypercube ($P = 2^{\log P}$) and `myid` the task's identifier (in the range $0..2^{\log P} - 1$). XOR denotes an exclusive or operation, and OP is the user-supplied operator, used to combine local data with the data arriving from the $i$th neighbor in the hypercube.

binary labels of two nodes that are neighbors in the $d$th dimension differ only in the $d$th place; hence, the expression `myid XOR 2^i` yields the $i$th neighbor of node `myid`.

A particular parallel algorithm is defined by the operator OP used to combine `state` and `message` at each step in the template. In the following, we shall show how this template can be used as a basis for parallel vector reduction, matrix transposition, and sorting algorithms.

## 11.2   Vector Reduction

Recall that in Section 2.4.1 we developed a parallel algorithm to sum $P$ values distributed among $P$ tasks. This algorithm is essentially Algorithm 11.1 with an addition operator used as OP. That is, the algorithm maintains a partial sum as the local `state` in each node, and in each step accumulates a partial sum received from another node into this partial sum. After $\log P$ steps, the sum of the $P$ input values is available in every node.

This same algorithm can be used to perform a reduction using *any* commutative associative operator, such as multiplication or maximum; the commutative associative operator is used as OP in Algorithm 11.1. The algorithm can also be used to implement a barrier operation, which synchronizes the tasks that execute it. In this case, the values communicated are simply null tokens, and the operation performed on each pair of incoming messages is a synchronization operation that waits for the two tokens to be available.

In the related *vector reduction* problem, each of $P$ tasks supplies a vector of $N$ values and $N$ separate reductions are performed to produce a vector of $N$ results. As illustrated in Figure 11.1, these $N$ reductions can be achieved in $\log P$ steps by using Algorithm 11.1. The operator OP is defined as follows: take two vectors of $N$ values as input and apply the commutative associative operator $N$ times to produce a vector of $N$ results. The per-processor cost of this *simple exchange* algorithm is

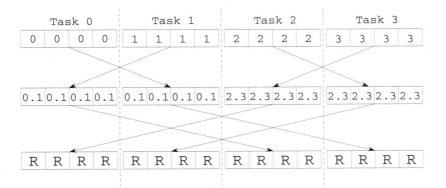

**Figure 11.1** Using the hypercube algorithm to reduce four vectors of length $N = 4$ distributed among four tasks. The computation is performed in $2 = \log 4$ steps, with each task in each step exchanging $N$ data values with a neighbor and performing $N$ combine operations. The labels in the boxes denote the origin of the values that they contain; hence, 0.1 and 2.3 represent intermediate results obtained when contributions from task 0 and 1, or 2 and 3, are combined. R represents the final reduced values.

$$T_{\text{simple exchange reduction}} = \log P(t_s + N(t_w + t_{op})), \tag{11.1}$$

where $t_{op}$ is the cost of applying the reduction operator. This algorithm is efficient for small $N$, when message startup costs dominate. However, for larger $N$ it is inefficient, since it performs many redundant operations.

An alternative *recursive halving* algorithm utilizes the same hypercube communication structure but applies a divide-and-conquer technique to reduce message volume (Figure 11.2). In effect, Algorithm 11.1 is applied twice. In the reduction phase, each processor communicates (and combines) $N/2$ data in the first stage, half as much ($N/4$) in the second, and so on, so that each processor communicates a total of $N(P-1)/P$ data in $\log P$ steps. The global sum is then complete, and the vector of $N$ reduced values is evenly distributed over the $P$ processors. This process is reversed (without the reductions) to broadcast the result. Communication cost is

$$T_{\text{recursive halving reduction}} = t_s 2 \log P + (t_w 2 + t_{op})N \frac{P-1}{P}. \tag{11.2}$$

The recursive halving algorithm sends twice as many messages as the simpler algorithm does, but less data. It also performs less computation. Hence it will be more efficient for certain values of $N$ and $P$ and on certain machines. A robust hybrid algorithm can be designed that starts with the recursive halving approach and switches to an exchange algorithm after a certain number of stages so as to avoid some of the broadcast communication.

We can use similar techniques to define an efficient *vector broadcast* algorithm. Here, the problem is to replicate $N$ values located in a single task (the "root") in each of $P - 1$ other tasks. A simple algorithm uses the binary tree communication structure illustrated in Figure 2.8. The root task first sends the data to two other tasks; each of these tasks forwards

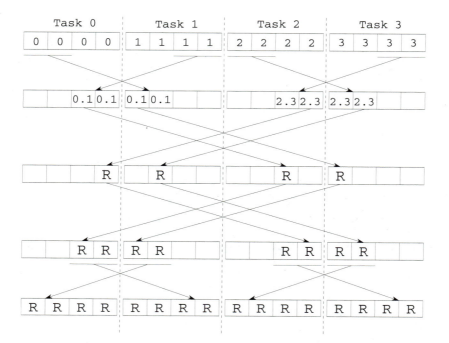

**Figure 11.2**   Using the recursive halving algorithm to reduce four vectors of length $N = 4$ distributed over four tasks. In the first $2 = \log N$ stages, values are combined to compute the $N$ reduced values, represented as R; these values are distributed over the four tasks. In the third and fourth stages, the process is reversed in order to broadcast the values.

the data to two other tasks, and so on, until the data are completely distributed. Total cost is approximately

$$T_{\text{vector broadcast I}} = \log P (t_s + t_w N).$$

This algorithm is efficient for small $N$ and $P$. For larger problems and processor configurations, it has the disadvantage that most processors are idle most of the time and the total time is dominated by the $t_w N \log P$ term. In these situations, it can be more efficient to break the message into pieces and then to route these pieces separately by using the hypercube communication structure. Communication costs are then approximately as follows (the chapter notes provide pointers to descriptions of this algorithm):

$$T_{\text{vector broadcast II}} = 2(t_s \log P + t_w N).$$

## 11.3   Matrix Transposition

The transposition of a two-dimensional $N \times N$ matrix $A$ yields a matrix $A'$ of the same size, in which $A'_{ji} = A_{ij}$. If $A$ and/or $A'$ are distributed between multiple tasks, then execution of the transpose operation may involve communication. We consider here a one-dimensional, columnwise decomposition of the input and output matrices among $P$ tasks. Notice that this transposition requires all-to-all communication.

One commonly used transposition algorithm proceeds in $P - 1$ steps, with each task exchanging $N^2/P^2$ data with another task in each step, for a per-processor communication cost of

$$T_{\text{simple transpose}} = t_s(P - 1) + t_w(P - 1)\frac{N^2}{P^2}. \tag{11.3}$$

This algorithm was used in the convolution example in Section 4.4. An alternative algorithm, described here, uses the hypercube communication template to reduce message startup costs at the expense of increased data transfer costs. The basic idea is similar to that used in the recursive halving reduction algorithm, but because the operator used to combine messages in the transpose is "append" rather than "reduce," message sizes do not become smaller as the transpose proceeds.

The algorithm proceeds as follows. Tasks are partitioned into two sets. Corresponding pairs of tasks in the two sets exchange the one half of their data that is destined for tasks in the other set. Tasks $0..(P/2) - 1$ communicate the lower half of their data, while tasks $(P/2)..P - 1$ communicate the upper half. This partitioning and exchange process is repeated until each set contains a single task. See Figure 11.3 for more details.

As each of the $\log P$ messages has size $N^2/(2P)$, the communication cost is:

$$T_{\text{hypercube transpose}} = t_s \log P + t_w \log P \frac{N^2}{2P}. \tag{11.4}$$

A comparison of Equations 11.3 and 11.4 shows that the hypercube algorithm sends about $P/\log P$ fewer messages but $(\log P)/2$ times more data. In most situations, the data transfer term dominates, and the $\mathcal{O}(P)$ algorithm is to be preferred. However, we can expect the $\mathcal{O}(\log P)$ algorithm to be competitive on small problems and when message startups are expensive and transfer costs are low.

## 11.4 Mergesort

Sorting is a common and important problem in computing. Given a sequence of $N$ data elements, we are required to generate an ordered sequence that contains the same elements. Here, we present a parallel version of the well-known mergesort algorithm. The algorithm assumes that the sequence to be sorted is distributed and so generates a distributed sorted sequence. For simplicity, we assume that $N$ is an integer multiple of $P$, that the $N$ data are distributed evenly among $P$ tasks, and that $P = 2^d$ is an integer power of two. Relaxing these assumptions does not change the essential character of the algorithm but would complicate the presentation.

The sequential mergesort algorithm is as follows; its execution is illustrated in Figure 11.4.

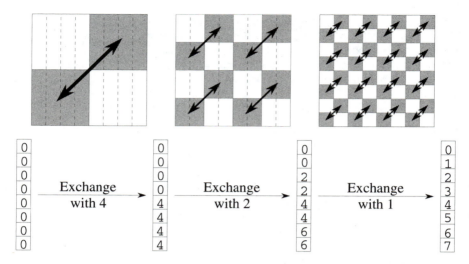

**Figure 11.3**   The three steps of the $\mathcal{O}(\log P)$ matrix transpose algorithm when $P = N = 8$. Initially, each task has a single column of the matrix. After the transpose, each task has a single row. In each step, each task exchanges one half of its data; this data is shaded in the upper part of the figure. The lower part of the figure shows the origin of the eight values held by task 0 at each step of the algorithm. Task 0 sends elements 4–7 in its first message and receives four elements from task 4; these are stored in locations 4–7. In the second step, task 0 exchanges both elements 2–3 (its own) and 6–7 (from task 3) with task 2. In the third step, it exchanges elements 1 (its own), 3 (from task 2), 5 (from task 4), and 7 (from task 6) with task 1.

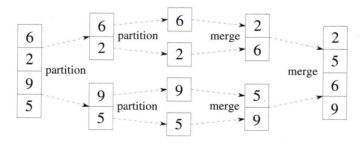

**Figure 11.4**   Mergesort, used here to sort the sequence [6,2,9,5]. The two partition phases each split the input sequence; the two merge phases each combine two sorted subsequences generated in a previous phase.

1. If the input sequence has fewer than two elements, return.
2. Partition the input sequence into two halves.
3. Sort the two subsequences using the same algorithm.
4. Merge the two sorted subsequences to form the output sequence.

The merge operation employed in step (4) combines two sorted subsequences to produce a single sorted sequence. It repeatedly compares the heads of the two subsequences and outputs the lesser value until no elements remain. Mergesort requires $\mathcal{O}(N \log N)$ time to sort $N$ elements, which is the best that can be achieved (modulo constant factors) unless data are known to have special properties such as a known distribution or degeneracy.

We first describe two algorithms required in the implementation of parallel mergesort: compare-exchange and parallel merge.

**Compare-Exchange**   A compare-exchange operation merges two sorted sequences of length $M$, contained in tasks $A$ and $B$. Upon completion of the operation, both tasks have $M$ data, and all elements in task $A$ are less than or equal to all elements in task $B$. As illustrated in Figure 11.5, each task sends its data to the other task. Task $A$ identifies the $M$ lowest elements and discards the remainder; this process requires at least $M/2$ and at most $M$ comparisons. Similarly, task $B$ identifies the $M$ highest elements.

Notice that a task may not need all $M$ of its neighbor's data in order to identify the $M$ lowest (or highest) values. On average, only $M/2$ values are required. Hence, it may be more efficient in some situations to require the consumer to request data explicitly. This approach results in more messages that contain a total of less than $M$ data, and can at most halve the amount of data transferred.

**Parallel Merge**   A parallel merge algorithm performs a merge operation on two sorted sequences of length $M2^d$, each distributed over $2^d$ tasks, to produce a single sorted sequence of length $M2^{d+1}$ distributed over $2^{d+1}$ tasks. As illustrated in Figure 11.6, this is achieved by using the hypercube communication template. Each of the $2^{d+1}$ tasks engages in $d + 1$ compare-exchange steps, one with each neighbor. In effect, each node executes Algorithm 11.1, applying the following operator at each step.

```
if ( myid AND 2^i > 0 ) then
   state = compare_exchange_high(state,message)
else
   state = compare_exchange_low(state,message)
endif
```

In this code fragment, AND is a bitwise logical and operator, used to determine whether the task is "high" or "low" in a particular exchange; myid and i are as in Algorithm 11.1.

**Mergesort**   We next describe the parallel mergesort algorithm proper. Each task in the computation executes the following logic.

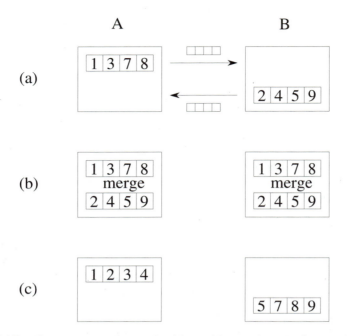

**Figure 11.5**   The compare-exchange algorithm, with $M = 4$. (a) Tasks $A$ and $B$ exchange their sorted subsequences. (b) They perform a merge operation to identify the lowest and highest $M$ elements, respectively. (c) Other elements are discarded, leaving a single sorted sequence partitioned over the two tasks.

```
procedure parallel_mergesort(myid, d, data, newdata)
begin
  data = sequential_mergesort(data)
  for dim = 1 to d
    data = parallel_merge(myid, dim, data)
  endfor
  newdata = data
end
```

First, each task sorts its local sequence using sequential mergesort. Second, and again using the hypercube communication structure, each of the $P = 2^d$ tasks executes the parallel merge algorithm $d$ times, for subcubes of dimension $1..d$. The $i$th parallel merge takes two sequences, each distributed over $2^{i-1}$ tasks, and generates a sorted sequence distributed over $2^i$ tasks. After $d$ such merges, we have a single sorted list distributed over $2^d$ tasks.

**Performance**   Parallel mergesort uses the hypercube communication template at multiple levels. We review these uses and develop a performance model. We assume $N$ data distributed over $P = 2^d$ tasks (that is, $d = \log P$), with $N$ an integer multiple of $P$. Hence, the total number of compare-exchanges is

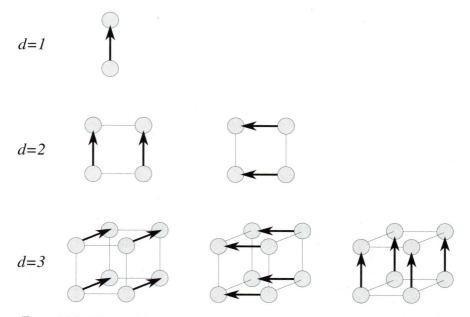

$d=1$

$d=2$

$d=3$

**Figure 11.6** The parallel merge operation, performed in hypercubes of dimension one, two, and three. In a hypercube of dimension $d$, each task performs $d$ compare-exchange operations. Arrows point from the "high" to the "low" task in each exchange.

$$\sum_{i=1}^{d} i = \frac{d(d+1)}{2}.$$

Because each compare-exchange requires one message containing $N/P$ data, the per-processor communication cost is

$$T_{comm} = t_s \frac{d(d+1)}{2} + t_w \frac{N}{P} \frac{d(d+1)}{2}.$$

The computation costs comprise the initial intraprocessor sort and the comparisons performed during the interprocessor communication phase. The former involves a total of $N \log(N/P)$ comparisons, while the latter requires at most $(Nd(d+1)/2)$ comparisons, thereby giving computation costs summed over $P$ processors of

$$T_{comp} \le t_c N \left( \log \frac{N}{P} + \frac{d(d+1)}{2} \right) = t_c N \left( \log N + \frac{d(d-1)}{2} \right).$$

Because the algorithm is perfectly balanced, we can assume that idle time is negligible. Thus, we obtain the following model for parallel execution time:

$$T = \frac{T_{comp}}{P} + T_{comm}$$

$$= t_c \frac{N}{P} \left( \log N + \frac{d(d-1)}{2} \right) + t_s \frac{d(d+1)}{2} + t_w \frac{N}{P} \frac{d(d+1)}{2}$$

$$\approx \left( t_c \frac{N}{2P} + t_s + t_w \frac{N}{P} \right) \frac{(\log P)^2}{2} \quad \text{if } (\log P)^2 \gg \log N.$$

## 11.5  Summary

The hypercube communication template (Algorithm 11.1) allows information to be propagated among $P$ tasks in just $\log P$ steps. Each algorithm considered in this case study has exploited this property to perform some form of all-to-all communication. For example, in matrix transposition each task requires values from every other task; in sorting, the position of each value in the final sequence depends on all other values. Many other parallel algorithms can be naturally formulated in terms of the same template, once the need for all-to-all communication is recognized.

The hypercube template described in this chapter is one of the most useful communication structures in parallel computing. Another useful structure that we have encountered is nearest-neighbor exchange on a two-dimensional torus: this template can be used to implement finite difference computations, matrix multiplication (Section 4.6), and graph algorithms. The manager/worker load balancing structure (Section 2.5.2) is a third example of a template.

Learning to recognize and apply templates such as the hypercube, torus, and manager/worker can greatly simplify the task of designing and implementing parallel programs. When designing a parallel algorithm, we can first seek to formulate communication requirements in terms of known communication structures; if we are successful, the design problem then reduces to that of specifying the application-specific part of the algorithm. A similar strategy can be applied when implementing designs that have been formulated in terms of templates.

### Exercises

1. Execute the hypercube summation algorithm by hand for $N = 8$, and satisfy yourself that you obtain the correct answer.

2. Use Equations 11.1 and 11.2 to identify problem size, processor count, and machine parameter regimes in which each of the two vector reduction algorithms of Section 11.2 will be more efficient.

3. Implement the hybrid vector reduction algorithm described in Section 11.2. Use empirical studies to determine the vector length at which the switch from recursive halving to exchange algorithm should occur. Compare the performance of this algorithm with pure recursive halving and exchange algorithms.

4. A variant of the parallel mergesort algorithm performs just $\log P$ compare-exchange operations and then switches to a parallel bubblesort [174]. In the bubblesort phase, tasks are connected in a logical ring and each task performs compare-exchange operations with its neighbors until a global reduction shows that no exchanges occurred. Design an implementation of this algorithm, using hypercube and ring structures as building blocks.

5. Implement the modified parallel mergesort of Exercise 4. Compare its performance with regular parallel mergesort for different input sequences and for a variety of $P$ and $N$.

6. Extend Equations 11.3 and 11.4 to account for bandwidth limitations in a one-dimensional mesh.

7. Modify the performance models developed for the convolution algorithm in Section 4.4 to reflect the use of the hypercube-based transpose. Can the resulting algorithms ever provide superior performance?

8. Use the performance models given in Section 11.2 for the simple and recursive halving vector reduction algorithms to determine situations in which each algorithm would give superior performance.

9. Design and implement a variant of the vector sum algorithm that does not require the number of tasks to be an integer power of 2.

10. Develop a CC++, Fortran M, or MPI implementation of a "hypercube template." Use this template to implement simple reduction, vector reduction, and broadcast algorithms. Discuss the techniques that you used to facilitate reuse of the template.

11. Implement a "torus template" and use this together with the template developed in Exercise 10 to implement the finite difference computation of Section 4.2.2.

12. Develop a performance model for a 2-D matrix multiplication algorithm that uses the vector broadcast algorithm of Section 11.2 in place of the tree-based broadcast assumed in Section 4.6.1. Discuss the advantages and disadvantages of this algorithm.

13. Implement both the modified matrix multiplication algorithm of Exercise 12 and the original algorithm of Section 4.6.1, and compare their performance.

## Chapter Notes

Leighton [187] discusses basic properties of hypercubes and describes many parallel algorithms that use a hypercube communication structure. The recursive halving vector reduction algorithm considered in Section 11.2 is described by Fox et al. [111] and the hybrid algorithm by van de Geijn [289]. Vector broadcast algorithms are described by Bertsekas and Tsitsiklis [35] and Johnsson and Ho [160]. The parallel mergesort algorithm, often called bitonic mergesort, is due to Batcher [30]; Akl [8] provides a good description. Fox et al. [111] describe a multicomputer implementation of this algorithm and of the variant discussed in Exercise 4. Other algorithms that are conveniently formulated in terms of a hypercube communication structure include the fast Fourier transform [20, 21, 110, 192,

277], parallel prefix [238], and various computer vision [238] and linear algebra computations [159]. See also the book by Kumar et al. [179] and papers by Bertsekas et al. [36], McBryan and van der Velde [197], and Saad and Schultz [248, 249].

The book by Kumar et al. [179] describes parallel versions of several sorting algorithms, including quicksort [153], one of the most commonly used sorting algorithms on sequential computers. Their parallel quicksort algorithm partitions processors according to the number of elements lesser than or greater than the pivot at each step. Fox et al. [111] describe an alternative parallel quicksort algorithm that uses regular processor partitions. They address load imbalance by performing some preliminary processing to identify pivots that approximately bisect the input sequence. Knuth [174] and Aho et al. [7] are good references for sequential sorting algorithms. In addition to standard algorithms such as mergesort and quicksort, Knuth describes various specialized algorithms designed to exploit certain properties of the data to be sorted. Kumar et al. [179] explain how many of these can be adapted for parallel computers. For example, if data are highly redundant (that is, they have many identical items), we can count items on each node, then do a global sum to obtain total counts. If the input data distribution is known, a parallel bucketsort can be used. Each processor knows the location of each bucket and sends its data to the appropriate location.

The online version provides access here to additional information on hypercube algorithms.

# 12 Further Reading

The literature on parallel programming and parallel computing is large and expanding rapidly. We have provided numerous references to this literature in the chapter notes. Here, we provide additional pointers.

Numerous books on parallel computing provide other perspectives or more detailed treatments of topics covered only briefly here. Of particular interest are the texts by Quinn [235] and Kumar et al. [179], both of which complement *Designing and Building Parallel Programs* by describing a wide range of parallel algorithms and communication structures; both also include excellent bibliographies. The Association for Computing Machinery [1] has published a bibliography of relevant material. Fox et al. [111, 113] describe a range of parallel algorithms, focusing on developments in the Caltech Concurrent Computation Project. Books by Akl [8], Gibbons and Rytter [119], JáJá [157], Leighton [187], Miller and Stout [209], and Smith [267] provide more theoretical treatments.

Texts describing parallel computer architecture include those by Almasi and Gottlieb [11], DeCegama [75], Hwang [156], Reed and Fujimoto [242], Suaya and Birtwistle [272], Stone [269], and Tabak [278]. See also the survey articles by Duncan [87, 88] and a chapter in Hennessy and Patterson's [134] book on computer architecture.

Books providing general introductions to parallel programming or describing particular approaches include those by Andrews [14], Andrews and Olson [15], Ben Ari [32], Carriero and Gelernter [48], Chandy and Taylor [55], Foster and Taylor [107], Gehani and Roome [117], Hatcher and Quinn [136], Koelbel et al. [176], and Wallach [291]. See also the survey articles by Karp [166] and Bal, Steiner, and Tanenbaum [23]. Feo, Cann, and Oldehoeft [95] describe SISAL, a functional programming language for parallel computing.

Kumar et al. [179] describe many parallel numeric algorithms and provide detailed references to the literature. Books by Bertsekas and Tsitsiklis [35], Carey [46], Dongarra et al. [82], Fox et al. [111], Golub and Ortega [122], Lakshmivarahan and Dhall [184], and van der Velde [290] address various aspects of parallel algorithms in numerical analysis and scientific computing. Survey articles in this area include those by Gallivan, Plemmons, and Sameh [116] (dense matrix algorithms); Demmel, Heath, and van der Vorst [77] (dense matrix algorithms); and Heath et al. [140] (sparse matrix algorithms).

Useful resources in other areas include the books by Akl and Lyons [9] (computational geometry), Banerjee [26] (VLSI design), Dew, Earnshaw, and Heywood [78] and Ranka and Sahni [238] (computer vision), Gupta [128] (production systems), and Kowalik [178] (artificial intelligence). An article by Manber [195] discusses concurrent data structures, while Singhal [260] surveys deadlock detection algorithms.

Keeping up to date with the most recent developments in parallel computing is made difficult by the large number of journals and conferences. *IEEE Parallel and Distributed Technology* magazine covers many topics of interest to parallel programmers. *IEEE Computational Science and Engineering* magazine focuses on the use of high-performance computers in science and engineering. *IEEE Transactions on Parallel and Distributed Systems* emphasizes parallel hardware and algorithms. *Concurrency: Practice and Experience* contains a mixture of application and algorithm papers, typically with an empirical flavor. Other relevant journals include *International Journal of Parallel Programming*, *Journal of Parallel Algorithms and Applications*, *Journal of Parallel and Distributed Computing*, and *Parallel Computing*. In addition, the following journals often include relevant articles: *Communications of the ACM*, *Computer*, *Future Generation Computer Systems*, *IEEE Transactions on Computers*, *IEEE Transactions on Software Engineering*, *International Journal of Supercomputer Applications*, *Journal of Distributed Systems*, *New Generation Computing*, *Scientific Programming*, *SIAM Journal of Scientific and Statistical Computing*, and *SIAM Review*.

The proceedings of various conferences in the field are also of interest. See, in particular, the proceedings of the annual Supercomputing conference and the SIAM Conference on Parallel Processing for Scientific Computing; both include papers on applications, tools, and algorithms for parallel computers, with an emphasis on scientific computing. Other relevant meetings include the Conference on Parallel Computational Fluid Dynamics, CONPAR, Frontiers of Massively Parallel Processing, the International Conference on Parallel Programming, the International Parallel Processing Symposium, PARCO, and the ACM Symposium on Principles and Practice of Parallel Programming.

The online version provides access here to online bibliographies and other sources of information on parallel computing.

# 13 About the Online Version

The World Wide Web is a distributed hypertext system that utilizes the Internet to provide access to multimedia resources (text, sound, images, and video). Users navigate between the pages of a Web document using browsers such as Mosaic, which provides a convenient point-and-click interface. *Designing and Building Parallel Programs (Online)* allows readers to access resources described in this book (such as programming tools) and to learn more about topics discussed in the book.

*Designing and Building Parallel Programs (Online)* is accessible to anyone with a Web browser on their computer and with access to the Internet. It can be found at the following Uniform Resource Locator (URL):

```
http://www.mcs.anl.gov/dbpp/
```

It is likely to be mirrored at other sites as well; consult this URL or send electronic mail to dbpp@aw.com to receive an automatic reply containing up-to-date information. If you do not have a Web browser, see Section 13.1.

*Designing and Building Parallel Programs (Online)* comprises four distinct but tightly linked components:

1. The content of *Designing and Building Parallel Programs*. This comprises the text of the book and hypertext links to the Web Tours described in Section 13.2.

2. Information on how to access most of the *Parallel Tools* described in the book and additional tutorial material on these tools.

3. A set of *Web Tours* that provides links to additional resources on the Internet that are related to this book's contents, such as parallel computer architecture, parallel algorithms, applications of parallel computers, and other tools for building parallel programs.

4. A variety of *Educational Materials*, including the example programs included in the text, Postscript versions of the figures, and teaching materials contributed by others.

While the text itself is reasonably static, the other resources continue to evolve to incorporate information about new machines, descriptions of interesting new applications of parallel computers, exercise sets developed in universities, etc. We welcome reader contributions.

## 13.1    Obtaining a Web Browser

The most popular Web browser is the Mosaic system developed at the National Center for Supercomputer Applications. This is free software and available for most machines by anonymous ftp at address `ftp.ncsa.uiuc.edu`, directory `Mosaic`. Commercial Web browsers are also available. Send electronic mail to `dbpp@aw.com` for the latest information on availability.

If you cannot obtain access to a Web browser, you can still access many of the parallel tools and educational resources described in this book via anonymous ftp from `ftp.mcs.anl.gov` in directory `pub/dbpp`. (Use the ftp program to connect to the system `ftp.mcs.anl.gov`, log in as `anonymous`, and give your email address as password. Then type `cd pub/dbpp` and `get README` to obtain a README file with more information.)

## 13.2    Web Tours

The online resources are organized as a series of *Web Tours*, including the following:

1. *Parallel Computers and Computation*: parallel applications, parallel computer architecture, and parallel programming models
2. *Designing Parallel Algorithms*: parallel program design and software engineering
3. *A Quantitative Basis for Design*: performance analysis and the architecture and performance of parallel and distributed computer systems
4. *Putting Components Together*: modular programming, parallel program design, and parallel libraries
5. *Compositional C++*: programming in CC++, including a public-domain compiler, a tutorial, and example programs
6. *Fortran M*: programming in FM, including a public-domain compiler, a tutorial, and example programs
7. *High Performance Fortran*: programming in HPF, including the HPF specification, information about compilers, and example programs
8. *Message Passing Interface*: programming in MPI, including public-domain implementations, a tutorial, and example programs
9. *Performance Tools*: performance tools, including public-domain implementations, documentation, tutorials, and examples of performance tool output
10. *Random Numbers*: random number generation on parallel computers
11. *Hypercube Algorithms*: hypercube algorithms and templates
12. *Further Reading*: online bibliographies and other sources of information on parallel computing

# References

[1] ACM. *Resources in Parallel and Concurrent Systems*. ACM Press, 1991.

[2] G. Adams, D. Agrawal, and H. Siegel. A survey and comparison of fault-tolerant multistage interconnection networks. *IEEE Trans. Computs.*, C-20(6):14–29, 1987.

[3] J. Adams, W. Brainerd, J. Martin, B. Smith, and J. Wagener. *The Fortran 90 Handbook*. McGraw-Hill, 1992.

[4] A. Aggarwal and J. S. Vitter. The input/output complexity of sorting and related problems. *Commun. ACM*, 31(9):1116–1127, 1988.

[5] G. Agha. *Actors*. MIT Press, 1986.

[6] G. Agrawal, A. Sussman, and J. Saltz. Compiler and runtime support for structured and block structured applications. In *Proc. Supercomputing '93*, pages 578–587, 1993.

[7] A. Aho, J. Hopcroft, and J. Ullman. *The Design and Analysis of Computer Algorithms*. Addison-Wesley, 1974.

[8] S. G. Akl. *The Design and Analysis of Parallel Algorithms*. Prentice-Hall, 1989.

[9] S. G. Akl and K. A. Lyons. *Parallel Computational Geometry*. Prentice-Hall, 1993.

[10] E. Albert, J. Lukas, and G. Steele. Data parallel computers and the FORALL statement. *J. Parallel and Distributed Computing*, 13(2):185–192, 1991.

[11] G. S. Almasi and A. Gottlieb. *Highly Parallel Computing*. Benjamin/Cummings, second edition, 1994.

[12] G. Amdahl. Validity of the single-processor approach to achieving large-scale computing capabilities. In *Proc. 1967 AFIPS Conf.*, volume 30, page 483. AFIPS Press, 1967.

[13] S. Anderson. Random number generators. *SIAM Review*, 32(2):221–251, 1990.

[14] G. R. Andrews. *Concurrent Programming: Principles and Practice*. Benjamin/Cummings, 1991.

[15] G. R. Andrews and R. A. Olsson. *The SR Programming Language: Concurrency in Practice*. Benjamin/Cummings, 1993.

[16] ANSI X3J3/S8.115. Fortran 90, 1990.

[17] S. Arvindam, V. Kumar, and V. Rao. Floorplan optimization on multiprocessors. In *Proc. 1989 Intl Conf. on Computer Design*, pages 109–113. IEEE Computer Society, 1989.

[18] W. C. Athas and C. L. Seitz. Multicomputers: Message-passing concurrent computers. *Computer*, 21(8):9–24, 1988.

[19] J. Auerbach, A. Goldberg, G. Goldszmidt, A. Gopal, M. Kennedy, J. Rao, and J. Russell. Concert/C: A language for distributed programming. In *Winter 1994 USENIX Conference*. Usenix Association, 1994.

[20] A. Averbuch, E. Gabber, B. Gordissky, and Y. Medan. A parallel FFT on an MIMD machine. *Parallel Computing*, 15:61–74, 1990.

[21] D. Bailey. FFTs in external or hierarchical memory. *J. Supercomputing*, 4:23–35, 1990.

[22] J. Bailey. First we reshape our computers, then they reshape us: The broader intellectual impact of parallelism. *Daedalus*, 121(1):67–86, 1992.

[23] H. E. Bal, J. G. Steiner, and A. S. Tanenbaum. Programming languages for distributed computing systems. *ACM Computing Surveys*, 21(3):261–322, 1989.

[24] V. Bala and S. Kipnis. Process groups: A mechanism for the coordination of and communication among processes in the Venus collective communication library. Technical report, IBM T. J. Watson Research Center, 1992.

[25] V. Bala, S. Kipnis, L. Rudolph, and M. Snir. Designing efficient, scalable, and portable collective communication libraries. Technical report, IBM T. J. Watson Research Center, 1992. Preprint.

[26] P. Banerjee. *Parallel Algorithms For VLSI Computer-Aided Design*. Prentice-Hall, 1994.

[27] U. Banerjee. *Dependence Analysis for Supercomputing*. Kluwer Academic Publishers, 1988.

[28] S. Barnard and H. Simon. Fast multilevel implementation of recursive spectral bisection for partitioning unstructured problems. *Concurrency: Practice and Experience*, 6(2):101–117, 1994.

[29] J. Barton and L. Nackman. *Scientific and Engineering C++*. Addison-Wesley, 1994.

[30] K. Batcher. Sorting networks and their applications. In *Proc. 1968 AFIPS Conf.*, volume 32, page 307. AFIPS Press, 1968.

[31] BBN Advanced Computers Inc. *TC-2000 Technical Product Summary*, 1989.

[32] M. Ben-Ari. *Principles of Concurrent and Distributed Programming*. Prentice-Hall, 1990.

[33] M. Berger and S. Bokhari. A partitioning strategy for nonuniform problems on multiprocessors. *IEEE Trans. Computs.*, C-36(5):570–580, 1987.

[34] F. Berman and L. Snyder. On mapping parallel algorithms into parallel architectures. *J. Parallel and Distributed Computing*, 4(5):439–458, 1987.

[35] D. Bertsekas and J. Tsitsiklis. *Parallel and Distributed Computation: Numerical Methods*. Prentice-Hall, 1989.

[36] D. P. Bertsekas, C. Ozveren, G. D. Stamoulis, P. Tseng, and J. N. Tsitsiklis. Optimal communication algorithms for hypercubes. *J. Parallel and Distributed Computing*, 11:263–275, 1991.

[37] G. Blelloch. *Vector Models for Data-Parallel Computing*. MIT Press, 1990.

[38] F. Bodin, P. Beckman, D. B. Gannon, S. Narayana, and S. Yang. Distributed pC++: Basic ideas for an object parallel language. In *Proc. Supercomputing '91*, pages 273–282, 1991.

[39] S. Bokhari. On the mapping problem. *IEEE Trans. Computs.*, C-30(3):207–214, 1981.

[40] G. Booch. *Object-Oriented Design with Applications*. Benjamin/Cummings, 1991.

[41] R. Bordawekar, J. del Rosario, and A. Choudhary. Design and evaluation of primitives for parallel I/O. In *Proc. Supercomputing '93*, pages 452–461. ACM, 1993.

[42] Z. Bozkus, A. Choudhary, G. Fox, T. Haupt, and S. Ranka. Fortran 90D/HPF compiler for distributed memory MIMD computers: Design, implementation, and performance results. In *Proc. Supercomputing '93*. IEEE Computer Society, 1993.

[43] W. Brainerd, C. Goldberg, and J. Adams. *Programmer's Guide to Fortran 90*. McGraw-Hill, 1990.

[44] R. Butler and E. Lusk. Monitors, message, and clusters: The p4 parallel programming system. *Parallel Computing*, 20:547–564, 1994.

[45] D. Callahan and K. Kennedy. Compiling programs for distributed-memory multiprocessors. *J. Supercomputing*, 2:151–169, 1988.

[46] G. F. Carey, editor. *Parallel Supercomputing: Methods, Algorithms and Applications*. Wiley, 1989.

[47] N. Carriero and D. Gelernter. Linda in context. *Commun. ACM*, 32(4):444–458, 1989.

[48] N. Carriero and D. Gelernter. *How to Write Parallel Programs*. MIT Press, 1990.

[49] N. Carriero and D. Gelernter. Tuple analysis and partial evaluation strategies in the Linda pre-compiler. In *Languages and Compilers for Parallel Computing*. MIT Press, 1990.

[50] R. Chandra, A. Gupta, and J. Hennessy. COOL: An object-based language for parallel programming. *Computer*, 27(8):14–26, 1994.

[51] K. M. Chandy and I. Foster. A deterministic notation for cooperating processes. *IEEE Trans. Parallel and Distributed Syst.*, 1995. to appear.

[52] K. M. Chandy, I. Foster, K. Kennedy, C. Koelbel, and C.-W. Tseng. Integrated support for task and data parallelism. *Intl J. Supercomputer Applications*, 8(2):80–98, 1994.

[53] K. M. Chandy and C. Kesselman. CC++: A declarative concurrent object-oriented programming notation. In *Research Directions in Concurrent Object-Oriented Programming*. MIT Press, 1993.

[54] K. M. Chandy and J. Misra. *Parallel Program Design*. Addison-Wesley, 1988.

[55] K. M. Chandy and S. Taylor. *An Introduction to Parallel Programming*. Jones and Bartlett, 1992.

[56] B. Chapman, P. Mehrotra, and H. Zima. Programming in Vienna Fortran. *Scientific Programming*, 1(1):31–50, 1992.

[57] B. Chapman, P. Mehrotra, and H. Zima. Extending HPF for advanced data-parallel applications. *IEEE Parallel and Distributed Technology*, 2(3):15–27, 1994.

[58] D. Y. Cheng. A survey of parallel programming languages and tools. Technical Report RND-93-005, NASA Ames Research Center, Moffett Field, Calif., 1993.

[59] J. Choi, J. Dongarra, and D. Walker. PUMMA: Parallel Universal Matrix Multiplication Algorithms on distributed memory concurrent computers. *Concurrency: Practice and Experience*, 6, 1994.

[60] A. Choudhary. Parallel I/O systems, guest editor's introduction. *J. Parallel and Distributed Computing*, 17(1–2):1–3, 1993.

[61] S. Chowdhury. The greedy load-sharing algorithm. *J. Parallel and Distributed Computing*, 9(1):93–99, 1990.

[62] M. Colvin, C. Janssen, R. Whiteside, and C. Tong. Parallel Direct-SCF for large-scale calculations. Technical report, Center for Computational Engineering, Sandia National Laboratories, Livermore, Cal., 1991.

[63] D. Comer. *Internetworking with TCP/IP*. Prentice-Hall, 1988.

[64] S. Cook. The classification of problems which have fast parallel algorithms. In *Proc. 1983 Intl Foundation of Computation Theory Conf.*, volume 158, pages 78–93. Springer-Verlag LNCS, 1983.

[65] T. Cormen, C. Leiserson, and R. Rivest. *Introduction to Algorithms*. MIT Press, 1990.

[66] B. Cox and A. Novobilski. *Object-Oriented Programming: An Evolutionary Approach*. Addison-Wesley, 1991.

[67] D. Culler et al. LogP: Towards a realistic model of parallel computation. In *Proc. 4th Symp. Principles and Practice of Parallel Programming*, pages 1–12. ACM, 1993.

[68] G. Cybenko. Dynamic load balancing for distributed memory multiprocessors. *J. Parallel and Distributed Computing*, 7:279–301, 1989.

[69] W. Dally. *A VLSI Architecture for Concurrent Data Structures*. Kluwer Academic Publishers, 1987.

[70] W. Dally and C. L. Seitz. The torus routing chip. *J. Distributed Systems*, 1(3):187–196, 1986.

[71] W. Dally and C. L. Seitz. Deadlock-free message routing in multiprocessor interconnection networks. *IEEE Trans. Computs.*, C-36(5):547–553, 1987.

[72] W. J. Dally et al. The message-driven processor. *IEEE Micro.*, 12(2):23–39, 1992.

[73] C. R. Das, N. Deo, and S. Prasad. Parallel graph algorithms for hypercube computers. *Parallel Computing*, 13:143–158, 1990.

[74] C. R. Das, N. Deo, and S. Prasad. Two minimum spanning forest algorithms on fixed-size hypercube computers. *Parallel Computing*, 15:179–187, 1990.

[75] A. L. DeCegama. *The Technology of Parallel Processing: Parallel Processing Architectures and VLSI Hardware: Volume 1*. Prentice-Hall, 1989.

[76] J. del Rosario and A. Choudhary. High-Performance I/O for Parallel Computers: Problems and Prospects. *Computer*, 27(3):59–68, 1994.

[77] J. W. Demmel, M. T. Heath, and H. A. van der Vorst. Parallel numerical linear algebra. *Acta Numerica*, 10:111–197, 1993.

[78] P. M. Dew, R. A. Earnshaw, and T. R. Heywood. *Parallel Processing for Computer Vision and Display*. Addison-Wesley, 1989.

[79] D. DeWitt and J. Gray. Parallel database systems: The future of high-performance database systems. *Commun. ACM*, 35(6):85–98, 1992.

[80] E. W. Dijkstra. A note on two problems in connexion with graphs. *Numerische Mathematik*, 1:269–271, 1959.

[81] E. W. Dijkstra, W. H. Seijen, and A. J. M. V. Gasteren. Derivation of a termination detection algorithm for a distributed computation. *Information Processing Letters*, 16(5):217–219, 1983.

[82] J. Dongarra, I. Duff, D. Sorensen, and H. van der Vorst. *Solving Linear Systems on Vector and Shared Memory Computers*. SIAM, 1991.

[83] J. Dongarra, R. Pozo, and D. Walker. ScaLAPACK++: An object-oriented linear algebra library for scalable systems. In *Proc. Scalable Parallel Libraries Conf.*, pages 216–223. IEEE Computer Society, 1993.

[84] J. Dongarra, R. van de Geign, and D. Walker. Scalability issues affecting the design of a dense linear algebra library. *J. Parallel and Distributed Computing*, 22(3):523–537, 1994.

[85] J. Dongarra and D. Walker. Software libraries for linear algebra computations on high performance computers. *SIAM Review*, 1995. to appear.

[86] J. Drake, I. Foster, J. Hack, J. Michalakes, B. Semeraro, B. Toonen, D. Williamson, and P. Worley. PCCM2: A GCM adapted for scalable parallel computers. In *Proc. 5th Symp. on Global Change Studies*, pages 91–98. American Meteorological Society, 1994.

[87] R. Duncan. A survey of parallel computer architectures. *Computer*, 23(2):5–16, 1990.

[88] R. Duncan. Parallel computer architectures. In *Advances in Computers*, volume 34, pages 113–152. Academic Press, 1992.

[89] D. L. Eager, J. Zahorjan, and E. D. Lazowska. Speedup versus efficiency in parallel systems. *IEEE Trans. Computs.*, C-38(3):408–423, 1989.

[90] Edinburgh Parallel Computing Centre, University of Edinburgh. *CHIMP Concepts*, 1991.

[91] Edinburgh Parallel Computing Centre, University of Edinburgh. *CHIMP Version 1.0 Interface*, 1992.

[92] M. A. Ellis and B. Stroustrup. *The Annotated C++ Reference Manual*. Addison-Wesley, 1990.

[93] V. Faber, O. Lubeck, and A. White. Superlinear speedup of an efficient parallel algorithm is not possible. *Parallel Computing*, 3:259–260, 1986.

[94] T. Y. Feng. A survey of interconnection networks. *IEEE Computer*, 14(12):12–27, 1981.

[95] J. Feo, D. Cann, and R. Oldehoeft. A report on the SISAL language project. *J. Parallel and Distributed Computing*, 12(10):349–366, 1990.

[96] M. Feyereisen and R. Kendall. An efficient implementation of the Direct-SCF algorithm on parallel computer architectures. *Theoretica Chimica Acta*, 84:289–299, 1993.

[97] H. P. Flatt and K. Kennedy. Performance of parallel processors. *Parallel Computing*, 12(1):1–20, 1989.

[98] R. Floyd. Algorithm 97: Shortest path. *Commun. ACM*, 5(6):345, 1962.

[99] S. Fortune and J. Wyllie. Parallelism in random access machines. In *Proc. ACM Symp. on Theory of Computing*, pages 114–118. ACM, 1978.

[100] I. Foster. Task parallelism and high performance languages. *IEEE Parallel and Distributed Technology*, 2(3):39–48, 1994.

[101] I. Foster, B. Avalani, A. Choudhary, and M. Xu. A compilation system that integrates High Performance Fortran and Fortran M. In *Proc. 1994 Scalable High-Performance Computing Conf.*, pages 293–300. IEEE Computer Society, 1994.

[102] I. Foster and K. M. Chandy. Fortran M: A language for modular parallel programming. *J. Parallel and Distributed Computing*, 25(1), 1995.

[103] I. Foster, M. Henderson, and R. Stevens. Data systems for parallel climate models. Technical Report ANL/MCS-TM-169, Mathematics and Computer Science Division, Argonne National Laboratory, Argonne, Ill., 1991.

[104] I. Foster, C. Kesselman, and S. Taylor. Concurrency: Simple concepts and powerful tools. *Computer J.*, 33(6):501–507, 1990.

[105] I. Foster, R. Olson, and S. Tuecke. Productive parallel programming: The PCN approach. *Scientific Programming*, 1(1):51–66, 1992.

[106] I. Foster, R. Olson, and S. Tuecke. Programming in Fortran M. Technical Report ANL-93/26, Mathematics and Computer Science Division, Argonne National Laboratory, Argonne, Ill., 1993.

[107] I. Foster and S. Taylor. *Strand: New Concepts in Parallel Programming*. Prentice-Hall, 1989.

[108] I. Foster, J. Tilson, A. Wagner, R. Shepard, R. Harrison, R. Kendall, and R. Littlefield. High performance computational chemistry: (I) Scalable Fock matrix construction algorithms. Preprint, Mathematics and Computer Science Division, Argonne National Laboratory, Argonne, Ill., 1994.

[109] I. Foster and B. Toonen. Load-balancing algorithms for climate models. In *Proc. 1994 Scalable High-Performance Computing Conf.*, pages 674–681. IEEE Computer Society, 1994.

[110] I. Foster and P. Worley. Parallel algorithms for the spectral transform method. Preprint MCS-P426-0494, Mathematics and Computer Science Division, Argonne National Laboratory, Argonne, Ill., 1994.

[111] G. Fox et al. *Solving Problems on Concurrent Processors*. Prentice-Hall, 1988.

[112] G. Fox, S. Hiranandani, K. Kennedy, C. Koelbel, U. Kremer, C. Tseng, and M. Wu. Fortran D language specification. Technical Report TR90-141, Dept. of Computer Science, Rice University, 1990.

[113] G. Fox, R. Williams, and P. Messina. *Parallel Computing Works!* Morgan Kaufman, 1994.

[114] P. Frederickson, R. Hiromoto, T. Jordan, B. Smith, and T. Warnock. Pseudo-random trees in Monte Carlo. *Parallel Computing*, 1:175–180, 1984.

[115] H. J. Fromm, U. Hercksen, U. Herzog, K. H. John, R. Klar, and W. Kleinoder. Experiences with performance measurement and modeling of a processor array. *IEEE Trans. Computs.*, C-32(1):15–31, 1983.

[116] K. Gallivan, R. Plemmons, and A. Sameh. Parallel algorithms for dense linear algebra computations. *SIAM Review*, 32(1):54–135, 1990.

[117] N. Gehani and W. Roome. *The Concurrent C Programming Language*. Silicon Press, 1988.

[118] G. A. Geist, M. T. Heath, B. W. Peyton, and P. H. Worley. A user's guide to PICL: A portable instrumented communication library. Technical Report TM-11616, Oak Ridge National Laboratory, 1990.

[119] A. Gibbons and W. Rytter. *Efficient Parallel Algorithms*. Cambridge University Press, 1990.

[120] G. A. Gibson. *Redundant Disk Arrays: Reliable, Parallel Secondary Storage*. MIT Press, 1992.

[121] H. Goldstine and J. von Neumann. On the principles of large-scale computing machines. In *Collected Works of John von Neumann, Vol. 5*. Pergamon, 1963.

[122] G. H. Golub and J. M. Ortega. *Scientific Computing: An Introduction with Parallel Computing*. Academic Press, 1993.

[123] A. Gottlieb, R. Grishman, C. P. Kruskal, K. P. McAuliffe, L. Rudolph, and M. Snir. The NYU ultracomputer: Designing a MIMD, shared memory parallel computer. *IEEE Trans. Computs.*, C-32(2):175–189, 1983.

[124] S. Graham, P. Kessler, and M. McKusick. gprof: A call graph execution profiler. In *Proc. SIGPLAN '92 Symposium on Compiler Construction*, pages 120–126. ACM, 1982.

[125] A. S. Grimshaw. An introduction to parallel object-oriented programming with Mentat. Technical Report 91 07, University of Virginia, 1991.

[126] W. Gropp, E. Lusk, and A. Skjellum. *Using MPI: Portable Parallel Programming with the Message Passing Interface*. MIT Press, 1995.

[127] W. Gropp and B. Smith. Scalable, extensible, and portable numerical libraries. In *Proc. Scalable Parallel Libraries Conf.*, pages 87–93. IEEE Computer Society, 1993.

[128] A. Gupta. *Parallelism in Production Systems*. Morgan Kaufmann, 1987.

[129] J. L. Gustafson. Reevaluating Amdahl's law. *Commun. ACM*, 31(5):532–533, 1988.

[130] J. L. Gustafson, G. R. Montry, and R. E. Benner. Development of parallel methods for a 1024-processor hypercube. *SIAM J. Sci. and Stat. Computing*, 9(4):609–638, 1988.

[131] A. Hac. Load balancing in distributed systems: A summary. *Performance Evaluation Review*, 16(2):17–19, 1989.

[132] G. Haring and G. Kotsis, editors. *Performance Measurement and Visualization of Parallel Systems*. Elsevier Science Publishers, 1993.

[133] P. Harrison. Analytic models for multistage interconnection networks. *J. Parallel and Distributed Computing*, 12(4):357–369, 1991.

[134] P. Harrison and N. M. Patel. The representation of multistage interconnection networks in queuing models of parallel systems. *J. ACM*, 37(4):863–898, 1990.

[135] R. Harrison et al. High performance computational chemistry: (II) A scalable SCF code. Preprint, Mathematics and Computer Science Division, Argonne National Laboratory, Argonne, Ill., 1994.

[136] P. Hatcher and M. Quinn. *Data-Parallel Programming on MIMD Computers*. MIT Press, 1991.

[137] P. Hatcher, M. Quinn, et al. Data-parallel programming on MIMD computers. *IEEE Trans. Parallel and Distributed Syst.*, 2(3):377–383, 1991.

[138] M. Heath. Recent developments and case studies in performance visualization using ParaGraph. In *Performance Measurement and Visualization of Parallel Systems*, pages 175–200. Elsevier Science Publishers, 1993.

[139] M. Heath and J. Etheridge. Visualizing the performance of parallel programs. *IEEE Software*, 8(5):29–39, 1991.

[140] M. Heath, E. Ng, and B. Peyton. Parallel algorithms for sparse linear systems. *SIAM Review*, 33(3):420–460, 1991.

[141] M. Heath, A. Rosenberg, and B. Smith. The physical mapping problem for parallel architectures. *J. ACM*, 35(3):603–634, 1988.

[142] W. Hehre, L. Radom, P. Schleyer, and J. Pople. *Ab Initio Molecular Orbital Theory*. John Wiley and Sons, 1986.

[143] R. Hempel. The ANL/GMD macros (PARMACS) in Fortran for portable parallel programming using the message passing programming model – users' guide and reference manual. Technical report, GMD, Postfach 1316, D-5205 Sankt Augustin 1, Germany, 1991.

[144] R. Hempel, H.-C. Hoppe, and A. Supalov. PARMACS 6.0 library interface specification. Technical report, GMD, Postfach 1316, D-5205 Sankt Augustin 1, Germany, 1992.

[145] M. Henderson, B. Nickless, and R. Stevens. A scalable high-performance I/O system. In *Proc. 1994 Scalable High-Performance Computing Conf.*, pages 79–86. IEEE Computer Society, 1994.

[146] P. Henderson. *Functional Programming*. Prentice-Hall, 1980.

[147] J. Hennessy and N. Joupp. Computer technology and architecture: An evolving interaction. *Computer*, 24(9):18–29, 1991.

[148] V. Herrarte and E. Lusk. Studying parallel program behavior with upshot. Technical Report ANL-91/15, Mathematics and Computer Science Division, Argonne National Laboratory, Argonne, Ill., 1991.

[149] High Performance Fortran Forum. High Performance Fortran language specification, version 1.0. Technical Report CRPC-TR92225, Center for Research on Parallel Computation, Rice University, Houston, Tex., 1993.

[150] W. D. Hillis. *The Connection Machine*. MIT Press, 1985.

[151] W. D. Hillis and G. L. Steele. Data parallel algorithms. *Commun. ACM*, 29(12):1170–1183, 1986.

[152] S. Hiranandani, K. Kennedy, and C. Tseng. Compiling Fortran D for MIMD distributed-memory machines. *Commun. ACM*, 35(8):66–80, 1992.

[153] C. A. R. Hoare. Quicksort. *Computer J.*, 5(1):10–15, 1962.

[154] C. A. R. Hoare. *Communicating Sequential Processes*. Prentice Hall, 1984.

[155] G. Hoffmann and T. Kauranne, editors. *Parallel Supercomputing in the Atmospheric Sciences*. World Scientific, 1993.

[156] K. Hwang. *Advanced Computer Architecture: Parallelism, Scalability, Programmability*. McGraw-Hill, 1993.

[157] J. JáJá. *An Introduction to Parallel Algorithms*. Addison-Wesley, 1992.

[158] J. Jenq and S. Sahni. All pairs shortest paths on a hypercube multiprocessor. In *Proc. 1987 Intl. Conf. on Parallel Processing*, pages 713–716, 1987.

[159] S. L. Johnsson. Communication efficient basic linear algebra computations on hypercube architectures. *J. Parallel and Distributed Computing*, 4(2):133–172, 1987.

[160] S. L. Johnsson and C.-T. Ho. Optimum broadcasting and personalized communication in hypercubes. *IEEE Trans. Computs.*, C-38(9):1249–1268, 1989.

[161] M. Jones and P. Plassmann. Parallel algorithms for the adaptive refinement and partitioning of unstructured meshes. In *Proc. 1994 Scalable High-Performance Computing Conf.*, pages 478–485. IEEE Computer Society, 1994.

[162] R. Kahn. Resource-sharing computer communication networks. *Proc. IEEE*, 60(11):1397–1407, 1972.

[163] M. Kalos. *The Basics of Monte Carlo Methods*. J. Wiley and Sons, 1985.

[164] L. N. Kanal and V. Kumar. *Search in Artificial Intelligence*. Springer-Verlag, 1988.

[165] A. Karp and R. Babb. A comparison of twelve parallel Fortran dialects. *IEEE Software*, 5(5):52–67, 1988.

[166] A. H. Karp. Programming for parallelism. *IEEE Computer*, 20(9):43–57, 1987.

[167] A. H. Karp and H. P. Flatt. Measuring parallel processor performance. *Commun. ACM*, 33(5):539–543, 1990.

[168] R. Katz, G. Gibson, and D. Patterson. Disk system architectures for high performance computing. *Proc. IEEE*, 77(12):1842–1858, 1989.

[169] W. J. Kaufmann and L. L. Smarr. *Supercomputing and the Transformation of Science.* Scientific American Library, 1993.

[170] B. Kernighan and D. Ritchie. *The C Programming Language.* Prentice Hall, second edition, 1988.

[171] J. Kerrigan. *Migrating to Fortran 90.* O'Reilly and Associates, 1992.

[172] C. Kesselman. *Integrating Performance Analysis with Performance Improvement in Parallel Programs.* PhD thesis, UCLA, 1991.

[173] L. Kleinrock. On the modeling and analysis of computer networks. *Proc. IEEE,* 81(8):1179–1191, 1993.

[174] D. Knuth. *The Art of Computer Programming: Volume 3, Sorting and Searching.* Addison-Wesley, 1973.

[175] D. Knuth. *The Art of Computer Programming: Volume 2, Seminumerical Algorithms.* Addison-Wesley, 1981.

[176] C. Koelbel, D. Loveman, R. Schreiber, G. Steele, and M. Zosel. *The High Performance Fortran Handbook.* MIT Press, 1994.

[177] S. Koonin and D. Meredith. *Computational Physics.* Addison-Wesley, 1990.

[178] J. S. Kowalik. *Parallel Computation and Computers for Artificial Intelligence.* Kluwer Academic Publishers, 1988.

[179] V. Kumar, A. Grama, A. Gupta, and G. Karypis. *Introduction to Parallel Computing.* Benjamin/Cummings, 1993.

[180] V. Kumar, A. Grama, and V. Rao. Scalable load balancing techniques for parallel computers. *J. Parallel and Distributed Computing,* 22(1):60–79, 1994.

[181] V. Kumar and V. Rao. Parallel depth-first search, part II: Analysis. *Intl J. of Parallel Programming,* 16(6):479–499, 1987.

[182] V. Kumar and V. Singh. Scalability of parallel algorithms for the all-pairs shortest-path problem. *J. Parallel and Distributed Computing,* 13(2):124–138, 1991.

[183] T. Lai and S. Sahni. Anomalies in parallel branch-and-bound algorithms. *Commun. ACM,* 27(6):594–602, 1984.

[184] S. Lakshmivarahan and S. K. Dhall. *Analysis and Design of Parallel Algorithms: Arithmetic and Matrix Problems.* McGraw-Hill, 1990.

[185] L. Lamport. Time, clocks, and the ordering of events in a distributed system. *Commun. ACM,* 21(7):558–565, 1978.

[186] H. Lawson. *Parallel Processing in Industrial Real-time Applications.* Prentice Hall, 1992.

[187] F. T. Leighton. *Introduction to Parallel Algorithms and Architectures.* Morgan Kaufmann, 1992.

[188] M. Lemke and D. Quinlan. P++, a parallel C++ array class library for architecture-independent development of structured grid applications. In *Proc. Workshop on Languages, Compilers, and Runtime Environments for Distributed Memory Computers.* ACM, 1992.

[189] E. Levin. Grand challenges in computational science. *Commun. ACM,* 32(12):1456–1457, 1989.

[190] F. C. H. Lin and R. M. Keller. The gradient model load balancing method. *IEEE Trans. Software Eng.,* SE-13(1):32–38, 1987.

[191] V. Lo. Heuristic algorithms for task assignment in distributed systems. *IEEE Trans. Computs.*, C-37(11):1384–1397, 1988.

[192] C. Loan. *Computational Frameworks for the Fast Fourier Transform.* SIAM, 1992.

[193] D. Loveman. High Performance Fortran. *IEEE Parallel and Distributed Technology*, 1(1):25–42, 1993.

[194] E. Lusk, R. Overbeek, et al. *Portable Programs for Parallel Processors.* Holt, Rinehard, and Winston, 1987.

[195] U. Manber. On maintaining dynamic information in a concurrent environment. *SIAM J. Computing*, 15(4):1130–1142, 1986.

[196] O. McBryan. An overview of message passing environments. *Parallel Computing*, 20(4):417–444, 1994.

[197] O. A. McBryan and E. F. V. de Velde. Hypercube algorithms and implementations. *SIAM J. Sci. and Stat. Computing*, 8(2):227–287, 1987.

[198] S. McConnell. *Code Complete: A Practical Handbook of Software Construction.* Microsoft Press, 1993.

[199] C. Mead and L. Conway. *Introduction to VLSI Systems.* Addison-Wesley, 1980.

[200] P. Mehrotra and J. Van Rosendale. Programming distributed memory architectures using Kali. In *Advances in Languages and Compilers for Parallel Computing.* MIT Press, 1991.

[201] J. D. Meindl. Chips for advanced computing. *Scientific American*, 257(4):78–88, 1987.

[202] Message Passing Interface Forum. Document for a standard message-passing interface. Technical report, University of Tennessee, Knoxville, Tenn., 1993.

[203] Message Passing Interface Forum. MPI: A message passing interface. In *Proc. Supercomputing '93*, pages 878–883. IEEE Computer Society, 1993.

[204] M. Metcalf and J. Reid. *Fortran 90 Explained.* Oxford Science Publications, 1990.

[205] R. Metcalfe and D. Boggs. Ethernet: Distributed packet switching for local area networks. *Commun. ACM*, 19(7):711–719, 1976.

[206] J. Michalakes. Analysis of workload and load balancing issues in the NCAR community climate model. Technical Report ANL/MCS-TM-144, Mathematics and Computer Science Division, Argonne National Laboratory, Argonne, Ill., 1991.

[207] B. Miller et al. IPS-2: The second generation of a parallel program measurement system. *IEEE Trans. Parallel and Distributed Syst.*, 1(2):206–217, 1990.

[208] E. Miller and R. Katz. Input/output behavior of supercomputing applications. In *Proc. Supercomputing '91*, pages 567–576. ACM, 1991.

[209] R. Miller and Q. F. Stout. *Parallel Algorithms for Regular Architectures.* MIT Press, 1992.

[210] R. Milner. Calculi for synchrony and asynchrony. *Theoretical Computer Science*, 25:267–310, 1983.

[211] nCUBE Corporation. *nCUBE 2 Programmers Guide, r2.0*, 1990.

[212] nCUBE Corporation. *nCUBE 6400 Processor Manual*, 1990.

[213] D. M. Nicol and J. H. Saltz. An analysis of scatter decomposition. *IEEE Trans. Computs.*, C-39(11):1337–1345, 1990.

[214] N. Nilsson. *Principles of Artificial Intelligence.* Tioga Publishers, 1980.

[215] Grand challenges: High performance computing and communications. A Report by the Committee on Physical, Mathematical and Engineering Sciences, NSF/CISE, 1800 G Street NW, Washington, DC 20550, 1991.

[216] D. Nussbaum and A. Agarwal. Scalability of parallel machines. *Commun. ACM*, 34(3):56–61, 1991.

[217] R. Paige and C. Kruskal. Parallel algorithms for shortest paths problems. In *Proc. 1989 Intl. Conf. on Parallel Processing*, pages 14–19, 1989.

[218] C. Pancake and D. Bergmark. Do parallel languages respond to the needs of scientific programmers? *Computer*, 23(12):13–23, 1990.

[219] Parasoft Corporation. *Express Version 1.0: A Communication Environment for Parallel Computers*, 1988.

[220] D. Parnas. On the criteria to be used in decomposing systems into modules. *Commun. ACM*, 15(12):1053–1058, 1972.

[221] D. Parnas. Designing software for ease of extension and contraction. *IEEE Trans. Software Eng.*, SE-5(2):128–138, 1979.

[222] D. Parnas and P. Clements. A rational design process: How and why to fake it. *IEEE Trans. Software Eng.*, SE-12(2):251–257, 1986.

[223] D. Parnas, P. Clements, and D. Weiss. The modular structure of complex systems. *IEEE Trans. Software Eng.*, SE-11(3):259–266, 1985.

[224] J. Patel. Analysis of multiprocessors with private cache memories. *IEEE Trans. Computs.*, C-31(4):296–304, 1982.

[225] J. Pearl. *Heuristics—Intelligent Search Strategies for Computer Problem Solving.* Addison-Wesley, 1984.

[226] G. F. Pfister, W. C. Brantley, D. A. George, S. L. Harey, W. J. Kleinfelder, K. P. McAuliffe, E. A. Melton, V. A. Norlton, and J. Weiss. The IBM research parallel processor prototype (RP3): Introduction and architecture. In *Proc. 1985 Intl Conf. on Parallel Processing*, pages 764–771, 1985.

[227] P. Pierce. The NX/2 operating system. In *Proc. 3rd Conf. on Hypercube Concurrent Computers and Applications*, pages 384–390. ACM Press, 1988.

[228] J. Plank and K. Li. Performance results of `ickp`—A consistent checkpointer on the iPSC/860. In *Proc. 1994 Scalable High-Performance Computing Conf.*, pages 686–693. IEEE Computer Society, 1994.

[229] J. Pool et al. Survey of I/O intensive applications. Technical Report CCSF-38, CCSF, California Institute of Technology, 1994.

[230] A. Pothen, H. Simon, and K. Liou. Partitioning sparse matrices with eigenvectors of graphs. *SIAM J. Mat. Anal. Appl.*, 11(3):430–452, 1990.

[231] D. Pountain. *A Tutorial Introduction to OCCAM Programming.* INMOS Corporation, 1986.

[232] A research and development strategy for high performance computing. Office of Science and Technology Policy, Executive Office of the President, 1987.

[233] The federal high performance computing program. Office of Science and Technology Policy, Executive Office of the President, 1989.

[234] M. Quinn. Analysis and implementation of branch-and-bound algorithms on a hypercube multicomputer. *IEEE Trans. Computs.*, C-39(3):384–387, 1990.

[235] M. Quinn. *Parallel Computing: Theory and Practice.* McGraw-Hill, 1994.

[236] M. Quinn and N. Deo. Parallel graph algorithms. *Computing Surveys*, 16(3):319–348, 1984.

[237] M. Quinn and N. Deo. An upper bound for the speedup of parallel best-bound branch-and-bound algorithms. *BIT*, 26(1):35–43, 1986.

[238] S. Ranka and S. Sahni. *Hypercube Algorithms for Image Processing and Pattern Recognition*. Springer-Verlag, 1990.

[239] V. Rao and V. Kumar. Parallel depth-first search, part I: Implementation. *Intl. J. of Parallel Programming*, 16(6):501–519, 1987.

[240] D. A. Reed. Experimental Performance Analysis of Parallel Systems: Techniques and Open Problems. In *Proc. 7th Intl Conf. on Modeling Techniques and Tools for Computer Performance Evaluation*, 1994.

[241] D. A. Reed, R. A. Aydt, R. J. Noe, P. C. Roth, K. A. Shields, B. W. Schwartz, and L. F. Tavera. Scalable Performance Analysis: The Pablo Performance Analysis Environment. In *Proc. Scalable Parallel Libraries Conf.*, pages 104–113. IEEE Computer Society, 1993.

[242] D. A. Reed and R. M. Fujimoto. *Multicomputer Networks: Message-Based Parallel Processing*. MIT Press, 1989.

[243] A. Reinefeld and V. Schnecke. Work-load balancing in highly parallel depth-first search. In *Proc. 1994 Scalable High-Performance Computing Conf.*, pages 773–780. IEEE Computer Society, 1994.

[244] B. Ries, R. Anderson, W. Auld, D. Breazeal, K. Callaghan, E. Richards, and W. Smith. The Paragon performance monitoring environment. In *Proc. Supercomputing '93*, pages 850–859. IEEE Computer Society, 1993.

[245] A. Rogers and K. Pingali. Process decomposition through locality of reference. In *Proc. SIGPLAN '89 Conf. on Program Language Design and Implementation*. ACM, 1989.

[246] K. Rokusawa, N. Ichiyoshi, T. Chikayama, and H. Nakashima. An efficient termination detection and abortion algorithm for distributed processing systems. In *Proc. 1988 Intl. Conf. on Parallel Processing: Vol. I*, pages 18–22, 1988.

[247] M. Rosing, R. B. Schnabel, and R. P. Weaver. The DINO parallel programming language. Technical Report CU-CS-501-90, Computer Science Department, University of Colorado at Boulder, Boulder, Col., 1990.

[248] Y. Saad and M. H. Schultz. Topological properties of hypercubes. *IEEE Trans. Computs.*, C-37:867–872, 1988.

[249] Y. Saad and M. H. Schultz. Data communication in hypercubes. *J. Parallel and Distributed Computing*, 6:115–135, 1989.

[250] P. Sadayappan and F. Ercal. Nearest-neighbor mapping of finite element graphs onto processor meshes. *IEEE Trans. Computs.*, C-36(12):1408–1424, 1987.

[251] J. Saltz, H. Berryman, and J. Wu. Multiprocessors and runtime compilation. *Concurrency: Practice and Experience*, 3(6):573–592, 1991.

[252] J. Schwartz. Ultracomputers. *ACM Trans. Program. Lang. Syst.*, 2(4):484–521, 1980.

[253] C. L. Seitz. Concurrent VLSI architectures. *IEEE Trans. Computs.*, C-33(12):1247–1265, 1984.

[254] C. L. Seitz. The cosmic cube. *Commun. ACM*, 28(1):22–33, 1985.

[255] C. L. Seitz. Multicomputers. In C.A.R. Hoare, editor, *Developments in Concurrency and Communication*. Addison-Wesley, 1991.

[256] M. S. Shephard and M. K. Georges. Automatic three-dimensional mesh generation by the finite octree technique. *Int. J. Num. Meth. Engng.*, 32(4):709–749, 1991.

[257] J. Shoch, Y. Dalal, and D. Redell. Evolution of the Ethernet local computer network. *Computer*, 15(8):10–27, 1982.

[258] H. Simon. Partitioning of unstructured problems for parallel processing. *Computing Systems in Engineering*, 2(2/3):135–148, 1991.

[259] J. Singh, J. L. Hennessy, and A. Gupta. Scaling parallel programs for multiprocessors: Methodology and examples. *IEEE Computer*, 26(7):42–50, 1993.

[260] M. Singhal. Deadlock detection in distributed systems. *Computer*, 22(11):37–48, 1989.

[261] P. Sivilotti and P. Carlin. A tutorial for CC++. Technical Report CS-TR-94-02, Caltech, 1994.

[262] A. Skjellum. The Multicomputer Toolbox: Current and future directions. In *Proc. Scalable Parallel Libraries Conf.*, pages 94–103. IEEE Computer Society, 1993.

[263] A. Skjellum, editor. *Proc. 1993 Scalable Parallel Libraries Conf.* IEEE Computer Society, 1993.

[264] A. Skjellum, editor. *Proc. 1994 Scalable Parallel Libraries Conf.* IEEE Computer Society, 1994.

[265] A. Skjellum, N. Doss, and P. Bangalore. Writing libraries in MPI. In *Proc. Scalable Parallel Libraries Conf.*, pages 166–173. IEEE Computer Society, 1993.

[266] A. Skjellum, S. Smith, N. Doss, A. Leung, and M. Morari. The design and evolution of Zipcode. *Parallel Computing*, 20:565–596, 1994.

[267] J. R. Smith. *The Design and Analysis of Parallel Algorithms*. Oxford University Press, 1993.

[268] L. Snyder. Type architectures, shared memory, and the corollary of modest potential. *Ann. Rev. Comput. Sci.*, 1:289–317, 1986.

[269] H. S. Stone. *High-Performance Computer Architectures*. Addison-Wesley, third edition, 1993.

[270] B. Stroustrup. *The C++ Programming Language*. Addison-Wesley, second edition, 1991.

[271] C. Stunkel, D. Shea, D. Grice, P. Hochschild, and M. Tsao. The SP1 high-performance switch. In *Proc. 1994 Scalable High-Performance Computing Conf.*, pages 150–157. IEEE Computer Society, 1994.

[272] R. Suaya and G. Birtwistle, editors. *VLSI and Parallel Computation*. Morgan Kaufmann, 1990.

[273] J. Subhlok, J. Stichnoth, D. O'Hallaron, and T. Gross. Exploiting task and data parallelism on a multicomputer. In *Proc. 4th ACM SIGPLAN Symp. on Principles and Practice of Parallel Programming*. ACM, 1993.

[274] X.-H. Sun and L. M. Ni. Scalable problems and memory-bounded speedup. *J. Parallel and Distributed Computing*, 19(1):27–37, 1993.

[275] V. Sunderam. PVM: A framework for parallel distributed computing. *Concurrency: Practice and Experience*, 2(4):315–339, 1990.

[276] Supercomputer Systems Division, Intel Corporation. *Paragon XP/S Product Overview*, 1991.

[277] P. Swarztrauber. Multiprocessor FFTs. *Parallel Computing*, 5:197–210, 1987.

[278] D. Tabak. *Advanced Multiprocessors*. McGraw-Hill, 1991.

[279] A. Tantawi and D. Towsley. Optimal load balancing in distributed computer systems. *J. ACM*, 32(2):445–465, 1985.

[280] R. Taylor and P. Wilson. Process-oriented language meets demands of distributed processing. *Electronics*, Nov. 30, 1982.

[281] Thinking Machines Corporation. *The CM-2 Technical Summary*, 1990.

[282] Thinking Machines Corporation. *CM Fortran Reference Manual, version 2.1*, 1993.

[283] Thinking Machines Corporation. *CMSSL for CM Fortran Reference Manual, version 3.0*, 1993.

[284] A. Thomasian and P. F. Bay. Analytic queuing network models for parallel processing of task systems. *IEEE Trans. Computs.*, C-35(12):1045–1054, 1986.

[285] E. Tufte. *The Visual Display of Quantitative Information*. Graphics Press, 1983.

[286] J. Ullman. *Computational Aspects of VLSI*. Computer Science Press, 1984.

[287] Building an advanced climate model: Program plan for the CHAMMP climate modeling program. U.S. Department of Energy, 1990. Available from National Technical Information Service, U.S. Dept of Commerce, 5285 Port Royal Rd, Springfield, VA 22161.

[288] L. Valiant. A bridging model for parallel computation. *Commun. ACM*, 33(8):103–111, 1990.

[289] R. A. van de Geijn. Efficient global combine operations. In *Proc. 6th Distributed Memory Computing Conf.*, pages 291–294. IEEE Computer Society, 1991.

[290] E. F. van de Velde. *Concurrent Scientific Computing*. Number 16 in Texts in Applied Mathematics. Springer-Verlag, 1994.

[291] Y. Wallach. *Parallel Processing and Ada*. Prentice-Hall, 1991.

[292] W. Washington and C. Parkinson. *An Introduction to Three-Dimensional Climate Modeling*. University Science Books, 1986.

[293] R. Williams. Performance of dynamic load balancing algorithms for unstructured mesh calculations. *Concurrency: Practice and Experience*, 3(5):457–481, 1991.

[294] S. Wimer, I. Koren, and I. Cederbaum. Optimal aspect ratios of building blocks in VLSI. In *Proc. 25th ACM/IEEE Design Automation Conf.*, pages 66–72, 1988.

[295] N. Wirth. Program development by stepwise refinement. *Commun. ACM*, 14(4):221–227, 1971.

[296] M. Wolfe. *Optimizing Supercompilers for Supercomputers*. MIT Press, 1989.

[297] P. H. Worley. The effect of time constraints on scaled speedup. *SIAM J. Sci. and Stat. Computing*, 11(5):838–858, 1990.

[298] P. H. Worley. Limits on parallelism in the numerical solution of linear PDEs. *SIAM J. Sci. and Stat. Computing*, 12(1):1–35, 1991.

[299] J. Worlton. Characteristics of high-performance computers. In *Supercomputers: Directions in Technology and its Applications*, pages 21–50. National Academy Press, 1989.

[300] X3J3 Subcommittee. *American National Standard Programming Language Fortran (X3.9-1978)*. American National Standards Institute, 1978.

[301] J. Yan, P. Hontalas, S. Listgarten, et al. The Automated Instrumentation and Monitoring System (AIMS) reference manual. NASA Technical Memorandum 108795, NASA Ames Research Center, Moffett Field, Calif., 1993.

[302]  H. Zima, H.-J. Bast, and M. Gerndt. SUPERB: A tool for semi-automatic MIMD/SIMD parallelization. *Parallel Computing*, 6:1–18, 1988.

[303]  H. Zima and B. Chapman. *Supercompilers for Parallel and Vector Computers*. Addison-Wesley, 1991.

# Index

# Books of Related Interest

*Scientific and Engineering C++* by John J. Barton and Lee R. Nackman, Addison-Wesley Publishing Company, 1994   ISBN 0-201-53393-6

*Distributed Systems: Concepts and Design,* Second Edition by George Coulouris, Jean Dollimore, Tim Kindberg, Addison-Wesley Publishing Company, 1994   ISBN 0-201-62433-8

*Distributed Systems,* Second Edition, Edited by Sape Mullender, Addison-Wesley Publishing Company, 1993   ISBN 0-201-62427-3

*An Introduction to Parallel Algorithms* by Joseph JáJá, Addison-Wesley Publishing Company, 1992   ISBN 0-201-54856-9

To learn more about these and other Addison-Wesley titles please visit the aw gopher site via the Internet: gopher aw.com to connect.